THE ORIGINS OF THE COLD WAR IN ASIA

THE ORIGINS OF
THE COLD WAR IN ASIA

Edited by
Yōnosuke Nagai
Akira Iriye

COLUMBIA UNIVERSITY PRESS
UNIVERSITY OF TOKYO PRESS
1977

© UNIVERSITY OF TOKYO PRESS, 1977

UTP Number 3031-36219-5149
ISBN 0-86008-178-8

American edition published by
Columbia University Press
New York   Guildford, Surrey   March 2 78
ISBN: 0-231-04390-2   DEC 19 '77
Library of Congress Catalog Card Number: 77-7467
Printed in Japan

77-7467

Contents

Preface

The essays in this volume (with the exception of four noted below) were originally presented at an international symposium on "The International Environment in Postwar Asia," held in Kyoto from November 27 to 30, 1975. The symposium was part of a larger activity, a three-year project known as "Basic Studies on the International Environment," which was supported through a grant by the Japanese Ministry of Education, Science and Culture. The project, funded for 1973–76, was an enormous undertaking, the first attempt by Japanese historians and social scientists to engage in a collective research endeavor to study the recent past. Hayashi Kentarō, president of Tokyo University, served as project director, and Nagai Yōnosuke, professor of political science at the Tokyo Institute of Technology, as chief coordinator. Nagai established a project secretariat at his university to coordinate research activities by the participants, who ultimately numbered nearly two hundred. He was assisted by two associate coordinators: Professors Homma Nagayo of the University of Tokyo and Nakajima Mineo of the Tokyo University of Foreign Studies.

These researchers showed an interest in postwar international relations in Asia in part because of their concern with the present. In order to understand the emerging structure and orientation of Asian-Pacific affairs in the 1970s, they felt it would be of fundamental importance to go back to the roots of the Cold War confrontation in Asia. But the project participants were also drawn to this topic because of the recent partial opening of archives in the United States, Great Britain, and Japan and because of their interest in applying analytical concepts and models to empirical data. A systematic cooperative effort was an ideal setup for collecting and analyzing these data from various angles.

The Kyoto symposium was intended as a landmark, bringing together not only the project participants but also several prominent specialists from the United States and Great Britain. Organized under the supervision of Professor Hosoya Chihiro of Hitotsubashi University, it was attended by over one hundred specialists and interested observers—an impressive turnout when one recalls that the conference coincided with a week-long strike of the national railway system. Altogether fourteen papers were presented, and each of the eight sessions was filled with serious and enlightening, if at times heated, debate. The summary appended at the end of this volume gives only a partial view of that debate. (A 174-page edited transcript of the symposium proceedings is available in Japanese.) The participants—those who presented papers and all others—agreed that this was a remarkable conference, raising Cold War historiography to a higher level than had been attained theretofore. The success of the symposium owed itself to a great extent to the organizing skill and efficient teamwork of the program committee (Professors Hosoya Chihiro, Nagai Yōnosuke, Nakajima Mineo, Homma Nagayo, Asada Sadao, and Yano Tōru), and to the devoted staff work by the project secretariat.

The editors have selected twelve papers from that symposium for inclusion in this volume in revised form. Professor D. C. Watt's opening remarks at the conference have also been reproduced with his permission. In addition, the editors have asked four others (Professors Itō, Nakajima, Tanigawa, and Yamamoto) to contribute. All four were members of the larger project and presented modified versions of these papers at other meetings. We would have liked to have included essays by other participants, but decided to publish first the papers that had been revised and made available to us by October 1, 1976. It is hoped that other products of the symposium and of the entire project will in time be printed for wider circulation, and that in the meantime this volume will add significantly to the literature on the Cold War in general and postwar Asian international affairs in particular.

The editors are grateful to all the contributors to this volume for their cheerful cooperation, and to Nina Raj of the University of Tokyo Press for her unfailing support of the undertaking from beginning to end. Various individuals and institutions were involved with the translation and revision of a number of the papers by Japanese contributors. Our appreciation goes to Kanō Tsutomu, J. Victor Koschmann, Pat Murray, and the staff of *The Japan Interpreter*; Mark D. Ericson; and the staff of *Japan Echo*. We would like to acknowledge the financial support received from the Ministry of Education, Science and Culture for the publication of this book.

Note on Chinese, Japanese, and Korean names: All these names are given in this book in traditional fashion, i.e., the family name preceding the given name.

THE ORIGINS OF THE COLD WAR IN ASIA

Introduction
The Historian's Tasks and Responsibilities

D. C. Watt

In introducing this conference, I speak for all the guest historians from outside Japan, and as the sole representative of historical work in Europe. Speaking in my first capacity, may I say for all of us how grateful we are and how honoured we feel to be invited to this conference. We accepted the invitation with high expectations of our Japanese colleagues. The quality of the papers we are to discuss has in no way disappointed us.

I am a European historian. More than that, I am a European historian who has specialized in the history of international relations and is the product of an approach which enjoins the abandonment of nationalistic approaches to historical problems. I am too a historian who has specialized in the study of contemporary history and who is well aware of the very special problems faced by students of contemporary history in seeking to attain that degree of separation from the emotional and empathetic problems of the age he studies which historians of the more distant past enjoy as an inevitable consequence of their distance in time from the period they study. My remarks therefore will be devoted firstly to recalling the special obligations which lie upon us as historians examining one of the major sets of historical events of our own lifetimes. From this, I will turn to the present state of Cold War studies, dominated as they are by the various American schools of historiography. This will lead to a brief examination of the elements present in the American approach to world politics which strike a European as significantly different from what may loosely be called the European approach. And finally I propose to make some brief points about the Cold War as a subject of historiographical study.

The contemporary historian (i.e., the historian whose field of study is the world of which he is a contemporary) is under an obligation both to his profession and to his employers to maintain the standards and practices by which historians judge work to be objective. I say "to his employers" not only because the work of all contemporary historians is of much more immediate relevance to the public which consumes and, in one way or another, pays for our work. Contemporary historians are much more likely to find themselves consulted by, even directly employed by, governments, as we are in the case of this conference which we are attending. This is not to argue that the acceptance of money from governments makes a historian a paid stooge. It does make it the more essential for him to guard himself and his work from the suspicion of financially induced orthodoxy.

The historian who works in the contemporary field finds himself accompanied by a horde of fellow travellers. Not only is he accompanied by fellow academics from the disciplines of sociology, political science, economics, social psychology, and the like who seek to understand the present in terms of the immediate past and fall so often into the unhistorical error of projecting the values of the present back into the past. He will find himself surrounded by a horde of others with less respectable motives, intent on establishing their own orthodoxies for reasons entirely unhistorical if not directly antihistorical. A historian has to remember that time and causal explanations based on sequences of events in time move only in one direction. Behind lies the already unrolled tapestry of the past. The present and the future lie in that part of the tapestry which is even now being unrolled. It only unrolls one way; and the process of unrolling is inalterably continuous.

The contemporary historian, to vary the metaphor, is at work permanently at the ongoing frontier of history. His aim is to settle on some part of that frontier, to explore it, to map it, perhaps to build his own homestead of settlement, above all to join it onto the ordered, settled, law-abiding civilized areas already settled. But like the would-be settlers of geographical frontiers in the past, he works in an area populated also by claim-jumpers, confidence trickers, gamblers, would-be establishers of utopias, refugees from a past they feel has rejected them, even vigilantes intent on establishing their own versions of order without law. On the one hand he faces the "instant historians" intent on stripping a period rapidly of the immediately obvious evidence, putting a distortion on it which may take generations of patient, painstaking work to correct. On the other he faces the more numerous groups, which will inevitably include many defectors from his own confraternity, who hope to influence the present and the immediate future by establishing their own versions of the immediate past and eliminating if they can, by whatever means their society allows, those who will not subscribe to it or whose work looks likely to cast doubt upon it. The contemporary historian who is true to the canons and standards of his profession cannot hope to escape unpopularity, though he would be wise not to court it deliberately. If he is not true to the standards of his profession, he is worthless.

Having said that, let me turn to the present state of Cold War studies in the noncommunist world. Historical study of the Cold War is at present dominated by the historians of the United States. Three sets of causes have combined to produce this state of affairs. Of all the participants in the Cold War, the United States government and society afford the most open and immediate access to historical evidence bearing on the formation of official policy. My American colleagues will immediately point out that this access is by no means universal, that attempts have been made to limit it and control it, and that major areas of deception have recently been uncovered. All of this is true. But by contrast, for example with the practice even of Britain and France, let alone the Soviet Union, the evidence available for the study of American policy in the Cold War is as the Nile delta contrasted with the circumambient desert.

The second set of causes has to do with the American defeat in Vietnam. While the immediate political impact of that defeat was dissipated in the electoral disaster which overtook Senator George McGovern's campaign in the presidential elections of 1972 and the nemesis which overtook his successful rival eighteen months later, the cultural shock of the defeat will clearly last much longer. Particularly striking is its effect on different generations of American historians, especially on those who lived through the controversies of the late 1940s, the defeated supporters of Henry Wallace, those who took refuge in the study of the past from the excesses of McCarthyism, and on those who only came of age in the early 1960s, to whom the imperatives of the 1940s and the memories of East Berlin and Budapest were inconceivable arguments used to buttress an alien, incomprehensible, and incredibly mismanaged war to which their generation was expected to sacrifice their freedom and their affluence. The present state of Cold War studies in America is dominated by precisely that state of retrospective politics of which contemporary historians should most beware.

This is greatly exacerbated by the third set of causes which arise from the position of the historian in American society. We are all familiar with the role of the historians in the growth of nationalism in nineteenth-century Europe, especially among the national groups which emerged among the decaying ruins of the Hapsburg and Ottoman empires. In extreme cases, so great was the strength of history in European culture that historians invented a past and forged the necessary documents where they could not uncover them. Bulgarian nationalism, for example, began with the establishment of a journal of Bulgarian history. In Germany Ranke and Treitschke, in Britain Stubbs and Seeley put history to the work of establishing the peculiar nature of German and British political traditions. The court historian of despotism was succeeded by the historian of the modern nation-state, specializing in the history of the institutions and national character of the nation.

The role of Ranke and Treitschke in Germany, of Stubbs and Seeley in Britain was taken in America by the frontier school. Since America in the late nineteenth century was a country settled by immigrants from an ever-increasing number of separate national traditions, to identify what was specifically American in American society, to provide Americans with the sense of national identity they or their forebears had abandoned with the *genus loci* of the lands from which they had emigrated, they concentrated on not heredity but environment, on not traditional national character but the effects of the experience of new settlement on a nation of immigrants. Whereas to call oneself English, French, German, or Japanese was to make a descriptive statement, to call oneself American was a normative statement. The norms by which these were judged were those of a secular religion, the priests of which were the teachers of American history, the teachers of a history in which the American nation progressed to its position as a world power, free, open, and democratic, through a series of moral conflicts: with Britain in the war of independence; with the old Europe on the issue of the Monroe Doctrine; with slave owners in the war of the states; with corruption, big-city bossism, xenophobia, robber-baronries in the 1880s and 1890s; with European imperialism and its would-be imitators in America in the first two decades of the twentieth century; with retrogressive particularism and poverty in the 1930s; and with European totalitarianism thereafter. Through all of this America grew stronger, by overcoming the repeated intrusion of practices contrary to American ethics.

This progress was defeated in Indochina. America's defeat came, and came deservedly, because America was fighting on the wrong side and in a way contrary to the ideals of Americanism. It is difficult not to see in the reaction of many American revisionists to this defeat an atavism akin to that of Islamic fundamentalists to the impact of European power. This is a reaction with which those of us who were not and are not conditioned by the moral imperatives of American education and society can sympathize and which we can understand. But there is no reason why we should follow these imperatives. They are not issues of history but of the secular theology of American national self-consciousness; insofar as they are historical, they belong not to the history of the Cold War in the period 1945–60 but to the history of American domestic politics in the period 1964–74.

In assessing American policy in the Cold War years, especially in the years 1945–55, the non-American historian must therefore seek for and consider elements which do not necessarily figure very prominently in the revisionist debate. Three elements are sufficiently striking as to require comment here. The first is the element of social Darwinism in the popular American view of the U.S. role in world politics, the reverse side of that belief in American history as the record of ethical progress through struggle which was so abruptly defeated in Vietnam. Elements of this are to be found at all levels, from President Roosevelt's rejection of France after 1940 downward. But it appears particularly strong in the popular attitude in the Senate and elsewhere to those

European countries which became dependent on American financial aid, and in the attitude of the American armed services, whose senior personnel began, especially after 1949, to play so important a part in the day-to-day conduct of America's relations with her allies and associates. And while those who conducted American foreign relations at the top in the Truman administration remained comparatively free from the point of view that American strength gave the United States the right to dismiss or override the views or interests of her smaller allies and associates and to dictate to them for their own good, it was to manifest itself increasingly strongly among that constant stream of new entrants into the American foreign policy-making elite which is so marked a feature of American, as contrasted with European, democratic politics.

The second element lies in the dichotomy between the leadership and outlook of the American armed forces and the rest of American political society, that doctrine of the separation of the military from the political sphere, which is the least happy of America's inheritance from European despotism. Its effect, seen from the point of view of those foreign countries concerned with their relations with the United States, is to introduce into those relations an alternation, even a discontinuity, of behaviour between that influenced by "military" and that influenced by "political" considerations. America's allies found such alternation at the very least mystifying and baffling. It could not but prove a source of constant suspicion to those who saw themselves as America's adversaries. Divisions among the military—as, for example, that between the chiefs of staff in 1950–51 and General MacArthur on the issue of Europe or Asia first—could obscure that alternation by making it appear that the president's closest military advisers accepted the primacy of political arguments. But in fact, as often as not, the unity of one military school of thought with that of the political leadership represented the acceptance by the latter of the primacy of the former.

This is particularly noticeable in the misunderstanding, so often apparent in American calculations, of the nature of power in international politics. In the early part of the postwar period this manifested itself as much in an overestimation of British power as it did in the miscalculation of Soviet power. American calculations of power tended, like American naval strategists in the school of

Admiral Mahan, to concentrate on the "one big war" and on calculations of total war potential. The circumstances of the Cold War were to show that "power" was equivalent only to what was immediately disposable in excess of existing commitments and capable of being sustained on that basis. In some circumstances, a spare brigade, a couple of squadrons, and the very limited quantity of sea or air transport necessary to bring force quickly to bear where it is required represents far more power than an army corps tied up by the need to balance similar forces across a strategic frontier. In others, the financial and industrial strength of a historic empire is weakness compared with the multifarious commitments which outmatch it at all points. There was thus a tendency greatly to overestimate British strength in the years 1945–49 and to fail to realize how desperately it was stretched and how greatly American action contributed in various ways to that process. From 1949 there was a similar tendency to overestimate Soviet strength and to demand from America's allies in NATO a military effort to match that strength, which was completely beyond their potential to create or to sustain. Ultimately, as America's own strategic planners were to discover the hard way in the years 1964–68, the power of a nation depends on the willingness of its people to sustain and support the policies of those to whom its political system has given the prerogative of decision making. Power becomes ability to implement decisions; where there is no united popular will, however achieved, the successful implementation of the policy-makers' decisions becomes impossible. There is no power where there is no will.

The third element in American policy making, which is to a non-American historian most striking, is the absence from American debate and from much of American behaviour of any sense of the rules, conventions, and restraints accepted among European nations in the classic period of the balance of power and still accepted as valid in the middle decades of the twentieth century. In his study of Anglo-American relations in the 1890s, A. E. Campbell remarked on the difference between the British reaction to President Cleveland's message to Congress on the Venezuelan boundary dispute with Britain and the Kaiser's telegram of congratulation to President Kruger, the Boer leader, on the failure of the Jameson raid. Of the two, President Cleveland's language was the more intemperate. British opinion largely ignored President Cleveland to concentrate on the Kaiser. The reason, explains Campbell, is that President Cleveland, being American, and therefore outside the conventions of intra-European international relations, was assumed not to understand the implications of his action. The Kaiser, by contrast, or so it was assumed, understood the implications of his action only too well. No action was taken in the American case. The Kaiser was answered by the mobilization of a special naval squadron.

Again it is often forgotten that the reason why Britain declared war on Nazi Germany in 1939 rather than waiting, as did the United States and the Soviet Union, for a German attack on her, was that Hitler's actions since 1935 had convinced Britain's policy-makers and British opinion that he was intent on establishing German supremacy and recognized no other restraint on his action than that of superior force. What convinced them was his constant use of radio propaganda to abuse and subvert his neighbours, his insistence on unilateral action rather than negotiation through established international institutions, and his total disdain of the accepted conventions of international behaviour in time of peace.

In the circumstances of 1945–48 the most obvious inheritor of Hitler's refusal to accept any conventions of international behaviour other than those which were of immediate tactical advantage to him appeared to be the USSR. Since the Soviet Union's attitude to the external non-Soviet world was largely reminiscent of the division of the world accepted by classical Islamic law between the abode of peace (*Dar al-Islam*) and the abode of chaos (*Dar al-Harb*), between whom no treaties can be valid for more than a few years, Soviet behaviour was bound to strike European observers as the new embodiment of that destructive national self-centredness which they had so recently and so expensively buried beneath the ruins of the *Führerbunker* in Berlin. (In a sense the processes of détente over the last decade or so have centred around the slow and uncertain establishment of a new set of rules and conventions to govern, at least in part, relations between the Soviet and non-Soviet worlds.)

What the historian has to recognize is that in certain important respects the image of the world entertained by substantial sections of American opinion and translated into practice by much of the

American policy-making apparatus was the mirror image of that entertained by the Soviet Union. The American picture was however more subtle in that the external American world fell not into one but a number of categories. The Soviet world and that of its coerced satellites were only one such area. To this was to be added that of the new emergent nations, of which India was only the largest and most significant, and whose behaviour subsequent to the achievement of independence was to be so disappointing to American expectations. The older nations of Europe, including Britain, made up yet a third category. American policy-makers saw no incongruity in counting these as allies and fellow members of the "Free World" while at the same time intervening in their domestic politics or attempting to use their dependence on American Marshall aid to school their behaviour (as in the case of the conflict between the Netherlands and Indonesia) in a way consonant with American views of international morality. Any attempt to discuss the attitudes of the non-Soviet participants in the Cold War has to recognize and take account of the strains imposed on the alliance politics of the Western bloc by this attitude among American policy-makers, and the reactions of their partners to it, as well as the mutual suspicions and restraints on action the recognition of this source of strain imposed on policy-makers on both sides of the Atlantic.

The last set of considerations that must govern us as contemporary historians has to do with the nature of the subject under discussion, the Cold War itself. There can be no doubt that it was a genuine clash of ideologies, and that the Soviet role in its origins was more than the purely reactive role depicted by some U.S. revisionists. There were far-reaching incompatibilities between the systems of internal government and of international relations which each of the two principal groups of policy-makers, in Washington and London, believed to be in their interest and in accordance with their ideals. No one who spent, as I did, the years 1947–48 on the ground in Central Europe—listening to the groundswell of fears, rumours, and reports; meeting the floods of refugees from the democratic parties of Eastern Europe, especially from Czechoslovakia and Hungary; following Soviet policy in East Germany and in Soviet-occupied Austria—can dismiss the Cold War as an invention of one section of President Truman's policy-makers. Seen from London, what is most striking is the slowness and weakness of the American response to what in British eyes was the misuse by the Soviet Union of the dominance in East and Central Europe won by their armies, and their determination to tolerate no one but the most obedient and brainwashed of puppets in the governments of the areas they occupied. The evidence for a determined and continuous policy aimed at the establishment of Soviet power as far west of the Oder-Neisse as was possible stretches well back into the war period, at least as far as the Teheran Conference and the preceding Soviet victories.

The Cold War can be said to have taken its origins in Europe in two senses. In the first place, it was the consequence of the destruction of the major powers of Europe as a result of the outcome of the 30 years of civil war in Europe between Britain, France, and Germany. Without this there could have been no Soviet-American confrontation in Central Europe. In the second, both of the superpowers, America and Russia, are ideological constructs, making claims on the loyalties of humanity far outside the bases of national citizenship to which individual loyalty was owed in the classic European system of international politics. Both ideologies embody heretical deviations from the two main strands of European traditional political culture involved in the civil war: particularist, participatory, pluralist, elective democracy in which sovereignty is exercised under the restraint of law; and universalist, collectivist empire in which prerogative is exercised by a single ruler or caucus of rulers in the name of the collectivity. Law comes second to the interests of the state, monist and monopolist, single-valued in its morality, and the practice of sovereignty is legitimized by plebiscite where it had once been exercised by divine right.

The spread of the Cold War to East and Southeast Asia and the Pacific littoral was the immediate consequence of the U.S.-Soviet confrontation arising from the occupation of Korea. In the longer run, however, it sprang from the period of European hegemony in East and Southeast Asia and the challenge to and destruction of that hegemony by the empire of Japan. Japan brought East and Southeast Asia into the scope of the European civil war and its outcome by her attempt to take advantage of that civil war to pursue her own policy of expansion to the point where the resistance of the United States was directly aroused; this despite the lessons of Japanese experience in pursuing a similar course during World War I.

As a result of the destruction of the European great powers in the 30 years of European civil war, Europe became the anvil rather than the hammer, the object rather than the subject, of international politics, the confrontation and political battlefield of the superpowers. Japan, failing to pursue a policy of moderate expansion, found herself after 1945 in a similar position.

This was, however, to be complicated by the final victory of the Chinese Communists in the 35-year war of the Chinese revolution. This brought China into the position of dominant successor state to Japan on the Asian mainland, a development which Japanese policy had been designed to prevent since the 1890s. Since the United States had succeeded to Japan's position as the dominant maritime power of the western Pacific, Sino-American confrontation was almost inevitable, and was made such by the identification of the Chinese Communist party with the Soviet bloc.

The consequent Sino-Soviet alignment was to last a little less long and was to break up much more dramatically than the North Atlantic alliance, which was its Euro-American analogue. Both were casualties of the end of the 1950s. The public breach in the European case came with the famous press conference held by President de Gaulle in January 1963 in which Britain's application to join the European Economic Community was rejected as a consequence of the Anglo-American agreement on the *Polaris* missiles. In the Sino-Soviet case it came with the Soviet decision to sign a partial test-ban treaty with America and Britain the following July. The North Atlantic alliance remained formally in being, and U.S. relations with most of the powers of Western Europe remained cordial; but historians, especially those who view subsequent developments from London's viewpoint, let alone from that of Paris, cannot help but recognize a definite separation of U.S. and European policies, stemming in part from the U.S. military involvement on the mainland of Southeast Asia, consequent to the U.S. decision in 1954 to take on the role of successor to the European hegemony dismantled at the Geneva Southeast Asian conference, and in part from the financial weakness which affected the overseas balance of payments of the United States from 1960 onward and from the impact of that financial weakness on Europe.

From the vantage point of 1975–76, it is clear that to depict the Cold War, even in its earliest years after the denouement of the European civil war in 1945, as a bilateral conflict between the groups of ideologically opposed powers is a grotesque and misleading oversimplification. Even before the end of its first European phase in 1954–55 with the Geneva conference on Southeast Asia and the first summit conference the following year, there were three groups of participants. With the Bandung Conference that same year, and the beginnings of Afro-Asian nonalignment and Chinese cultivation of it, the Cold War becomes four- or five-way; indeed it is possible to argue that after 1955 the form in which U.S.-Soviet rivalry is expressed has changed so radically that the "Cold War" is an entirely misleading way to describe it. If the term is essential, then a distinction should be drawn between the "first Cold War," which drew to its end between 1953–55, and the second, which followed the period of thaw in which the Soviet Union had to bring Polish and Hungarian nationalism to heel and the United States had to bring down the last Anglo-French attempt to exercise power outside Europe in the Suez enterprise, and can be said to have opened with Khrushchev's first Berlin "ultimatum" in November 1958.

This recognition of the pluralist nature even of the "first Cold War" brings me to my last point: that the Japanese participants in this conference should reflect on the similarities between the Japanese and European positions relative to the superpowers hitherto recognized as the main protagonists in the Cold War. It would be my contention that there is more in common between the Japanese and West European experiences and attitudes than there is between these and the experiences and attitudes of either of the superpowers; and that to explore these issues would form a fruitful basis for cooperation and possibly a future conference between Japanese and British historians.

The Roots of Cold War Doctrine
The Esoteric and the Exoteric

Nagai Yōnosuke

The Paradox of the Containment Line

The structural features of the Cold War seem to have been symbolized by the term "containment line." This expression has a dual meaning. First, it connotes a "geographic" defense or demarcation line, namely, one dividing the world into national spheres of influence in accordance with the traditional interstate system. Second, it suggests an "ideological" symbolic line which has been created for the purpose of making artificial distinctions along strategic Cold War lines. A central problem for the Truman administration in the winter of 1949–50 was the question of how to draw a containment line in the latter sense of the term across the Asian region like the one designed with more calculation by the North Atlantic Treaty. As evidenced by various diplomatic documents, including NSC 8, NSC 13/2, NSC 34, NSC 48/2, as well as the text of a speech delivered by Secretary of State Dean Acheson at the National Press Club in January 1950, the Truman administration's approach to Asia before the outbreak of the Korean War had been quite similar to that of the Nixon Doctrine in such points as the high esteem for rising Asian nationalism, the Asians' spirit of self-help, insistence on the principle of noninterference in the domestic affairs of states on the East Asian mainland, etc. However, the North Korean attack against South Korea across the 38th parallel in June 1950 forced Washington to abandon its policy based on a relatively "limited notion of contain-

15

ment" and opened the way to the unlimited "globalization and militarization of containment." Why did all this happen?

While I have no intention of elaborating here on the origins of the Korean War, attention must be focused on something pointed out by Marshall Shulman: "The Communist attack against South Korea, instead of being interpreted primarily in the local context of developments in Asia, came to be understood in the West, and I believe wrongly, as an indication of heightened Soviet militancy generally, which might also manifest itself by overt aggression in Europe and elsewhere."[1] It seems not unlikely that North Korea's incursion into the south, comparable to the North Vietnamese armed offensives against South Vietnam, was primarily aimed at taking advantage of the "localization of conflict" in the wake of the withdrawal of both U.S. and Soviet troops from the Korean peninsula in order to unleash a revolutionary upheaval in South Korea and eventually to overthrow Rhee Syngman's tottering regime. However, the view that the North Koreans launched the attack as an "independent act without Soviet authorization" must be dismissed as "childish nonsense," as Charles Bohlen admitted in his memoirs. For it would be only natural to ask, "How could an army, trained in every respect by the Soviet Union, with Soviet advisers at every level, and utterly dependent on Moscow for supplies, move without Soviet authorization?"[2] Nevertheless, we can accept Charles Bohlen's conclusion on the Korean War as being closer to the truth: "There was little chance of the Soviet Union's repeating the invasion in any place, such as Germany. The Soviet action in Korea was limited strictly to Korea."[3]

Yet the reaction shown by the Truman administration in the 24 hours after the outbreak of the war was, as Ernest May sharply pointed out, entirely contrary to the policy it had pursued until then. In the words of May: "The answer is not that American policy had changed, nor, though close to the truth, that there were two policies which happened to collide. Rather, it is that the United States had two *kinds* of policies—the 'calculated' vs. the 'axiomatic.' "[4] According to him, while the Acheson speech represented the "calculated policy"—formulations based on means-end calculations—the action taken by Truman in the Korean War, like Dulles's unexpected reaction to the Suez crisis of 1956, was not on that level, although the two kinds of policies were tightly interwoven. It was an instinctive reaction that expressed the national style, deeply rooted in American experience and tradition—a phenomenon similar to that of the man who, faced with a crisis, suddenly finds himself speaking with the provincial accent of his childhood. Ernest May's suggestion as to where the problem lay might be right. Still, it seems possible to say that, seen from a more comprehensive viewpoint, the whole decision-making process in the United States before the outbreak of the Korean War, including Congress and public opinion, already contained a domestic momentum toward the "globalization and militarization of containment," which, catalyzed by events at home and abroad from 1949 through 1950, was growing daily.

Historical "events" are not facts. It is a question of the frame of reference through which the accidental happening on the Korean peninsula is perceived. In fact, the whole frame of reference for policy-makers as illustrated by the NSC 68 paper suggests that even if there had been no Korean War, a similar development would have been enough to integrate the strategic views of several of the opinion elite in the government. In view of this, the Korean War is more pertinently interpreted as an event that had a strong "catalyzing effect" on the formation of a "Cold War consensus," rather than "as one that marked the true 'turning point' in America's foreign policy."[5]

Despite my inclination to give greater emphasis to the role of contingencies in history, I am reluctant to accept John L. Gaddis's speculations as to what effects the Korean War did not have. "The policies of Truman, Marshall and Acheson, had they been allowed to run their course," Gaddis argues, "might have resulted in the evolution of a multipolar world operating on the balance-of-power game principle . . . a world not too different, ironically enough, from that now apparently sought by Henry Kissinger and Richard M. Nixon."[6] In my opinion, Gaddis overestimates the calculated level of foreign policy on the one hand and overemphasizes the "accidental event" in history on the other. In a sense, this is rather like attributing the responsibility for the mass bombings that devastated Dresden, Tokyo, Hiroshima, and Nagasaki during World War II not to the Anglo-American military strategy with its emphasis on technology but to the mistake committed by 10 of the 170 German bombers that raided London on the night of August 24, 1940.[7]

In spite of the substantial changes in the power realities of today's multipolar world, Nixon and Kissinger had to pay a high price at home, in the form of the Watergate incident and the subsequent resignation of the president, for the evolution into a "balance of power" diplomacy. It seems noteworthy that throughout the Cold War, such "realists" as George F. Kennan, who had an aversion to "public diplomacy" in democracies and a yearning for the nineteenth-century type of cool-cabinet diplomacy, had to experience frustrations in the peculiar political culture of the United States. Notwithstanding Kennan's warnings in the concluding part of his famous long telegram of February 22, 1946,[8] the United States, by projecting its own universalism into Soviet intentions through a kind of mirror image, began gradually to build up a sort of "crisis theology" among the elite, which turned out to be similar in nature to the enemy ideology. As a result of this, American actions were a typical case of self-fulfilling prophecy by making a reality of what Stalin had termed "capitalist encirclement." No doubt the Russians made a similar self-fulfilling prophecy on their side.

The present paper aims at analyzing the symbolic interaction between the esoteric doctrine of Cold War, which stems from what might be called "epidemiological geopolitics," and public opinion.[9] I do not share the views of Athan Theoharis and other revisionists who advanced a sort of conspiracy theory in which Truman's policy was defined not as an attempt to win public support for his foreign policy but as a deliberate symbol manipulation to conceal the failures of the domestic reform measures by diverting public attention to the threat of an external enemy.[10] For it may be generally said that revisionist historians commit the fallacy of speculating about the intentions of the actors directly from the outcome (as perceived in hindsight), ignoring the ironic contrast between what the Truman administration thought it was doing and what it actually achieved, the gap between the administration's intentions and the eventual outcome.

The Epidemiological Nature of Containment

No fewer than eight times, from the autumn of 1945 through February of 1946, the United States received a series of communications from Ho Chi Minh, asking American support at the UN for the same free status that the United States was giving the Philippines.[11] At that time the United States was beginning to take up the position that dealing with the Soviet Union with "patience and firmness" was the only effective policy, short of war, to counter the Russian challenge in Europe. It was an irony of history that while Washington made no response to Ho Chi Minh's overtures, a long cable received from George F. Kennan, then the American chargé d'affaires in Moscow, on February 22, 1946, evoked a reaction from Washington officials that was described as "nothing less than sensational." The telegram, which Kennan himself described as being "like one of those primers put out by alarmed Congressional committees or by the Daughters of the American Revolution, designed to arouse the citizenry to the dangers of the Communist conspiracy,"[12] was copied on the orders of Secretary of the Navy James Forrestal to be read by the president and hundreds, if not thousands, of higher officers in the armed services. Kennan's esoteric interpretation of Russian external activities gave a clear direction and theoretical endorsement to the frame of reference that was already taking shape among Washington officials.

When Franklin D. Roosevelt was president, he would pay little regard to the function of the State Department and would let America's foreign policy be executed by a small group of aides who were amateurs in the matter of diplomacy. Under such circumstances, the guiding principle of foreign policy was a sort of "hubris of worldwide do-goodism"[13] fraught with the kind of universalistic rhetoric that could be seen in the Four Freedoms, the Atlantic Charter, the UN Charter, and so on. Kennan and other professionals in the State Department were of the generation that not only shared the memory of humiliation throughout the thirties but also, being very much "realists" in believing in Realpolitik, had often harbored dissatisfaction with Roosevelt's concern over public opinion in domestic politics. President Truman, unlike his predecessor, positively appointed professionals of the State Department to positions of trust, initiating significant changes in the line-up of American foreign policy personnel. Thus the department's professionals for the first time found themselves filing papers and memoranda with a prospect of influencing decision making in the White House.[14]

Before proceeding to an examination of the "frame of acceptability" used by Washington officials in approving the telegram, it is perhaps worthwhile to review a sort of epidemiological way of thinking represented by the telegram.[15] The propagation and dissemination of religious, ideological, and cultural symbols is discussed, more often than not, as being analogous to the spread of epidemic diseases. Kennan's telegram has a typical epidemiological structure in that it seeks the pathogenic organism, claims to have discovered the medium of the pathogenic bacteria, calls for a strengthening of the healthy body against an attack by the bacteria, and stresses public education in hygiene and improvement of antiepidemic facilities, mode of life, and environmental circumstances. I might point out, however, that Kennan, without examining the most important epidemiological question of whether communism is an "endemic" disease peculiar to the political culture of the Soviet Union and other underdeveloped countries, or an "epidemic" that might plague the whole world, propounded his theory on the premise that communism *is* an epidemic. Particularly conspicuous from the standpoint of rhetoric are such sentences in his telegram as: "Much depends on health and vigor of our society. World Communism is like malignant parasite which feeds only on diseased tissue," and "We must study it with the same courage, detachment, objectivity, and the same determination not to be emotionally provoked or unseated by it with which a doctor studies unruly and unreasonable individuals."

On the analogy of a theological system, Kennan made a clear distinction between the exoteric doctrine officially announced by the Soviet leadership, which stressed its concept of capitalist encirclement, and the esoteric doctrine of the Kremlin, which had deep roots in the history and environment of Russia. Suggesting that it was a mistake to understand Soviet diplomacy in terms of capitalist encirclement, Kennan said: "At the bottom of the Kremlin's neurotic view of world affairs is a traditional and instinctive Russian sense of insecurity." He went on to define the officially announced line of the Soviet government and party as "not based on any objective analysis of the situation *beyond Russia's border*" which "arises mainly from basic inner-Russian necessities." In the end Kennan dismissed "Marxist dogma" as nothing more than a "perfect vehicle for sense of insecurity."

To be sure, Kennan's esoteric interpretation of Soviet conduct, isolating the "pathogenic bacteria," prompted the U.S. to do away with its previous "symptomatic treatment," thus opening a way to a more fundamental cure—the freedom of a nonmilitary unilateral action aimed at containing, first and foremost, the spread of the "bacteria" themselves. This is evident in the light of a memorandum which was carried in *Foreign Relations* (vol. I, 1946).[16] According to the memorandum, Kennan's telegram prompted Washington to realize that it had erred in "adopting a firm and friendly attitude in dealing with the Soviet government" due to the administration's two current misapprehensions about Soviet motivations, namely, "capitalist encirclement" and "suspicions." "Its source *lies with the border* of the Soviet Union," and, therefore, the Soviet's unilateral actions would continue unaltered irrespective of the changes in the actions and attitudes of the United States and other Western countries, it was asserted. In conclusion, the memorandum acknowledged no need to take account of the Russian disapproval of the presence of American troops on the peripheries of the Soviet Union, including China, Cuba, and Iceland.

SWNCC 282 (March 27, 1946)[17] stated that "the maintenance of such a world peace will depend on mutual cooperation among Britain, Russia and the United States." But SWN 4096, dated February 21, 1946, the day before the arrival of Kennan's telegram, reflected a radical change in the government's posture toward the Soviet Union. It said: "From a military point of view, the consolidation and the development of the power of Russia is [*sic*] the greatest threat to the United States in the feasible future,"[18] adding that "the adoption of a firm and friendly attitude in our dealings with the Soviet Government was strongly endorsed with, however, emphasis upon firmness."

At about the same time, President Truman instructed Clark Clifford, then the most influential presidential adviser, to prepare

a summary of American relations with the Soviet Union in consultation with the Secretary of State, the Secretary of War, the
Attorney General, the Secretary of the Navy, Fleet Admiral
William Leahy, the Joint Chiefs of Staff, Ambassador Edwin
Pauley, the director of the Central Intelligence Agency, and
others who had special knowledge in this field. They produced a
report which quoted from Kennan's telegram the part dealing
with the basic inner-Russian necessities underlying Soviet actions.[19] The report said: "The language of military power is the
only language which disciples of power politics understand. . . .
Compromise and concessions are considered, by the Soviets, to be
evidences of weakness and they are encouraged by our 'retreats'
to make new and greater demands." Arguing that "in order to
maintain our strength at a level which will be effective in restraining the Soviet Union, the United States must be prepared to wage
atomic and biological warfare," it suggested that "war with
USSR" could be a total war. The report concluded that the
American objective should be to convince the Russians that "we
are too strong to be beaten and too determined to be frightened."

David Riesman, discussing the deepest difference between British and American realism, once pointed out that America's was
often "pseudo-realism" that sprang from fear about masculinity
and that "American men seem constantly pursued by the fear of
unmanliness and therefore feel the need to present themselves as
hard and realistic."[20] As is clear in the rhetoric of the Clifford
report, compromise and concessions are always evidence of weakness and unmanliness for the American. It is with this in the background that a type not to be found among British realists, a proponent of tragic realism as brilliant as Reinhold Niebuhr, whom
Kennan once called "the father of us all," was born.[21] As Kennan
later admitted that "it was I who was naive," it was primarily
due to the mood prevalent in the United States as well as to timing
that his opinion caught the public fancy.[22] At any rate, the accuracy of Kennan's analysis seemed to be substantiated in the case
of the handling of the Iranian crisis, increasing even further the
Truman administration's confidence in its new policy of "patience
with firmness." In an attempt to win public support for its new
policy line, the administration began formulating the "Truman
Doctrine" as an "exoteric doctrine"—a symbol for external pre

sentation to the general public fraught with universalistic rhetoric.

Also published at the time was Kennan's famous X-Article titled "The Sources of Soviet Conduct" in *Foreign Affairs*, which greatly contributed to the molding of public opinion. However, because of the intrinsic ambiguity of the magic word "containment," the article was nothing more than a strange combination of an ideology and geopolitics, which Lloyd C. Gardner in his comment linked to the "Presbyterian elder wrestling with the Bismarckian geopolitician."[23]

As already mentioned, the dual meaning of "containment line" in terms of geography and ideology marked the logical culmination of the development from epidemiological geopolitics. As is suggested by the term "cordon sanitaire," a predecessor to the term "iron curtain" used by Churchill in his famous speech at Fulton, Missouri, on March 5, 1946, the world "containment" has a negative, hygienic sense of protecting the healthy body against the spread of epidemic disease.

Historically, American politicians and businessmen have often used "healthy" as a favorite catchword symbolizing their political stance. Other expressions used in describing the degree of health of a political body were such metaphors as "the disease of Liberty" (Thomas Jefferson), "the scourge of war" (Abraham Lincoln), and, probably the most famous of all, "quarantine," used by Franklin D. Roosevelt in his speech in the autumn of 1937. Giving a classic definition of "epidemiological geopolitics," Roosevelt said, "When an epidemic of physical disease starts to spread, the community approves and joins in a quarantine of the patients in order to protect the health of the community against the spread of the disease."[24] Needless to say, Roosevelt used this political expression to demonstrate the U.S. posture of "strong neutrality" without sanctionary measures like armed intervention so as to awaken the Congress and the general public, still persisting in the attitude of isolationistic neutrality, to the "epidemic of world lawlessness" being spread by the Japanese militarists, Mussolini, and Hitler. President John F. Kennedy also used the word "quarantine" as a political euphemism for a blockade in peacetime in his speech delivered in October 1962 at the time of the Cuban missile crisis. Thus, "containment" too became a magic word with which to

appeal to the general public for support of the Truman administration's attitude of "patience with firmness" vis-à-vis the USSR.

True, Kennan's memoirs contained nebulous points as regards
whether the threat of the Soviet Union implied a military expansion beyond the borders of its sphere of influence in East Europe
or was ideological and political, as exemplified by the communist advances in France and Italy. Also left unanswered was the
question of whether the West's countermeasures against the Soviet
threat should be confined to economic and political means or centered on military force. At any rate, such ambiguities found in
Kennan's memoirs constituted a fatalistic contradiction of the
concept of a containment line.

In the SWNCC memorandum dated April 2, 1946, the containment line was construed as a dual line to cope with both direct and
indirect aggression, thus already evidencing the latent possibility
that, should the restrictions imposed on the utilization of resources,
money, and manpower be removed, the line would be bound to
extend itself unlimitedly.[25] At the root of epidemiological geopolitics was an admixture of the isolationistic mental climate resulting from American innocence and the nation's geographic
remoteness from the rest of the world; the security of the country,
insured up until the latter half of the nineteenth century because
of its geographical position and the British control of the seas;
and a sort of "fear of strangers" or "populist feeling" with its
endemic social psychology. In this light, one may clearly grasp the
"depth-psychological" reasons why the Cold War revisionists have
clung so persistently to W. A. Williams's special interpretation of
the Open Door policy as *an extension of Turner's old frontier thesis*.[26]
In fact, Acheson's speech made at the Congress in 1944, which is
frequently quoted by many of the revisionists under the theoretical
influence of W. A. Williams, has its value, not as an example of
verifying the Cold War policy as an extension of the Open Door
policy, but rather as convincing material in the field of social
psychology, appealing to the subconscious of fearful and anxious
congressmen, business leaders, and the general public. In the
speech Acheson told the Congress: "If you wish to control the entire trade and income of the United States, which means the
life of the people, you could probably fix it so that everything
produced here would be consumed here, but that would com-

pletely change our Constitution, our relation to property, human liberty, and our very conception of law." Apparently implied between the lines is a sense of fear that, should the ethics of free trade and free competition crumble, the vitality of the nation would be lost, and America's native culture, centered around small business, would precipitate a moral disintegration toward mass culture and bureaucratization. The Acheson speech also suggests that in order to maintain the physical health of the nation, it is necessary that the American people always keep the trailblazer attitude, seeking to discover "new frontiers" at home and abroad. Despite the essentially negative strategy it implied, George Kennan's X-Article also had a strong appeal for the people because it was fraught with such rhetoric as "stand up," "manfully," "not aggressively," "application of counterforce," "firm out," "vigilant containment," and so on.

As an alienated intellectual, Kennan himself was known to be obsessed with the fear of chaos intrinsic and latent in American society. At a meeting of the International Association for Cultural Freedom at Princeton in December 1968, Kennan asserted the necessity for the U.S. to seek a fundamental change at home, which he called "*dirigisme*," in order to achieve a full-fledged disengagement in its foreign policy.[27] Secretary of the Navy Forrestal had a high opinion of Kennan's emphasis on the ideological elements of Soviet conduct and encouraged him to write "Psychological Background of Soviet Foreign Policy," which was the basis of his X-Article. Forrestal's emotional obsession with communism is indicated by his insistence in the famous letter to Walter Lippmann that "the fundamental question in respect to our relations with Russia is whether we are dealing with a nation or religion."[28] As Lloyd C. Gardner suggested, his obsession came from the old fear that European radicalism would finally terrorize the world like a German head on the shoulders of a Russian peasant. He made it a German head on the shoulders of a Mongol warrior. His reference to Marx as a direct spiritual heir of Genghis Khan in the letter revealed Forrestal himself as a typical example of a man who thinks in terms of epidemiological geopolitics and betrays a fear resembling that of the Yellow Peril.[29] It is particularly to be noted that, as Roosevelt's usage of the word "quarantine" as political jargon suggests, there evidently was a latent fear on the part of the Anglo-Saxons, who were losing their strategic supremacy on the seas. Without a shadow of doubt, Forrestal was impressed with Kennan's paper because he found there the justification he had been seeking for extending American naval strength throughout the Mediterranean.

According to the German political scientist Carl Schmitt, world history, as far as Western civilization is concerned, has been the annals of "war between Sea and Land" in the symbolical sense, with the sea symbolized by "Leviathan" and the land by "Behemoth."[30] As established by the famous navel-strategy theory of Mahan, Anglo-Saxon strategic supremacy lay in the control of maritime supply routes and the encirclement of the continents. Liddel Hart observed that the "British way of war" was an exclusive reliance, based on their strategic supremacy at sea, upon such indirect, and essentially commerical, techniques as blockade, piracy, commando attacks, and gun-boat diplomacy, and the British refrained from the use of mass armies for intervention on land. Under this strategy, it was Britain's allies who were to pay the cost of the war in terms of human lives. Out of rational and hardheaded consideration of their national interests, the British sought to maintain the balance of power among the continental countries and would not allow any single power to assume a dominant position. However, Leviathan came to create technology within itself, and through a "spatial revolution," caused by the expansion of "informational" space and cosmic space due to the development of aircraft, missiles, and other means of communication, Britain has lost much of its strategic supremacy based on the dichotomy of sea and land. Exactly as the appearance of terms like "*la guerre froide*" (a French expression used in the thirties from which "Cold War" is said to derive) and "fifth column" would suggest, the rise of a new Behemoth on the Eurasian continent in the twentieth century, with gigantic manpower, ideological infiltration, and guerrilla tactics as its main weapons, began to cast a shadow of apprehension over the security of the United States. For, since the exposure of a spy incident in Canada in February 1946, the rapid spread of an unusual mental climate which Edward Shils described as the "torment of secrecy" has been unavoidable in open American society, which consists essentially of pluralistic ethnic and religious groups.

The Way to the Militarization of Containment

On May 7, 1947, the State Department announced the establishment, effective May 5, of the Policy Planning Staff for insuring the formulation of a long-range policy. It was to function as a central machinery for implementing what George F. Kennan in his long telegram had termed "our political general staff work." Soon afterward, the National Security Council (NSC) came into being under the National Security Act of July 26, 1947.[31] With the help of these new organizations, Truman, Marshall, Kennan, and their associates were able to develop a long-range and systematic Cold War policy in the period from late 1947 through early 1948 (NSC 20/4, November 23, 1948).[32] One of the most difficult questions posed in the process of integrating the diverse views held by the White House, the Pentagon, and the State Department was how to resolve the fundamental contradictions of the concept of containment line. For the strategy of containment, intrinsically "negative, ideologically," excluded the possibility of employing the same measures as those used by the Soviet Union to dominate Eurasia through ideological warfare—propaganda, subversion, and systematic terrorism.

In order to win the hearts of the people, it was imperative for the administration to adhere to the axiomatic policy, originating in the Monroe Doctrine, of not resorting to the use of force. In order, too, to force the Kremlin into accepting a rule against trespass, Washington had no alternative but to draw an anti-Soviet defense line along "the existing boundary of the Soviet empire, not our borders or some intermediate line." Nor could it be replaced by the lines dividing the spheres of influence based on the traditional European state systems, a formula apparently sought by Stalin at Yalta. The containment line thus drawn not only provided the Soviet Union with an advantage of "shorter logistical lines of communication" as warned against by Walter Lippmann, but also substantiated Stalin's fear of capitalist encirclement, causing in turn a vicious cycle of a tougher Soviet diplomatic stance and greater American caution against communist expansion.

It seems fair to assume, as the revisionists emphatically asserted, that the communist ideology was essentially "endemic" and not "epidemic," and that the notion of a worldwide communist conspiracy was a projection of America's own universalism.[33] In the first place, a defense line to contain ideological infiltration through local communist parties would be a highly permeable one drawn on a topological space. Furthermore, in order to minimize the burden and cost involved in keeping the line intact, there would be no other choice for the United States but to establish a system of alliances through which to seek burden-sharing on the basis of the "defense of Europe first" strategy.

The new defense strategy formulated on the basis of these considerations naturally provided naval officers, airmen, and other guards of "Leviathan" with a good justification to win authorization for more spending on building carriers and bombers.[34] It must be noted that America's Cold War ideology, unlike the communists', was principally intended to provide its allies with a basic frame of reference for spelling out their respective interpretations of world developments, not with positive directions or directives for action. As Walter Lippmann aptly pointed out: "The movement of opinion is slower than the movement of events. Because of that, the cycle of subjective sentiments on war and peace is usually out of gear with the cycle of objective developments."[35] This holds true for the whole process of the Cold War days and also for the present global scene marked by détente.

With the start of the Cold War, the Truman administration came to reevaluate Japan as a possibe element contributing to the global anticommunist strategy. The administration's attempt to bring Japan, as well as Germany, "two of the greatest workshops of Europe and Asia" (Acheson's speech in Cleveland, Mississippi, in May 1947), into the strategic framework of the containment line was snagged, however, because of differences of view with the Eastern Commission, which retained much of a "pre–Cold War flavor" (see FEC 230), and also with the Supreme Command of the Allied Powers in Japan. Great Britain was found to be in no mood to welcome an economically powerful Japan, while Australia, New Zealand, and other Asian and Pacific countries were more concerned about a revival of Japanese militarism than the Soviet threat. Under such circumstances, it was a policy task of great proportions for the Truman administration in 1946 through 1948 to adjust the "time lags" and "standardize" an international recognition of the gravity of the Cold War.[36]

It seems fair to say that until the Czechoslovakian coup in February 1948, which brought home to the world the gravity of the East-West ideological confrontation and was an important factor in the formation of the NATO, the Truman administration had acted with prudence, exercising restraint in its conduct. Evidently, the administration had been well aware of a subtle difference between what the diplomatic elite in Washington had understood as the esoteric doctrine of Cold War strategy and the exoteric doctrine which had been propounded primarily to win public support. For example, the initial reaction of President Truman to the death of Jan Masaryk at a press conference in March 1948 was a cautious one. He said: "I cannot make my [*sic*] any official statement. . . . I think, though, that we should be careful, as General Marshall said, not to let any passions get the better of us until we know the facts."[37]

However, public opinion in the U.S. stiffened abruptly from the summer through the autumn of 1949 in the wake of the Communist takeover of the China mainland and the loss of America's nuclear monopoly. Symbolizing the agitated public opinion was the perjury case involving the State Department official Alger Hiss. As is clearly seen in NSC 20, the United States had maintained an ambiguous attitude as to where to draw a containment line across Asia. However, the loss of China to the Communist forces began compelling the U.S. government, through 1949 and 1950, to weigh seriously the question of a defense perimeter in Asia— not a provisional or expedient one like the Berlin Wall and the 38th parallel on the Korean peninsula, but one strategically well calculated. The new situation required a dispassionate strategic judgment of whether or not South Korea, Taiwan, and the Indochina penisula should be included in the projected containment line. Consequently, the National Security Council came out with a series of regional strategic decisions such as NSC 8 (for South Korea in April 1948), NSC 13/2 and NSC 13/3 (for Japan), NSC 34 (for China in September 1948), NSC 37/7 (for Taiwan in August 1948), NSC 48/1 and NSC 48/2 (for all of Asia in December 1949), NSC 64 (for Indochina in February 1950) and NSC 124/1 (for Southeast Asia in February 1952). Among them, NSC 48/1 and NSC 48/2, the latter of which was submitted to the president toward the end of 1949, are, along with NSC 68 (April

14, 1950), papers indispensable for grasping the administration's esoteric doctrine of Cold War that remained in force until the outbreak of the Korean War.

NSC 48/1 was drafted to "assess and appraise the position of the United States with respect to Asia on the basis of our national security interests."[38] Fully cognizant of Asia's distinct conditions and positions marked by "poverty, nationalism and revolution," it urged the formulation of a new Asia policy from the "Asiatic point of view" to assist the Asian peoples "in the development of truly independent, friendly, stable and self-sustaining states." Stating that the United States "should refrain from taking the lead in the movements which must necessarily be of Asian origin," the paper unequivocally set forth a policy of noninterference in the Asian mainland. With respect to global strategy, it defined Asia as "only one of several fronts on which the United States directly or indirectly confronts the U.S.S.R.," and said, "A successful strategic defense in the East must be assured with a minimum expenditure of military manpower and material in order that major effort may be expended in the West." Therefore, "the minimum position is considered to consist of at least our present military position in the Asian offshore island chain," and "the first line of strategic defense should include Japan, the Ryukyus and the Philippines." As Ernest May suggests, the United State gave "more considerations to Taiwan than to Korea, because Taiwan seemed at the time the more probable target for the next communist threat and partly, too, because Korea had been the subject of so much discussion in the Pacific."

As for Taiwan, the administration reaffirmed the conclusion drawn in NSC 37/7 of August 22, 1949, on the basis of estimates made by the Joint Chiefs of Staff (J.C.S.) and the CIA, that "the strategic importance of Formosa does not justify overt military action." NSC 48/1 also understood that "the colonial-nationalist conflict provides a fertile field for subversive communist movements, and it is now clear that Southeast Asia is the target for a coordinated offensive directed by the Kremlin." However, NSC 48/1 stated that the United States, as a Western power in any area where the bulk of the population had long been suspicious of Western influence, should so far as possible refrain from taking any lead in Southeast Asia. The United States should "encourage the people of India, Pakistan, the Philippines and other Asian states to take the leadership in meeting the common problems of the area." NSC 48/2 also pointed out the need to urge the French to remove barriers to "Bao Dai or other noncommunist nationalist leaders obtaining the support of a substantial proportion of the Vietnamese."

Secretary of State Acheson's speech of January 1950 before the National Press Club was, like the China White Paper, a popular edition of NSC 48. The speech, which later gained renown for its use of the term "defense perimeter," contained words of praise for Asian nationalism, a pledge of noninterference in affairs on the Asian continent, and prospect of an imminent rift between China and the Soviet Union. In short, the speech may well be called a predecessor to the Nixon Doctrine in that both clearly defined the national identity of the "Leviathan" America. It must be noted, however, that in an open contemporary society, news and information are nondiscriminatory, and that their spread cannot be restricted to particular audiences. To borrow the words of James Reston, "The Secretary of State is always talking to various audiences at the same time. He may be talking mainly to the American people, but his words are also studied with the greatest care in Moscow and Peking."[39]

How and in what frame of reference the Kremlin interpreted the Acheson speech and what effect it may have had on the outbreak of the Korean War are the questions which have remained unanswered. But the speech caused deep and far-reaching reverberations in the U.S., provoking China lobbyists in the Congress and providing the most powerful weapon to the Republicans to attack the Democratic administration. As Norman Graebner has suggested, "It has been said a neo-isolationist was the one who wanted to fight in China." Also chagrined at the state of affairs on the domestic front was Truman himself, who wrote: "To orthodox Republicans, the island of Formosa was more important than the island of England."[40]

General MacArthur and other army officers supporting the right-wing Republicans, who were resentful of the unduly belittled significance of the Pacific theater under the U.S. "Eurocentric" grand strategy during World War II and unsatisfied with the anti-climatic ending of Japan's surrender, tended to create a mental attitude which might be called a kind of psychological *"Zeigar-nik"* effect.[41] It was some thirteen thousand Catholics who had immigrated into the New World from East Europe, Ireland, and Italy over the period from 1900 to 1914 that were the chief promoters of the Roosevelt Revolution. The massive urbanization movements and the changeover of generations that took place from 1943 to 1953, as well as the subsequent "reappearance of the frontier in a new urban form as one of the most important political forces,"[42] were most dramatically demonstrated when Truman won an unexpected landslide victory in the 1948 presidential election. In its wake, the older generation, or prisoners of the past, who shared the memory of the Great Depression and the lesson of Munich, became unusually interested in international issues, thus presenting a phenomenon contrary to the original expectations held by Truman and Acheson. As the United States rose rapidly in postwar international politics as a hegemonic power to replace Great Britain and France, so did those segments of the American population rise up to middle-class status, acquiring in turn a sense of unreality and uncertainty as though they were hanging up in the air. As befitted their status as members of the middle class, who were supposed to have an opinion, the people came to have their own views of various external problems on the basis of a new outlook on the world. However, the official interpretations of world affairs as furnished by the government came into conflict with people's intolerance of ambiguity,[43] making them feel that the fundamental ambiguity of the containment policy itself constituted a threat to their self-assurance and sense of reality.

Especially from 1949 onward, the Democratic administration, faced with diverse developments within and without the country, seemed incapable of adequately coping with the threat of communism. The strange combination of the image of homosexuals with that of intellectuals clearly implicit in the symbolism of the "Hiss incident"—the State Department's "cooking-pusher Harvard-trained sissy"[44]—presaged a kind of mass hysteria seeking internal scapegoats to make up for the injured American illusion of omnipotence. It was in fact out of this hotbed that McCarthyism was born as a "revenge synthesis."[45]

The dramatic change in the popular mood across the United States was evident in the rapid decline of the spirit of bipartisanship as symbolized by Vandenberg's leadership in the passage of the Marshall Plan and the Truman Doctrine. It was with this domestic situation in the background that Truman signed a directive initiating the H-bomb program on January 30, 1950, and that the National Security Council decided to conduct a general strategic situation on January 5, 1950. Paul Nitze, who succeeded Kennan as Policy Planning Staff director, took the initiative in carrying on the research programs which resulted in the drafting of a paper known as NSC 68 in mid-March 1950. The paper was submitted to the president in April.

Back in the winter of 1949, differences of opinion had already been known to exist between the government officials concerned, including Kennan, Nitze, Bohlen, the J.C.S., and other military officers, over the military implications of containment. For one thing, Kennan, attaching importance to the political and economic aspects of the concept of containment, called for flexibility in diplomacy and opposed a general policy or long-run rigid planning which he said would inhibit the future freedom of action. It was his belief that a current budgetary ceiling of roughly $13.5 billion a year should be enough to meet all the military requirements in carrying out the containment policy. In his opinion, a localized, small, and unified task force, highly mobile and highly mechanized, would be best suited as a military strength to be maintained for carrying out a flexible containment policy.[46] On the other hand, the military establishment favored long-range planning, giving full consideration to arms development, the mobilization of manpower, and logistic requirements. Perhaps it was inevitable that NSC 68, drafted under the initiative of Nitze, a former member of the Strategic Bombing Survey, and Major General J. H. Landon, an air force member of the Joint Strategic Survey Committee, should have been based on "the airmen's concept of full-scale warfare." This tendency was clearly reflected in a briefing given at the Defense Department by General Richard C. Lindsay, deputy director for Strategic Plans of the Joint Staff. While acknowledging the Pentagon's position of acquiring capabilities to wage small wars as far as the budgetary limitations permitted, Lindsay said, "In order to be ready for the worst, they had given up special limited-war capabilities to concentrate on large-scale war capabilities, particularly the Strategic Air Command with its massive air atomic retaliatory capability."[47] This typical airmen's way of thinking on war proved to have a strong appeal to the Congress and grass-roots opinion in the United States. This was because the strategy of a "manly" attack at a freely chosen locality vital to the enemy and far from the national soil was in agreement with budgetary limitations, and also because the strategy, more than offering a way to deal the enemy an effective blow, minimized the sacrifice that had to be made in terms of manpower and time, resources of extreme scarcity for a metropolitan power.[48]

Even Dean Acheson, in an appraisal of the NSC 68 paper in later years, cited a staff members' criticism of the document as "the most ponderous expression of elementary ideas." Presumably this referred to such points as its clear statement of the concept of the zero-sum game in the polarization of power[49] and its mood of "crisis theology" as expressed in such phrases as "the will of God" and "the absolute power." He made an attempt at self-justification, however, by saying that "we need education in the obvious more than investigation of the obscure." However, the true source of the paper's mood of "crisis theology" was the necessity of assuming the existence of an enemy representing "absolute evil"—that is, an enemy deserving of annihilation—and hence the necessity of recognizing that a total H-bomb war could occur and of justifying preparations for such a war.

The document stands out most clearly for its emphasis on the extreme asymmetry in the means that the respective sides would choose and on the role of military strength in the containment policy. The objective, of course, was realization of coexistence with the USSR by employing a mix of soft and hard approaches. But more than anything else, it argued, U.S. military weakness had so far prevented the containment policy's success. In this connection, NSC 68 points out that the U.S. has "the greatest potential of any single nation in the world," but that "numerical inferiority in forces in being and in total manpower" leads to "a sharp disparity between our actual military strength and our commitment." This indicates the kind of specific considerations that evidently led to the conclusion that the only course of action left was the "rapid build-up of political, economic, and military strength in the Free World."

The document was by no means a product of normal organizational procedures on the national level. As Paul Y. Hammond has substantiated in a case study,[50] it was part and parcel of classical bureaucratic maneuvering on the intragovernmental level to secure larger budget allocations, and hence it exemplified the "hidden hand in a government" mediating between various groups' interests. Bohlen, believing that there was "absolutely no chance that its recommendation for a huge increase in defense spending would be adopted," desired at the least to make the draft more precise and accurate as "a useful exercise" to clarify the government's thinking on Cold War economic problems.[51] In response, Kennan stressed that no matter how accurate or rational the execution of planning, misapplication in the stage of execution could easily result in perversion of the intention, a basic apprehension that he had come to feel in the light of his experience in governmental policy making since 1947.[52] Moreover, as a professional diplomat who respected the esoteric art of "finesse" in diplomacy, he believed that judging the nature of the Soviet threat simply in terms of capability, without considering the nation's incessantly changing intentions, would give rise to oversimplification of an intolerable rigidity. At the polar extreme from Kennan was Nitze, who based his position on the fact that the budgetary ceiling imposed by Congress was excessively limiting U.S. diplomatic options. Anticipating that the military threat would be discounted, he wanted to sacrifice a measure of rationality in the analysis of NSC 68 in order to exaggerate the threat, thereby eliciting a reaction from opinion leaders commensurate with the threat, that is to say, a reaction that would be rational as measured against the actual threat.[53] Dean Acheson, in like manner, recalls that: "The purpose of NSC 68 was to so bludgeon the mass mind of 'top government' that not only could the President make a decision but that the decision be carried out. . . . Even so, it is doubtful whether anything like what happened in the next few years could have done had not the Russians been stupid enough to have instigated the attack against South Korea and opened the 'hate America campaign.' "[54]

Actually, NSC 68 was not designed as a blueprint for a limited war, such as the Korean conflict, but was built on the hypothesis of a total war. It is one of the ironies of history, however, that the document did become one of the blueprints for the expansion of military appropriations that dated from the initiation of fighting on the Korean peninsula. Without this development, adoption of the plan would have been virtually out of the question, for some time at least, due to the prevailing mood of "domestic affairs first" that had in its grips the president, the White House staff, and the Bureau of the Budget, all of whom were concerned first and foremost with their "political accountability." And in fact, NSC 68 remained unprogrammed and unapproved when the Korean War began.[55] As Gaddis has also made clear, the burden of proof at that time was on the shoulders of Kennan, Bohlen, and others who themselves feared the dominance of military considerations in U.S. foreign policy. The event, then, came to their rescue as the ultimate proof, and it tipped the balance of power in government from the State Department to the military.

Nevertheless, it should not be reasoned that in the absence of the unprogrammed Korean War, the U.S. Cold War strategy would have veered away from the NSC 68 orientation and toward that of NSC 48. The world view that was to become the fundamental distinguishing characteristic of U.S. foreign policy through the fifties and sixties, namely, the tendency to view world order as an undifferentiated whole, had already taken root in government and public opinion. Given the expectations of the European allies in those days and the domestic restraints, such a view had gained ground among a wide range of social groups and congressional cliques, and any consideration as to how or why the Korean War broke out was irrelevant. The president, who should be seen not so much as a prisoner of events but as a prisoner of domestic affairs whose freedom of choice was being eroded daily, did not need to write a prescription on the basis of the diagnosis submitted by his advisers; he had only to take the pulse of the nation.[56]

The Containment Line as a Symbol of the New Frontier

No sooner had he learned of the North Korean attack againt the south than President Truman decided to send U.S. ground forces to Korea, at the same time announcing increased military assistance to the French in Indochina and the interposition of naval forces to safeguard Taiwan. This resealed the interlock between the Cold War in Europe and the "hot" war in Asia. France's local colonial war hence became the front line of the global containment strategy, and the fighting likewise became part of the "just war for the Free World." Although the U.S. itself in the past had become the first of the "new nations" when it cast off Great Britain's colonial rule, and although it had enjoyed a brief honeymoon with Ho Chi Minh during World War II, the country's traditional anticolonialist policy was necessarily neutralized by the policy of bolstering its European allies, a policy given content as early as June–August 1944 when de Gaulle's French Committee of National Liberation had been recognized on the basis of the "Europe first" strategy.[57]

Meanwhile, a degree of domestic pressure was brought to bear by the loss-of-China campaign, and as a prerequisite to the formation of the European Defense Community (EDC), one of Washington's top strategic priorities in the early fifties, West Germany's membership in the community had to be brought about. This weakened the position of the United States, for it opened the government up to blackmail by the French government.[58] Acheson's call for Germany's rearmament in the fall of 1950, as a result of the Korean War, had the effect of more firmly linking the containment line in Europe to the extension in Asia which had suddenly been projected into the interior of the continent. Eventually, the Geneva conference caused the 17th parallel to be transformed into a political and territorial boundary, and the containment line's substantive significance was diluted while its symbolic significance as a barometer of U.S. concern and credibility was reinforced.

In time, borrowing the words of Alexander Kendrick, "the Mekong Valley would become a part of the New Frontier as the Tennessee Valley had been part of the New Deal."[59] Actually, the term "new frontier" here, later to become one of the key elements of the Kennedy administration's style, appeared earlier in a speech by Senator Vandenberg of Michigan on October 11, 1938, but in a totally different sense: "Eternal vigilance is the price of liberty. Every journey to the forbidden land begins with the first step. These 'new frontiers' that are offered to us are anti-constitutional, anti-democratic, anti-liberal frontiers. They are potential boundaries of the collectivist state." Such redefinition of terms is symbolic of the change in meaning of "containment line" that was to come about in 1966 in the Johnson administration under the "new Rusk doctrine." Even Secretary Dulles admitted that the type of aggression characteristic of the situation in Vietnam should not be categorized under the Monroe Doctrine principle as an "armed attack" but as a second type of aggression covered by paragraph 2, article IV of the SEATO treaty. The new Rusk doctrine, nevertheless, supplanted Dulles's interpretation with an expanding, unrestrained containment line that recognized neither time nor place.[60] A situation without a "front," where the daytime ruler of a given area was not necessarily the nighttime ruler, was one inherently inconceivable within the Western concept of a sovereign state, but in the midst of the governmental chaos in Indochina, the containment line could only exist as a fabrication. Americanization of the Vietnam War from 1965 on inevitably had to give birth to the Vietnamization of America. In this modern society of advanced communications, it proved impossible to stop the extension of the containment line until it had become the "wound within" by extending itself into the inner space of the American mind.

In this sense, Raymond Aron is correct when he states that "what led to the Vietnam tragedy was not the concept of containment nor perhaps the imperative of nonresort to force, but the growing tendency to substitute symbol for reality in the discrimination of interests and issues."[61] This tendency of Americans to project their democratic experience universalistically has another tendency as its corollary: the tendency to draw abstract generalizations and to derive broad principles from special local problems and unique experiences. If it can be concluded that the uniqueness of America will prove to be its ability to erase its uniqueness,[62] then the question follows, what lessons will America's next generation draw from the country's "unique" experience in Vietnam?

1. Marshall Shulman, *Beyond the Cold War* (New Haven: Yale University Press, 1966), p. 8.

2. Charles E. Bohlen, *Witness to History 1929–1969* (New York: Norton, 1973), p. 294.

3. Ibid., p. 292.

4. Ernest R. May, "The Nature of Foreign Policy: The Calculated vs. the Axiomatic," *Daedalus* (Fall 1962): 653–67.

5. *See* John Lewis Gaddis, "Was the Truman Doctrine a Real Turning Point?" *Foreign Affairs* 3 (January 1974): 386–402.

6. Ibid., p. 393.

7. Also, John L. Gaddis himself with reference to the decision to drop the bomb tells us: "Throughout the war Anglo-American military strategy had been to seek victory as quickly as possible through technology, not manpower. The decision to drop the bomb marked the logical culmination of that effort." John L. Gaddis, *The United States and the Origins of the Cold War 1941–1947* (New York: Columbia University Press, 1972), p. 245. *See also* A. J. P. Taylor, *English History 1914–1945*, II (New York: Oxford University Press, 1965).

8. "After all, the greatest danger that can befall us in coping with this problem of Soviet communism, is that we shall allow ourselves to become like those with whom we are coping." George F. Kennan, *Memoirs 1925–1950* (Boston: Little, Brown, 1967), Annexes, p. 559. See also *Foreign Relations of the United States* (henceforth cited *FR*), *1946*, VI, 709.

9. The terms "esoteric doctrine" and "exoteric doctrine" as used in this paper are borrowed from G. A. Almond, *The Appeals of Communism* (Princeton: Princeton University Press, 1954), chap. 3, pp. 62–96. In Almond's case study, such media as, for example, *Stalin's History of the Communist Party of the Soviet Union (Bolshevik)* are selected as giving the "internal representations" (esoteric doctrine) intended for the inner elite of the Communist party, while the American *Daily Worker* is selected as an example of an *external* communist source, a source directed to the mass membership of the party and nonparty sympathizers or potential sympathizers. In the present paper, partly out of space considerations, I have concentrated on the "esoteric" doctrine of the Cold War and have attempted a brief sketch of the logical structure, style, and rhetoric of such documents as George Kennan's long telegram, the Clifford report, NSC 20, NSC 48, and NSC 68.

10. *See* Athan Theoharis, "The Rhetoric of Politics: Foreign Policy, Internal Security, and Domestic Politics in the Truman Era, 1945–1950" and "The Escalation of the Loyalty Program," in *Politics and Policies of the Truman Administration*, ed. Barton J. Bernstein (New York: Watts, 1970), pp. 266–98; Theoharis, *Seeds of Repression: Harry S. Truman and Origins of McCarthyism* (New York: Quadrangle, 1971); Richard M. Freeland, *The Truman Doctrine and the Origins of McCarthyism* (New York: Knopf, 1972).

11. See *Pentagon Papers*, Senator Gravel edition (Boston: Beacon, 1971), 17–18. *See also* Edward R. Drachman, *United States Policy Toward Vietnam, 1940–1945* (Cranbury, N. J.: Associated University Presses, 1970), pp. 14–58.

12. Kennan, *Memoirs*, pp. 294–95.

13. *See* Stanley Hoffmann, "Revisionism Revisited," in *Reflections on the Cold War*, eds. Lynn H. Miller and Ronald W. Pruessen (Philadelphia: Temple University Press, 1974), p. 15.

14. *See* Ernest R. May, *"Lessons" of The Past* (New York: Oxford University Press, 1973), chap. 2, especially pp. 22–24. *See also* Dean Acheson, *Present at the Creation* (New York: Norton, 1969). Charles Bohlen points out in his memoirs that, in contrast with Roosevelt, Truman studied the files and papers prepared for him (*Witness to History*, p. 301).

15. Kennan, *Memoirs*, Annex C, or *FR*, *1946*, VI, 696–709.

16. *FR*, *1946*, I, 1167–71. This memorandum by the acting Department of State member (Matthews) to the State-War-Navy Coordinating Committee (subject: Political Estimate of Soviet Policy for Use in Connection with Military Studies) was prepared in response to a request submitted by the Joint Chiefs of Staff to the SWNCC on March 13.

17. This document was approved by the Joint Chiefs of Staff on September 19, 1945.

18. This document, SWN 4096 ("Foreign Policy of the United States"), was transmitted by the Joint Chiefs of Staff to the State-War-Navy Coordinating Committee as SM 5062, dated February 21.

19. "American Relations with the Soviet Union," a report prepared by Clark M. Clifford and submitted to Truman on September 24, 1946. *See* Arthur Krock, *Memoirs: Sixty Years on the Firing Line* (New York: Funk & Wagnalls, 1968), Appendix A.

20. David Riesman, "The American Crisis," in *Abundance for What? and Other Essays* (New York: Doubleday, 1964), pp. 35–36.

21. *See* Walter LaFeber, *America, Russia, and the Cold War 1945–1971*, 2d ed. (New York: Wiley, 1972), p. 54. *See also* Christopher Lasch, *The New Radicalism in America* (New York: Knopf, 1965).

22. Kennan, *Memoirs*, pp. 403–4. "The greatest mystery of my own role in Washington in those years, as I see it today, was why so much attention was paid in certain instances, as in the case of the telegram of February 1946 from Moscow and the X-Article. . . . The only answer could be that Washington's reactions were deeply subjective, influenced more by domestic-political moods and institutional interests than by any theoretical considerations of our international position. It was I who was naive."

23. *See* Lloyd C. Gardner, *Architects of Illusion* (New York: Quadrangle, 1970), p. 285.

24. Franklin D. Roosevelt's speech in Chicago in the fall of 1937. *See* William Safire, *The New Language of Politics: An Anecdotal Dictionary of Catchwords, Slogans, and Political Usage* (New York: Random House, 1968), p. 368.

25. *FR, 1946*, I, 1168.

26. *See* William Appleman Williams, *The Tragedy of American Diplomacy* (New York: Knopf, 1962). *See also* Richard S. Kirkendall, ed., *The Truman Period as a Research Field: A Reappraisal, 1972* (Columbia: University of Missouri Press, 1974), especially p. 14.

27. *See* Christopher Lasch, "The Cold War, Revisited and Re-Visioned," in *The New York Times Magazine*, 14 January 1968; or "Introduction" in Gar Alperovitz, *Cold War Essays* (Cambridge: Schenkman, 1970).

28. *See* Gaddis, *United States and Origins of Cold War*, p. 299.

29. *See* Gardner, *Architects*, pp. 273–74.

30. Carl Schmitt, *Land und Meer: Eine Weltgeschichtliche Betrachtung* (Stuttgart: Reclam Verlag, 1954).

31. *FR, 1947*, I, 712, 733, 760.

32. NSC 20 has not yet been released, but an outline is given in Frederick S. Dunn, *Peace-Making and the Settlement with Japan* (Princeton: Princeton University Press, 1963), pp. 48–52. A part of NSC 20/4 is appended to NSC 68, released in February 1975.

33. According to S. Hoffmann, "Whereas it was the Soviet Union that behaved according to a classical theory of power politics, it was the United States that behaved not at all like a classical great power playing a balance of power game but like an ideological power with a global vision" (Hoffmann, "Revisionism Revisited," p. 11). Historians, liberal realists, and revisionists now generally agree on the limited nature of Stalin's objectives. However, to quote Hoffmann, "The Soviet Union's policy was to a large extent defensive and cautious, but was pursued so vigorously that to many Americans and West Europeans, it looked like the policy of Genghis Khan reincarnate" (Ibid., p. 17).

34. *See* May, "*Lessons*," p. 30.

35. Walter Lippmann, *The Public Philosophy* (London: Hamish Hamilton, 1955), pp. 25–26.

36. See *FR, Japan, 1948*, VI, and Dunn, *Peace-making*, pp. 53–143.

37. *Public Papers of the Presidents: Harry S. Truman, 1948* (Washington: 1964), pp. 178–79.

38. NSC 48/1, p. 226.

39. James Reston, *The Artillery of the Press* (New York: Harper and Row, 1966), p. 39.

40. Harry S. Truman, *Memoirs* (New York: Doubleday, 1958), p. 466.

41. *See* David Riesman, "Reflections on Containment and Initiatives," in *Abundance For What?* p. 53.

42. *See* Samuel Lubell, *The Future of American Politics*, 2d ed., rev. (New York: Doubleday, 1956), p. 69. For the relationship between domestic politics and the foreign policy of Cold War in the Truman era, *see also* Alonzo L. Hamby, *Beyond the New Deal: Harry S. Truman and American Liberalism* (New York: Columbia University Press, 1973). For the present state of research relating to domestic policy in this period, *see* Alonzo L. Hamby, "The Clash of Perspectives and the Need for New Syntheses," in *Truman Period as Research Field*, ed. Kirkendall, pp. 113–48. As pointed out in Hamby's article, although research using such sophisticated methods as quantitative analysis has appeared (the systematic study by the University of Michigan's Survey Research Center is but one example), Samuel Lubell's "more humanized and highly convincing" study, based on a detailed field survey carried out over many years, is still the classic work in this field (Ibid., pp. 122–23).

43. The concept of "intolerance of ambiguity" has been developed by Else Frankel Brunswik and co-workers. Also, David Riesman suggested, "These newly prosperous ones want to see the world clearly bounded in blacks and whites; they have been brought up conventionally, to make use of conventional categories, and fluidity of boundaries threatens their self-assurance and their very hold on reality." *See* Daniel Bell, ed., *The Radical Right* (New York: Doubleday, 1964) pp. 110–11.

44. *See* David Riesman's article in ibid., p. 119.

45. *See* Samuel Lubell, *The Revolt of the Moderates* (New York: Harper, 1956).

46. *See* Kennan, *Memoirs*, pp. 355–67. Also, in the summer of 1949, Kennan had advocated concentration on the development of a small, mobile task force, approximately the size of two divisions, to meet and to deter military challenge on the Soviet perimeter. On the rearmament of Japan, see *FR, 1948*, VI, 692–93. On Charles Bohlen's concept of containment, *see* Bohlen, *Witness to History*, p. 319.

47. *See* Paul Y. Hammond, "NSC 68: Prologue to Rearmament," in *Strategy, Politics, and Defense Budgets*, W. Schilling, P. Hammond, and G. Snyder (New York: Columbia University Press, 1962), p. 288.

48. *See* Yōnosuke Nagai, "Time as a Political Resource," *Japan Echo* 2, no. 3 (1975).

49. NSC 68 pointed out that "the assault on free institutions is world-wide now, and in the context of the present polarization of power a defeat of free institutions anywhere is a defeat everywhere" (p. 8).

50. On the fashionable concept of "bureaucratic politics" and studies based on this model, *see*, in particular, Richard Neustadt, *Alliance Politics* (New York: Columbia University Press, 1970); G. Allison, *Essence of Decision* (Boston: Little, Brown, 1971); Charles E. Lindblom, "Bargaining: The Hidden Hand in Government," RM-1434-RC, Rand Corporation, 22 February 1955; H. Arkes, *Bureaucracy, the Marshall Plan and the National Interest* (Princeton: Princeton University Press, 1972); John D. Steinbruner, *The Cybernetic Theory of Decision* (Princeton: Princeton University Press, 1972).

51. Bohlen, *Witness to History*, p. 291.

52. Hammond, "NSC 68," p. 370.

53. Ibid., p. 371.

54. Acheson, *Present at Creation*, pp. 373–76, especially p. 374.

55. Paul Y. Hammond, "The Role of NSC 68 in the Korean Rearmament," in *Strategy, Politics, and Defense Budgets*, Schilling, Hammond, and Snyder.

56. In their memoirs, George F. Kennan, Charles Bohlen, Dean Acheson, and others all try to justify their own positions in the light of hindsight. The words of the British political scientist Stuart Hampshire evoke a response of deep-felt sympathy from Japanese students of politics, who had the bitter experience of the militarization

of Japan before the war. On the question of why presidential advisers—"the best and the brightest"—in the Kennedy–Johnson era lost sight of the real situation in Vietnam to an even greater degree than the general public, Hampshire wrote, "One reason is not often enough mentioned, I think. Neither American Presidents nor the American people have learned by long experience, as European governments, they must distrust chiefs of staff and military leaders and advisers as being liable always to be wrong about foreign policy. De Gaulle, Eisenhower, and Churchill, the first two because they were generals themselves, and Churchill because of World War I, knew that the plans and forecasts of their generals were apt to be wrong and biased in favor of more bombing, more fighting" ("The Meaning of Vietnam," in *New York Review of Books*, 12 June 1975).

57. *See* Drachman, *United States Policy Toward Vietnam*, p. 112.

58. George Kahin and John W. Lewis, *The United States in Vietnam* (New York: Delta Books, 1967), p. 44.

59. Alexander Kendrick, *The Wound Within* (Boston: Little, Brown, 1974), p. 133.

60. Kahin and Lewis, *United States in Vietnam*, pp. 300–3.

61. Raymond Aron, *The Imperial Republic* (Englewood Cliffs, N.J.: Prentice-Hall, 1974), p. 309.

62. Daniel Boorstin points out that "the first charm and virgin promise of America were that it was so different a place, but the fulfilment of modern America would be its power to level times and places, to erase differences between here and there, between now and then. And finally, the uniqueness of America would prove to be its ability to erase uniqueness " *The Americans: The Democratic Experience* (New York: Random House, 1973), p. 307.

American Policy-Makers, Public Opinion, and the Outbreak of the Cold War, 1945–50

Walter LaFeber

When World War II ended in August 1945, Washington officials harbored no doubts about who had emerged as the dominant power. As the president's chief of staff reported on a nationwide radio broadcast, "Today we have the biggest and most powerful navy in the world. . . . We have the best equipped and most completely mechanized ground force in the world. The army and navy together have the world's largest and most efficient air force." Finally, Admiral William D. Leahy observed, "We possess, with our British allies, the secret of the world's most fearsome weapon."[1] Leahy might have added that American economic strength was even greater, relative to the resources of other nations, than the military superiority. The question was not which nation held the high cards in international diplomacy. Nor, consequently, was the question which nation had the greatest freedom of action and choice in the development of its game plan. Rather, it was who in the United States would play these cards and what the stakes would be.

During the next five years, as American foreign policy moved from an uneasy coexistence with its wartime partners to costly war in Korea, those questions were clearly answered. (How the cards would be played, that is, which tactics would be employed, would not be answered until 1947). Indeed, these two questions were answered before World War II ended. By the spring of 1945, President Harry S. Truman and a small number of advisers controlled foreign policy, allowing their final decisions to be determined by neither public opinion nor Congress. This executive group set the stakes, or objectives, of American diplomacy. It could do so because little effective public debate was waged over the objectives. Differences developed largely over tactics. Given the narrowness of the debate, therefore, the executive proved able to persuade or circumvent Congress and the public, or, if necessary, to compromise without losing any of the essentials of its policy.

Franklin D. Roosevelt's administration set the precedent, particularly in its policy toward Poland, that focal point of the early Cold War. Roosevelt held off pressing a Polish settlement with Stalin and Churchill until early 1945 (despite Soviet recognition of the communist Lublin regime in late 1944) because of his need to retain Soviet military cooperation, his hope of winning Stalin to American positions on the United Nations, and his knowledge that the prying of the Red Army out of Poland had to await the right opportunity. That opportunity seemed to arise at the Yalta Conference when the president, along with Churchill, pressed for a reorganized Polish government and free elections. A tenuous agreement was reached, but by late March the Soviets had refused to allow more than three Western Poles in the regime. Roosevelt sent a tough note to Stalin on April 1, following this five days later with a letter to Churchill suggesting that recent British-American military successes "will permit us to become 'tougher' " in dealing with the Russians.[2]

Harry Truman became "tougher" in mid-April. In consulting with a small number of advisers between April 15 and 23, the new president discovered that only a minority warned against a showdown with the Soviets over Poland. Many of the advisers agreed with Averell Harriman, American ambassador to Russia. Since at least the autumn of 1944, Harriman had urged the White House to use economic and other pressures against Stalin to prevent "the establishment of totalitarianism" in Eastern Europe.[3] Despite a confrontation with Soviet Foreign Minister V. M. Molotov and an exchange of blunt letters with Stalin, however, Truman could not reopen Poland on his terms. Nor did the president succeed in getting his way in Rumanian and Bulgarian affairs.

As early as March, or two weeks before Roosevelt's death, State Department officials were toughening their own approach.

Their instrument was the Declaration of Liberated Europe, proposed by Roosevelt at Yalta, which pledged each power to "consult together" on policy affecting liberated states. The language was so loose that Stalin and Churchill finally saw no harm in signing it. The declaration has since been dismissed by some as a Rooseveltian sop to American opinion; the State Department, however, tried to use it as a blunt instrument to force Rumania open. The Russians accurately interpreted the declaration as virtually meaningless, but Washington did not give up.[4] Since Churchill had acknowledged in October 1944 that Stalin could control Rumania, the new British government of Clement Attlee did little to support the American position. But Attlee did even less in Bulgaria, where a Russian-controlled election had angered Washington officials. British Foreign Office officials saw the central problem as reconciling "the U.S. Government to the idea of concluding peace treaties with unrepresentative governments" and to "secure such concessions as we can from the Soviet Government both in order to help us bring the U.S. Government into line and to give us a more satisfactory line of retreat" so that a break with the Soviets could be avoided.[5] By at least the autumn of 1945, the United States had replaced England as the leading anti-Soviet force in the Anglo-Saxon coalition.

In taking these advanced positions, Washington policy-makers were well ahead of public and congressional opinion. After the Yalta agreements on Poland were made public, the State Department Public Studies Division noted that "5 out of 6 of those with opinions [on the Polish agreement thought it was] 'about the best that could be worked out under the circumstances.' " Press and radio comment generally agreed. In March, Americans' trust of Russia reached one of the highest points during the war. By late April, after disputes over Poland and the United Nations Charter had been aired, the number of Americans who trusted Russia dropped but slightly (57 percent to 51 percent). In late May, this slid to 45 percent, but the State Department believed that pro-Soviet opinion began rising again in June. By October 54 percent (including 71 percent of the college educated, a group the State Department Public Studies Division considered particularly important) believed the USSR could be trusted to cooperate after the war. Throughout the spring commentators divided, with Senator Robert Taft (Republican of Ohio) and "the habitually anti-Soviet press" (to use the State Department's term) criticized for "reckless and irresponsible" talk by such liberal observers as *The Washington Post, Milwaukee Journal*, Max Lerner, and Martin Agronsky. In the autumn, a majority of Americans blamed Russia for Big Three troubles; many "prominent commentators," as the State Department called them (including such commentators as Walter Lippmann), censured the United States and Russia equally for the failure of the Foreign Ministers Conference in September. Administration policy had toughened months before, but most Americans remained divided in opinion, while the State Department perceived many of the most knowledgeable observers as opposed to the tougher policy.[6]

Most striking, in August 84 percent of Americans polled believed Russia should receive $6 billion in credits through either government or private channels, and only 9 percent opposed the credit. Another survey revealed that 60 percent disapproved of a loan to Great Britain. The wording of the poll on Soviet credits was skewed to increase vastly the "approval" percentage, but the figure was nevertheless impressive. So too was a late-1945 survey revealing that exactly the same number of Americans (60 percent) now disapproved of a large loan to either Russia or Great Britain. The Truman administration moved rapidly to make such a loan to the British, but never seriously negotiated a similar deal with Stalin. In the areas of loans, lend-lease, and general economic policy, mass public opinion obviously little affected policy-makers, for it was too uninformed and divided.[7] Besides, Truman, having long before lost his faith that Stalin wished to cooperate, had assumed a hard line on Polish, Eastern Europe, and economic issues.

Nor does the administration's position at the start of the Cold War seem to have been significantly shaped by congressional sentiment about Russian issues. The most important Senate voice on Poland, as well as most foreign policy problems, was Senator Arthur Vandenberg of Michigan, the ranking Republican on the Foreign Relations Committee. Vandenberg made headlines in January when he announced in a Senate speech that he had exchanged his "isolationism" for the internationalism of the UN. Those words guaranteed Senate ratification of the UN Charter. Of equal importance in the speech, but less noted in the newspapers, Vandenberg asked for a four-power treaty to disarm Germany and Japan so that "postwar Soviet expansion" would be "as illogical as it would be unnecessary."[8]

This proposal clearly aimed at a disarmed Germany that would allow the withdrawal of Russian troops from Soviet-styled "security" zones in Eastern Europe, opening the entire area to both Russians and Americans on an equal basis. In this sense, Vandenberg's proposal resembled George Kennan's "disengagement" ideas of 1949 and after, Walter Lippmann's proposal for joint American-Russian withdrawal from Central Europe in 1947, and Henry Wallace's plea in 1946 for a settlement that would produce "open doors" in the Soviet zone. The White House rejected all of these proposals, starting with Vandenberg's, and probably for the same reasons: after the experiences of the 1930s no one could be certain Germany would remain neutral and disarmed, and no one could guarantee that Soviet troops would remain in a disengaged position after U.S. troops withdrew across the Atlantic. In the first of many such occasions, Vandenberg was embraced by the president, sent to an international conference as a member of a large, State Department–dominated delegation, and lauded for his cooperation with the executive; meanwhile the policy-makers quietly ditched his German plan.

Vandenberg was no more effective on the Polish issue. Here his motivation was, in part, a large number of Polish-Americans in his home state. Vandenberg publicly and privately condemned the Yalta agreement on Poland, but the political threat posed by the Polish-Americans was probably not decisive in the senator's actions, and certainly was insignificant in the executive's policy. The Polish-American voters were rock-ribbed Democrats. Vandenberg had largely ignored them in 1940, winning handsomely as he would triumph again in 1946 without even having to campaign. In 1944 Polish-Americans were not pleased with a Democratic administration's policies in Eastern Europe, but they nevertheless voted overwhelmingly for a Democratic president, a voting performance that was repeated in 1948. Overall, this ethnic group had inadequate leadership to play any important catalytic role in the Cold War's origins. As a Republican, Vandenberg did not provide the leadership; indeed he acted more as a buffer for Democratic policy-makers, articulating the Polish-Americans' anger, moderating extreme demands, and, in all (in the words of one scholar), acting "as a kind of wailing wall" for these constituents.[9]

Concern for Polish-American voters, or other voting groups, appears with surprising rarity in White House or State Department policy papers on Central and Eastern Europe. Indeed, in this context the most striking characteristic of these memoranda is a set of rationales and terms of discourse which are used by policy-makers and a few well-informed private citizens but which are unused and probably unknown to the overwhelming majority of the public and Congress. Before Yalta, for example, the official American position on Poland was phrased not in terms of sentiment or domestic politics, but with emphasis on (1) "the early return of trade to a multilateral basis under the freest possible conditions," and (2) "interest in general European economic stability." Politically, "in the situation which is likely to prevail in Poland and the Balkan states after the war, the United States can hope to make its influence felt only if some degree of equal opportunity in trade, investment, and access to sources of information is preserved."[10]

Such differences in the terms of discourse between policy-makers and others are not unusual. The "others," after all, are usually spokesmen for particularistic interest groups. These "functionalists" include congressmen whose horizons are necessarily limited by the composition of their constituency and the next election. Policy-makers in the executive, however, have responsibility not for particularistic groups (whether these groups are part of the domestic scene or of overseas alliances), but for an entire system. These "cosmopolitan" policy-makers must have a larger view that takes in all the "functionalists," yet an approach that can sacrifice some of the latter if necessary for the benefit of the entire community.[11]

In mid-1945, for example, the British moved to offset Soviet expansion not by confronting Stalin in Eastern Europe, but by designing a regional plan of their own in Western Europe. The State Department opposed this scheme devised by America's closest ally, arguing that "basic United States policy has been to oppose spheres of influence in Europe," and thus "American policy must be attuned to events in Europe *as a whole* and to the consequences of general European conditions on the stability of Great Britain."[12] Few in the United States (and evidently in the United Kingdom) had this kind of vision or were willing to play for such high stakes. Consequently, Americans outside the executive not only generally exerted little influence on policy, but usually did not even use the same vocabulary as policy-makers.

Because of these differences, the State Department and congressmen (or the mass of the knowledgeable public) might arrive at the same conclusions in 1945 (for example, reopen Poland), but the policy-makers had taken a quite different route and for different reasons. The congressmen may have been motivated by simple anticommunist sentiment or particular constituent interest. The State Department, however, saw Poland as part of a much larger problem. As one top official summarized policy on Europe during 1944–45: "The government of the United States should . . . take the view that it desires to see Europe west of the Russian border as finally drawn, established as a cooperative continental system economically unified in certain major particulars." As noted above, the State Department hoped to use multilateral trading pacts to keep Europe open. Congress, while agreeing with the objective, attacked reciprocal trade agreements in 1945–46. As for the mass of opinion, in *Fortune*'s fine phrase, "although 94% of the public do not know exactly what reciprocal trade agreements mean, a majority nevertheless feels that such agreements are desirable."[13] Perhaps something like this was in Dean Acheson's mind when he once dismissed "world opinion," "not because people do not know the facts—facts are not necessary to form opinion—but because they do not know that the issues exist."[14] When mass opinion, "functionalists," and "cosmopolitans" talk past one another in this fashion, the first two have little chance of shaping the policies of the third.

In early 1946, Stalin's tough speech of February 9, the Iranian crisis, and Russia's refusal to join the World Bank and International Monetary Fund brought a sharp upturn in mass anti-Soviet sentiment. Yet the opinion was divided and complex. Some leading newspaper and radio commentators interpreted Stalin's speech as emphasizing "butter rather than guns," and while Walter Lippmann concluded that Stalin now was forcing the United States to rebuild Western Europe as a counterweight to Russian expansion, others sharply disagreed. Even the hard liners were divided among themselves. Lippmann only wanted to rebuild the remaining noncommunist world, while others (the Alsops, the Scripps-Howard papers, Dorothy Thompson) constituted a "get tough with Russia" school.[15]

In the Iranian crisis, the State Department perceived opinion as focusing little attention on the issue of Russian expansion, but rather on how the United Nations would stand up under the strain.[16] When Vandenberg asked for "more firmness and candor," and Secretary of State James Byrnes warned against any nation taking unilateral action against another state, some believed these speeches marked a "turning point in American policy toward Russia." But commentators then praised them for "focussing attention upon UNO as the agency through which solutions can be worked out." (In reality, the Truman administration and Vandenberg were rapidly losing hope for the world organization. But as the UN lost its importance in official policy, 67 percent of Americans as late as January 1947 thought the best chance for peace was the organization, and only 28 percent placed confidence in trying unilaterally to stay ahead of the Russians by building atomic bombs.) Similar faith in the UN was expressed when most Americans applauded the tough administration stand on the Turkish Straits question in late August. Some commentators even asked for internationalization of the straits, a solution Truman would not consider.[17]

Throughout 1946 opinion followed, not shaped, American policy. As the State Department perceived the situation, and as polls reflected it, commentators and the mass of Americans were divided, emphasized aspects of policy (as the UN) which the administration had privately deemphasized, and supported a tough response in crises but wanted no war. Hopefully affairs with Stalin could somehow be worked out. Most important, as the year progressed, Truman's foreign policy ran into increasing opposition from American liberals, that amorphous group on which any Democratic nominee would have to depend in the 1948 presidential election. The State Department declared that " 'liberal' sources" opposed Truman's using the UN as a theater in which to embarrass Stalin over the Iranian problem; opposed his cutting the Soviets out of Japanese occupation policy; opposed his plan for international control of atomic energy as too "nakedly national-istic"; opposed the president's intention to raise Germany's level of production; and, finally, many liberals broke with or severely criticized him for firing Henry Wallace as secretary of commerce in September because of Wallace's blasts at American foreign policy.[18] Wallace had attacked that policy throughout 1946, and Truman may well have kept the secretary as long as possible be-cause the president desperately needed liberal political support as he developed a tougher policy toward the Soviets.[19] Phrased an-other way, if national opinion had any effect at all on administra-tion policy, Truman's political need for support from such liberals as Wallace and leading radio and newspaper commentators may actually have restrained the administration from moving into as strong an anti-Soviet position as Truman wished.

Another restraint also hobbled the president. By at least late 1946 he had been forced by Russian opposition to give up hope of immediately reopening Eastern Europe. American policy, indeed, would have to move rapidly to save war-devastated, near-bankrupt Western and Central Europe from an economic collapse that could throw political power into the hands of communist or radical socialist parties. Such a policy, however, re-quired immediate, massive economic aid. Military responses, such as those which the administration used in Iran and the Turkish Straits crises, would not solve the fundamental problems of recon-structing Europe. The stakes of the game had therefore changed from the whole of Europe to the most vital areas of Western and Central Europe. The manner in which Truman could play his cards had also changed. No longer would a mere military response, or appeals through the UN, suffice.

Large sums of economic aid were required, and to obtain them Truman would have to confront Congress. As the result of the 1946 elections this was a Congress dominated by Republican conservatives who hated communism, but who were fully com-mitted to slashing the federal budget and the taxes of their con-stituents. (The hatred of communism, moreover, had to be quali-fied. In the 1946 campaign the major attention was devoted to domestic, not international, communism.) Restrained by a divi-sion of opinion in 1946, Truman now faced the greatest restraint upon his anticommunist policies: the reluctance of Congress to pay for programs that were immediately required. The State Department believed public opinion supported Congress. Noting in January 1947 that 72 percent of Americans now approved rebuilding the peaceful industry of Germany (a nation that was moving to the center of the administration's reconstruction policies), the Public Affairs Division added, "There is doubtless a gap between approval in principle and popular support for funds to implement the program."[20]

Truman also had other problems. His personal popularity reached a low of 32 percent in November 1946. In December, only 22 percent of the public thought foreign policy was the most important of all issues.[21] Opinion sympathetic to the Soviets had reached a new low in the polls during October when only 32 percent believed Russia could be trusted to cooperate, but in January 1947 this rose suddenly to 43 percent. In late 1946, moreover, 74 percent believed both the United States and Russia were to blame for global misunderstandings. The State Department noted that radio and press commentators were "encouraged by the 'easing of tension between Russia and the West' " as the Soviets turned inward to rebuild. Prospects for peace "are deemed much brighter."[22] The Soviets apparently would not give Truman the crisis he needed to rally support for his new policies.

The opportunity nevertheless arose in mid-January 1947 when the British told the State Department they would no longer be able to help the Greek government in a revolutionary struggle against left-wing Greeks who were being aided by the Yugoslav Communist government. Policy-makers seized on this, in the words of one official finding "release from the professional frustrations of years,"[23] frustrations that evidently included domestic unconcern as well as the Soviets. As Clark Clifford, the president's top political adviser, put it, Truman would deliver a speech that would be "the opening gun in a campaign to bring people up to [the] realization that the war isn't over by any means."[24]

The administration conceived and executed the plans with great care and skill.[25] Truman, Secretary of State George Marshall, and Under Secretary Dean Acheson met with congressional leaders in late February. In this famous session, Acheson convinced the congressmen, especially Vandenberg, to support the president by dramatically outlining a global crisis in which the

Russians were "aggressive and expanding" with the intention of snuffing out freedom country by country until "freedom anywhere in the world would have only a poor chance of survival." Only the United States, acting unilaterally, could break up the Soviet design for world conquest.[26]

The congressmen were convinced, not consulted. The administration had already decided its policies before Acheson advanced this argument for them. The Greek struggle would be defined not as a civil war, which it was, but as part of a larger ideological struggle requiring a major political, economic, and military commitment. Because of this concern for a general commitment, the key economic factors were omitted from the Truman Doctrine speech in which he asked Congress for $400 million of immediate aid to help Greece and Turkey. Acheson struck paragraphs mentioning American oil interests in the Mediterranean area from the draft of the speech because he wanted a general principle accepted, not a debate that would bog down over particulars. But the economic factors were laid out with clarity in a message delivered by the president at Baylor University just a week before the Truman Doctrine speech.[27] In this way, the administration shaped the debate to its advantage by focusing congressional and public debate on the general ideological (that is, anticommunist) issues in the second speech delivered before a joint session of Congress.

The address nevertheless generated intense debate. Both conservatives and liberals ripped into Truman's request.[28] Many critics especially disliked the bypassing of the UN. Vandenberg quieted these complaints by framing a provision that paid lip service to the organization while keeping the policy entirely in American hands. The most interesting debate erupted over the military component of the doctrine. On this public opinion was notable. Although 56 percent of those who had heard of the doctrine approved of it (with 32 percent opposed), 54 percent opposed sending American military advisers to Greece and only 37 percent approved. As the State Department itself noted, 53 percent opposed sending even military supplies to Greece and 54 percent opposed sending them to Turkey.[29]

A similar division existed in the administration. George Kennan objected not only to the sweeping language of Truman's speech (as did the other State Department expert on Soviet affairs,

Charles Bohlen), but fought sending any military aid to Turkey. Secretary of War Robert Patterson agreed. Acheson was able to overrule both men, and consequently only $128 million of the $400 million finally consisted of economic aid. American military officials were sent to both countries. By December the State Department privately noted that "an important segment of opinion," led by Walter Lippmann and such radio commentators as William Shirer and Quincy Howe, opposed the military commitments, but more Americans (54 percent) approved these commitments than ever before. Only one of every three Americans polled, however, were even aware of the military aid being sent.[30]

Truman's handling of the issue was masterful. When condemned for aiding repressive, nondemocratic governments in Greece and Turkey, the administration responded that the choice was "between a totalitarianism and an imperfect democracy." Cabinet members actively campaigned among Congress, businessmen, and commentators. In one of his rare attempts to do so during his presidency, Truman worked systematically to convince radio spokesmen and newspaper editors. In these appearances he emphasized the nonmilitary aspects of the doctrine and, later, the Marshall Plan. In dealing with Congress he gave the legislators a stark alternative. As Congressman Francis Case of South Dakota later told him: "The situation was regarded as an accomplished fact. You had spoken to the world. The Senate had acted. At least 75 members, I judge, would have voted against final passage, myself included, had it not been that we thought it would be like pulling the rug out from under you or Secretary of State Marshall."[31]

The Truman Doctrine is a landmark in American postwar history. It publicly redefined the administration's view of the world crisis, led to a global military commitment by the United States, and greatly augmented presidential power at the expense of Congress. It also created a broad American consensus on the need to fight the Cold War aggressively. Since that consensus lasted a quarter century, the doctrine may well be the most significant milestone in America's post–World War II years. With extraordinary success, the administration developed a strong anticommunist line, carried it out, and then, of course, acquiescence to the policy (including its military aspects, once strongly opposed) came back to the State Department as "public opinion" and served to justify the whole procedure.[32]

Truman's popularity began to climb. By late spring, 54 percent of those polled thought foreign policy (instead of inflation, taxes, meat shortages, or other domestic embarrassments) was the main issue confronting the country. The president had succeeded in redefining the issues and creating a consensus on the most important foreign policy. It was a brilliant performance.

Perhaps it was too brilliant. Truman succeeded partly because he took advantage of a domestic scare over internal communist subversion. The administration seized this issue, publicizing the threat of subversion so widely that some scholars now believe the president's actions contributed to the rise of McCarthyism and the witch hunts in the post-1948 era.[33] In foreign policy, Truman's tactics were so effective that public opinion became staunchly and heavily anti-Russian. The State Department emphasized the importance of the high percentage of college-educated who rather suddenly moved into this anti-Soviet category. By the end of 1947, 40 percent of those polled wanted the United States to cooperate with the UN to "tell Russia that any further move into Greece will be considered a declaration of war against the rest of the world."[34] The sentiment was noteworthy since most Americans had been reluctant to send military aid unilaterally to Greece itself. In Congress, many Democrats trumpeted the crusade. John McCormack of Massachusetts warned that without the doctrine, the Soviets would overrun Europe, Asia, and then "actually reach our shores." McCormack was using the terms of Acheson's lecture to the congressional leaders in late February and working out the logical conclusion.[35]

These references to Asia were another sign that Truman had perhaps oversold his doctrine. From late 1945 until early 1948, public opinion and the knowledgeable public strongly supported his China policy, whether that policy was mediating between Chiang and the Communists in 1945–46, or American withdrawal from the talks in 1947.[36] By mid-1948, however, the State Department noted new public concern over China, as Mao Tse-tung's armies moved rapidly to victory. Liberal and middle-of-the-road commentators not only warned that Asia was "a happy hunting ground" for communists, but some asked that help immediately be sent to Southeast Asia before the communists also triumphed there.[37] Congressmen demanded that more aid be given than Truman thought necessary. The president nevertheless continued withdrawing from China, while Indochina policy was not precisely defined until early 1950. Meanwhile popular support for sending more military aid to Chiang grew from 32 percent to 55 percent in the first five months of 1948. Both Congress and the public had apparently taken the Truman Doctrine at its word and now wanted its military parts extended to Asia. The essentials of the president's policy, however, did not change radically in China between early 1947 and 1949.

As Mao completed his triumph in the summer of 1949, American opinion divided evenly over whether to continue sending aid to Chiang, who was even then setting up new headquarters on Formosa. The 43 percent who approved sending aid, however, could be a nucleus of a large group who later condemned Truman's handling of China.[38] On the more important question of whether Mao's government should be recognized, opinion sharply divided. In a July 1949 poll, 19 percent favored recognition, 41 percent opposed, while 25 percent said they were not familiar with the Chinese civil war. Knowledgeable radio and newspaper observers, however, as well as many scholars, disagreed with mass opinion. Such important newspapers as *The Wall Street Journal*, *San Francisco Chronicle*, *Christian Science Monitor*, *Louisville Courier-Journal*, and *The Washington Post* urged consideration of recognition even after the Communists imprisoned American Consul Angus Ward and seized United States property.[39] Truman had actually made a decision not to recognize Mao several months earlier, in midsummer 1949. Divided opinion, with the antirecognition forces led by vocal congressmen and the Hearst and Scripps-Howard chains, once again allowed Truman to do what he believed global policy, not public attitudes, required. But the importance and number of those who wanted a harsher policy in Asia than the administration advocated grew sharply after the Truman Doctrine proclamation. These hard liners would disturb, then nearly wreck, administration policy, but only after the Korean War broke out in mid-1950.

Although polls during these years showed that most Americans opposed helping Japan "get back on her feet," once again opinion divided between the mass opinion and attentive observers. As early as August 1946, as the Chinese situation deteriorated, a few commentators urged the restoration of Japanese industry so the nation could be a "buffer for democracy in the Orient." In 1947 the administration moved rapidly to construct such a buffer, despite the State Department's perception of public opposition: "Japan is thought to be fairly well equipped to resume her 'old, dangerous' role in Asia," is the way the Public Studies Division evaluated majority opinion. After the Truman Doctrine, however, the public, especially commentators, at least caught up with the administration. Although some critics persisted, the State Department believed in early 1948 that the rebuilding of Japan was generally "welcomed."[40]

Although opinion tended to differ somewhat with Truman on Japanese and Chinese issues, in Europe and on defense policy he skillfully used the consensus created by his doctrine. The president was aided by Stalin's belligerent reaction to the doctrine, to the Marshall Plan, and to Tito's defection from the Soviet bloc. The rise in American support for Truman after the Communist coup in Czechoslovakia was especially sharp, with liberal spokesmen who had opposed the doctrine now in some instances declaring that the takeover was the "last straw" and a "deadly parallel" with the 1938 Munich crisis.[41] The administration helped along such sentiment by releasing in early 1948 captured German documents on Nazi-Soviet relations during 1939–41.

At this point in the Cold War (1948–49), Truman guided the nation to a new policy course. Military means received increasing emphasis while economic approaches and the use of diplomatic negotiations were downgraded as tactics. In perspective this is a significant turn since it led first to the establishment of the North Atlantic Treaty Organization (NATO), America's first peacetime alliance since the eighteenth century, and then to secretly drawn plans that soon became transformed into a defense budget that varied between $35 billion and $50 billion during the 1950s and early 1960s. The defense budget thus mushroomed three to four times over the budget of 1948. Again, as after the doctrine, public opinion marched even with, if not at times ahead of, the administration. Months before the national debate occurred over NATO, a majority of Americans not only wanted to protect Western Europe against attack, but the State Department noted that "53% . . . favor a promise to back up the Brussels powers with our armed forces 'in case Communists inside these countries try to seize control by force.' " In sharp contrast to opinion in late 1946, in early 1948 a private State Department survey showed that when Americans were asked what gives "us the best chance of avoiding a future war with Russia," only 10 percent said trying to meet Russia's point of view and only 10 percent favored using the Marshall Plan. Sixty-six percent, however, replied "strengthening our own armed forces." At the same time, 73 percent of those polled felt the United States was "too soft" on the Soviets. During the first weeks of the Berlin blockade the public position was adamant. When asked whether Americans should force their way through the blockade if necessary to get food and coal to Berlin, 86 percent said yes, 8 percent thought not.[42]

Truman's actions during 1947–48 had so shaped foreign policy issues in his favor that the Republicans did not even try to use European policies against him in 1948. Thomas E. Dewey, however, did note in several speeches the growing disenchantment with Chinese affairs. Truman's triumph publicly legitimated the Cold War in the United States,[43] although the turn toward the president's victory in the diplomatic realm had started with the Truman Doctrine.

By 1949 the State Department's survey of press and radio opinion noted "increasing agreement" with Secretary of State Dean Acheson's statements that building "situations of strength" was prerequisite to negotiating agreements. And fewer of these observers wanted specific issues negotiated than demanded that the entire broad conflict with the Soviet Union be settled. This resembled the State Department's exceedingly general, and unattainable, goals in all of Eastern Europe during 1945. Sixty-one percent disapproved of any Truman-Stalin meeting when the general public was asked.[44] This sentiment was consistent with the assumptions of NSC 68, a comprehensive plan secretly drawn up by the executive after the Soviets exploded their first atomic bomb in August 1949. The document proposed no negotiations with Stalin until the American defense budget quadrupled, military defenses were constructed globally, and even the Russian people arose to change their system.[45] Those demands seemed to make negotiations improbable for some time.

The outbreak of war in Korea provided the perfect opportunity for the administration to make real the plans of NSC 68. As the State Department Public Affairs Division noted privately, "In its deep impact on public opinion the Korean conflict has aroused almost unanimous support in the country for measures that will assure victory in Korea and enable the country to be prepared for other Soviet-inspired aggressions." By July 1950, American policy-makers prepared plans for the most significant act in the conflict, moving beyond the 38th parallel in an attempt to unify, or "liberate," North Korea. Such a move would also establish Western military force on the boundary of Communist China. The State Department noted that such important public leaders as Senator Robert Taft and General Dwight Eisenhower urged the crossing of the 38th, and reunification plans were "supported by a number of commentators" and "influential observers." By August only "a few" were perceived as opposing this course, including the much maligned *Chicago Tribune*, which warned, "We shall be face to face with the hordes of Russia and Red China with a new line more explosively dangerous than the 38th parallel ever was." By mid-September, 54 percent of those polled approved going beyond the 38th.[46] Apparently the "commentators" and "influential observers" were more belligerent than the mass of Americans.

The crossing of the parallel resulted in an enlarged war, costly in blood and costly politically for Truman. "The rude shock of the [American] military retreats in Korea, coupled with a widely shared impression of apathy among our European allies," the State Department Public Studies Division noted in December 1950, "have awakened some doubts that American power should be irrevocably committed in Europe and Asia."[47] Truman, Acheson, and later Eisenhower nevertheless succeeded in stopping the debate by negotiating an armistice in Korea while strengthening U.S. military commitments in both Europe and Asia. Americans were settling in for a long period of frigid weather in international affairs.

Looking back at his years in the State Department, one associate of Acheson's believed that "almost 80 percent of your time, if you are on a policy job, is management of your domestic ability to have policy, and only 20 percent, maybe, dealing with the foreign. . . ."[48] The 80 percent figure is questionable, but the significant word is "management." Between 1945 and 1950, policy-makers seldom if ever followed public opinion, or the opinion of "knowledgeable" or "attentive" publics. From early 1945 until March 1947 these opinions were either too fragmented, too general, uninterested in foreign affairs, antimilitary, or (especially among liberals) sympathetic to cooperating with Russia to determine the thinking of policy-makers.

By early 1947 the stakes changed. Stalin, viewing the choice as either controlling Eastern Europe or surrendering Soviet security and perhaps undermining his own political power, dropped the Iron Curtain. Truman determined to secure the noncommunist world. To obtain the necessary support at home he sharply redefined the globe in ideological terms. The nation responded. It indeed responded so fervently that opinion raced ahead of the administration on Asian and some military issues, although the policy-makers never lost control of policy and seldom, if ever, trimmed plans because of public opinion.

Not surprisingly, the Truman Presidential Library's files on public opinion polls are virtually nonexistent. Truman demonstrated little interest in such material. In May 1947 he told the Association of Radio News Analysts, "Our Government is not a democracy, thank God. It's a republic. We elect men to use their best judgment for the public interest."[49] After leaving office, Dean Acheson was more blunt: "If you truly had a democracy and did what the people wanted, you'd go wrong every time."[50] Truman and Acheson often thought of the 1930s, when, in their view, mass antiwar sentiment prevented Roosevelt from taking strong steps to avoid World War II. These feelings were buttressed by key foreign service officers, such as George Kennan, who felt that as experts they, not the public or "the convulsive reactions of politicians to an internal political life dominated by vocal minorities," should command foreign policy making.[51] These officers received their opportunity between 1945 and 1950.

Acheson's opinion of Congress was almost as low as his view of the public. Congress's function was "vital," he noted in 1953, but the legislature is composed of people "who don't know and don't care and are just generally raising hell around." His view of Vandenberg was gentler and not unfavorable because the Michigan senator "was eminently capable of receiving and using" the ideas of others so that a "national consensus could support policy."[52] The devotion of the Democratic congressional leadership to administration policy was seldom tested since the leaders almost totally supported the president's initiatives.[53]

State Department officials spent an inordinate amount of time on Capitol Hill, but their testimony should not be confused with consultation. Even consultation, in the view of the executive, frequently meant only to "inform," or so believed Francis O. Wilcox, who served as an official in both the Senate Foreign Relations Committee staff and the State Department. "The script is usually much the same," Wilcox has written. "This is the situation; this is what we [in the State Department] are going to do about it. Members of Congress may comment if they desire, but only rarely are they in a position to change anything."[54]

In 1945 and 1946 Congress made some impact on foreign economic policy, particularly with regard to Export-Import Bank funds and trade agreements. But it remains to be demonstrated that the legislators significantly altered the administration's broad view toward the Soviet Union. That view seemed to change with new foreign developments or the executive's perception of the West's socioeconomic needs, not with pressure from Congress. In any case, scholars may well be mistaken in identifying a "congressional point of view." As Wilcox has noted, "Congress is composed of 535 strong-minded individuals among whom one can usually find somebody who subscribes to almost any point of view within the realm of rational American political discourse."[55]

Individual senators such as Vandenberg did gain a role, but when the major, specific policies are examined (for example, the Truman Doctrine or even NATO), his importance seems to have been in having the policy adopted by Congress, not in the conception of the policy's essentials. Moreover, throughout 1945 and 1946, the Senate Foreign Relations Committee had a professional staff of one clerk (serving half-time), an assistant clerk, a secretary, and another part-time secretary. The committee, in Wilcox's phrase, "was almost entirely dependent upon the executive branch for information about foreign policy, for the preparation of committee reports, and for professional assistance of all kinds."[56] Only after the Legislative Reorganization Act of 1946 did the Foreign Relations Committee begin to build an adequate and independent staff.

American foreign policy between 1945 and 1950 developed through a series of stages. First, the wartime alliance split in 1945 over the issue of Eastern Europe. Second, as a result of the Iranian and Turkish Straits crises of 1946, American leaders concluded that Soviet expansionism would yield only to counterforce. Third, the counterforce was initially applied in the eastern Mediterranean and Western Europe in 1947–48 through aid to Greece and Turkey and with the passage of the Marshall Plan. Fourth, in 1949 and 1950 American officials turned more to military tactics and less to economic devices in order to unite the West and contain the Soviets. Fifth, simultaneously between 1947 and 1950, U.S. policy began to view Asia as increasingly important (although not of equal importance with Europe). Through the rebuilding of Japan, the attempt to isolate China, a new colonial policy focusing on Southeast Asia, and increased military commitments, Americans were fighting a two-front Cold War before Korea erupted in June 1950.

The most portentous of these steps was the third, for it created the domestic consensus in the United States that made possible the militarization and Asianization of American Cold War policy. The key to understanding U.S. foreign policy in 1947 seems not to be public opinion, congressional pressure, private interest groups, or bureaucratic politics (although bureaucratic infighting provides a better insight than the other three). The key is to be found in the minds and actions of a small number of executive policy-makers whose view of history, understanding of the Soviet Union, determination of the American system's requirements, and evaluation of U.S. power primarily shaped the nation's foreign policy.

1. Leahy quoted in Balfour to Foreign Office, 19 August 1945, FO 371 AN 2740/35/45, Public Record Office, London, England.
2. U.S. Department of State, *Foreign Relations of the United States* (henceforth cited

FR), *1945*, V, 194–96; Roosevelt to Churchill, 6 April 1945, in Francis L. Loewenheim, Harold D. Langley, and Manfred Jonas, eds., *Roosevelt and Churchill: Their Secret Wartime Correspondence* (New York: Saturday Review Press, 1975), p. 705.

3. "Special Information for the President," from Stettinius, 5 April 1945, Lot File 53 D 44, National Archives, Record Group 59 (henceforth cited NA, RG 59), Washington, D.C.; Diary of Henry Stimson, 23 April 1945, Papers of Henry Stimson, Yale University, New Haven.

4. Daily Staff Summary, 28 March and 3 April 1945, Lot File, NA, RG 59; "Memorandum for the Secretary," 20 August 1945, Staff Officers Summary, Lot File, NA, RG 59.

5. Minutes on Halifax to Foreign Office, 22 November 1945, FO 371 R 19813/5063/67, Public Record Office, London.

6. U.S. Department of State, *Fortnightly Survey of International Affairs*, 20 March 1945, pp. 3–4; ibid., 9 May 1945, pp. 1–2; ibid., 23 May 1945, p.1; ibid., 9 June 1945, pp. 2–3; ibid., 21 June 1945, p.3; *Public Opinion Quarterly* 9 (Spring 1945): 103. Although extensive studies have broken down the various "publics" in American opinion, this paper generally notes only two: mass opinion as reflected in polls, and knowledgeable commentators in the press and radio industry. These two categories only are used because (1) reliable data can be found for these categories (reliable, that is, given the nature on the techniques in the late 1940s); (2) although there are studies of interest-group opinion on policy (for example, business and labor), most of the studies are not concerned with demonstrating how policy-makers perceived that opinion or how it affected policy making; (3) this paper is necessarily limited in space; (4) little evidence exists that policy-makers devoted much attention to the need for following public or special interest group opinion. An excellent essay that clears away much underbrush is Ernest R. May, "An American Tradition in Foreign Policy: The Role of Public Opinion," in *Theory and Practice in American Politics*, ed. William H. Nelson (Chicago: University of Chicago Press, 1964).

The key source used in this paper is the Department of State's *Fortnightly Survey of International Affairs*, changed to *Monthly Survey* in March 1947. This was compiled by the Public Studies Division, Office of Public Affairs. The author of this paper is indebted to H. Schuyler Foster, who produced the *Survey* from 1945 to 1963, and who allowed the author to investigate files in his office. This paper relies on the *Survey* for the following reasons: (1) since it was compiled in the department and circulated among top officials on a "confidential" basis, it serves as perhaps our record of how the department itself perceived opinion; (2) it not only included published polls, but conducted private surveys and, most important, used public comment correspondence arriving in the department, assessed congressional opinion, noted editorials from several hundred daily newspapers and columns of leading journalists, surveyed fifty magazines and periodicals, and—especially notable—systematically covered transcripts of radio comment and debate. (Henceforth this periodical will be cited as *Survey*.)

Additional evidence on American opinion toward the Soviets is in *Survey*, 6 September 1945, p. 2; ibid., 19 October 1945, pp. 5–6; *Public Opinion Quarterly* 9 (Fall 1945): 388.

7. *Public Opinion Quarterly* 9 (Fall 1945): 383; ibid., 9 (Winter 1945–46): 533.

8. Good analyses are in John Lewis Gaddis, *The United States and the Origins of the Cold War, 1941–1947* (New York: Columbia University Press, 1972), pp. 168–69; and Lloyd C. Gardner, *Architects of Illusion* (Chicago: Quadrangle, 1970), pp. 49–50.

9. John N. Cable, "Vandenberg: The Polish Question and Polish Americans, 1944–1948," *Michigan History* 57 (Winter 1973): 296–310; Shelden A. Silverman, "At the Water's Edge: Arthur Vandenberg and the Foundation of American Bipartisan Foreign Policy" (Ph.D. diss., University of California, Los Angeles, 1967), pp. 211–12, 237; Peter H. Irons, "America's Cold War Crusade: Domestic Politics and Foreign Policy, 1942–1948 (Ph.D. diss., Boston University, 1973), pp. 331–32; *FR, Conference of Berlin*, I, 26–59.

10. *FR, Conferences at Malta and Yalta, 1945*, 235–36.

11. I have borrowed and adapted these terms and approaches from an important essay by Thomas J. McCormick, "The State of American Diplomatic History," in *The State of American History*, ed. Herbert J. Bass (Chicago: Quadrangle, 1970), pp. 127–40.

12. *FR, Conference of Berlin*, I, 262–64.

13. The "top official" quoted is Adolf A. Berle, "Diplomacy and the New Economics," in *Dimensions of Diplomacy*, ed. E. A. J. Johnson (Baltimore: Johns Hopkins Press, 1964), pp. 93–95; *Fortune* quoted in *Survey*, 21 August 1945, p. 7; on congressional attitudes and views of reciprocal trade pacts, *see* Richard M. Freeland, *The Truman Doctrine and McCarthyism* (New York: Knopf, 1972).

14. Dean Acheson, "The American Image Will Take Care of Itself," *The New York Times Magazine*, 28 February 1965, p. 95.

15. *Survey*, 26 February 1946, p. 3; ibid., 6 March 1946, p. 1; *Public Opinion Quarterly* 10 (Summer 1946): 264.

16. *Survey*, 7 February 1946, p.1; ibid., 20 March 1946, p. 2. Americans at first saw the Iranian deadlock as a British setback; see *Survey*, 8 January 1946, p. 3.

17. Ibid., 20 March 1946, p. 1; ibid., 20 August 1946, p. 5; ibid., 4 September 1946, pp. 1–2; *Public Opinion Quarterly* 11 (Spring 1947): 140.

18. *See* especially the following issues of *Survey*: 4 April 1946, p.1; 19 April 1946, p. 1; 19 October 1945, pp. 1, 2, 4–5; 3 October 1946, pp. 1–2.

19. Ronald Radosh, "The Economic and Political Thought of Henry Wallace" (M.A. thesis, State University of Iowa, 1960), pp. 80–129.

20. Herbert S. Parmet, *The Democrats: The Years After FDR* (New York: Macmillan, 1976), pp. 62–63; *Survey*, 22 January 1947, p.5.

21. Richard J. Barnet, *Roots of War* (New York: Atheneum, 1972), p. 245.

22. *Survey*, 20 December 1946, and 7 January 1947, p.1; *Public Opinion Quarterly* 11 (Spring 1947): 138–61; Daily Staff Summary, 17 March 1947, Lot File, NA, RG 59.

23. Joseph M. Jones, *The Fifteen Weeks* (New York: Harcourt, Brace, 1955), pp. 146–47.

24. Quoted in Gaddis, *U.S. and the Cold War*, p. 350.

25. Richard J. Barnet, *Intervention and Revolution* (New York: World, 1968), p. 117.

26. Jones, *Fifteen Weeks*, pp. 139–43.

27. "Memorandum with Reference to Speech of the President at Baylor University," 10 February 1947, Baylor University folder, Box 28, Papers of Clark Clifford, Harry S. Truman Library, Independence, Missouri.

28. Jones, *Fifteen Weeks*, pp. 175–78; "Personal Memorandum for Clark Clifford," from J. Donald Kingsley, n.d., Greece and Turkey—Assistance to under Public Law 75, Truman Papers, Truman Library.

29. *Survey*, April 1947, p.2; *Public Opinion Quarterly* 11 (Summer 1947): 285–86. H. Schuyler Foster has given a State Department official's view of how American opinion was changed in "American Public Opinion and U.S. Foreign Policy," *Department of State Bulletin* 41 (30 November 1959).

30. George Kennan, *Memoirs, 1925–1950* (Boston: Little, Brown, 1967), pp. 315–22; *FR, 1947*, V, 109; Thomas Paterson, *Soviet-American Confrontation* (Baltimore: Johns Hopkins Press, 1974), p. 202; *Survey*, December 1947, pp. 5–6. For the discussion on sending troops, *see* "Memorandum of Conversation," 26 December 1947, in *FR, 1947*, V, 466–69.

31. Susan M. Hartmann, *Truman and the 80th Congress* (Columbia: University of Missouri Press, 1971), pp. 58, 60–64; Elmer E. Cornwell, Jr., *Presidential Leadership of Public Opinion* (Bloomingon: Indiana University Press, 1965), pp. 164–68.

32. Bernard C. Cohen, *The Public's Impact on Foreign Policy* (Boston: Little, Brown, 1973), pp. 180–81. Cohen's works, and especially this volume, comprise the most valuable material on policy-makers' views of public opinion.

33. This issue is discussed at length in Freeland, *Truman Doctrine*, and several of Athan Theoharis's books, especially *Seeds of Repression: Harry S. Truman and the Origins of McCarthyism* (New York: Quadrangle, 1971).

34. *Survey*, April 1947, pp. 2–4; ibid., October 1947, pp. 3–4; *Public Opinion Quarterly* 11 (Winter 1947–48): 650.

35. Quoted in Irons, "America's Cold War Crusade," p. 43.

36. *See* the following *Survey* issues: 8 January 1946, pp. 3–4; 18 October 1946, p.5; 7 February 1947, pp. 4–5.

37. Ibid., June 1948, p. 7.

38. Ibid., August 1949, p.2.

39. Ibid., November 1949, pp. 2–3; *Public Opinion Quarterly* 13 (Fall 1949): 551.

40. The background is in Akira Iriye, *The Cold War in Asia* (Englewood Cliffs, N.J.: Prentice-Hall, 1974), pp. 147, 149, 174; *Survey*, 20 August 1946, p. 3; ibid., March 1947, pp. 8–9; *Public Opinion Quarterly* 13 (Fall 1949): 548. On the rebuilding issue, *Survey*, January 1948, pp. 9–10.

41. *Survey*, February 1948, pp. 6–7.

42. Ibid., April 1948, pp. 4–5; *Public Opinion Quarterly* 14 (Winter 1950–51): 809.

43. *See* Robert Divine's detailed analysis, *Foreign Policy and U.S. Presidential Elections, 1940–1948* (New York: Watts, 1974), pp. 247–48, 276.

44. *Survey*, March 1949, pp. 5–6; ibid., March 1950, p. 2.

45. "NSC 68. A Report to the National Security Council by the Executive Secretary on United States Objectives and Programs for National Security, April 14, 1950."

46. *Survey*, July 1950, pp. 1–3; ibid., August 1950, p. 4; ibid., October 1950, p. 5.

47. Ibid., December 1950, p. 1.

48. Princeton Seminar transcript, 8–9 July 1953, Papers of Dean Acheson, Truman Library.

49. *Public Papers of the Presidents of the United States, Harry S. Truman . . . 1947* (Washington, 1963), p. 238.

50. Dean Acheson, *Pattern of Responsibility* (Boston: Houghton Mifflin, 1952), p. 17; *The Washington Post*, 30 September 1969, p. Bl.

51. Kennan, *Memoirs*, p. 185; *see also* Cohen, *Public's Impact*, pp. 155–56.

52. Dean Acheson, *Sketches From Life of Men I Have Known* (New York: Harper, 1959), pp. 127–31.

53. Malcolm Jewell, *Senatorial Politics and Foreign Policy* (Lexington: University of Kentucky Press, 1962), pp. 56–59, 112–14.

54. Francis O. Wilcox, *Congress, the Executive and Foreign Policy* (New York: Harper and Row, 1971), pp. 40–41.

55. Ibid., p. 21.

56. Ibid., p. 74.

The United States and the Cold War
The Cold War Era in American History

Aruga Tadashi

The purpose of this essay is to discuss the Cold War in the context of American political and diplomatic history. The Cold War was an American creation as well as its adversary's. The intellectual and psychological framework of American foreign policy, deeply rooted in the American tradition, played a significant role in the development of the international situation usually referred to as the Cold War. It was an aspect of American intellectual tradition to define the national interest in terms of morally justifiable principles. When Americans became internationalists, they sought to create a new world order based on their universal principles. This universalism could not reconcile itself with the ruthless defense of particular interests by the Soviet Union. Having seen Soviet violations of American principles, Americans developed an image of the Soviet Union as a sinister expansionist power with which no friendly dialogue was possible. Because of psychological residues of isolationism, however, they could not effectively mobilize American power to contain the expansion of Soviet influence without evoking the image of a quasi war. They needed a kind of war image to engage themselves actively in power politics and carry on an extensive foreign-aid policy. War symbolism inherent in the term "Cold War" had an important meaning in the context of American politics. The Cold War made it possible for Americans to integrate their nation permanently into global international politics.

This is not a criticism of American foreign policy. It is my opinion that, given the bipolar nature of the postwar world and the ideological and psychological tradition of the two superpowers, the development of the Cold War was almost inevitable. My interest here is to explain the U.S. response to the postwar international situation in terms of the country's political and diplomatic tradition and assess the meaning of the Cold War in American history. For the purpose of this paper, I define the Cold War in the American context: hostile relationship between the United States and a communist power, in which the United States viewed its adversary as an aggressive power whose policy was entirely incompatible with American interests, attributed most of the troubles in the world to the aggressor's design for world domination, and considered that the latter's expansionist drive could be counteracted only by an active, vigilant employment of American power.

Diplomacy of Principles

American wartime diplomacy can be characterized as a diplomacy of principles. Indeed, this was the character of the whole of American diplomatic history. As the examples of the Monroe Doctrine and the Open Door policy indicate, American diplomacy always defined national interests in terms of principles. When Americans entered World War I, it became their aim to reconstruct the Old World in accordance with American principles. When they felt that their aim had been thwarted by European statesmen, however, they retreated from Wilsonian internationalism into the traditional posture of isolationism. The collapse of the Versailles system simply hardened their determination to stay away from European conflicts. After the outbreak of World War II, especially after the French defeat, Americans began increasingly to recognize the serious nature of the German threat. But most of them were not willing to go beyond aiding Britain by means short of war. In order to become a full-fledged participant in the European war, Americans needed a vision of a new peaceful world order. Franklin D. Roosevelt began talking about this vision with his "Four Freedoms" speech in January 1941. Then in August 1941, Roosevelt, together with Winston S. Churchill, announced the Atlantic Charter, a joint statement of their principles to reconstruct the world order. Such a statement endorsed by the British leader was prerequiste for American entry into the war. The Atlantic Charter, which asserted such principles as denial of territorial aggrandizement, guarantee for each nation of the right of self-determination, creation of an open, liberal economic system, and international cooperation to preserve peace and security, became an important document in the diplomacy of World War II, since it served as a point of departure for American postwar planning.

The cooperation of the two major allies, Britain and the Soviet Union, was essential to creating the postwar world order which Americans envisioned. Although Britain shared many political values with America, its imperialism did not exactly conform to the American vision of a liberal democratic international order. During the war years and also after the war, American diplomacy put pressure on Britain to liberalize its empire, especially in its economic aspect. Because of close Anglo-American cooperation and the degree of Britain's dependence on American power, American leaders were not worried about the future of Anglo-American relations.[1]

The prospect of Soviet support for the American postwar system was questionable, however. Its communist ideology and its totalitarian state system did not fit the American liberal international order. U.S.-Soviet relations had never been intimate. Stalin's purge and the Nazi-Soviet Pact of 1939 alienated most liberals hitherto sympathetic to the Soviet experiment in socialism and strengthened in America the negative image of the Soviet Union. But American leaders understood that Soviet cooperation was not only needed to defeat the Axis powers but also indispensable for realizing their postwar vision of a peaceful world order. They hoped that, if Soviet leaders were convinced of American friendship, they would discard their old distrust of the Western democracies and cooperate with Americans in reconstructing the postwar world.[2] The Roosevelt administration offered lend-lease assistance to the Soviet Union on conditions more generous than those for Britain. It did not attempt to exact any quid pro quo.[3] Soviet acceptance of the Atlantic Charter principles seemed to be enough for the time being. Administration spokesmen refrained from making any critical comment on the Soviet Union and tried to deal with Russians with delicacy. In addition, American endorsement of Soviet territorial aspirations might have been an effective way to convince Soviet leaders of American good will. But such endorsement was contrary to the very principles on which Americans wanted to reconstruct the world. Cordell Hull and State Department policy-makers sought to postpone all decisions among the Allies on territorial matters in Europe until the end of the war. It was their hope that Soviet expansionist aspirations would by then be mitigated as Soviet leaders became impressed with American friendship and the promise of a system of collective security.[4]

It was encouraging therefore that the Soviet leaders accepted in the Moscow declaration the American idea of establishing an international organization to preserve peace and general security. In the first summit meeting at Teheran, Roosevelt was pleased with Joseph Stalin's friendly attitude. The latter disclosed Soviet territorial aims in Eastern Europe but did not seem to have any interest in exporting communism beyond the Soviet border. He also vaguely intimated his aims in East Asia, but Roosevelt did not consider them unreasonable. Neither did he feel that the United States could prevent the Russians from gaining such territories as they were determined to take since the Red Army was winning on the Eastern front. He simply wanted to make the Russian aims somewhat more congenial to American principles.[5]

When the Red Army began to liberate Eastern Europe in 1944, it became necessary for the American government to reach an agreement with the Soviet Union on the political problems of the region, especially Poland. Although some policy-makers had been aware of the possibility that the Soviet Union might seek domination of Eastern Europe, it was not American policy to limit the areas to be liberated by the Red Army by maneuvering Anglo-American military strategy for such a political purpose. Such an attempt was not only against the traditional American concept of military strategy; it would also defeat the American purpose of building up the three-power unity for the postwar era.[6] The friendly attitude of the United States as a powerful nation and the moral force of its principles were the bargaining materials American leaders sought to employ in their attempt to ameliorate Soviet behavior. At Yalta, Roosevelt had no desire to spoil Big Three unity by taking an inflexible position on Polish and other Eastern European problems. Knowing the strength of the Soviet position and its special interest in Poland, he did not resist the Soviet stand on the problem of the Soviet-Polish frontier. He conceded much in agreeing to make the Soviet-supported Warsaw government the core of the new provisional government of national unity. Since Stalin agreed to reorganize the Warsaw government by adding noncommunist members and let the government hold a free election, Roosevelt could feel that he had obtained the best possible settlement. He could also be satisfied with the joint declaration on liberated Europe, which affirmed the right of self-determination for liberated peoples and announced the Allied policy to let them hold a free election to form a democratic government. Although Roosevelt could not approve spheres of influence in principle, he recognized them implicitly. He was willing to accept Soviet predominance in Eastern Europe—and for that matter in Manchuria, as the Far Eastern agreement indicated—but he certainly hoped that the Russians would use moderate means for establishing it.[7] Thus the Yalta agreements were a precarious compromise between American universalist principles and the Soviet desire to establish a dominant position in Eastern Europe. It was soon to crumble in the face of political realities.

As the dispatch of the Harry Hopkins mission indicated, President Harry S. Truman hoped to continue his predecessor's policy of cooperation with the Soviet Union. But he was susceptible to the opinion that a tough posture, not a mere show of friendliness, would win Russian respect and procure Russian cooperation.[8] Believing that the Soviet Union needed the United States more than the United States needed the Soviet Union, Truman took a more uncompromising posture at Potsdam. The Western powers were in a stronger bargaining position in regard to most problems other than Eastern Europe. Regarding the German reparation issue, for instance, the most important question at the conference, the Western powers obtained a grudging Russian consent to their formula without substantial compromise.[9] It was otherwise as to Eastern European problems. Irritated by Soviet behavior there, the Americans made a diplomatic offensive to implement the principles of the Declaration on Liberated Europe. But the Russians were unyielding. The Potsdam communiqué simply covered the deadlock with a vague agreement which really meant they had agreed only to disagree.[10]

American leaders hoped that the country's possession of atomic bombs and ability to provide financial assistance would induce the Russians to soften their attitude. But the hope proved to be illusory in the Council of Foreign Ministers meeting held in London in the fall of 1945. Desiring to revive three-power unity, James Byrnes went to Moscow in December 1945 and obtained Russia's minor concessions in Rumania and Bulgaria in a package deal which covered various issues including the occupation of Japan and international control of atomic weapons.[11] But congressional leaders such as Tom Connally and Arthur Vandenberg were critical of this deal, regarding it as an appeasement. Truman, who had not been consulted by Byrnes, tended to agree with them. By that time, Truman himself was "tired of babying the Soviets." Byrnes soon turned to a tougher posture toward the Soviet Union.[12]

It is significant that the Cold War developed first from U.S.-Soviet clashes in Eastern Europe, where American interests were very small compared with Russian interests. This does not mean that American policy was aggressive, although it certainly appeared to be so to the Soviet eye. American interest in Eastern Europe was mainly "a matter of principles," as Averell Harriman wrote to Truman.[13] Once a matter of principle became involved, American diplomacy could not willingly compromise. As Anthony Eden commented, "Soviet policy is amoral: United States policy is exaggeratedly moral, at least where non-American interests are concerned."[14] While the United States did not force a showdown with the Soviet Union in Eastern Europe and eventually acquiesced in the *fait accompli*, Soviet behavior in the region led American policy-makers to the conclusion that friendly relations with the Soviet Union would be impossible. Their moralistic approach to foreign affairs, together with their experience with the Axis powers and their misgivings of the communist ideology, led them to view the Soviet Union as an immoral aggressive power bent on world domination.

By early 1946, Truman came to believe that he should not play compromise any longer, since "unless Russia is faced with an iron fist and strong language, another war is in the making."[15] In a similar vein, Clark Clifford, a special adviser to Truman, synthesized the view of top policy-makers in a memorandum in September 1946. Soviet leaders were "conducting their nation on a course of aggrandizement designed to eventual world domination." "The language of military power" was the only language which they could understand.[16] The American origins of the Cold War lay in the intellectual characteristics of U.S. foreign policy which led to such a perception of the Soviet Union.

Creation of a War Image

By mid-1944, the experience of World War II had induced the American people once again to embrace internationalism. This did not mean that most Americans were now willing to contribute generously to the economic recovery and development of other nations or to involve themselves actively in the affairs of various parts of the world. American internationalism regarded the UN as the core of the new international order. It hopefully expected that this organization could transform anarchic international politics into something like parliamentary politics. Such a change would make it possible for the United States to play the role of the leading nation with a minimum amount of burdens and obligations. American internationalism, like isolationism, reflected the traditional American desire to enjoy the fruits of an empire without assuming its burdens. In a sense, the UN was a new way of running away from the troublesome problems of the world.

Because of the nature of their internationalism, Americans were not prepared to support extensive foreign-aid programs or a policy of power politics vis-à-vis the Soviet Union which would require a substantial expense. Americans were willing to give a limited amount of aid to relieve the people in war-devastated areas, but they did not want to subsidize the economic recovery of other nations. Congressional pressure limited the scope of UNRRA's activities to relief purposes. Congress supported the establishment of the International Bank for Reconstruction and Development, but it wanted the bank to make only businesslike loans. Congress specified that lend-lease funds could not be used to finance post-war reconstruction. Given such congressional narrow-mindedness, it was no wonder that the Truman administration quickly terminated the lend-lease program at the end of war.[17]

The American public was not receptive to the idea of giving a sizable amount in loans to Britain and the Soviet Union for their postwar reconstruction.[18] The Truman administration itself was not so generous in this matter; it was willing to provide a loan only in return for the acceptance by the other party of the principle of multilateralism. The British made a major concession to it in the Anglo-American financial agreement of 1945.[19] The Truman administration recognized the importance of the loan as a means for stimulating the recovery of the British economy and international trade. As for financial aid to the Soviet Union, the administration lacked a positive interest because of its dissatisfaction with Soviet behavior in Eastern Europe and Iran. But the administration had to clarify its stand on the matter to build up congressional support for the British loan. Therefore it proposed to the Soviet Union that it would provide credits if the Russians were willing to cooperate with the United States in liberalizing Soviet-American economic relations and the economy of Eastern European nations. The Truman administration took quite an uncompromising stand on the matter. Henry Wallace advised Truman to soften it, but this advice was not heeded.[20] The administration's toughness pleased conservatives in Congress. Yet they did not favor the British loan either. An economic argument was not enough to persuade many conservatives. The loan was approved by Congress only after supporters of the loan succeeded in persuading a sufficient number of members by the political argument that the loan could make Britain stand against the Soviet Union in Europe.[21]

Conservatives supported Truman's tough policy toward the Soviet Union, but they were not willing to underwrite an expensive program. If mere diplomatic pressure brought forth Soviet retreat, as happened in Iran, they would praise it as a success. If a strong stand did not bring any desirable result, as in Eastern Europe, they would still regard it as better than appeasement. But they were not prepared to underwrite a costly aid program which the "tough" policy entailed. They were willing to pursue anti-Soviet power politics, but only on a very limited scale. Liberals were more generous, but were opposed to playing power politics vis-à-vis the Soviet Union. Many of them were critical of Truman's tough policy, believing that if Truman had pursued Roosevelt's friendly approach to the Russians, U.S.-Soviet friction could have been avoided. Although they did not wholly approve of Soviet behavior in Eastern Europe or in Iran, they applied their moral standards more critically to British and American behavior and maintained that the Truman administration had no moral basis to challenge the Soviet Union in these areas. They considered British imperialism a more dangerous threat to peace than Soviet communism, and criticized the tendency of the administration to side with Britain. Since they were a considerable political force in the Democratic party, Truman did not want to alienate them. In spite of his own anti-Sovietism, he refrained from publicly endorsing Churchill's "Iron Curtain" speech in March 1946. He wished to retain Wallace's loyalty until he was forced to dismiss him for his public criticism of the administration's foreign policy in September 1946. However, those liberals critical of Truman's diplomacy were weakened by the midterm election of 1946 which elected a Republican Congress. Anti-Soviet, anticommunist liberals were gaining strength. Sensing the vulnerability of softness toward communism, the CIO's national convention declared that they would not tolerate communist interference. By 1947 it became opportune for Truman to strike out in an openly anti-Soviet stance to lead the public.[22]

In such a domestic context, the Truman administration was confronted with the issue of the impending British retreat from Greece in early 1947. Administration leaders decided to take over the historic British role to stop Russian expansion into the East Mediterranean by providing Greece and Turkey with economic and military aid. The amount of the aid was not so large in terms of American capacity to pay. But such an aid program toward faraway countries in peacetime was unprecedented. For conservatives it would look like a giveaway policy; for anti–Cold War liberals, a play in power politics as a British proxy. The best strategy Truman and his advisers conceived for winning congressional support for the program was to dramatize the critical nature of the international situation threatened by aggressive "totalitarianism." As Vandenberg advised, Truman had to "scare hell out of the country."[23] The peoples of a number of countries, Truman observed in his speech before Congress, such as Poland, Rumania, and Bulgaria, had already had totalitarian regimes imposed upon them. Now Greece and Turkey were in similar danger. Then the whole of the Middle East would be threatened, and the European countries struggling to preserve their freedom and independence would also be profoundly shaken. "It must be the policy of the United States," Truman asserted, "to support free peoples who are resisting attempted subjugation by armed minorities or by outside pressures." Conforming to American tradition, the Truman Doctrine defined American interest in a universalistic manner.[24] With this speech, the Truman administration embarked on a campaign to win mass support for a positive policy to contain Soviet expansion into strategic areas.

Bernard Baruch felt that the speech was "tantamount to a declaration of an ideological or religious war." Adopting the term "Cold War" invented by his ghost writer, Baruch declared in a speech in April 1947: "Let us not be deceived—today we are in the midst of a cold war." The term "Cold War" was taken up by American journalism and quickly gained wide currency.[25] Indeed, it was really an image of quasi war that the Truman administration needed to begin an energetic expensive policy of containment. By invoking the symbol of totalitarianism, Truman tried to connect his policy with the American struggle against the Axis powers during World War II. Now the popular use of the term "Cold War" with its war symbolism well served the administration's purposes. If the situation were like a war, then Americans would be willing to give extensive aid to their friends. They could also involve themselves actively in the global power struggle.

In spite of its dramatic presentation, the Greece-Turkey aid program was only a secondary one in the energetic foreign policy which the Truman administration was about to formulate. During the spring of 1947, planning for a large-scale foreign aid program went on within the State Department. The result was the Marshall Plan, an ambitious plan of economic aid for Europe. Such a program, saving West European nations from economic distress and facilitating their move toward economic recovery and political stability, would effectively serve American interests in Europe. In the announcement of this plan, George Marshall emphasized a humanitarian motivation and presented it as a single plan for all of Europe, not merely for countries outside the Iron Curtain.[26] Since his speech was for European audiences, Marshall deemphasized the anti-Soviet and anticommunist connotations of the program. This approach could gain liberal support at home, but not conservative support which was essential to get the program through Congress. Thus administration leaders had to emphasize the anti-Soviet, anticommunist aspect of the program when they submitted it to Congress. Without effective American help, Marshall warned the Senate Foreign Relations Committee in January 1948, Western Europe would "take on a new form in the image of the tyranny that we fought to destroy in Germany." If Americans were not willing effectively to assist in the reconstruction of Western Europe, they "must accept the consequence of its collapse into the dictatorships of police states." This argument was still not enough to move Congress.

It was the coup d'état in Czechoslovakia in February 1948 that provided the administration with a crisis atmosphere to get the European recovery program quickly enacted.[27] Again, Truman addressed Congress in person in March 1948. Indicting the Soviet Union for having "destroyed the independence and democratic character of a whole series of nations in eastern and central Europe," Truman warned of the Soviet Union's clear design to extend this destruction to the remaining free nations of Europe. Drawing an ominous picture of the situation in Europe, he urged Congress to enact not only the European recovery program but also such measures as universal military training and a renewal of selective service.[28] An atmoshere of war scare was created, and Congress dutifully enacted the administration programs for the policy of containment.[29]

Having emphasized the menace of communist totalitarianism abroad, the Truman administration naturally adopted a program for preventing communist subversion at home. Anticipating a Republican demand for it, Truman instituted a federal employee loyalty program. But this did not prevent the issue of communist subversion from being exploited by the Republicans. The anti-communist direction of the Truman administration was inevitably criticized by the popular-front liberals. In order to isolate them from the bulk of liberal Democratic voters, Truman took a pro-welfare, pro-labor stance on domestic issues. The Republican Congress would not support this, but his adoption of such a stance would attract many liberals to his side.[30] This strategy proved to be successful. In spite of the defection of anti–Cold War liberals and Southern white supremacists from the Democratic party, Truman won an upset victory over Thomas Dewey, the Republican candidate, in the presidential election of 1948. With Henry Wallace's crushing defeat, Cold War consensus was established in America.

In June 1948, Soviet leaders, probably acting defensively from their own perspective, precipitated another crisis by closing surface traffic between West Berlin and the western part of Germany. The prolonged Berlin blockade helped the Truman administration obtain the ratification of the North Altantic Treaty, the first peacetime alliance for the United States. A successful Soviet atomic explosion in the fall of 1949 led the administration, as the famous NSC 68 of April 1950 demonstrated, to plan strengthening American military power.[31] Soon the Korean War broke out and the United States intervened, greatly expanding American efforts in the military aspect of the containment policy. By the mid-fifties, when international tensions were somewhat reduced, American military commitments had been extended to a global scale, and the Cold War had become routinized in the American mind.

The Coming of the Cold War in Asia

The Truman administration began the Cold War in Europe and created a quasi-war atmosphere in order to mobilize public support for its epoch-making European policy. The Cold War in Asia, on the other hand, developed in spite of its attempt to limit American involvement. It is true that the United States became involved in hot wars in Asia while the Cold War remained cold in Europe. But this does not mean that American policy was more aggressive in East Asia than in Europe. Neither does it mean that East Asia was more important for the United States than Europe. For the Truman administration, East Asia was obviously a secondary theater of the Cold War. Ironically, this very fact brought forth the situation in which the United States was compelled to intervene by military means. Instability in nascent Asian states, which was contrasted with the relative stability of European states, was another cause of hot wars in Asia.

Traditionally, the United States had a limited involvement in East Asian affairs, and the Truman administration did not see any necessity to change the traditional posture. Its foreign policy was definitely a Europe-first policy. Japan, the only Asian power which had challenged American interests in Asia and the Pacific, had been defeated and was under U.S. control. Southeast Asia was far removed from Soviet influence, and except for the Philippines, it still remained a Western European sphere. For the United States, Asian problems primarily meant China and Korea.

China had been the historic center of American interest in East Asia, expressed in the principle of the Open Door policy. But it was also an implicit aspect of the policy to make only a limited effort for the defense of the principle. It was the American hope during World War II to make China a stabilizing power in postwar Asia, and this eagerness procured a half-hearted British and Soviet consent.[32] But the Roosevelt administration, having adopted a Europe-first strategy, did not give substantial aid to China. Administration leaders were aware that the real China was far from being qualified for a great-power status, but they hoped that a unified, stable, and democratic government could somehow develop out of a Nationalist-Communist coalition. The Truman administration inherited this hope. The United States sent marine corps to help Nationalist forces to reach major cities ahead of Communist forces to accept the surrender of the Japanese army.[33] But it was a temporary measure, and the creation of a Nationalist-Communist coalition through American good offices remained the basic goal. During 1946, the Marshall mission continued its attempt to get an agreement from the two rival parties in forming a unified government, but when Marshall's effort ended in failure, the administration retreated into a passive, wait-and-see posture. Administration leaders did not apply the Cold War framework to the Nationalist-Communist rivalry in China.[34]

Policy-makers in the State Department did not see a vital American interest in China, which they regarded as a vast underdeveloped country not particularly rich in natural resources. The absence of an efficient government and the sheer size of the country, which might raise the price of effective aid prohibitively high, made them doubly reluctant to consider a new aid program for China.[35] Japan, with its proven industrial skill, seemed to be a more valuable stake in the Cold War. The United States, they reasoned, could afford to lose China, but not Japan. By 1948, the aim of America's policy shifted to rebuilding Japan as a future partner in East Asia.[36] However, there were many in Congress, mostly Republicans, who felt that China was being unduly slighted by the administration in its foreign-aid program. Their attitude reflected a traditional American sentiment—detachment from Europe and attachment to Asia represented by China. Since Truman had announced a doctrine of universal scope, it was difficult for the administration to apply the framework of the Cold War selectively. In order to get the approval of the European aid program in Congress, Marshall promised to prepare a China aid program; as a result, simultaneous with the approval of the $4 billion European recovery program in Congress in April 1948, a China aid program of $460 million was also enacted. Policy-makers in the State Department, seeing no utility in the aid program, considered it a mere sop to domestic political prejudice.[37] A program of this size could placate pro-Chinese elements in Congress who, being financial conservatives, did not have a massive China aid program in mind. There were in fact few real Asia-firsters. But the program, committing the United States to aiding the Nationalist regime, certainly antagonized the Chinese Communists. The administration's desire to avoid taking the Cold War into China was thus undermined.

The visible deterioration of the Nationalists' position by early 1949 reawakened dissatisfaction of pro-Nationalist legislators with the administration's China policy. In order to defend itself, the Truman administration published the China White Paper in August 1949, in which Dean Acheson argued that "nothing that this country did or could have done within the reasonable limits of its capabilities could have changed" the result of the civil war in China.[38] But the State Department, with no faith in its own aid program, had not administered it efficiently. Pro-Nationalists argued that, if more timely aid had been given, it could have saved Chiang Kai-shek. Against the administration's clear desire to wash its hands of the Chinese civil war, they demanded new aid to Chiang. They insisted on including military aid for the Nationalists in the general military assistance bill. Again a concession was necessary to get the bill enacted in Congress and a fund of $75 million was earmarked to be used by the president at his discretion in "China and the Far East."[39]

The Truman administration had to review its policy toward Asia in view of the Communist victory in China. It was moving toward strengthening noncommunist forces in China's periphery through economic and military aid.[40] In this connection, the Defense Department favored giving some military aid to the Nationalists in Taiwan. There were, of course, voices in Congress arguing for the defense of the island. Acting on Acheson's advice, however, Truman decided not to give any military aid to the Nationalist refuge. To clarify the government's position, Truman announced in January 1950 the policy of nonintervention.[41] There was some hope in official Washington that Mao might become another Tito. But the conclusion of the Sino-Soviet alliance in February 1950 made a Sino-Soviet split unlikely in the near future. The outbreak of the Korean War led Truman to extend the Cold War framework overtly to the problem of Taiwan. Reversing his announced policy, he dispatched the Seventh Fleet to the Taiwan Strait to prevent Communist take-over of the island.[42]

Although Korea had been one of the focal points in U.S.-Soviet conflicts, the Truman administration and the Joint Chiefs had not given it strategic importance sufficient to justify the maintenance of American forces. Therefore the United States had proposed a simultaneous U.S.-Soviet withdrawal from Korea, and it had been carried out.[43] But this withdrawal without stabilizing the border between the two Koreas had increased the possibility of a hot war in the peninsula. The North Korean and Soviet leaders presumably supposed in the early summer of 1950 that the North Korean army might be able to establish a *fait accompli* before the United States could effectively intervene. Probably they also felt that such a chance would soon be lost forever as the United States was about to strengthen the defenses of the western Pacific region.[44]

No matter what had been the administration's estimate of the strategic value of South Korea, administration leaders could not tolerate a massive invasion by northerners into the south. American inaction against what appeared to be an outright aggression by a Soviet proxy would seriously damage the power and prestige of the United States throughout the world.[45] The latter promptly decided to intervene. But the consideration of greater American interests in Europe precluded involvement in an extensive war in Asia. A misjudgment of China's reaction led the decision to advance into the north. Confronted with Chinese intervention, administration leaders were determined to continue the war as a local war with limited means. They were willing to lose Korea rather than becoming involved in a major war.[46] Even after U.S. forces took the offensive again, they no longer favored an advance into the north.

China's intervention, certainly a defensive action from its own viewpoint, made that country in American eyes an aggressive power cooperating with the Soviet Union for communist world domination. The Cold War in Asia now reached a fully developed stage. Both the North Koreans and the Chinese Communists were regarded as agents of aggression for international communism directed by Soviet leaders. Leftist rebels in Indochina and Southeast Asia in general were also viewed in the same light.[47]

Because of the existence of a quasi-war atmosphere developed through a series of crises, Americans willingly supported their country's military intervention in Korea. But involvement in a hot war was unpleasing. As unpleasing were restrictions imposed by the administration in the conduct of this limited war. Taking advantage of the popular displeasure, the Republicans attacked the Truman administration's record in East Asia—its failure to give more aid to the Nationalist regime to prevent the victory of the Communists in China and to deter the aggression in Korea by a clear warning to the communist leaders.[48] This Republican strategy helped them to win the election of 1952. Popular dissatisfaction with the results of Truman's East Asian policy gave impetus to McCarthyism, which distinguished itself from former wartime nativist movements by its partisan attacks on the government. Anticommunism invoked by the Truman administration had come home to roost in the form of McCarthyism.

The Republicans, who had favored giving more weight to Asia in American foreign policy, proceeded to institutionalize the Cold War in Asia by concluding defense treaties with the Republic of Korea, the Nationalist regime in Taiwan, and the Philippines. Because of their fiscal conservatism, however, they wanted to wage the Cold War in Asia with limited resources. When the

Democrats realized that developing areas had become major theaters of the Cold War, they began to feel that the Republican program was inadequate. With their return to power in 1961, the Democrats committed more of American resources to the Cold War in Asia than the Republicans had done. A result of their policy was the deepening American involvement in the Vietnam War.

It may be said that the Cold War with the Soviet Union ended with John F. Kennedy's 1963 American University speech and the conclusion of the partial nuclear test-ban treaty immediately thereafter. Thenceforth American-Soviet rivalry became like a more or less normal rivalry between two major powers. The Cold War with China, on the other hand, continued. The Kennedy and Johnson administrations regarded the People's Republic of China as an expansionist power bent on communist aggrandizement by inciting national liberation movements in developing areas if not by using its own military forces. Thus they emphasized the need to prevent a communist takeover in South Vietnam.

The acceptance by the public and by Congress of military involvement in Vietnam indicated the complete routinization of the Cold War in the American mind. Unlike the time of the Korean War, which followed the war scare of 1948, Americans did not have a serious sense of threat to their security. U.S.-Soviet tensions had been reduced, and new tensions had developed between the two communist superpowers. China's involvement in Vietnam, in spite of its image as an expansionist power, did not seem to be substantial. Nevertheless, Americans were so accustomed to the use of American military force in the Cold War that they were willing to support armed intervention in Vietnam. Because of the lack of a sense of serious threat, however, they could not support a large-scale war in Vietnam for a prolonged period. When they realized that the degree of involvement was growing out of proportion to the degree of the threat, they began to question the moral and practical basis of the war in Vietnam. The increasing unpopularity of the war resulted in President Johnson's decision to retire and the Democratic defeat in the presidential election of 1968. The excess of military involvement in Vietnam destroyed the Cold War mentality of Americans. A reorientation of American foreign policy was now needed. The Nixon administration responded to this necessity by achieving a détente with the People's Republic of China and by a gradual disengagement from Vietnam. The Cold War in Asia was definitely over by the time of President Nixon's visit to Peking.

The Meaning of the Cold War Era in American History

With the passing of the Cold War into a historic era, it may now be possible to assess its meaning in American history. Until recently, the United States has been a young nation with robust pride and moral self-righteousness. Taking pride in the moral superiority of the principles of their government, Americans assumed that their foreign policy stood for worthy principles. Enjoying the favorable international environment which accorded them free security and free expansion, they could dispense with power politics and regard it as one of the evils of the Old World.

When Americans realized that they could no longer remain isolated after the outbreak of World War II, they tried, as they had done in World War I, to recreate the peaceful international environment they had enjoyed in the past by reconstructing the world order in accordance with American principles. Because of their belief in the universal applicability of these principles, American leaders tended to view anyone who challenged them as a sinister aggressive power, and were determined to employ military force to contain the expansion of Soviet power. Because of the residual isolationist psychology, however, the American public was reluctant to support large-scale foreign aid programs or an active engagement in power politics. American leaders had to invoke an image of a quasi war to mobilize mass support for their energetic policy of containment in Europe. Only by invoking a war image could Americans integrate themselves permanently into global international politics. Armed with a sense of moral superiority and confidence in their own power, they engaged themselves in an incessant play of power politics to contain the Soviet Union, the People's Republic of China, and leftist revolutionary movements allegedly allied with or manipulated by one of the communist powers. In the course of pursuing this policy, Americans routinized their diplomatic and military intervention in troubled areas.

It seems that the Cold War era was the last phase of the long first period in American history, in which Americans combined a simplistic image of the world with moral self-righteousness. In other words, it was the last era in which Americans could still retain their innocence. With the passing of the Cold War era, this long first period also came to the end. The bitter experience in Vietnam was a major catalyst for this change. The war not only forced Americans to realize the limits of their power but also shook their belief in the moral basis of American foreign policy. Almost simultaneously with the end of the Vietnam War, new issues like shortages of cheap sources of energy became very important and began to undermine the existing structure of international politics. A simplistic image of the world was no longer feasible. Whereas it had been considered America's mission to spread the gospel of American ways of life—liberal democracy and affluent living— throughout the world, liberal democracy had not spread to developing countries; even in the advanced countries, the future viability of liberal democracy had often been questioned. Now it became doubtful whether the limited quantities of natural resources would allow the rest of the world to enjoy an American standard of affluence.

As the American dream was frustrated abroad, complacence with the American way of life began to be shaken at home. The protest of black Americans reminded white Americans of a moral defect in liberal democracy. Stimulated by the black protest movement, various minority groups began to assert their rights and promote their own ways of life. Along with racial conflicts, such phenomena as the rising crime rate, political assassinations, and urban decay put the American belief in progress in doubt. Americans also began to reconsider the value of their traditional quest for affluence in the light of many environmental problems. The American people no longer indulge themselves in an image of their country as a good, moral, and peaceful country into which they can retreat with comfort. Return to isolationism is no longer feasible. Knowing that their country, like the rest of the world, is ridden with problems that are difficult to solve, they are now exploring ways to cope with domestic and international problems in a troubled world.

I would like to thank Professors George McT. Kahin, Asada Sadao, Akira Iriye, and Nakajima Mineo for their comments on the original version of this paper. In revising the paper for this book, I have had the benefit of learning from the other papers published together here.

1. Cordell Hull, *The Memoirs of Cordell Hull* (New York: Macmillan, 1948), II, pp. 1234–38; Robert E. Sherwood, *Roosevelt and Hopkins* (New York: Harper, 1948), pp. 363, 511–12, 716, 866; William Hardy McNeill, *America, Britain and Russia: Their Cooperation and Conflict: 1941–1946* (London, 1953; New York: Johnson Reprint, 1970), pp. 139–41, 319, 334; Herbert Feis, *Churchill, Roosevelt, Stalin: The War They Waged and the Peace They Sought* (Princeton: Princeton University Press, 1957), pp. 68, 120, 124, 214–15, 274, 556; Earnest F. Penrose, *Economic Planning for Peace* (Princeton: Princeton University Press, 1953), pp. 87–115; Richard N. Gardner, *Sterling-Dollar Diplomacy: The Origins and the Prospects of Our International Economic Order*, new ed. (New York: McGraw-Hill, 1969), pp. 4–23, 55–62 150–53, 203–4.

2. Hull, *Memoirs*, II, pp. 1464–65, 1468; Sherwood, *Roosevelt and Hopkins*, pp. 372–73; Harriman to Roosevelt, 5 July 1943; *Foreign Relations of the United States* (henceforth cited *FR*), *Tehran, 1943*, 15; Harriman to Hull, 13 March 1944, *FR, 1944*, IV, 951; John Lewis Gaddis, *The United States and the Origins of the Cold War: 1941–1947* (New York: Columbia University Press, 1972), pp. 40–42, 47–52.

3. George C. Herring, Jr., *Aid to Russia, 1941–1946: Strategy, Diplomacy, the Origins of the Cold War* (New York: Columbia University Press, 1973), pp. 1–109.

4. Hull, *Memoirs*, II, p. 1170; British-Soviet negotiations, State Dept. memorandum, 4 February 1942, *FR, 1942*, III, 505–12; memorandum of conversation, by Durbrow, 3 February 1943, *FR, 1943*, III, 500–505; Lynn Etheridge Davis, *The Cold War Begins: Soviet-American Conflict over Eastern Europe* (Princeton: Princeton University Press, 1974), pp. 18–37, 83–85.

5. Roosevelt-Stalin meeting, Bohlen minutes, 1 December 1943, *FR, Tehran, 1943*, 594–95; Charles E. Bohlen, *Witness to History: 1929–1969* (New York: Norton, 1973), pp. 150–51; Feis, *Churchill, Roosevelt, Stalin*, p. 255; Gaddis, *Cold War*, pp. 137–38.

6. Walter Millis, ed., *The Forrestal Diaries* (New York: Viking, 1951), p. 36; Kent Roberts Greenfield, *American Strategy in World War II: A Reconsideration* (Baltimore: Johns Hopkins Press, 1963), pp. 16–20; Davis, *Cold War Begins*, pp. 68–69.

7. Suggested U.S. policy regarding Poland: 3rd plenary meeting, Matthews minutes, 6 February 1945; 5th plenary meeting, Bohlen minutes, Matthews minutes, 8 February 1945; 6th plenary meeting, Bohlen minutes, Matthews minutes, 9 February 1945; communiqué of conference; declaration on liberated Europe, *FR, Yalta, 1945*, 230–34, 677–81, 776–79, 790, 842–43, 854, 973, 977–78; Sherwood, *Roosevelt and Hopkins*, p. 870; Edward R. Stettinius, Jr., *Roosevelt and the Russians: Yalta Conference* (New York: Doubleday, 1949); Diane Shaver Clemens, *Yalta* (New York: Oxford University Press, 1970), pp. 173–215; Davis, *Cold War Begins*, pp. 172–201.

8. I think it is reasonable to assume that Truman then really wanted, as he wrote in his memoir, *Memoirs by Harry S. Truman*, vol. I, *Years of Decisions* (New York: Doubleday, 1955), pp. 229, 258–60, to maintain friendly relations with the Soviet Union, though through negotiations with a tougher posture. For a similar interpretation, *see* Gaddis, *Cold War*, pp. 198–243.

9. Informal meeting of the foreign ministers, State Dept. minutes, 23 July 1945; Byrnes-Molotov meeting, Bohlen minutes, 27 July 1945; Truman-Molotov meeting,

Bohlen minutes, 29 July 1945; Byrnes-Molotov meeting, 30 July 1945, Bohlen minutes; 11th plenary meeting, State Dept. minutes, 31 July 1945; communiqué of the conference, *FR, Potsdam, 1945*, II, 271–80, 295–98, 450–52, 471–76, 480, 512–14, 1485–86; McNeill, *America, Britain and Russia*, pp. 623–24.

10. Proposal by U.S. delegation, 17 July 1945; proposal by the Soviet Union, 20 July 1945; 3rd meeting of the foreign ministers, State Dept. minutes, 20 July 1945; proposal by U.S. delegation, 21 July 1945; 8th plenary meeting, Thompson minutes, 24 July 1945; Byrnes-Molotov meeting, Bohlen minutes, 30 July 1945; proposal by U.S. delegates, 30 July 1945, *FR, Potsdam, 1945*, II, 150–55, 363–64, 480–83, 630, 643–44, 646–47, 698; Davis, *Cold War Begins*, pp. 288, 299; Herbert Feis, *Between War and Peace: The Potsdam Conference* (Princeton: Princeton University Press, 1960).

11. James Byrnes, *Speaking Frankly* (New York: Harper, 1947), pp. 108–22; George Curry, *James Byrnes* (*The American Secretaries of State and Their Diplomacy*, vol. 14) (New York: Cooper Square Pub., 1965), pp. 147–83. For the communiqué of the Moscow conference, see *FR, 1945*, II, 815–24.

12. Curry, *Byrnes*, pp. 167–68, 186, 200–202, 361n; Truman, *Years of Decisions*, pp. 551–52; Dean G. Acheson, *Present at the Creation: My Years in the State Department* (New York: Norton, 1969), pp. 135–37.

13. Harriman to Truman, 8 June 1945, *FR, Potsdam, 1945*, I, 61. Several scholars, including William A. Williams (*The Tragedy of American Diplomacy*, rev. ed., 1962) and Gabriel Kolko (*The Politics of War*, 1968) have emphasized economic aspects of the American interest in Eastern Europe. It seems to me that they exaggerate policy-makers' concern for the open door in Eastern Europe as a prime motivation behind their policy for the region. Policy-makers' attachment to the Atlantic Charter principles was much deeper than their concern for economic interest.

14. Anthony Eden, *The Reckoning: The Memoirs of Anthony Eden* (Boston: Houghton Mifflin, 1965), p. 406. As William McNeill has aptly pointed out, the United States itself devoted considerable attention to building up a sphere of influence. The Good Neighbor policy in Latin America, whatever the subjective intention of the Americans might be, was a policy of sphere-building. American leaders would certainly have admitted that the western hemisphere was virtually a U.S. sphere. But they would have emphasized their self-restraint in intervening in the internal affairs of lesser nations. *See* McNeill, *America, Britain and Russia*, p. 317.

15. Truman, *Years of Decisions*, p. 552.

16. Cited by Gaddis Smith, *Dean Acheson* (*The American Secretaries of State and Their Diplomacy*, vol. 16) (New York: Cooper Square Pub., 1972), pp. 34–35. *See also* George Kennan's famous long telegraph from Moscow, which influenced policy-makers in Washington. Kennan to Byrnes, 22 February 1946, *FR, 1946*, VI, 696–709.

17. Herring, *Aid to Russia*, pp. 146, 155, 188–92, 230–33; Bradford Westerfield, *Foreign Policy and Party Politics: Pearl Harbor to Korea* (New Haven: Yale University Press, 1955), pp. 129–45; Gardner, *Sterling-Dollar Diplomacy*, pp. 176–80; Penrose, *Economic Planning*, pp. 155–56; Richard M. Freeland, *The Truman Doctrine and the Origins of McCarthyism: Foreign Policy, Domestic Politics, and Internal Security, 1946–1948* (New York: Knopf, 1970), pp. 22–69.

18. George H. Gallup, *The Gallup Poll: Public Opinion: 1935–1971* (New York: Random House, 1972), I, 530, 561. In the polls conducted in December 1945, a $5 billion British loan and a $6 billion Soviet loan received equally 27 percent approval, 60 percent disapproval, and 13 percent no opinion.

19. For negotiations leading to the Anglo-American financial agreement, *FR, 1945*, VI, 1–203; Gardner, *Sterling-Dollar Diplomacy*, pp. 188–223.

20. Herring, *Aid to Russia*, pp. 250–68; Thomas G. Paterson, *Soviet-American Confrontation: Postwar Reconstruction and the Origins of the Cold War* (Baltimore: Johns Hopkins Press, 1973), pp. 46–56. For diplomatic contacts regarding the possibility of American loans and credits to USSR, *FR, 1946*, VI, 818–65; for the American conditions for granting credits, Byrnes to Orekhov, 21 February 1946, ibid., pp. 828–29.

21. *Congressional Quarterly Almanac, 1946* (Washington, D.C.: Congressional Quar-

terly Service, 1946), pp. 271–76, 473–76, 484–85; Gardner, *Sterling-Dollar Diplomacy*, pp. 236–54.

22. Alonzo L. Hamby, *Beyond the New Deal: Harry S. Truman and American Liberalism* (New York: Columbia University Press, 1973), pp. 88–113, 157–68; Westerfield, *Foreign Policy and Party Politics*, p. 219.

23. Truman, *Memoirs*, vol. II, *Years of Trial and Hope* (New York: Doubleday, 1956), pp. 104–9; Joseph M. Jones, *The Fifteen Weeks* (New York: Viking, 1955), pp. 59–77, 89–170; Acheson, *Present at Creation*, pp. 217–25; Eric F. Goldman, *The Crucial Decade and After* (New York: Vintage Books, 1960), p. 59.

24. *Public Papers of the Presidents: Harry S. Truman, 1947* (Washington, 1961), pp. 76–80.

25. Goldman, *Crucial Decade*, p. 60; Freeland, *Truman Doctrine*, p. 101.

26. Jones, *Fifteen Weeks*, pp. 199–205, 223, 245–55, 281–84; Acheson, *Present at Creation*, pp. 226, 235; George F. Kennan, *Memoirs; 1925–1950* (Boston: Little, Brown, 1967), pp. 325–53.

27. Freeland, *Truman Doctrine*, p. 255; Westerfield, *Foreign Policy and Party Politics*, pp. 274–86; Robert H. Ferrell, *George C. Marshall* (*The American Secretaries of State and Their Diplomacy*, vol. 15) (New York: Cooper Square Pubs., 1966), pp. 128–31; *Congressional Quarterly Almanac, 1947*, pp. 607–18; ibid., *1948*, pp. 170–98, 214, 220–21.

28. *Public Papers, Truman, 1948*, p. 182.

29. Freeland, *Truman Doctrine*, pp. 264–76; Bert Cochran, *Harry Truman and the Crisis Presidency* (New York: Funk & Wagnalls, 1973), p. 197.

30. Hamby, *Beyond New Deal*, pp. 209–11; Freeland, *Truman Doctrine*, pp. 115–16.

31. Paul Y. Hammond, "NSC–68, Prologue to Rearmament," in *Strategy, Politics, and Defense Budgets*, Warner R. Schilling et al. (New York: Columbia University Press, 1962), pp. 271–378.

32. Memorandum of U.S.-British conversations by Hopkins, 22 March 1943, 27 March 1943, *FR, 1943*, II, 35–36, 39; Roosevelt-Stalin meeting, Bohlen minutes, 29 November 1943, *FR, Teheran, 1943*, pp. 530–32.

33. For the meaning of American military activities in China immediately after Japan's surrender, J. C. S. to Wedemeyer, 18 September 1945, Vincent to Acheson, 27 September 1945, Acheson to Vincent, 28 September 1945, *FR, 1945*, VII, 565, 570–71.

34. Warren I. Cohen, *America's Response to China: An Interpretative History of Sino-American Relations* (New York: Wiley, 1971), pp. 185–96; Jones, *Fifteen Weeks*, pp. 195–97; *China White Paper* (Standford: Stanford University Press, 1967), pp. 380–84.

35. *China White Paper*, p. 383; Kennan, *Memoirs*, p. 374; Goldman, *Crucial Decade*, p. 73.

36. Kennan, *Memoirs*, pp. 374–94; Akira Iriye, *The Cold War in Asia: A Historical Introduction* (Englewood Cliffs, N. J.: Prentice-Hall, 1974), pp. 173–76; Frederick S. Dunn, *Peace-Making and the Settlement with Japan* (Princeton: Princeton University Press, 1963), pp. 54–70.

37. Westerfield, *Foreign Policy and Party Politics*, pp. 256–66; Goldman, *Crucial Decade*, p. 77; Arthur H. Vandenberg, Jr., ed., *The Private Papers of Senator Vandenberg* (Boston: Houghton Mifflin, 1952), pp. 522–26.

38. *China White Paper*, p. xvi.

39. Westerfield, *Foreign Policy and Party Politics*, pp. 266–68, 343–69.

40. Department of Defense, *United States-Vietnam Relations* (12 books, Washington, 1971), Book 8, NSC 48/1 (23 December 1949), and NSC 48/2, (30 December 1949).

41. Ibid.; Acheson, *Present at Creation*, pp. 407–9; Tang Tsou, *America's Failure in China, 1940–50* (Chicago: University of Chicago Press, 1963), pp. 514–19, 527–38; statement by Truman and remarks by Acheson, 5 January 1950, *Department of State Bulletin* 22 (16 January 1950), pp. 79–81.

42. Truman, *Years of Trial and Hope*, p. 339; Acheson, *Present at Creation*, pp. 407–9. For a persuasive analysis of this reversal of policy, *see* John Lewis Gaddis's essay in this book.

43. America's Korea policy before the war is discussed in Gaddis's article; Kamiya Fuji, *Gendai kokusai seiji no shikaku* (Tokyo: Yūhikaku, 1966), pp. 32–68; Soon Sung Cho, *Korea in World Politics: 1940–1950* (Berkeley: University of California Press 1967).

44. For a persuasive analysis of the political process leading to the outbreak of the war, *see* Okonogi Masao's essay in this book.

45. Truman, *Years of Trial and Hope*, p. 339; Acheson, *Present at Creation*, p. 405; Glenn D. Paige, *The Korean Decision*, Japanese ed. (Tokyo: Simul Press, 1971), pp. 138–86.

46. Statement on the situation in Korea, 27 June 1950, *Public Papers, Truman, 1950*.

47. For the official American view of the war in Indochina, *see*, for example, Truman's special message to Congress on mutual security program, 24 May 1951, *Public Papers, Truman, 1951*, p. 309.

48. Barton J. Bernstein, "Election of 1952," in *History of American Presidential Elections: 1789–1968,* ed. Arthur M. Schlesinger, Jr. (New York: Chelsea House, 1971), pp. 3219, 3241, 3254.

Britain and the Cold War in the Far East, 1945–58

D. C. Watt

For Britain the Cold War in the Far East became a reality in 1948, the same year that the Cold War in Europe produced its greatest moments of crisis, with the Soviet coup in Prague, the first grouping together of the West European powers in a collective military security pact, the Brussels Treaty Organisation, and the Soviet blockade of Berlin. It began not in China, but in Malaya with the Malayan Chinese Communist rising in June 1948, a rising British intelligence was inclined to believe was the consequence of a Soviet decision and concerted with Asian communist organizations at the Calcutta Conference of the World Federation of Democratic Youth in February of that same year.[1] British policy-makers had anticipated Soviet pressures in Europe from the date at which forward planning for the postwar era began in 1942, and had made it a cardinal feature of British policy to secure American participation in any postwar security system.[2] They had laid equal force on the need to secure Soviet membership in such a system[3] on the long-established principle (so often appealed to by those who regretted the termination of the Anglo-Japanese alliance) that potential adversaries are far better tied to one by treaty than left to languish in alienated isolation. Seen from London the main feature of the years 1945–47 was not the inevitable escalation of the Cold War consequent on American misperception of Soviet motives so beloved of revisionist historians in the United States, but a desperate and frustrating effort to prevent the ebbing away of American interest, involvement, and commitment to Europe prophesied by Franklin D. Roosevelt at Yalta.

Under the impact of wartime propaganda most British opinion, despite much first-hand friction, had come to entertain much the same mythology of shared ideals and purposes in relation to the United States as it did in relation to the Soviet Union (though perhaps not quite so strongly). As the truth about the vast gulf between Soviet perceptions of the external world and those current in Britain sank into British opinion generally, so the mythology in relation to the United States increased in strength. The continuing close association between Britain and the United States dictated after 1947 by Soviet pressures against European economic recovery, in Germany and on the frontiers of Greece and Turkey, was very much eased for the Labour government after 1948 by the apparent continuation of Roosevelt's New Deal into Truman's Fair Deal and his victory in the 1948 presidential elections. But as McCarthyism grew in the United States, the very deep disagreements with the Truman administration, which arose over the policy and strategy to be followed in the Far East, can now be seen as marking the beginnings of the separation between the two English-speaking powers which was to manifest itself in 1972 with British accession to the European community. More disagreements were in fact to lead to a short period of Anglo-Soviet cooperation in the establishment of a truce in Southeast Asia and Korea at Geneva in 1954 and in the restraint exercised on their American and Chinese partners during the first offshore islands crisis the following year. Since the Geneva summit of 1955, at which this latter instance of cooperation manifested itself, is taken by many historians, myself included, to mark the end of the Cold War, properly defined, in Europe, it makes a useful point at which to end this discussion of the Far East.

A full picture of British policy in the Far East during the period reviewed here will not be possible until the year 1986 (at the earliest), when the operation of the thirty-year rule established by the Public Records Act of 1968 will result in the opening to academic research of the Cabinet and Foreign Office records for 1955. Any judgment made now must necessarily therefore be made only *ad interim*, based as it must be on access to official records only up to December 1945, supplemented thereafter by a limited collection of unpublished private papers and diaries, and of memoirs and parliamentary statements and papers.[4] These do, however, present a remarkably consistent picture of British policy and of British perceptions of international events, which the full release of the archives will certainly flesh out, but whose general lines, it is hoped, will not be very much altered.

To understand British policy in the Far East and in Southeast Asia in the years reviewed here, it is essential first to identify those responsible for the making of that policy and then to analyse the assumptions on which they based their formulation of that policy. The British foreign policy-making elite[5] of the years 1945–55 had shared the common experience of the 1930s and of World War II, though most of them inevitably had been far closer to the centres of policy making during this latter period. At the political level the senior members of the Labour cabinet had been in opposition during the 1930s; and although they had performed a perhaps less heroic role in opposing the policies of "appeasement" than their party mythology allowed, they shared in the view which saw "appeasement" not as the prewar attempts to avoid a confrontation in Europe by the management and alleviation of sources of potential crises, but as a craven betrayal and abandonment for highly dubious reasons of the only system of institutions, rules, and conventions for interstate relations possible for the restraint of aggression and the suppression of tyranny, and the achievement of enduring peace. They had supported the British declaration of war against Germany in September 1939 as the only course of action possible against a regime that had so palpably and repeatedly been in breach of and determined to destroy that system. They had joined the Churchill-led national government in 1940 and played a major part in its labours. Successful in the general elections of 1945 and 1950, they were to hold office until the autumn of 1951, when the Conservative party under Churchill's octogenarian leadership returned to power. By that time they had revolutionized British society at least so far as its systems of reward for enterprise and succour for the unfortunate were concerned. Two of their ablest and most powerful leaders, Ernest Bevin and Sir Stafford Cripps, died in office as a result of their labours after long and debilitating illnesses. Social reformers in domestic politics, they were, by long experience, set in hostility to the small native British Communist party, which they saw essentially as a divisive and disruptive force, tending (and intending) to destroy that single-minded solidarity which they believed to be the greatest strength of the Labour movement in a system of government and class that was by definition hostile to them and their aims. They found little difficulty, despite initial belief that "Left could speak to Left," in transferring that hostility to the Soviet government, especially when they found the Soviet Union wilfully challenging and thwarting (as it seemed to them) their efforts to bring about British and European recovery. It was only gradually, however, that they came to put the actual Soviet threat before their fears of a revived threat from the defeated Germany. They were nationalists and patriots for an empire they were determined to remake into a multiracial community of civilized self-governing states. To abandon that empire was the last thing they were prepared to concede. On its continuous functioning depended, they believed, the well-being of all its inhabitants, but especially the well-being of the British working classes. In practice their policy in the Far East and in Southeast Asia differed hardly at all from that of their Conservative successors. Where differences are discernible, they can be ascribed mainly to differences of personality and political method between Bevin and his successor in the 1951 Labour government as foreign secretary, Herbert Morrison, on the one hand, and Eden, on the other, Eden being much more instinctively inclined to negotiation than either of his Labour predecessors.

Below the political level lies the professional level of advisors-administrators, Treasury, Chiefs of Staff, Board of Trade, Colonial Office, Commonwealth Office, and Foreign Office being the most important. In times when Far Eastern problems seem of low priority, the main source of both advice on and implementation of policy would be the Far Eastern division of the Foreign Office. This was very much influenced by a small group of advisers with long experience of China in many cases, of whom Sir John Pratt and G. F. Hudson were the most prominent.[6] These men tended to be heavily influenced by their admiration for and alienation from Chinese society and traditions, which they tended to see as *sui generis.* The idea that Western ideas could be grafted onto Oriental roots and that China could become a Western-style democracy struck them in the short run as palpable nonsense. They believed Western models of a centralized state to be something totally unknown to China; accepting therefore that China would always present the outward appearance of division and dissension, they thought policy predicated (as was that of the United States) on the emergence of a strong central government, however desirable that might seem, to be based on so great an improbability as to verge on the absurd. They were dominated, in fact, by a view of national characteristics which made these the only desirable and reliable guides to national behaviour. They differed in their estimates as to how far China would become "communist" on the Soviet model, in so far as they disagreed as to whether the distinguishing features of Soviet Marxism-Leninism were of Occidental or Oriental origin. They were, however, agreed in foreseeing the Sino-Soviet schism. They rarely succumbed to the myth which depicted the Chinese Communists as "agrarian reformers" which took such strong hold of some American Sinophiles for a crucial period in the mid-1940s. Where such ideas crept into British politics they came via a younger, more naive group of individuals. They thought of the Chinese Communist movement as "a rival Chinese Nationalist party rather than a communist party interested in class war and revolution."[7] In early 1945 Hudson predicted victory by the Chinese Communists in north China even before the Japanese surrender opened the way for their take-over in Manchuria. But even when Mao's own faithfulness to Marxist-Leninist orthodoxy was recognized, the Far Eastern division appears to have been able to convince their political masters that Chinese nationalism would prove stronger than the ties of socialist solidarity.[8]

The data from which any British discussion of affairs in the Far East started can best be discussed under four headings: Britain's decline in military and economic power and America's military and economic strength; the importance of conducting a Commonwealth foreign policy; Britain's stake in Southeast Asia; and Britain's stake in China and Hong Kong.

Britain ended World War II in a state of virtual bankruptcy and with the status and commitments of a superpower. At the end of 1945 British forces still occupied Germany, Austria, Italy, and Greece in Europe and maintained lines of communication through

France and the Netherlands. In Africa they were spread between Libya, Egypt, Ethiopia, and Somalia. In western Arabia they occupied Palestine, Syria, Jordan, Iraq, and southern Persia. In India, Burma, and Ceylon they faced the onset of self-government. In Southeast Asia they occupied Malaya and Singapore. They were still facing a situation of war and disorder in Indonesia though they had just about pulled out of southen Indochina. They had reoccupied Hong Kong. And they had regular garrisons throughout Africa, the Pacific islands, and the West Indies. To convert Britain's totally mobilized war economy to peace and to the export drive necessary to repair the ravages of war and pay off the enormous sterling balances accumulated by India, Egypt, and others required a major switch of manpower from the armed forces to industry. The manpower budget was in constant deficit. The road to recovery was expected to be long and hard. The last thing any British government, let alone one committed to a major programme of social reform such as that which took office after the general election of July 1945, could desire was continuing international disorder such as to require the continuing presence in the armed forces of large numbers of men and the continuing diversion into war production of a sizable part of Britain's financial and industrial effort. Yet the course of Anglo-Soviet relations on the one hand and the growth of anti-British feeling in the Middle East on the other seemed to make this inevitable.

British military priorities inevitably put Europe first, the Middle East second, and Southeast Asia and the Far East third. The Far East, it was accepted, would be an area of American primacy. During most of the 1930s British diplomatists and statesmen had done their utmost to engage the United States in the Far East as a means of balancing Japanese power, with which Britain was no longer able to cope and alliance with which had been prohibited in 1921 and 1934 by American pressure backed by Americophile sentiment in Britain, Canada, and South Africa. During the war years Britain's planners in the Foreign Office accepted that Britain's predominating position in China was a thing of the past. As Hudson wrote in a minute of December 31, 1943:

Apart from the advantages accruing to the USA in China from the circumstances of the war, there seem two fundamental reasons for expecting a predominance of American, as opposed to British, influence in post-war China: (1) the fact that the USA will be in a position to grant loans and credits on far more favourable terms than we can, and (2) the absence of territorial or quasi-territorial issues between China and the USA in contrast to the Sino-British disputes over Hong Kong and Tibet . . . and those which are likely to arrive later over Malaya?[9]

In 1942, as a memorandum of July 7, 1945, pointed out,[10] the Combined British and American Chiefs of Staff had agreed to China falling within the American sphere of influence, and it was expected that the "ascendancy of the United States in building up China's war effort" would project itself into the postwar period. All that Britain could provide for the military occupation of Japan was a single brigade group, and that had to be withdrawn later.

In July 1948 the British Chiefs of Staff felt obliged to advise the prime minister that the state of Britain's armed forces was "a cause of grave concern," a phrase which two months later had become "a cause of the gravest alarm."[11] Two years later, as North Korean forces marched across the 38th parallel, the Chiefs of Staff submitted a memorandum to the cabinet on the "Ability of the Armed Forces to meet an Emergency,"[12] which stated flatly that if war should break out in Europe in July 1951, the whole of Western Europe would be overrun and a similar position to that existing in 1948 would come about. War was likely to begin with a heavy air bombardment, a threat which the RAF would be far below the minimum level to meet. In November 1950[13] the Chiefs of Staff warned against any movement into North Korea north of the so-called "waist" of the country, following this in December and January (1951)[14] with the most stringent of warnings against any involvement in war with China. Under the circumstances it is hardly surprising that Britain's military strength in the Far East and Southeast Asia was measurable in battalions rather than in army corps and that Britain was forced to defer to American strength.

Deferring was one thing. Leaving the Asia-first school to capture the conduct of American foreign and strategic policy was another. To secure American political, economic, and, where necessary, military strength to balance Soviet military predominance in Europe was a major element both in British reactions to the Marshall proposals of 1947 and in the efforts made to secure American military participation in the North Atlantic Treaty Organisation. Korea raised the nightmare prospect of American involvement in a land war against China and of Soviet moves in Europe to take advantage of such involvement. This anxiety was expressed by Attlee in a message to President Truman of July 6, 1950,[15] and in the consequent military conversations between Lord Tedder, Sir Oliver Franks, General Omar Bradley, and Philip Jessup of the State Department. The Chinese intervention in early November[16] increased these fears. They played a large part in the motivation of Attlee's visit to Washington.[17] Similar concern for the balance between France and West Germany, if French troops remained tied down in Indochina while West Germany was driven to rearm, played an important part in British determination to prevent an escalation of the war in Indochina and secure a compromise settlement in 1954.[18]

Within the rigid confinement imposed by Britain's continuing military and economic weakness, there were, however, other motives at work. The first of these lay in Britain's continuing commitment to the notion of the Commonwealth as a military, political, and economic community. Before 1939 this community had consisted of the four white settler dominions, Canada, South Africa, Australia, and New Zealand, and the British empire over India, to which from the 1900s onwards Britain had been in some sense committed to granting dominion status. From Versailles onwards the British government had insisted on India enjoying separate representation at international conferences and at the League of Nations. And India had maintained quasi-diplomatic representation in Washington. The granting of independence to India, Burma, Pakistan, and Ceylon in 1947 did not immediately alter the British assumption that the defence of India was as continuing a British responsibility as the defence of Australia and New Zealand.[19] Whether any hopes were pinned on Indian forces continuing to be available for purposes of Commonwealth defence cannot be said in the present state of the evidence. British hopes had been pinned on the white dominions before and had experi-

enced disappointment.[20] They were pinned again on Australia
and New Zealand taking over more responsibilities in the Far
East in 1948, but Australia and New Zealand, rejecting Britain,
concluded the ANZUS pact with the United States two years
later. The hopes of India, rebuffed in 1948–49, when India's sole
military concerns lay with her Islamic neighbour, Pakistan, were
still strong enough to bend Eden's policy toward the proposed
Southeast Asian security pact in 1954.[21]

The disappointment of Britain's military hopes of India in no
way diminished the political importance of India for British
foreign policy. The granting of independence to India and the
other Asiatic dominions in 1947 was seen by British policy-makers,
not only on the Labour side of the House of Commons, as a major
step towards the transformation of the Commonwealth from an
organization of British settler states into a truly multiracial community. Concern for Asiatic opinion and for the evidence of a
white-coloured split in the UN came very easily to those conscious of the effective use of pan-Asiatic themes made by Japanese
imperial propaganda before and during World War II. It was to
loom large in British anxieties during the Korean fighting as the
command of the UN forces in Korea and the general direction of
American foreign policy seemed to deviate more and more from
the idea of a joint UN and towards a nativist American foreign
policy.[22] It played a crucial part in the initial decision by the
British government to oppose the American draft resolution of
January 1951 condemning Chinese "aggression" in Korea and
calling for sanctions against China.[23] This decision, reversed
in February 1951 after American assurances that a peaceful
settlement was their aim, and an amended draft resolution had
emerged, split the cabinet into a pro-American minority and an
anti-American majority, provoked Hugh Gaitskell, the future
leader of the Labour party, into threatening his resignation, and
was resolved after consultation with Commonwealth premiers and
the mediation with the U.S. government of the Canadian states-
man Lester Pearson.[24]

Virtually all sources presently available on the reaction of the
British cabinet, the foreign policy-making elite, and general public to the increasing "Americanisation" of the war in Korea make
it clear that this marked a period of intense disillusionment in

Britain with the notion that America could be regarded as part of the general continuum of West European ideals and attitudes to international politics which it had hitherto been assumed were a general and universal norm from which deviance was, as with Hitler and Stalin, possible but undesirable and therefore inimical. The disillusionment led to many and diverse reactions, being masked in many instances by the continuing need for American military support in Europe, in others by a resuscitation of the prewar distinction between "good" Americans (i.e., progressive, internationalist, New Deal–Fair Deal) and "bad" Americans (i.e., isolationist, trigger-happy, anti-welfare state, business-conscious). That this was essentially a debate about how far it was realistic to continue with prewar assumptions of progress towards a state of interstate relations in which all showed the same respect for the same rules and conventions governing interstate intercourse was not generally realized, though it was to become steadily more apparent during the Eisenhower regime, largely owing to the degree to which anti-Americanism became identified in domestic British politics with hostility to British membership in NATO and, paradoxically, to British maintenance of its own nuclear weapons programme. In terms of Far Eastern policy it was to lead to the period of Anglo-Soviet cooperation in 1954–55 already noted, and to the disastrous (for Britain) estrangement of Eden and Dulles. Labour and Conservative attitudes to the Commonwealth, not as a "third force" as that term is usually understood, but as a much closer approximation to the ideal international community—attitudes which were only finally transferred from the realm of genuine ideal to that of political rhetoric during the late 1960s after the failure of the African members of the Commonwealth to conform in any way to those ideals—represent a straightforward continuation of these attitudes and presuppositions about the "international community" with which Britain entered both World War II and the Cold War.

Britain's policy was inevitably governed by her interests in Southeast Asia and in Hong Kong. It was axiomatic that the British colonial possessions in Malaya and Singapore should be protected from external intervention and remain under British rule until such time as a further transfer of power in an area where there was already a good deal of indirect rule seemed timely. The principal British anxiety lay with the presence of large Chinese minorities in these territories, who had already proved in the inter-war years to be sensitive to political developments in China itself and who might provide larger-scale material for subversion for a Soviet-dominated China. In January 1949, six months after the rising by the Malayan Nationalist Communist army had begun, a Foreign Office memorandum for the State Department called communist control of all China a "grave danger" for Malaya in that it would bring militant Communist Chinese influence very close to Malaya's borders, Thailand and Indochina being regard-ed as "poor buffers." It would, in addition, immensely improve morale among the MCA, have a depressing effect on morale in the Chinese community generally, and have adverse repercussions among the Malays.[25] Lord Strang, touring Southeast Asia in February 1949, in preparation for taking over as permanent under-secretary in the Foreign Office, expressed himself in very similar lines about the "menace" Communist victory in China brought for Southeast Asia with "its great Chinese communities."[26]

As for Hong Kong, this had of course been a constant burden on Anglo-American relations during the period in which American hopes of Chiang Kai-shek and the Kuomintang were at their highest. At that time Churchill had robustly rebuffed various American initiatives and pressures.[27] These seem to have slackened off during the period in which both American and Kuomintang energies were concentrated on the civil war in China, but with the onset of victory for the Communist forces the question came at once to the fore again. In January 1949 the Foreign Office pre-sciently noted that the retention of Hong Kong under British rule might depend on whether the new regime found the existence of a "well-organised and well-run British port convenient for their trade with the outside world."[28] In May 1949, as Communist forces occupied the border between Hong Kong and China and the British river gunboat, HMS *Amethyst*, was taken into armed Chinese custody, and as Chinese Nationalist forces attempted to blockade the treaty ports of the Pacific coast of China, a major crisis arose over Hong Kong. The chancellor of the exchequer, Sir Stafford Cripps, wanted it abandoned. The bulk of the cabinet, with a public opinion already dangerously inflamed by the *Amethyst* in-cident, rejected this as defeatism. But diplomatic enquiries seem to have revealed a total lack of support from either the United States, Canada, India, or Australia. The Chiefs of Staff pronounced the place indefensible against major attack and wanted a call-up of the army reserve. They seemed rather inclined to fear a combination of military threat and internal subversion on the lines of Soviet pressure on Berlin, and wanted substantial reinforcements dispatched against a possible attack in September.[29] Some troops were dispatched, in fact, and the crisis passed. In September, Bevin told Acheson in Washington that while Britain would be prepared to discuss the future of Hong Kong with "a friendly and stable government of a unified China," the conditions under which such discussions could take place did not then exist and were unlikely to come into existence in the foreseeable future. "Until conditions change, we intend to remain in Hong Kong," he remarked.[30]

Mention of Hong Kong and Southeast Asia leads inevitably to the subject of Anglo-American disagreement in the Far East and of British perception of American policy. Any discussion of this subject must begin with a geopolitical point which is so simple as to largely have escaped notice so far in discussions of British and American relations with Southeast Asia and the Far East. For the United States China is less the Far East than the Far West. It lies at the extreme of American western expansion on the Pacific frontiers of America, approached from Hawaii or Alaska—Japan, Formosa, and the Philippines being the outer bastions of the western hemisphere. For Britain, Southeast Asia and Hong Kong lie at the extreme eastern end of a maritime and continental route leading via the Middle East, the Gulf, India, Burma, and Malaya to Singapore and Hong Kong. For America the Far East is the boundary of the Pacific; for Britain, it is an extension of the Indian Ocean via the Straits of Malacca and the South China Sea. India with its Tibetan frontiers on China lay athwart the map every time British politicians or planners turned to an atlas. Even without the Commonwealth connection and the Labour cabinet's idealization of Nehru and Krishna Menon, India could not have helped being a major factor in British perceptions of the Far East. Geopolitically, for the United States, India lay beyond China, and was an irritating irrelevance in the Far Eastern scene. For Britain the strategy of "peripheral" containment by the states of the "seagirt periphery, the Rimland which skirts the Heartland of Europe and

Asia,"[31] as defined by the leading British geopolitician, Sir Halford Mackinder, before World War I in *Democratic Ideals and Reality* (reissued by Penguin in paperback), came naturally. As Lord Strang wrote, summing up his tour of South and Southeast Asia in February 1949:

> The importance of our maintaining control of this periphery from Oslo to Tokyo, of denying it to Communism and, if possible, of defending it against attack was brought home to one the further one travelled. . . . What seemed important from the point of view of the framing of policy was that we should try to look at the periphery as a whole. . . . There was also the conviction that in spite of divergencies of outlook we must aim at having not merely a United Kingdom but a Commonwealth policy.[32]

Nothing here, it should be noted, of American foreign policy— though it is always possible that the collective "we" conceals the long-prevalent British assumption that British foreign policy, or, more strictly, thinking about foreign policy—was shared by the forces of sanity and responsibility in America, subject though these were to periodic disruption by the darker forces in American populism.

That even "sane" and "responsible" American policy-makers saw American interests differently from those of Britain, while formulating them in much the same universalist concepts as did the British, was, and still often is, one of the most fruitful sources of resentment, misunderstanding, and ill-feeling between Britain and the United States. Whether policy-makers saw matters purely in terms of competitive national interests, as at least the older professional diplomatists and advisers of the Far Eastern department of the Foreign Office did, or whether they saw matters in the universalist terms shared by the political leadership, a constant element on the British side was, to put not too fine a point on it, the contempt displayed in private for American naivety, ignorance, and sheer professional incompetence. This contempt became more and more loaded with fear as American leadership became more and more formally institutionalized into collective defence arrangements.

These disagreements began over the nature of Chinese politics. British advisers simply did not believe that these allowed for the establishment of a state based on democratic principles. As Sir Eric Teichman wrote in 1943:

> It is at present impossible in China . . . for any Government to function on the basis of true democratic politics. The people are not sufficiently advanced for the exercise of universal suffrage and the popular government by the counting of heads. . . . Criticism of the Kuomintang government and its lack of popular basis must therefore be largely destructive because no practical alternative exists. . . . For the characteristics of the Chinese will persist, whatever guise or colouring they may adopt. And unfortunately in the condition in which China finds herself centralised government can only be maintained by high-handed administrative methods unsupported by the rule of law.[33]

In the course of the same report, reviewing the development of Sino-American contacts, Sir Eric referred to the "growing cynicism, dissatisfaction and disillusionment with the Chinese and their affairs amongst American diplomats, soldiers, airmen, technicians, and journalists in China" as "American direction, energy, and drive come more and more into contact with Chinese individualism, business avarice, and official corruption and ineptitude," noting that it "did not seem to have had the least effect on the sentimental enthusiasm for China in America," but expressed fears for the future. This theme, fear of American disillusionment with China great enough to overturn the course of events in the Far East, was to continue to haunt the British observers. The military collapse of the summer of 1944 was a cause of increased anxiety, as, for example, in Lord Halifax's telegram in August 1944, and Scott's minute on it: "I hope the slump in Chinese stock in the U.S.A. does not mean a lessening of enthusiasm for the Far Eastern war."[34] Hudson noted the reverse side of this in October 1944, commenting on an article by Pearl Buck:

> She is quite right about the disastrous effect on Sino-American relations of the sojourn of the US Army Air Force in

China, eating up Chinese farm cattle and six eggs a man per day and ridiculing everything Chinese. A letter from an educated Chinese, serving as an interpreter with an American unit in Yunnan, recently intercepted by postal censorship, throws a vivid light on the mutual exasperation produced by this particular form of inter-allied cooperation.[35]

As the war in the Far East turned towards its end, British policymakers grappled again with the question of how to reestablish British influence in China when Britain's "liquid foreign resources" were less than those of China itself. A long minute by Edward Hall-Patch referred to the dangers of a reaction in Congress against "lavish U.S. public expenditure in China for uncertain returns."[36] As for intervention by the "US private banker and merchant," he wrote:

> The combination of Chinese nationalism and subtlety with the inexperience of the US banker and merchant is not one which should cause us undue alarm. The established British enterprises in China made handsome profits in the years after the last war. They did not make these profits out of the Chinese but out of the American bankers and merchants who dashed into the Chinese market with no experience of its pitfalls.

Unfortunately at this point the supply of Foreign Office minutes runs out. But that the contempt continued can easily be documented from other sources. This is hardly the place for a study of Anglo-American relations in the Far East,[37] a zone admitted to be primarily of American responsibility. But the experience of watching America's vain efforts first to prevent the intensification of the civil war in China between the Kuomintang and the Chinese Communists and then to mediate did nothing to alter British views of American expertise and judgment. To these were to be added an increasing resentment of American pressure. In April 1950, Kenneth Younger referred to "a number of relatively small issues which raise the question of our relations with the United States and our capacity to resist undue pressure from them."[38]

The initial defeat of American forces by the North Koreans caused some misgivings about American military competence,[39] though these soon disappeared in the course of MacArthur's brilliant Inchon landing. They were to be violently revived by the debacle which overtook the UN forces at the hands of the first Chinese offensive at the end of November 1950.[40] As reports began to filter back from British reporters and from British officers serving with the 27th brigade in Korea, British reactions were a mixture of contempt for the way in which American forces had retreated in headlong disorder[41] and panic at the prospect of nuclear weapons being placed in the hands of a military command as seemingly divorced from reality as General MacArthur appeared to be.[42] The role of the 1st battalion, the Gloucester regiment, in holding the left flank of the retreat in April 1951 before the second Chinese offensive, if anything, confirmed chauvinist British opinion of the military incompetence of American force once their superiority in *matériel de guerre* was cancelled out. Matters were not improved by the very marked contrast between the ability of the American and British other ranks captured by the Chinese to resist brainwashing techniques; by the controversy over the American use of napalm; or by the verbal bellicosity of some of MacArthur's epigones and successors.

To this was added criticism of the dogmatic naivety of the American approach to the communists as being all alike, no matter what their nationality, and all bound "to dance to Moscow's tune" and that it was "mere wishful thinking to hope for any accommodation with communists," war with the communist powers being "inevitable and likely to occur relatively soon, say within three to five years."[43] That this reaction was not simply confined to the Labour side of the House can be seen from Anthony Eden's rejection of Dulles's overtures in April 1954 as being far too vague and ill defined, amounting to a demand for British support for a policy Dulles had not thought out yet.[44]

These criticisms of American naivety can be paralleled from the war years when Franklin D. Roosevelt was attempting to make China into the "fourth horseman," the fourth policeman in his vision of a postwar world policed by the four leading powers of the Grand Alliance. That this view ill accorded with the British view of China has already been abundantly demonstrated. That British criticism of American hopes of China should have led American Sinophiles to regard Britain as determined to maintain

China's internal divisions was an added source of resentment, especially as these allegations were to become the stock-in-trade first of the Rooseveltian Left, reaching their most extreme form in General Patrick Hurley,[45] and then of the supporters of Chiang Kai-shek and the China lobby. General MacArthur's testimony to the Senate committee on the situation in the Far East concerning British trade with Communist China was particularly resented,[46] especially when British radio revealed British trade with China to have been much less than that permitted by MacArthur between China and occupied Japan. No wonder that in 1953 the subject of China was top of the basic brief produced by the British Information Services in America for British official visitors under the heading "Sixteen Striking Questions."[47]

The biggest difference between American and British policy-makers in this period, however, seems to have arisen from their different attitudes to the Cold War in general and to the Cold War in the Far East in particular. It is worth debating on this at some length if only because of the way in which current writing in the United States on the Cold War seems to be standing the old Cold War orthodoxy on its head, or substituting myopia of the left eye for myopia of the right.

The first point to make is that British policy-makers started with a series of norms in their thinking about the pattern of the postwar world. These norms developed naturally out of the development of international law and custom over the previous century or so. They included the assumption that the major powers would pay mutual respect to one another's interests; that negotiation and arbitration were the most desirable way of resolving clashes of interest; that breaches in these norms of behaviour were uncharacteristic actions dictated only by a deliberate intention to depart from them only for the time it took to resolve a particular dispute by abnormal means; that acceptance of these norms was the distinguishing mark between a civilized state and one which had not yet come into the comity of nations. Among these norms was the convention that while xenophobia against individual foreign states or against all foreigners was a normal phenomenon of domestic politics, governments would not encourage or pander to it as a way of solving their domestic political difficulties. Foreign interests would enjoy at least the same degree of protection against arbitrary action as domestic interests. The international system was seen as a single system from which there could well be individual cases of deviance, as with both the United States and the Soviet Union at different times in the interwar years. But since the system had originally been designed to accommodate states of very different types of government, it was expected that those outside the system would gradually accommodate themselves to the demands, the not very onerous demands, of its membership. If one state or regime continually violated these norms, it was assumed that it was intent on replacing the system (which was one of balanced disharmony between states or, in some cases, aggregations of states linked by patron-client relationships) by a universal empire under itself.

Now it cannot be emphasized too often that the present period represents the substitution for this concept (which certainly informed those responsible for the original charter of the UN) of a quite different one involving the coexistence of two, three, or more quite equal subsystems, the norms of behaviour within these subsystems being quite different in all respects either from those obtaining within other subsystems or from those governing relations between them. Indeed it would not be an altogether inaccurate statement to say that whereas there are still universal institutions and agreed conventions and rules covering many of the minor areas of international contact, the major areas of contact between those subsystems are still the subject of essentially normative disputes. For the younger generation of historians, especially American historians, the idea of a world divided into subsystems is so general that it is difficult for them to understand and easy to deny the significance of the normative element in British and American thinking in the 1940s, especially since for much of the interwar period American governments deliberately remained outside the system as it then existed, while during the wartime period American policy on the postwar period oscillated uneasily between the four poles of a quadrilateral formed by British thinking, American national, strategic, and economic interests, the "lessons of the past," and the desirability of securing Soviet support for whatever system of relationships could be evolved for the postwar world. To present-day historians of the Cold War, that conflict seems so obviously the product of an attempt to insist on the adoption of a normative system within which American national strategic and economic interests could be accommodated, that the norms themselves are taken simply as rhetorical covering for underlying strategic and economic "realities."

Such a view is an understandable reaction to the volume of persuasive noise with which the normative conflict has been shrouded in the 25 to 30 years since the end of World War II, a volume that increased its decibel content *pari passu* with its steady loss in persuasive content. It is, however, necessary to point out that any attempt to translate this reaction into historiographical re-examination of the early years of the Cold War is as much an unhistorical attempt to mask "politics projected into the past" as history, as anything ground out by the historical hacks of any totalitarian regime past, present, or to come; since it can only make sense on the assumption that the subjects of historical investigation live backwards in time.

The point here is that the norms envisaged by British (and American) policy-makers as having been in part so breached by the Axis powers that a more effective system would have to be set up at war's end to embody and revivify them were perfectly real to those policy-makers, being a logical development from the application of their education and past experience to what seemed to be the prospects for the future. That they generally fitted perceptions of the economic and political interests of the citizens of the countries for whom the policy-makers spoke is hardly surprising, given the responsiveness of policy-makers even in authoritarian states to the perceived needs of at least that section of the citizen body without whose collaboration authority would be nullified. The degree to which each group of policy-makers was responsive to such perceptions can best be gauged not by the correspondence of perceptions to norms but by the degree of non-correspondence. It would be a valuable and productive study to see how far American or British policy-makers failed to respond to such perceptions in given cases (and a distinct change from all those monographs on individual cases where such correspondence exists).

One of the principal British objections to American foreign policy, particularly that of the first Roosevelt administration, was that it seemed to respond to domestic perceptions and to no others.

It was assumed that this would be overcome in time, by a process usually referred to in internal British memoranda as "education," the pupil in this case being the American electorate. As "education" proceeded, so America would become more and more suited to membership in the international community. In the years of Europe's collapse, the need for American participation to balance the vacuum created by Hitler in the heart of the continent meant for Britain's policy-makers a need to reformulate institutions and accept the American formulation of norms if that was the only way to secure that participation. In contemplating this vacuum, Britain's policy-makers suffered from two fears: that a defeated Germany would revive and refill it in such a way as to demand a third European war to control it; or that a Soviet Union would fill it, without in any way changing its own ideological rejection of the prewar norms. While the British planners, especially the military, worried greatly over the second possibility,[48] it was the first which governed British policy in Europe at least up to the autumn of 1947.[49] What changed this was the Soviet reaction to the Marshall proposals, coupled with the Soviet resistance to German economic recovery, moves which convinced the senior members of the Labour cabinet that they were dealing not simply with Soviet "cussedness," with Soviet refusal to see any interest but their own perception of their own interests, but with a deliberate attempt to continue to keep the economics of the West European states in the state of emaciation they had reached in the spring of 1947, in order to secure the maximum political advantage for their stooges on the West European political scene.[50]

The vital element in the Cold War that the British cabinet perceived had begun with the Soviet reaction to the Marshall Plan, the Cominform declaration of October 1947, the breakdown of the Foreign Ministers Conference in Moscow in December 1947, and the coup in Prague in February 1948 was the element of "infiltration." As Bevin told the cabinet in March 1948:

> It has really become a matter of the defence of western civilisation or everyone will be swamped by the Soviet method of infiltration. Unless positive and vigourous steps are taken it may well be that within the next few months or even weeks, the Soviet Union will gain political and strategic advantages

which will set the great Communist machine in action leading to the establishment of World dictatorship or to the collapse of organized society over great stretches of the globe.[51]

This same belief that amongst the various Soviet Cold War techniques "infiltration" may be found runs throughout such analyses as we have of subsequent British thinking. The North Korean attack across the 38th parallel was seen by Attlee as "a new step in the technique by which totalitarian communism is seeking to advance across the earth," and Britain had to "face the possibility that the technique which was used in Korea may be repeated."[52] Britain was confronted with "an attempt to impose communist regimes by force on an ever-widening number of countries." Reflecting on the lessons of Korea, Kenneth Younger wrote in 1951 of the "need to provide against the possibility of Soviet expansion both in Europe and the East promoted by a mixture of subversion and armed force." "Even where one would wish to support revolutionary forces," he continued, "Soviet policy makes it virtually impossible to do so because it follows up social revolution in any country by tying that country to the Soviet Union and cutting it off from the rest of the world. One has seen this in Eastern Europe."[53] Economic disruption, subversion, limited force by proxy—these were the instruments of Soviet Cold War strategy as perceived by British policy-makers. To the Labour leadership of 1945–51, Soviet action was tragically unwelcome in that it threatened to thwart entirely the economic recovery of Britain on which the new welfare state of their reforms (which, together with control of the public utilities, coal and steel, composed their limited vision of socialism) depended.

Given the strength of the Soviet position in Europe and the possibilities of mischief open to the Soviets in West Europe, the Mediterranean, and the Middle East, the priority of Europe and the fear of military or political distraction away from Europe was of cardinal importance to British strategy. British military planning gave Europe and the Middle East priority[54] while insisting on the evacuation of British troops from Indochina and Indonesia. There seemed no very obvious threat to Southeast Asia, especially in the light of information provided to the British by the secretary-general of the Malayan Communist party, Loi Tak, who was a

British agent.[55] For Britain, as already noted, the Cold War spread to the East *before* the Chinese Communist victories of 1949 with the outbreak of the "emergency" in Malaya in July 1948.[56] With the Chinese Communist victories of 1949, the whole Indochinese question linked in. As the deputy high commissioner in India, Frank Roberts, told the American embassy in Delhi in November 1949,[57] Indochina was the key to the whole Southeast Asian situation. If Indochina fell under communist control, all of Southeast Asia save Malaya would succumb (an interesting early version of the Domino theory). A joint Anglo-American declaration was suggested as a deterrent to communist aggression against Indochina.[58]

It would appear from the scanty evidence available at the moment that the British expected at least a Chinese Communist victory in northern China from the autumn of 1945 onwards. The memorandum handed over to the State Department on January 10, 1949,[59] would, in normal Foreign Office practice, have been in gestation for at least two months, say since October 1948, and would have crystallized the development of thinking since the summer of 1948. It accepted Mao's devotion to Marxist-Leninist principles, and argued that while the economic deficiencies of China would provide some bargaining weapons with which to protect British economic interests in China, these could expect to suffer economic dislocation, antiforeign agitation, and close Chinese official control leading to eventual expropriation. Nevertheless Britain would encourage its traders to continue in China as long as possible in the hope of taking advantage of a Chinese "N.E.P." period. Britain looked for a Chinese evolution away from a communist regime of the Russian type, believing in what Strang called the "ineradicable Chinese passion for trade."[60] British representatives did their continuing best to get the Americans to plan in advance for the question of recognition,[61] but in vain. In July Bevin set up an interdepartmental committee, telling the U.S. ambassador, Lewis Douglas, of his intention to make the Near and Middle East secure before becoming too deeply involved in the Far East.[62]

Its first inclination was to leave matters for an American lead. But the total collapse of Kuomintang forces led the officials to produce a new formulation of British policy which received cabinet sanction at the end of August 1949.[63] The memorandum made three points, after recognizing the extent of the Communist victory and the doctrinal commitment of the current Chinese Communist leadership to the Soviet Union: first, that it would be disastrous to intervene in an attempt to prevent a complete Communist victory; intervention would rally Chinese xenophobia behind their new rulers and drive them further into Moscow's arms; secondly, the sole hope of encouraging a less anti-Western tendency in China was to give the new regime time to realize both its need for economic aid from the West and "the incompatability of Soviet imperialism with China's national interests"; thirdly, the need to establish an effective anticommunist front in Southeast Asia to prevent the encroachment of communist influence beyond China's borders. Bevin sought to urge the need for a "careful game" so as to "weaken the Soviet grip on China" in his visit to Washington in September, though without much noticeable effect.

The real crisis arose with the Chinese Communist regime's formal request for recognition on October 2. Britain waited a month for the meeting of all its Southeast Asian experts in a conference at Singapore, following this with consultations with her NATO allies and the high commissioners of the Commonwealth in London. The Singapore conference's unanimous recommendations,[64] immediate recognition combined with a propaganda drive throughout Southeast Asia and a strengthening of resistance to the spread of communism in the area, followed the pattern of British strategy already agreed on. A cabinet decision was taken on December 15,[65] and recognition followed on January 6, 1950.

The step of recognition was taken against the balance of public opinion, which split 45 percent against, 29 percent in favour in a Gallup poll published on November 28, 1949.[66] It was defended against Tory attack (Churchill's approval was not shared by the bulk of his party) by Labour spokesmen after the general election of February 1950, at a time when it was clear that the new Chinese regime was fulfilling the worst British expectations by its measures against all British economic interests in China and by the conclusion of Sino-Soviet treaties of alliance on February 14, 1950, and trade on April 19. Nevertheless, Bevin and Younger stuck to the need to promote trade, break Chinese dependence on the Soviet

Union, and respond to the Asian members of the Common-wealth.[67] The question of Formosa became an immediate source of conflict between Britain and the United States,[68] and was to continue as such, matching with British efforts to secure the succession of Communist China to the Kuomintang seat in the UN as a permanent member of the Security Council.

So far from separating China from the Soviet Union, the issue of recognition was beginning to drive a wedge between Britain and the United States, whether or not Britain's view that the Soviet walkout of the UN in January 1950 was dictated by the desire to keep China out of the UN was correct.[69] Fortunately for Anglo-American relations, the invasion of South Korea by troops from the north produced a new situation. The British assessment of this action was that the Soviets "must almost certainly have winked at, even if they had not provoked"[70] the North Korean action, but that they had not expected the instant American reaction nor the manner in which memories of the 1930s galvanized the UN into supporting the American reaction.[71] There was therefore "inconsiderable embarrassment as to their next move."[72] British efforts to prevent China taking the Soviet side continued through-out the period until the Chinese intervention focusing on Formosa and the Chinese seat at the UN. But what Younger referred to as the "ham-handedness and excitability of Americans," their re-luctance to pay "attention to the longer term issues," and their lack of interest in "our view that China if properly handled could in the long run be separated from Moscow"[73] defeated British efforts, as did the complete unwillingness of the Chinese to reply to any British advances. Chinese contempt for Britain was mani-fested by the outrageous behaviour of a Chinese delegation which visited Britain at this time, led by Liu Ning-i, a delegation which even the left-wing *Tribune* described as "the rudest ever to come to Britain."[74] Chinese intervention in Korea followed, greatly ex-acerbating both Anglo-Chinese and Anglo-American relations, the one at the level of public opinion, the other at the official level. Britain gradually abandoned her efforts both over Formosa[75] and over Communist China's admission to the UN.[76]

The Chinese commitment to Korea seems in retrospect to have begun a process of separating not an expansionist Marxist-Leninist Soviet Union from a traditional China, but a tradition-

alist Soviet Union from a Marxist-Leninist China, at least so far
as British experience is concerned. In November 1950, Sir Gladwyn Jebb recorded an informal Soviet warning that the Chinese
were quite as difficult with their allies as they were with their
Western opponents.[77] The unbending stance of the U.S. policy
towards China, one backed by public opinion for whom Korea was
primarily a Sino-American war, was matched by an equally inflexible Chinese stance. Between these neither Britain nor Russia,
both primarily concerned with the struggle over the rearmament
of West Germany, could achieve anything but ritual support. It
was the linkage of this with the deterioration of the French position
in Indochina and the French reluctance finally to commit themselves to their own European Defence Community proposals (while
their Indochinese commitments would leave them weakened vis-
à-vis a resurgent and rearming West Germany[78]) that finally
brought Britain and the Soviet Union together.

This is hardly the point at which to embark on a long dissertation
on the subject of British policy towards Indochina, nor is there
much in the way of documentation on which to base such discussion. British views of Ho Chi Minh before 1945 classified him
as a one-time Comintern agent who had reappeared as a member
of what official British reportage described as "Annamite" nationalists.[79] The British forces occupying southern Indochina in 1945
had taken the restoration of public order and French authority as
their principal task[80] until the arrival of French troops. Efforts
to promote talks between Vietminh representatives and French
officials broke down, in the British view, as a result of what was,
at the very least, the inability or unwillingness of the Vietminh
leadership to control their forces. The period of British involvement (and its scale) was much more limited than in Indonesia;
but the main lines of British policy, official nonintervention and
unofficial mediation with the aim of reconciling colonialists with
moderate nationalists, were the same in both territories.

Between 1946 and 1950, Britain remained an uninvolved but
anxious spectator of the progress of the Franco-Vietminh struggle.
The outbreak of the Malayan Chinese Communist rising in 1948
and the increasing evidence suggesting some kind of coordinated
Soviet strategy behind the various activities of the various armed
communist organisations in Southeast Asia (Malaya, Indonesia,

Indochina) focused their anxieties on Indochina as soon as the victory of the Communists in China and the expulsion of the Kuomintang forces brought Chinese Red Army forces to the Indochinese border. Roberts's early formulation of what was to become the Domino theory in November 1949 has already been noted.[81] It was in pursuance of this policy and in order to encourage American financial aid for the French in Indochina that the Labour government recognized the Bao Dai government as the legitimate government of Vietnam, an "associate state within the French Union,"[82] following on the ratification by the French Assembly of the Elysee agreement of March 8, 1949, between Bao Dai and the French president, Vincent Auriol. The move was defended in Parliament as simply a formal recognition of an existing legal situation in a speech by Younger notable for its less than whole-hearted rapture.[83] But the British decision was unavoidable, given their conviction that the Vietminh movement was irretrievably in the hands of the Indochinese Communist party (a Stalinist creation), their anxieties in Malaya, and their commitment to France in Europe with American financial involvement in support of France; all that could be done for the time being for the collective defence of Southeast Asia had been done. Further developments would depend on the degree to which Indian and American policy could be aligned, since Britain's hopes of Australia and New Zealand were to be rudely rebuffed by their decision to conclude the ANZUS defence agreements with America, not only without British participation but with hardly even the dignity of consultation. Since the British military assessments of July 1950[84] called on the Commonwealth to provide "the naval forces required for control of the sea communications in South East Asia and the Eastern Indian ocean," and the army could only provide a minimum garrison of two divisions, one of them largely composed of Gurkha mercenaries and the other subject to withdrawal in the event of war in Europe, the action of Australia and New Zealand is not altogether incomprehensible. It nonetheless represented a very major breach in the whole British concept of the Commonwealth. Britain was therefore forced into the role of an anxious but powerless observer of events in Indochina, relying only on the degree of Chinese involvement in Korea as the principal force preventing any major support for the Vietminh.

Army demoralization in the situation in Indochina in the years 1950–52 was stilled by the success of General de Lattre de Tassigny. And it was only after his death that the flow of pessimistic reports from Paris resumed.[85] For the time being British and American policy was directed to the common aim of warding off Chinese intervention while resisting French efforts to involve their allies still further, efforts which Eden warded off with more success for Britain than Acheson did for the United States. But both British and French military and political thinking seems during 1952 to have accepted the inevitability of evacuation, the main issue being only how respectable the terms could be. Paradoxically the acceptance of evacuation at the end required a bigger military in the interim, if only to secure a stronger bargaining position with the Vietminh. The other issue on which French and British thinking coincided was the need for a permanent military security organization in Southeast Asia.

The question of evacuation raised at once the issue of what should be evacuated. French thinking had at this time hardly crystallized beyond a general acceptance of the idea so far as Vietnam was concerned and that only as the worst kind of *pis aller*. British concern for Malaya added to the British conviction that central and southern Vietnam were different from the north and the experience of divided occupation in 1945 seemed to suggest partition backed by a guarantee in which it was hoped some at least of the Asian Commonwealth members would participate.[86] It would, however, be intensely misleading to see the proposals which Eden and the Foreign Office were to evolve in the first months of 1954 as being simply the fruit of anxieties over regional security in Southeast Asia. They were much more the product of two quite different forces: the aging Winston Churchill's desire for a general settlement, and the incoming Conservative administration's desire to restore Britain to a position of reasonable equality within the Anglo-American alliance. They were spurred on by the way in which Britain's own achievement of status as a power possessing fission weapons was almost immediately overtaken by both the American and Soviet achievement of fusion weapons; and the need to control the ruinously expensive acceleration of the arms race in both conventional and nuclear weapons and the competitive stockpiling which by greatly raising the world price of primary products had largely destroyed the effects of the 1949 devaluation and Britain's economic recovery. The desire to retain, or rather to reestablish, Britain's separate status as a world power necessarily involved its assertion. And the years of the last Churchill government mark a virtual end for the time being to the close consultation, at least on European matters, of the Bevin-Acheson period.

This process was enhanced by the Republican victory in December 1952 and the appointment of John Foster Dulles as secretary of state, an appointment which President Dwight E. Eisenhower's style of governing allowed largely to nullify British hopes of capitalizing on wartime ties of familiarity, friendship, and affection, or on Churchill's own prestige as the sole surviving architect of victory after Stalin's death in March 1953. Mr. Dulles's personality, his single-minded view of the Cold War, his doctrinaire refusal to distinguish between the various powers of the Sino-Soviet world, his dislike of neutrals or neutralism, his unlawyerlike lack of clarity as to his immediate aims, and his fear of being trapped into anything that might smack of appeasement made him the worst imaginable partner for Eden's oversubtle draftsmanship and willingness to compromise to avoid conflict. Too much should not, however, be laid at the door of personality alone. President Eisenhower's prestige was enormous and his success in securing an armistice in Korea was to enhance it greatly. But if he himself felt it safer to absorb the fundamentalists of the American Right rather than fight them, whoever he appointed as secretary of state would have had little chance of following Eden's path willingly.

As it was, however, the prospect of Dulles alongside Admiral Radford, as chairman of the U.S. Joint Chiefs of Staff, and Senator William Knowland, as majority leader in the Senate, reminded the British of nothing so much as Lord Wellington's comment on the British army before the battle of Waterloo.[87] It must, I think, be assumed, especially in the jockeying for power among Stalin's *diadochi* after his death, that they had a similar effect on the Soviet leadership. Dulles's speech of January 12, 1954, to the Council of Foreign Relations in New York in explanation of the "new look" in American defence policy, including the doctrine of "massive retaliation . . . instantly, by means and at places of our own choosing," must have underlined these anxieties. It is far from clear, however, whether the Chinese shared these anxieties.[88] Indeed the later exchanges between Khrushchev and the Chinese leadership would tend to suggest the reverse. It was certainly Molotov's contention, at his meeting at Geneva with Eden on May 4, 1954, that both Britain and the Soviet Union faced the problem of allies "whose views on Indochina were much more extreme than their own."[89] While nothing could have been better calculated to flatter Eden's vanity, flattery was not Molotov's usual forte, and the underlying evidence suggests that his anxieties were genuine. A Sino-American armed clash in Indochina would run the very strong risk of evoking the doctrine of "massive retaliation," the effect of which would have been to destroy Russia's effectiveness as a great power however it reacted.

Whatever the truth is about the apparent symmetry between the British and Soviet positions vis-à-vis their allies, the degree of Anglo-American disagreement is a matter of record. A detailed examination of the course of the Geneva conference is hardly called for.[90] The main point must be the marked disagreement between Britain and the United States as to the desirability of a conference at all; the strength with which Dulles clung to the hope of a military victory in Indochina even when it was clear that no real support for the necessary measures could any longer be found in France; Dulles's deep-rooted hostility to the idea of partition; his obsession with the idea that it would be enough to end Chinese intervention and aid to the Vietminh; his vain attempt to secure British participation, in an exercise of that calculated sowing of indecision in his adversary's mind that later came to be known as "brinkmanship," in his proposal to threaten air and naval action against China and in Indochina; his very low estimate of the chances of British success in Malaya; his appeal to a series of dubious historical precedents drawn from the history of the 1930s; and his obsession with the idea that the sole obstacle to the creation of an effective Vietnamese resistance to the Vietminh was the presence of the French "colonial" power.

What has perhaps attracted less attention is his continuous—and successful—efforts to thwart the British proposal for a regional security organization on prewar "Locarno" lines[91] to be backed by a collective alliance and to preserve instead the collective alliance on its own.[92] In this he was eventually successful, Eden unaccountably dropping the Locarno idea during the course of the Geneva conference. India, Ceylon, Burma, and Indonesia therefore refused to join, and SEATO became what it was to continue to be, a truncated, quasi-colonialist organization ineffective in any of the problems which were subsequently to threaten the peace of the area, and enjoying only the lowest of military priorities from its British and French members.

The final outcome of the Geneva conference was a marked triumph for the British policy of concentrating on an ending of the existing military confrontations and threats of confrontation in the post-Stalin era in Central Europe, Southeast Asia, and Korea. It was matched by the Soviet initiatives in settling firmly for a "two Germanies" policy and in conceding the Austrian state treaty. It did nothing, however, to end the Anglo-American tensions over and resulting from the Cold War. Anglo-American confidence remained constantly unsettled for the remainder of the Republican era, through Suez, the Berlin crisis, Harold Macmillan's failure to secure American support against the Common Market, and the abortive summit of 1960, as it did through the Quemoy-Matsu crises of the late 1950s. The basic difference lay on the British side in the conviction that Asian politics were not like those of Europe or America and required different methods and approaches if Asia were not to be alienated, and the changing American convictions that British colonialism would continue despite the withering away of the old imperial relationships and that America alone could speak free of the colonialist taint and provide a leadership that noncommunist forces in Asia would accept.

In these disagreements, especially in the 1950s, the United States succeeded in postponing the developments in the Sino-Soviet relationship anticipated by British observers as early as the middle 1940s, and then refused for another decade to take any advantage of them. While Geneva, the successful conclusion of the Malayan civil war, and the successful stand-off of Indonesian imperialism against the new Malaysia were to mark the last successes of Britain in Southeast Asia, the record of American policy argues some very basic malformation and malfunction of the foreign policy-making machinery in the United States at least in the years before Henry Kissinger's first and most startling appearance in Peking.

1. Anthony Short, *The Communist Insurrection in Malaya, 1948–60* (London: Muller, 1975), pp. 45–49. There had been trouble in Singapore in 1945–46 with the Chinese Communists, but it proved transitory.

2. Sir Llewellyn Woodward, *British Foreign Policy in the Second World War* (London: 1962), chs. 25, 26 *passim*.

3. Ibid., pp. 469–70.

4. The principal collections of private papers used here are those of Clement Attlee (University College, Oxford) and Hugh Dalton (London School of Economics, British Library of Political and Economic Science). I have, in addition, by the kindness of the Right Honourable Sir Kenneth Younger, been enabled to consult his journals for the years 1950–51, written while he was Minister of State in the Foreign Office. Some official documents of British origin have been published in the volumes of the series *Foreign Relations of the United States*, henceforth cited *FR*. Other sources are noted where first cited.

5. For a definition of the "foreign policy-making elite" *see* D. C. Watt, *Personalities and Policies: Studies in the Formulation of British Foreign Policy in the Twentieth Century* (London: Longman, 1965).

6. There are useful passages on these two in Brian Porter, *Britain and the Rise of Communist China: A Study of British Attitudes 1945–1954*, (London: Oxford University Press, 1967) esp. pp. 18–20, 114–15 on Hudson and pp. 17–18, 92–95 on Pratt.

7. Teichman to Foreign Office, 26 July 1943, FO 371/35780.

8. *See*, for example, the British Foreign Office memorandum of January 1949 in *FR, 1969*, IX, 6–11.

9. Minute on F 8611/74/10, FO 371/35780.

10. F 4171/186/10, FO 371/46211.

11. Viscount Montgomery of Alamein, *Memoirs* (London: 1958), p. 486.

12. Attlee papers, Box 35.

13. Bevin in Hansard, 5th Series, House of Commons Debates (henceforth cited *H. C. Deb.*), vol. 482, cols. 1459–61, 12 December 1950; K. Younger, *Socialist Foreign Policy* (London: Fabian, 1951), p. 25.

14. Dalton diary, entry of 18 January 1951.

15. Francis Williams, *A Prime Minister Remembers* (London: Heinemann, 1961), pp. 230–31.

16. The first intelligence of which appears to have reached the cabinet on about 5 November 1950: Dalton diary, entry 5 November 1950; Younger journal entry of 5 November 1950; Lord Gladwyn Jebb, *Memoirs* (London: Weidenfeld and Nicolson, 1974), p. 243.

17. Dalton diary, entries of 30 November, 9 December 1950.

18. Harold Macmillan, *Tides of Fortune* (London: Macmillan, 1969), p. 52. Anthony Eden, *Memoirs, Full Circle* (London: Cassell, 1960), p. 82.

19. Field Marshal Sir Claude Auchinleck in *Daily Mail*, 20 July 1948, cited by Philip Darby, *British Defense Policy East of Suez, 1947–1968* (London: Oxford University Press, 1973).

20. Watt, *Personalities and Policies*, pp. 154–56.

21. Eden, *Full Circle*, pp. 97, 153.

22. Cf. Dalton diary entry of 9 December 1950: "Gladwyn [Jebb] . . . puts on record that unless everything is peaceably settled soon, which looks unlikely, his estimate is that Russia and her satellites will withdraw from U.N. and with China form a new International Organisation. Counting at the start more than half the population of the world and aimed at others especially Asians to join this would be a very powerful magnet to many."

23.   *See* Dalton diary, entries of 25 January 9 and 15 February 1951; Younger journal, entries of 21 and 28 January, 4 February 1951.

24.   Lester B. Pearson, *Memoirs, 1948–1957, The International Years* (New York: Quadrangle, 1974) pp. 300–314.

25.   British Embassy, Washington, to Department of State, 10 January 1950, *FR, 1949*, IX, 6–11. In July 1945, a Foreign Office memorandum had commented, "An unfriendly China can also be a source of much trouble in our Far Eastern territories like Malaya and Burma where large Chinese populations reside." F 4171/186/10, FO 370/46211.

26.   William, 1st Baron Strang, *Home and Abroad* (London: Deutsch, 1956) p. 249.

27.   Woodward, *British Foreign Policy*, p. 428.

28.   Memorandum of 10 January 1949 in *FR, 1949*.

29.   Dalton diary, entries of 5 and 25 May, 1 June 1949; Alaxander in *H.C. Deb.*, vol. 466, cols. 208–10, 22 June 1949.

30.   Acheson memorandum, 13 September 1949, *FR, 1949, IX*, 81–85.

31.   Strang, *Home*, p. 240.

32.   Ibid. In October 1948, Bevin told Dalton that "he was trying to 'organise the middle of the planet,' West Europe, the Mediterranean, the Commonwealth. He has told Liaquat [Ali Khan, the leader of emergent Pakistan], that Pakistan should take the lead in organising the Arab states." Dalton diary, entry of 15 October 1948.

33.   Cited in note 7, above.

34.   F 3976/357/10, 20 August 1944, FO 371/41632.

35.   Pearl S. Buck, "Our Last Chance in China," *Common-Sense* (August 1944), included a Washington report of 18 September 1944, F 4552/357/10, FO 311/41632.

36.   F 1331/409/10, FO 371/46232, minute dated 10 March 1945.

37.   For C. F. Hudson's views *see* Porter, *Britain and Rise of Communist China*.

38.   The particular issue was the ownership of 70 aircraft in Hong Kong ordered from American producers by the Kuomintang government before its collapse, but not delivered. They were claimed by the Chinese Communist authorities, recognized by Britain as the legitimate government in China in succession to the Kuomintang. Younger journal, entry of 8 April 1950.

39.   Dalton diary, 3 August 1950.

40.   Ibid., 9 December 1950.

41.   Younger journal, entry for 7 January 1951.

42.   Dalton diary, 21 December 1950.

43.   Younger journal, entries of 5 August and 26 November 1950.

44.   Eden, *Full Circle*, pp. 83–84.

45.   For comments on General Hurley's resignation as U.S. ambassador in China and his allegations against Britain made in November 1945, *see* minutes in F 11528/36/10 of 4 December 1945, FO 371/46172.

46.   Porter, *Britain and Rise of Communist China*, pp. 119–20, citing Sir Hartley Shawcross in *H. C. Deb.*, vol. 487, cols. 1589, 2185–86, and Sir Oliver Franks on U.S. radio, *The Times*, 19 May 1951. MacArthur, it turned out, had been citing categories of goods in statistics returned by the Hong Kong government without revealing that against these categories, which were strategic, *nil* returns were listed.

47.   Sir Paul Gore-Booth, *With Great Truth and Respect* (London: Constable 1974), p. 189.

48.   Thus Churchill's satisfaction with the outcome of Yalta and his quasi-Chamberlainian belief that Stalin was a man of his word represented not so much satisfaction with the territorial and economic terms of the agreements (which were greeted in the

cabinet and Whitehall with, at best, modified rapture) as with the evidence Yalta, in his eyes, afforded him, that Stalin understood and accepted other views and needs than those of the Soviet and would therefore prove a reliable partner in the postwar system. For British military anxieties and Eden's rejection of them see Woodward, *British Foreign Policy*, pp. 473–74.

49. *See* citation of cabinet minutes in June 1947 on the rejection by Attlee and Bevin of a Chiefs of Staff report on the danger of war with Russia in favour of the view that a resurgent Germany was a greater danger, in Margaret Gowing, *Independence and Deterrence: Britain and Atomic Energy* (London: Macmillan, 1974), vol. 1, pp. 91, 186–87. In August 1947, the Ministry of Defence directed that the risk of a major war could be ruled out over the next five years and that the risk would only increase gradually during the next five years. Ibid.

50. Gowing, *Independence and Deterrence*, pp. 92, 213–14.

51. Cited, ibid., p. 214. On 1 March 1948 Attlee's office included among the notes for his speech of that day a reference to "the chaotic state of the world provoked by the spread of dictatorships in Eastern Europe and the Far East (please do not forget the Far East)." Attlee papers, Box 28.

52. Draft for speech of 12 September 1950, Attlee papers.

53. Younger journal, entry of 28 August 1951.

54. Montgomery, *Memoirs*, pp. 435–36.

55. Short, *Communist Insurrection*, pp. 39–41.

56. *See* first paragraph of this essay.

57. Donovan to State Department, 7 November 1949, *FR, 1949*, IX, 175–76.

58. Langdon to State Department, 7 November 1949, ibid., 176–77.

59. *See* note 8, above.

60. Strang, *Home*, pp. 244–45.

61. *See*, for example, the initiative of the British ambassador on 4 May 1949 citing precedents from the Spanish Civil War. Stuart to State Department, 4 and 5 May 1949, *FR, 1949*, IX, 15–17.

62. Douglas to Washington, 22 July and 29 July 1949, ibid., 52, 54–55.

63. *FR, 1949*, IX, 51–61. The memorandum is dated 17 August 1949. Cabinet approval was communicated to the Americans by Lord Strang on 1 September. Holmes to State Department, 1 September 1949, ibid., 70.

64. British notes, 8 and 24 November 1949, ibid., 186–87, 199–201.

65. Ibid., 225–26.

66. Porter, *Britain and Rise of Communist China*, p. 162.

67. *H. C. Deb.*, vol. 475, cols. 2081–84, 2186–87.

68. Porter, *Britain and Rise of Communist China*, pp. 68–69.

69. Bevin in *H. C. Deb.*, vol. 482, col. 1458, 14 December 1950.

70. Jebb, *Memoirs*, p. 230.

71. *See* Kenneth Younger, "Public Opinion and Foreign Policy," *British Journal of Sociology* 6 (June 1955); Attlee in *H. C. Deb.*, vol. 471, col. 493.

72. Jebb, *Memoirs* p. 230. A view echoed by Younger journal, entry of 22 July 1951.

73. Younger journal, entry of 5 August 1950; Dalton diary, entry of 2 September 1950.

74. Porter, *Britain and Rise of Communist China*, pp. 17, 155.

75. *H. C. Deb.*, vol. 487, cols. 2301–3, statement by Herbert Morrison.

76. Ibid., vol. 488, cols. 159–60, 11 June 1951, written statement by Kenneth Younger.

77. Jebb, *Memoirs*, p. 245.

78. Eden, *Full Circle*, p. 82.

79. The British embassy in Chungking to Foreign Office, enclosing report by Brewis, acting consul-general in Kunming, 18 July 1944, FO 371/41724, F 3713/66/61. Much of the documentation in which British views of the Vietminh before 1945 could be expected to be found remains closed to research as being of intelligence origins.

80. Cmnd. 2384, Miscellaneous no. 25 (1965), *Documents Relating to British Involvement in the Indo-China Conflict, 1945–1965*, pp. 7–8, and Document no. i.

81. *See* note 57, above.

82. British embassy in Paris to French Foreign Ministry, 7 February 1950, Cmnd. 2384 (1965), no. 8; Eden, *Full Circle* p. 80.

83. Ibid., no. 11.

84. *See* note 12, above.

85. Eden, *Full Circle*, p. 82.

86. Ibid., p. 87.

87. "I don't know what effect they will have on the enemy, but, my God, they scare me!"

88. The analysis in A. L. Hsieh, *Communist China's Strategy in the Nuclear Age* (Englewood Cliffs, N.J.: Prentice-Hall, 1962) is inconclusive. *See also* Robert F. Randle, *Geneva, 1954, The Settlement of the Indo-Chinese War* (Princeton: Princeton University Press, 1969), pp. 147–51; Eden, *Full Circle* p. 124.

89. Ibid., pp. 116–17, 121.

90. It is in any case well set out in ibid., pp. 107–45, and Randle, *Geneva*.

91. Here the "lessons of history" were clearly read quite differently by Dulles and Eden, the American equating Locarno with the Kellogg pact, Eden regarding it as a success. *See* Eden, *Full Circle*, p. 133.

92. Ibid., pp. 96, 98, 106.

Soviet Far Eastern Policy, 1945–50
Stalin's Goals in Korea

Robert M. Slusser

Soviet Historians and Their Concept of Their Task

At the beginning of July 1974 the Soviet Academy of Sciences' Scholarly Council on "The History of the Foreign Policy of the USSR and International Relations" held a meeting in Moscow. Reporting on the event, V. I. Miljukova states, "As a result of the discussion there was drawn up and adopted as a working document the basic directives of scholarly research on the problem of the history of the foreign policy of the USSR and international relations, *resulting first of all from the tasks formulated in the program of peace of the XXIV congress of the Communist party of the Soviet Union.*"[1]

The concept of historical scholarship which pervades this document helps to explain why in the Soviet Union historians consider it their duty not to analyze objectively the historical record, including the history of their own nation and its foreign policy, but rather to select from the raw data of history those facts and documents which can be used to present Soviet policy in the most favorable light. The results of such an approach can be seen in a recent report from Moscow of claims by Soviet historians that "the Soviet Union, in entering the Allies' war against Japan in 1945, opened the way for the successful rise of communist movements from Korea and China to Vietnam. In so doing, according to Moscow, it provided a new climate in Asia."[2]

Given this approach to historical scholarship it is not surprising that Soviet historians have provided little guidance on the problems of the formulation of Soviet foreign policy and its strategic goals. To the Soviet historian questions of this kind find their full answer in the portrayal of Soviet foreign policy as uniformly just, far-seeing, and in line with the progressive forces of historical change.

Even such an intelligent and well-informed critic of Stalin's policies as the dissident Soviet historian Roy Medvedev, although he notes that "the relations between the Soviet Union and the national liberation movements in Asia in 1944–47 have not yet been adequately studied,"[3] and although he considers that Stalin revealed "remarkable ineptitude" in his attitude toward the new national states of Asia and Africa in 1945–52,[4] can still write that "the Soviet army helped not only to free North Korea from the Japanese but also win a victory for the socialist movement in that part of the country,"[5] a statement to which no orthodox Soviet historian would object.

Meanwhile historians in other nations have been subjecting their nations' policies to rigorous scrutiny. In the United States the work of the so-called "revisionist" historians has produced an impressive body of writings. Sharply critical of American policies throughout the world, and making effective use of the abundant archival materials now available for research on U.S. policy, the revisionist historians have drawn a highly unfavorable picture of American foreign policy.

The work of the revisionists suffers, nevertheless, from a number of limitations, one of the most serious of which is their neglect of the Soviet side of the historical record. Few of the revisionists have made a thorough study of Soviet foreign policy, and in any case the impossibility of working in the Soviet archives rules out any real balance as between their detailed portrayal of U.S. policy and its Soviet counterpart. Yet to ignore or underestimate the significance of Soviet actions, policies, and strategic goals seriously limits the value of the revisionists' work.

In the present paper an attempt will be made to identify Soviet long-range goals in one of the key strategic areas in the Far East, the Korean peninsula. The reasons for concentrating on Korea can best be explained by first offering a brief survey of Soviet post-war policy in the Far East as a whole.

Postwar Soviet Goals in the Far East: An Overview

Seen from Moscow, the Far East in the first five years after World War II could be divided into four zones, characterized by their varying degree of significance to Soviet policy-makers. In the outer zone, comprising the former colonial nations of India and Southeast Asia, Soviet interests were engaged only indirectly and to a limited degree. If communism was a living force throughout this vast region in the early postwar period, it was not because of Stalin's concern for it, which was minimal, but because of the continuing vitality of the Leninist concept of a link between the communist revolution in the West and the national liberation movement in the colonies and dependent countries. Communist movements in this region, for example, the drive for Vietnamese independence led by Ho Chi Minh, were in reality the continuation of impulses generated during the Comintern period and owed little to Moscow's support in the period immediately following World War II.

Postwar Japan, from the Soviet standpoint, constituted a second zone of concern. Here Soviet interests were far more directly involved; the Soviets had entered the war against Japan at the last moment and had been richly rewarded for their brief but significant contribution to the defeat of Japan: southern Sakhalin, lost to Japan in 1905, was returned to Russia, and along with it the Kurile Islands, which Russia had never previously claimed. Soviet aspirations went much further than the acquisition of these outlying territories, however; as the moment of Japan's surrender neared in July and August 1945, Stalin asked for an occupation zone in Japan itself, a request which was rebuffed by Truman, who was determined that the postwar administration of Japan should be reserved exclusively to the United States. The most the Soviets were able to obtain was membership on the Allied Council in Tokyo and the Far Eastern Council in Washington, both of which were limited to strictly advisory roles.

Effectively barred from any voice in the postwar control of Japan, the Soviets apparently recognized that further efforts to increase their influence there would have little effect. Even the Japanese Communist party was allowed to function without any attempt at systematic guidance and control from Moscow, at least until early 1950, when a directive published in the Cominform journal called for an abrupt turn in the party's policies with regard to the U.S. occupation regime.[6]

Far closer to Soviet interests in the postwar period was the third zone, China. Here the situation was complicated by the presence of the strong, militant, and ideologically autonomous Chinese Communist party (CCP). In regard to China, Soviet strategic planners, as World War II drew to a close, had to reckon with the unpredictable consequences of the long-continuing though temporarily subdued conflict between the CCP and the Nationalist regime of Chiang Kai-shek's Kuomintang, and with the support for the latter provided by the United States.

At Yalta, in the secret agreement on Soviet entry into the war against Japan, Stalin won a number of valuable concessions from the Western allies at China's expense, including internationalization of the warm-water port at Dairen, with the "pre-eminent interests of the Soviet Union in this port being safeguarded," the lease of Port Arthur as a naval base, and joint Soviet-Chinese administration of the strategic railways in Manchuria.[7]

Stalin appears to have recognized, however, that long-term Soviet dominance of Manchuria would be difficult to achieve and that Soviet aims there could be better served by reducing its industrial potential and thus ensuring that any postwar Chinese government would present no threat to Soviet power in the Far East. This, at any rate, seems a reasonable interpretation of the action of the Red Army in the late months of 1945 in systematically stripping the industrial base which the Japanese had built up in Manchuria.[8]

A second result of the Soviet occupation of Manchuria was a fateful shift in the balance of military power in China between the Communists and the Kuomintang. The Red Army turned over to the Chinese Communist armies the bulk of the arms and equipment it had captured from the Japanese Kwantung army, thereby greatly strengthening the Communists, and at the same time it delayed the entry of the Nationalist armies into Manchuria until the Communists had established firm control there.[9]

Soviet dismantling of industry in Manchuria stands in sharp contrast to the Red Army's policies in North Korea, where the scope of dismantling was far smaller.[10] The reasons for this discrepancy must be sought in basic Soviet policies rather than in any inconsistency on the part of the commanders involved. A parallel from Europe which helps shed light on the matter is provided by events in Silesia, a heavily industrialized province of eastern Germany which the Red Army occupied early in 1945 but which the Soviet commander, Marshal Konev, was given explicit instructions by Stalin not to subject to the same kind of large-scale industrial dismantling which the Red Army was carrying out elsewhere in Soviet-occupied eastern Germany.[11] Stalin's purpose, it seems clear, was to strengthen postwar Poland's economic position and thereby to make it a faithful and loyal ally of the Soviet Union. A similar purpose, we can assume, lay behind the Soviet decision to spare the industrial plant of North Korea.

It is in Korea, then, which from the Soviet standpoint can be considered a fourth zone of concern in the Far East, that Stalin's postwar policy aims can be studied most effectively. The significance of Korea, with its warm-water ports in the southern part of the peninsula and its strategic location vis-à-vis both China and Japan, had been recognized by Russian policy-makers in the late nineteenth and early twentieth centuries.[12] Now, for the first time since 1905, conditions appeared to be favorable for the attainment of Russian goals in that area.

Stalin's Part in Allied Planning for Postwar Korea

It will be argued in this paper that Stalin in the period 1945–50 had certain definite goals in Korea; that he sought to attain these goals through a combination of military, diplomatic, and political means; and that the pursuit of these goals helps to explain the record of Soviet policy in Korea in the postwar period, including the decision on the outbreak of the Korean War. In presenting this thesis it is well to recognize that a fully documented case in support of it cannot be presented, owing in large part to the lack of adequate material from the Soviet state and diplomatic archives. It is possible, nevertheless, using the documentary materials now available from U.S. archives, together with memoirs, scholarly monographs, and contemporary documentation, to build an analysis of Soviet strategic goals in Korea which is internally consistent and which finds confirmation at a number of key points from recent Soviet publications based in part on archival materials. For the purposes of this paper it will be useful to trace the development of Allied planning for postwar Korea as it evolved between 1943 and 1945, since it was this framework which conditioned Stalin's thinking about the possibilities and opportunities open to the Soviets in Korea.

The first steps in this area were taken in March 1943, when President Franklin D. Roosevelt suggested to British Foreign Secretary Anthony Eden that trusteeship arrangements would prove suitable for Indonesia and Korea after the defeat of Japan.[13] Roosevelt's proposal, which Eden promised to study, appears to have reflected earlier thinking in the State Department to the effect that Korea was "not capable of self-government at the present time."[14] Consistent with this view was the State Department's opposition in April 1942 to recognition of the provisional government of the Republic of Korea, an émigré group then located in Chungking.[15]

Despite Eden's lack of enthusiasm for the trusteeship idea, a distaste which Churchill shared, the British deferred to Roosevelt by endorsing the concept in principle, while continuing to oppose it in specific instances. At the Cairo Conference in November 1943, the British acceded to Roosevelt's view that Korea should "in due course . . . become free and independent."[16] Although the trusteeship idea continued to dominate American thinking on Korea, it was not specifically mentioned in the Cairo declaration published on December 1, 1943, thus leaving open the exact form which Allied control would take in Korea in the period between the defeat of Japan and eventual Korean independence.[17]

The first Soviet participation in Allied planning for Korea occurred at the Teheran Conference in late November and early December 1943. Stalin, shown a draft of the Cairo declaration, "thoroughly approved the communiqué and all its contents," and said it was right that Korea should be independent.[18] Later, in the course of the luncheon at which Stalin made this observation, Churchill spoke in favor of giving the Soviet Union access to warm-water ports and asked Stalin's view on the question of such ports in the Far East. The ensuing conversation merits quotation *in extenso*:

> Marshal Stalin replied that of course the Russians had their views, but that it would perhaps be better to await the time when the Russians would be taking an active representation in the Far Eastern War. He added, however, that there was no [Soviet] port in the Far East that was not closed off, since Vladivostok was only partly ice-free, and besides covered by Japanese controlled Straits.
> The President [Roosevelt] said he thought the idea of a free port might be applied to the Far East besides, and mentioned Dairen as a possibility.
> Marshal Stalin said he did not think that the Chinese would like such a scheme.
> To which the President replied that he thought they would like the idea of a free port under international guaranty.
> Marshal Stalin said that that would not be bad.[19]

Despite deliberate prodding by Churchill, who sought to stimulate Stalin's appetite for the acquisition of warm-water ports, Stalin said nothing about Korea, an obvious candidate for Soviet aspirations in that respect, thereby initiating what was to become a series of meaningful silences on his part and that of other Soviet spokesmen concerning Soviet goals in Korea. Granted that it is always difficult in historical analysis to build a case on negative evidence, the fact remains that there was something strangely suggestive about the consistency with which Stalin and his associates avoided raising the problem of Korea's future in negotiations with the Western allies, confining themselves to probing their allies' plans for Korea without disclosing their own intentions.

Roosevelt left Teheran convinced that Stalin "saw 'eye to eye' with him on all major problems of the Pacific."[20] That a considerable element of wishful thinking entered into this evaluation, however, is indicated by the fact that in reporting to the Pacific War Council about the Teheran Conference, Roosevelt stated that "Marshal Stalin had specifically agreed ... that the Koreans are not yet capable of exercising and maintaining independent government and that they should be placed under a 40-year tutelage."[21] According to State Department archivists, however, no indication of such a statement by Stalin has been found in the diplomatic records of the Teheran Conference.[22]

In December 1944 U.S. Ambassador to Moscow W. Averell Harriman obtained from Stalin a comprehensive list of the concessions the Soviets would require as compensation for their entry into the war against Japan. According to Harriman, "[Stalin] said that Russia's position in the [Far] East should be generally re-established as it existed before the Russo-Japanese War of 1905."[23] Again, however, Stalin made no mention of Korea, an especially puzzling omission in view of his emphasis on reestablishing Russia's position in the Far East as it had existed before the Russo-Japanese War, a war which was in large part the result of Russia's refusal to moderate its ambition to achieve a position of dominance in Korea and control of the warm-water ports of southern Korea.

The probability that the Soviets would try to establish their control over postwar Korea had meanwhile led officials in the State Department to consider plans for joint U.S.-Soviet military occupation of that country, in order to forestall its total subjugation by the Soviets.[24] No concrete recommendations were adopted, however, and when the Allies met at Yalta in February 1945, the secret agreement on the entry of the Soviet Union into the war in the Pacific omitted reference to Korea entirely. Anxious to ensure Soviet entry into the Pacific War, Roosevelt met all of Stalin's demands, as reported by Harriman, but since Stalin's list of particulars had made no mention of Korea, that nation did not figure in the Yalta agreement.

In a meeting with Stalin during the conference, Roosevelt alluded briefly to the trusteeship proposal and suggested that it be exercised by the United States, the Soviet Union, and China, whereupon Stalin urged that Britain be included as well.[25] With regard to the duration of the trusteeship Roosevelt mentioned the figure of "twenty to thirty years," in reply to which Stalin said, "The shorter the period the better." Stalin then asked whether any foreign troops would be stationed in Korea, and when Roosevelt replied in the negative, "Marshal Stalin expressed approval."[26]

State Department concern over possible Soviet control of postwar Korea was not shared by U.S. military leaders. General Douglas MacArthur, in a conversation with a War Department visitor in February 1945, outlined what he regarded as probable zones for Soviet military action in the Far East, including "all of Manchuria, Korea, and possibly part of China."[27] At this stage, however, it seems clear that the Soviets had no inkling of the U.S. military leader's views. As of Feburary 1955, Stalin concurred in the U.S. proposal for a four-power trusteeship in Korea, though he favored a shorter period for its duration than did Roosevelt. Since he expressed the hope that foreign troops would not be stationed in Korea, the logical deduction is that he was not planning to rely on the Red Army for the attainment of Soviet goals in that nation.

The complacency with which U.S. military leaders viewed the probability of Soviet occupation of Korea was not shared by high officials in the Chinese Nationalist government. On May 20, 1945, a gloomy forecast was made by Dr. Chu Hein-ming, chief of the Russian department in the Chinese Ministry of Information. Dr. Chu, according to an American diplomat,

does not believe there is any chance to assure Korea's independence. . . . He believes that the Korean Communists, trained in the Soviet Union, have a far greater chance to take over the power in China [sic, error for Korea] than have the Chinese and our [i.e., U.S.] Korean protégés. The Soviets, says Dr. Chu, have withdrawn many Koreans from border regions to more remote provinces in Turkestan during the purge of 1937–38. Those Koreans of whom the Soviets did not feel quite sure during the purge have since been thoroughly trained and incorporated into the Soviet administration. Their administrative experience, combined with the military and political prestige of their Soviet sponsors, may easily bring them to power in Korea.[28]

In the State Department, meanwhile, U.S. planners were drawing up preliminary plans for Korean trusteeship.[29] Conscious of the fact that the Soviets had not yet formally endorsed the idea, Truman asked Harry Hopkins to include it in the conversations which he conducted with Stalin in late May and early June 1945. To Hopkins's satisfaction, Stalin on May 28 gave his formal assent to the U.S. proposal for a four-power trusteeship for Korea.[30] In the course of the same conversations Stalin provided some significant indications of his ideas on Soviet entry into the Pacific War:

> He said that in the main the Soviet armies would be in a sufficient state of preparedness and in position by August 8. However, *as to the actual date of operations he felt that would depend on the execution of the agreement made at Yalta concerning Soviet desires.* . . . He said *it was necessary to have these agreements* in order to justify entry into the Pacific war in the eyes of the Soviet people. Therefore, *if China would agree to these desires, the Soviet Union would be ready to commence operations in August.*[31]

Stalin thus clearly indicated that Chinese acceptance of the concessions at China's expense made to the Soviets at Yalta was a necessary prerequisite for Soviet entry into the war against Japan. In the course of his conversations with Hopkins, Stalin also expressed a desire for an occupation zone in Japan, a desire duly transmitted by Hopkins to Truman, who evaluated it in the light of his growing disenchantment with Soviet policy in Germany.[32]

Talks between Stalin and Chinese Foreign Minister Soong got under way in Moscow on June 30. A report from Harriman provides light on Stalin's thinking about Korea at this time: "As to Korea Stalin confirmed to Soong his agreement to establishing a four-power trusteeship. Molotov interjected that this was an unusual arrangement with no parallel and that it would be necessary to come to a detailed understanding. *Stalin stated that there should be no foreign troops or foreign policy in Korea.*"[33] Harriman then went on to report Soong's forebodings: "Soong understands that the Russians have 2 Korean divisions trained in Siberia. He believes that these troops will be left in Korea and that there will be Soviet trained political personnel who will also be brought into the country. Under these conditions he is fearful that even with a four-power trusteeship the Soviets will obtain dominance of Korean affairs."[34] Soong's pessimistic forecast can be taken as a well-informed and probably accurate evaluation of

Soviet plans for Korea as they stood just before the Potsdam Conference. The Soviet estimate of the situation, on this reading, included acceptance of a four-power trusteeship, a brief period of occupation followed by the withdrawal of all foreign troops, and the establishment of a Korean provisional government in which Soviet-trained Korean communists, working with native communists and those who would be returning from China, would have a favorable chance to win power.

Evidence based on unpublished documents from Soviet archives indicates that there was more to Soviet planning for Korea than Soong realized, and that definite strategic goals were involved. Early in July 1945 the State Defense Committee, the top Soviet wartime executive and policy-making body, adopted a decision on the development of ports in the Far East as an "especially important state task."[35] While the order can be interpreted as referring only to existing ports in Soviet territory, it seems probable that Stalin already had his sights fixed on acquiring access to warm-water ports in the Pacific, the lack of which he had complained about at Teheran.

Soviet interest in Dairen and Port Arthur had been recognized at Yalta, and the final legitimization of Soviet aspirations there awaited only the conclusion of a formal agreement with China. Yet Korea offered opportunities equally suitable for Stalin's purposes; furthermore, if Soviet dominance could be established in Korea it would not have to be shared with China, which made no claim for jurisdiction over Korea. As to Japan, its defeat would mean the removal of Russia's historical antagonist for the control of Korea. There remained only one power which might conceivably challenge the Russian advance into Korea, the United States. In his negotiations with U.S. officials, Stalin moved cautiously with regard to Korea, sounding them out on their plans but refraining from disclosing his own goals.

Until the Potsdam Conference, Stalin's view of Soviet opportunities in Korea was necessarily restricted to the U.S. proposal for a four-power trusteeship, to which he had added the corollary that foreign troops should be withdrawn from Korea as soon as possible. In the opening stages of the Potsdam Conference, however, it became clear to Stalin that the trusteeship proposal was encountering stiff opposition from the British. Efforts by

Molotov at the session of July 22 to open a discussion about trusteeship for the former Italian colonies in North Africa were impatiently brushed aside by Churchill, and an attempt by Stalin to turn the discussion to Korea was equally unsuccessful. The only concrete result of the discussion was an agreement that trusteeship matters should be referred to the Council of Foreign Ministers.[36]

Two days later Stalin and his military advisers learned something of great significance: the Americans had no immediate plans for the occupation of Korea. On July 24 the senior officers of the United States, Britain, and the Soviet Union held a meeting for the purpose of coordinating their strategy in the Far East in preparation for Russia's entry into the Pacific War. During the meeting General A. I. Antonov, Soviet chief of staff, asked the Americans "if it would be possible for the U.S. forces to operate against the shores of Korea in coordination with the Russian forces that would be making an offensive against the peninsula," to which General Marshall, the U.S. chief of staff, replied that "such amphibious operations had not been contemplated, and particularly not in the near future."[37] Foreseeing an embittered last-ditch Japanese defense of Korea, Marshall said it would be necessary first to establish airfields in Kyūshū, from which Korea could be controlled. Clearly the Americans were thinking in exclusively military terms, with heavy weight being given to the estimated casualty lists in operations against the Japanese army; long-term strategic goals were completely absent from their calculations, nor did they impute any such goals to the Soviets. The Americans contemplated a long drawn-out campaign in Korea, with neither themselves nor the Soviets making any early moves there.

At the end of the meeting Antonov thanked Marshall "for the very valuable information he had given him and said that it would be truly exploited."[38] In effect, the Americans had told the Soviet military leaders that they had no plans for the military occupation of Korea. Taken in conjunction with the earlier disclosure that the U.S. proposal for a four-power trusteeship was encountering opposition from the British, the effect was to alert Stalin and his military advisers to the fact that Soviet prospects in Korea were far more promising than they had previously believed. Regardless of whether or not a trusteeship was eventually established, the possibility loomed in the immediate future of a Soviet occupation of the entire peninsula, unopposed by U.S. military actions.

To understand the importance of this information for Soviet policy-makers it is necessary to take note of a significant development in Soviet planning for the postwar world which had taken place during the war, one which called for assigning primary emphasis to military action for the extension of Soviet influence and power. According to M. S. Handler, a *New York Times* correspondent with high-level contacts in the Yugoslav Communist party, "the role of making the revolution [abroad] was assigned to the Red Army. Communist parties outside the Soviet Union were to wait for the arrival of the Red Army. They were not to attempt a full-fledged revolution on their own. They were to act as auxiliaries to the Red Army."[39]

Until the American disclosures at the July 24 meeting, Soviet planning for postwar Korea had been based on the assumption that the Red Army would not be in a position to influence the course of postliberation political developments in that country. The information obtained at the July 24 meeting provided the basis for a quick revision of Soviet plans. Antonov's parting words indicate that he had immediately grasped the strategic implications of Marshall's disclaimer of U.S. interest in the occupation of Korea.

At a follow-up meeting on July 26 the Russians provided answers to a number of questions which Marshall had asked. As reported by Truman, "Agreement was also reached on lines to mark off areas of operation for the respective air and naval forces. These ran generally from the northern tip of Japan across extreme northern Korea. *No lines were set up for land operations since it was not anticipated by our military leaders that we would carry out operations in Korea.*"[40] If the Soviets had any plans for the occupation of Korea, they said nothing about them; the general atmosphere of the meeting, according to Truman, "was one of cooperation and friendship." Summing up the results of the meeting, he adds, "There was no discussion of any zones for ground operation or for occupation [in Korea] for *it was not expected that either Soviet or American ground troops would enter Korea in the immediate future.*"[41]

The Soviet military leaders' silence about Korea at the July 26 meeting can mean only one thing: that they had already formulated plans for the occupation of the entire country and that they did not wish to alert the Americans to the existence of these plans.

On the same day that the Soviet and U.S. military leaders held their second meeting, U.S. and British political leaders issued the Potsdam declaration calling on Japan to surrender and reaffirming the Cairo declaration, which had called for Korean independence "in due course."[42] Stalin did not sign the Potsdam declaration, since the Soviet Union was not yet at war with Japan, but when the Soviets entered the war on August 8, they formally endorsed it and thus associated themselves with the pledge of eventual independence for Korea.[43]

Contrary to what Stalin and other Soviet spokesmen had been consistently saying about the need to conclude an agreement with China before Soviet entry into the Pacific War, the Soviet declaration of war was announced while Soviet-Chinese negotiations were still in progress. This fact, together with evidence from diplomatic reports sent from Moscow by Harriman, makes it clear that the Soviets greatly accelerated their entry into the war.[44] The same conclusion is indicated by the speed with which the Red Army's operations against Japanese forces in Manchuria and Korea were launched. Amphibious landings were carried out in Korea on August 10, and on the following day Soviet marines, under cover of the Soviet Pacific Fleet, captured the naval base at Rashin (Nadjin) in northern Korea.[45]

The sudden shift in Soviet intentions on the timing of their entry into the Pacific War and the speed with which they moved to occupy the territories open to them point to a desire to achieve strategic goals which would be jeopardized if they delayed entering a war which was now rapidly approaching its conclusion. In particular the rapid Soviet occupation of Korea, which took the Americans completely by surprise, indicates that that country held a key position in Soviet strategic planning.

The American response was a hurried improvisation, the adoption of a demarcation line along the 38th parallel, with U.S. commanders taking the Japanese surrender south of the line, Soviet commanders to the north. Worked out in the War Department on the night of August 10–11, the provision for the 38th parallel was incorporated into the draft of General Order No. 1, then in course of preparation as the basic Allied document for the surrender of Japanese forces.[46]

On August 15, the draft was sent to the Soviet and British governments for their comments and approval. Stalin in his reply asked for a number of modifications, including provision for the surrender of Japanese forces in northern Hokkaidō to a Soviet commander, a proposal which was tantamount to a request for a Soviet zone of occupation in Japan. Stalin said nothing, however, about the 38th parallel in Korea, thereby tacitly acquiescing in the U.S. proposal.[47]

Various suggestions have been offered as to why Stalin accepted the U.S. proposal for the division of Korea when he might, it seems, have obtained control of the entire country (U.S. military forces did not enter Korea until September 8, by which date Soviet forces had reached the southern parts of the country). While the question is necessarily speculative, some of the relevant factors can be identified. It is noteworthy, for example, that Stalin still hoped that the United States would accept his request for a Soviet zone of occupation in Japan. That was a prize too valuable to be jeopardized by the appearance of undue greediness in Korea. Furthermore, to object to the proposed dividing line in Korea would have meant disclosing Soviet aspirations to control the entire peninsula and might provoke a drastic U.S. response. There is ample evidence that Stalin at this time was being careful to avoid any action which might incur the risk of a direct U.S.-Soviet confrontation. Finally, the U.S. proposal on the 38th parallel at least provided a legal basis for Soviet occupation of half the country, something which had previously been lacking; eventual control of the entire nation could still be maintained as a goal.

Stalin's tacit acquiescence in the U.S. proposal of the 38th parallel can thus be recognized as the final link in the chain of pregnant Soviet silences on Korea. Only at the last moment, and only because they felt they could not afford to wait, had Stalin and his military commanders inadvertently revealed the urgency of their desire to occupy Korea. It was this urgency, in turn, which finally alerted the Americans to the strategic importance of Korea and to the imminent danger that it was about to pass fully under Soviet control. On both sides the basic considerations were strategic; the interests of the Korean people were subordinated to great-power politics, and the ultimate outcome would depend on which side managed most effectively to identify its strategic goals with the interests of the Korean people.

Soviet Policy in Korea, 1945–50

The history of Korea from its liberation on August 15, 1945, to the outbreak of the Korean War on June 25, 1950, represents the logical working out of the conditions which had been imposed upon the country in the final days of World War II. Neither the Soviets nor the Americans had expected the division of the country, though a few U.S. officials had considered the possibility; neither side wanted it, and neither had made effective preparations for it.

Of the two occupying powers, it was the Soviets who proved to be the better prepared. While Soviet plans for Korea had had to be altered several times to take account of changes in the Soviet perception of U.S. policy and intentions, the basic Soviet goal had remained unchanged: domination of the entire country as a base for the extension and strengthening of Soviet power in the Far East. Acceptance of the 38th parallel made it necessary to postpone attainment of the basic objective and meanwhile to concentrate on a short-term goal, the establishment of a firm base in northern Korea. For that purpose the Soviet occupation forces moved rapidly to seal off northern Korea by setting up a fortified border along the 38th parallel.

By contrast the Americans were singularly unprepared for their role as an occupying power in southern Korea. As a result of their refusal to work with Korean émigré political groups and their plans for a trusteeship, they had neglected to prepare an effective policy for liberated Korea. Even when they belatedly recognized the need to establish a viable political structure in southern Korea, their efforts were hampered by their fear that a Korean provisional government would fall under communist domination, given the Soviet Union's tight military control of half the country and its firm backing for the Korean communists. U.S. military authorities therefore looked for supporters among the conservative and right-wing groups of Korea and thus allowed themselves to be maneuvered into the unhappy position of opposing the strong desire of many Koreans for immediate independence and the enactment of fundamental economic reforms.

The damage done by faulty planning and inept policies on the part of the U.S. occupation authorities in southern Korea was compounded by bungling U.S. diplomacy at the foreign minister level. The immediate Soviet goal, once partition had become an accomplished fact, was to solidify their control over the north and to block any attempt to implement the proposal for a four-power trusteeship. An important step toward attainment of this goal was taken at the meeting of the Council of Foreign Ministers in Moscow in December 1945, where the trusteeship proposal was given formal endorsement but with the additional complication of provision for a joint commission representing the two occupying commands, which was to make recommendations for an all-Korean provisional government on the basis of consultation with democratic Korean political parties and groups.[48]

The Korean response to publication of the Moscow communiqué was a wave of indignation and rejection directed against the trusteeship decision. Even the Korean communists, in both the north and south, joined in the protests—that is, until they had received instructions from the Soviets to reverse their stand.[49] This reversal, which cost the communists much popular support, was motivated not by Korean interests but by those of the Soviets. Its true significance became apparent only when the joint U.S.-Soviet commission began its long, unproductive, and ultimately sterile series of meetings. Support of the Moscow proposal for a trusteeship was now presented by the Soviets as a touchstone to determine whether or not a given Korean party or political group qualified as "democratic" and was thus eligible for consultation by the joint commission.[50] Since the communists, after the reversal of their initial stand, met this criterion, while no other significant Korean political group did, the Soviets were able to use the trusteeship proposal to establish an impassable obstacle to the work of the joint commission and, with it, to the establishment of the trusteeship. The net effect of Soviet action, thus, was to block the unification of Korea by peaceful means under international supervision.

With progress in the joint commission brought to a standstill, the Soviets were free to work toward the preparation of North Korea for its role in achieving the unification of the nation by force of arms. Three closely related processes were involved: the recruitment and training of a North Korean army, the triumph of the Soviet-sponsored Korean communist faction headed by Kim Il-sung over its rivals, and the establishment of a North Korean state, the Korean People's Democratic Republic (KPDR).[51] In all three processes the Soviet army proved indispensable for the attainment of Soviet goals.

Valuable contributions were also made by Soviet espionage agencies. In Seoul the Soviet consul, A. L. Shabshin, organized a network for photographing south Korean military installations and objects of military significance, meanwhile serving as liaison for the transmittal of directives from Pyongyang and Moscow to the South Korean Communists.[52] At a higher level, there are grounds for speculation that the Soviets obtained evidence of U.S. intentions of withdrawing from Korea and used it to shape their proposal for a withdrawal of *both* U.S. and Soviet forces.[53]

Loath to assume long-term political, economic, or military responsibility for South Korea, the United States in September 1947 presented the Korean problem to the UN General Assembly, over Soviet protest. Slowly and painfully, with grudging assistance from the United States and a measure of good will from the UN, the South Koreans in 1948 forged a viable state, the Republic of Korea, followed in short order by the formal establishment of its North Korean counterpart. The arming and training of the North Korean army meanwhile was making rapid progress; by 1949 a well-trained force of 135,000 men was under arms. In November 1948 the U.S. Ambassador to Seoul, John Muccio, warned Washington that invasion from the North appeared both probable and likely to succeed.[54]

Stalin and the Outbreak of the Korean War

The vexed question of Soviet responsibility for the outbreak of the Korean War has been hotly debated, with opinions ranging from the widespread Western position that the war was ordered from Moscow to the opposite assertion by Soviet writers that it resulted from an attack by South Korea.[55] Gradually, as tempers have cooled and as new evidence has become available, the complexity of the problem has become apparent and the outlines of a new interpretation have begun to emerge. It becomes increasingly clear that any attempt to solve the problem must take into account not only Soviet policy but also the tangled complexities of North Korean politics and that the once-dominant Western view of a war started on orders from Moscow must be drastically modified.

Yet the question of Soviet motives in the genesis of the war has so far resisted solution. This is not the place for a full-scale attack on the problem; what can be suggested is that the analysis of Soviet goals in Korea which has been offered in this paper provides a suitable basis for a new approach. Those goals, it has been argued here, were the domination of all of Korea in order to strengthen Soviet power and influence in the Far East. The division of Korea in August 1945 temporarily blocked achievement of Soviet goals but did not lead to their abandonment; rather, new ways were devised for their eventual realization.

As long as the Soviets enjoyed use of the naval bases at Port Arthur and Dairen, control of the South Korean ports might appear to be of secondary importance. The Chinese Communist victory in the Chinese civil war in 1949, however, completely altered the situation. Soviet control of the Manchurian ports might be tolerated by a weak Nationalist China; a victorious and triumphant Communist China could be expected to demand their return to full Chinese control. That this demand was in fact made by Mao Tse-tung when he came to Moscow in December 1949 we know from the fact that the return of the ports to China was provided for in the agreements signed by the USSR and the Chinese People's Republic on February 14, 1950. The Chinese Communist victory thus had the effect of depriving Stalin of some of the key strategic gains he had won in 1945 by skillful diplomacy and bold military action.

Since maintenance of the appearance of international communist amity was considered essential, there was no easy way Stalin could resist the Chinese demand for return of the Manchurian ports. The warm-water ports he had been forced to relinquish in China, however, could be replaced by those of southern Korea. The military force needed for the conquest of South Korea had been ready for action for some time; the North Korean leadership was eager to demonstrate its capacity for waging a short, victorious war; all that was needed was Stalin's final authorization.

The question thus is why Stalin decided to give Pyongyang the green light for an attack on the South.[56] A vital element in his evaluation of the situation was necessarily the possibility of U.S. counteraction. Providentially, as it must have seemed to the Soviets, an authoritative statement of U.S. disinterest in Korea was provided at just this time, in the form of Secretary of State Dean Acheson's much debated speech of January 12, 1950, in which he defined the U.S. "defense perimeter" in the Far East in a way that deliberately excluded Korea.[57] If there was any doubt left in the Soviets' minds about U.S. reluctance to come to South Korea's defense, it must have been removed a week later when the Congress defeated a government-sponsored bill providing for economic aid to South Korea.[58]

Once Stalin's approval had been obtained, the further development of events was no longer fully under Soviet control. There appears to be considerable merit to recent suggestions that the timing of the North Korean attack was determined by internal conflicts in the Korean communist movement, and that the actual outbreak of the war took the Soviets by surprise.[59] The problem urgently needs further work. The purpose of the present paper has been to focus attention on Stalin's long-term goals in Korea, and thereby, incidentally, to shed new light on the question of Soviet motives in the Korean War.

One final word. As the result of developments during the Korean War, in particular the entry of Communist China into the war, the Soviets were able to obtain a postponement of the February 1950 agreements on the return of the Manchurian ports to

China. It was not until 1955 that a Soviet delegation, headed by N. S. Khrushchev, finally negotiated the transfer of the ports to the Chinese People's Republic. As long as Stalin lived, therefore, the Soviets maintained their strategic position in the Far East, and Stalin's long-term strategic goals remained intact.

1. V. I. Miljukova, "V naučnom sovete po istorii vnešnej politiki SSSR i meždunarodnych otnošenij," *Voprosy istorii* 9 (1974): 150–51. Similarly, E. M. Zhukov writes, "Soviet historians consider it their highest duty in the Tenth Five-Year Plan to concentrate their efforts on the solution of the tasks set by the Twenty-fifth Congress of the CPSU." E. M. Zhukov, "Osnovnye itogi i zadači istoričeskich issledovanij v svete rešenij XXV s'ezda KPSS," *Voprosy istorii* 4 (1967): 10.

2. Christopher S. Wren, "Moscow's renewed interest in Asia," *New York Times*, 14 September 1975, section 4, p. 5. For examples of the kind of articles Wren had in mind, *see* I. I. Gaglov, "Kommunističeskaja partija—organizator pobedy nad militaristskoj Japoniei," *Voprosy istorii KPSS* 9 (1975): 3–17, and A. Mikhailov, "Victory in the Far East and the Destinies of the Chinese Revolution," *International Affairs* 9 (Moscow, 1975): 38–47.

3. Roy Medvedev, *Let History Judge: The Origins and Consequences of Stalinism* (New York: Knopf, 1971), p. 473.

4. Ibid., p. 478.

5. Ibid., p. 473.

6. "For a lasting peace, for a people's democracy," 6 January 1950.

7. Max Beloff, *Soviet Policy in the Far East 1944–1951* (London: Oxford University Press, 1953), p. 25.

8. Edwin W. Pauley, *Report on Japanese Assets in Manchuria to the President of the United States, July 1946* (Washington, D.C.: U.S. Government Printing Office, 1946).

9. Beloff, *Soviet Policy*, pp. 41–48.

10. *See* Pauley's letter to Truman, quoted in Harry S. Truman, *Memoirs*, vol. 2 (Garden City: Doubleday, 1956), p. 322.

11. Geoffrey Jukes, *The Soviet Union in Asia* (Berkeley: University of California Press, 1973), pp. 215–16, citing I. S. Konev, *Sorok pjatyj* (Moscow: Voenizdat, 1968), pp. 3–4.

12. In a marginal noted dated 25 March/6 April 1895, Nicholas II wrote, "It is absolutely necessary that Russia should have a port which is free and open during the entire year. This port must be on the mainland (southeastern Korea) and must be connected with our existing possessions by a strip of land." *Krasnyj archiv* 52 (1932): 76. Czarist Russia's interest in Korea is summarized in Loh Keie-hyun, "Territorial division of Korea—a historical survey," *Korean Affairs* 3 (April 1964): 105–13. *See also* Chang Sung-hwan, "Russian designs in the Far East," in *Russian Imperialism from Ivan the Great to the Revolution*, ed. Taras Hunczak (New Brunswick, N.J.: Rutgers University Press, 1974), p. 305.

13. Bruce Cumings, "American Policy and Korean Liberation," in *Without Parallel: the American-Korean Relationship since 1945*, ed. Frank Baldwin (New York: Pantheon Books, 1974), p. 41.

14. Akira Iriye, *The Cold War in Asia: A Historical Introduction* (Englewood Cliffs,

N. J.: Prentice-Hall, 1974), p. 74, citing a State Department report of 11 April 1942.

15. Cho Soon Sung, *Korea in World Politics 1940–1950: An Evaluation of American Responsibility* (Berkeley: University of California Press, 1967), pp. 14–15.

16. Ibid., pp. 18–21.

17. Beloff, *Soviet Policy*, p. 155.

18. *Foreign Relations of the United States* (henceforth cited *FR*), *The Conferences at Cairo and Tehran, 1943*, 566.

19. Ibid., p. 567. A recent article on Teheran calls attention to Stalin's "disturbing hint suggesting that his aspirations might further expand with expanding opportunities." Vojtech Mastny, "Soviet War Aims at the Moscow and Teheran Conferences of 1943," *Journal of Modern History* 47 (September 1975): 500.

20. *FR, Conferences at Cairo and Tehran*, 869.

21. Ibid.

22. Ibid.

23. Beloff, *Soviet Policy*, pp. 23–24. *See also* W. Averell Harriman and Elie Abel, *Special Envoy to Churchill and Stalin 1941–1946* (New York: Random House, 1975), pp. 379–80.

24. Cumings, "American Policy and Korean Liberation," p. 44.

25. *FR, The Conferences at Malta and Yalta, 1945*, 770. *See also* Beloff, *Soviet Policy*, p. 155; Lee Won-sul, "American Preparedness on the Korean Question in 1945," *Bulletin of the Korean Research Center, Journal of Social Sciences and Humanities* 22 (June 1965): 62; and Arthur L. Grey, Jr., "The Thirty-Eighth Parallel," *Foreign Affairs* 29 (April 1951).

26. *FR, Conferences at Malta and Yalta*, 770.

27. Herbert Feis, *The Atomic Bomb and the End of World War II* (Princeton: Princeton University Press, 1966), p. 13, citing U.S. Department of Defense, *Entry of the Soviet Union into the War against Japan: Military Plans, 1941–1945* (Washington, D.C.: U.S. Department of Defense, 1955).

28. *FR, 1945*, VII, 872.

29. Ibid., 887.

30. *FR, The Conference of Berlin (the Potsdam Conference), 1945*, I, 47.

31. *FR, 1945*, VII, 888. Italics added.

32. Beloff, *Soviet Policy*, p. 108.

33. Truman, *Memoirs*, vol. 1, pp. 316–17.

34. Ibid., p. 317. See also *FR, 1945*, VII, 914.

35. *Istorija Kommunističeskoj partii Sovetskogo Sojuza v šesti tomach*, vol. 5, book 1 (Moscow: Politizdat, 1970), p. 624.

36. *FR, Potsdam Conference*, II, 252–53. 264.

37. Ibid., 351.

38. Ibid., 352. For an analysis of the July 24, 1945, meeting, which closely parallels the one offered in this paper, *see* Lee Won-sul, "American Preparedness" (note 25, above), p. 59. I differ, however, from Lee's view that "as regards Korea, the Russians did not, in spite of their age-old imperialistic ambition over the peninsula, have specific designs until the Potsdam Conference, partly due to their preoccupation with the question of Manchuria." Lee, in my view, does not give adequate weight to the significant silences by Soviet spokesmen as to their aspirations in Korea at Teheran, Yalta, Potsdam, and elsewhere.

39. M. S. Handler, "The New Pattern of Soviet Aggression," in *The Korean War*, ed. Lloyd C. Gardner (New York: Quadrangle, 1972), p. 107.

40. Truman, *Memoirs*, vol. 1, p. 383, Italics added.

41. Ibid., vol. 2, p. 317. Italics added.

42. Ibid., vol. 1, p. 391.

43. Text of the Soviet declaration of war is given in U.S. Department of State, *The Record on Korean Unification 1943–1960* (Washington, D.C.: U.S. Government Printing Office, 1960), pp. 43–44.

44. Truman, *Memoirs*, vol. 1, p. 425.

45. Beloff, *Soviet Policy*, p. 37. According to a recent Soviet study, the Soviet's Far Eastern offensive "developed with incredible speed." A. Mikhailov, "Victory in the Far East" (note 2, above), p. 43. Another recent Soviet study states that between 11 and 21 August 1945 Soviet forces "seized the most important ports and naval bases on the eastern shores of Korea. . . . " V. K. Pak, "Osvoboditel'naja missija Sovetskoj Armii v Koree," *Voprosy istorii* 9 (1975): 106.

46. Grey, "Thirty-Eighth Parallel": 482–87. *See also* Cumings, "American Policy and Korean Liberation," pp. 46–47.

47. Text of Stalin's reply is in *Correspondence between the Chairman of the Council of Ministers of the U.S.S.R. and the Presidents of the U.S.A. and the Prime Ministers of Great Britain during the Great Patriotic War of 1941–1945* (Moscow: Foreign Languages Publishing House, 1957), vol. 2, p. 266. For analysis and interpretation, *see* Grey, "Thirty-Eighth Parallel," pp. 485–86; Truman, *Memoirs*, vol. 1, p. 444; Cumings, "American Policy and Korean Liberation," p. 47.

48. The text of Part 3, "Korea," of the communiqué issued at the end of the Moscow Conference of Foreign Ministers is given in *Record on Korean Unification* (note 43, above), pp. 47–48. For analysis *see* George Ginsburgs, "The U.S.S.R. and the Issue of Re-unification," International Conference on the Problems of Korean Unification, *Report* (Seoul: Asiatic Research Center, Korea University, 1971), pp. 111–12.

49. Koon Woo Nam, *The North Korean Communist Leadership, 1945–1965: A Study of Factionalism and Political Consolidation* (University: University of Alabama Press, 1974), p. 31.

50. Ginsburgs, "The U.S.S.R. and Issue of Re-unification," p. 215.

51. Nam, *North Korean Communist Leadership*, provides a well-documented analysis of these developments.

52. Robert A. Scalapino and Chong-sik Lee, *Communism in Korea* (Berkeley: University of California Press, 1974), p. 277, and report by Richard J. H. Johnston, *New York Times*, 29 June 1950, p. 3. Shabshin's wife, F. I. Shabshina, is a leading Soviet specialist on Korea, the author of the most important scholarly study on the subject published since 1945: "Koreja posle Vtoroj mirovoj vojny," in *Krizis kolonial'noj sistemy; nacional'no-osvoboditel'naja bor'ba narodov Vostočnoj Azii*, ed. E. M. Zhukov (Moscow: Izdatel'stvo Akademii nauk SSSR, 1949), pp. 249–89. *See also* her book, *Južnaja Koreja 1945–1946 gg. Zapiski očevidca* (Moscow: "Nauka," 1974).

53. The evidence is indirect but highly suggestive. On September 25, 1947, the U.S. Joint Chiefs of Staff sent a memorandum to the secretary of state in which they argued that "from the standpoint of military security the U.S. has little strategic interest in maintaining the present troops and bases in Korea." Truman, *Memoirs*, vol. 2, p. 325. On the following day the Russian representative to the joint commission in Seoul suddenly proposed that all occupation troops be withdrawn early in 1948. Ibid., p. 324. Truman apparently saw no connection between these events. Beloff calls the Soviets' September 26 proposal "abrupt" (*Soviet Policy*, p. 170) but fails to see the connection with the Joint Chiefs' memorandum, which he discusses elsewhere (ibid., p. 180).

54. *FR, 1948*, VI, 1325–26.

55.   For a recent attempt to deny or cast doubt on the responsibility of North Korea for the outbreak of the Korean War, *see* Karunakar Gupta, "How did the Korean War Begin?" *China Quarterly* 52 (October–December 1972): 699–716. *See also* commentaries on Gupta's article by Chong-sik Lee, W. E. Skillend, and Robert R. Simmons, with a rejoinder by Gupta, ibid. 54 (April–June 1973): 699–716. *See also* Okonogi Masao, "The Korean War as a War of National Liberation," a paper presented at a symposium at Kyoto, 5 December 1974, as summarized in *Basic Studies on the International Environment, 1973–1975* (Tokyo: Tokyo Institute of Technology, 1975), pp. 37–39. A recent Soviet article adroitly avoids the question of which side started the Korean War by use of the noncommittal expression, "Military operations broke out on the Korean Peninsula on June 25, 1950." V. Tikhomirov, "People's Korea: 30 Years." *International Affairs* 9 (Moscow 1975) 49. Tikhomirov's article is also noteworthy for its flat misstatement with regard to the origin of the 38th-parallel division in Korea: he maintains that it was agreed to at the Potsdam Conference (ibid., p. 48).

56.   Despite their questionable origin, the so-called Khrushchev memoirs provide a basically convincing account of the relationship of Stalin to the outbreak of the Korean War. See *Khrushchev Remembers* (Boston: Little, Brown, 1970), pp. 367–69. The memoirs shed no light, however, on Stalin's motives for acceding to the North Korean request for authorization to attack South Korea.

57.   Text of the speech in *Department of State Bulletin* 22, no. 551, 23 January 1950, pp. 115–16. For Acheson's own commentary on the speech and the controversy which it generated, *see* his *Present at the Creation: My Years in the State Department* (New York: Norton, 1969), pp. 355–58.

58.   Philip E. Mosely, *The Kremlin and World Politics* (New York: Vintage, 1960), p. 327.

59.   Robert R. Simmons, "The Korean Civil War," in *Without Parallel*, ed. Baldwin, pp. 143–53.

The Genesis of the Cold War
Confrontation over Poland, 1941–44

Itō Takayuki

The Cold War in Asia has its own indigenous background, but one should not overlook that it was closely connected with events in other parts of the world. Weren't the Anglo-American concessions in Eastern Europe toward the end of World War II connected with the Soviet assent to participate in the war against Japan? Wasn't the Soviet toleration of American unilateral actions in the Allied Council for Japan a counterpart of Western acquiescence in similar Soviet conduct in the Allied control commissions for Rumania, Bulgaria, and Hungary? Finally, would the violent American reaction to the outbreak of the Korean War have been thinkable but for their bitter experiences in Eastern Europe? Indeed, it is one of the most significant features of the Cold War that any event in one part of the world, as a function of the worldwide confrontation of the two superpowers, inevitably becomes dependent on events in other parts of the world.

But our concern with Eastern Europe is based not only on the existence of such direct causal relations between the events in both parts of the world, but also on the fact that events in Eastern Europe created a basic pattern of Cold War confrontations in the world. Although debate over the origins of the Cold War has produced an immense amount of literature, almost all writers agree at least on one point: the Allied controversy over the future of Eastern Europe was a major cause.[1] It might be possible to say that a prototype of all subsequent Cold War confrontations is found in wartime Eastern Europe. However, for the very reason that confrontation in Eastern Europe falls in the opening period of the Cold War, it has a number of characteristics which distinguish it from other confrontations, especially those in Asia, which fall at a mature stage of the Cold War. One might say that there was something like an evolution from a usual to a Cold War confrontation in Eastern Europe. This study will discuss how this evolution took place. If this problem is clarified, it will greatly help define the specific character of the confrontation in Eastern Europe and its meaning for subsequent developments in other areas.

Of all the troubling issues concerning Eastern Europe that the Allied powers had to deal with during World War II, those concerning Poland were most obdurate and are considered by many writers a direct cause of the Cold War. "Poland," points out R. Divine, "more than any other issue, gave rise to the Cold War."[2] "The Cold War began," establishes A. Ulam, "just as had World War II, with Poland providing the immediate cause of the conflict."[3] What were the aims of the contending parties regarding Poland? Why did the Polish issue strain inter-Allied relations so much that the wartime alliance was brought almost to the verge of dissolution and even open conflict toward the end of the war?

The repetitious argument in the controversy over Poland always came to the same two issues: (1) In what territorial confines was Poland to exist? (2) Who was to govern Poland? The first issue had a long history. Russians, Germans, and Poles had for centuries been struggling for supremacy in east Central Europe. The territorial aspect of the conflict, therefore, can be considered a continuation of this old struggle, with one traditional party, the Germans, absent, but with the Anglo-Americans as a third party which had been completely unknown in that area until World War II. Here were involved national, rather than ideological, interests. Neither was the second issue quite a new issue. The Russian czars had always had their candidates for the Polish crown and tried to impose them on Poland. The Prussian kings and the Austrian emperors were not outdone in such intrigues. But the conflict during World War II added a new aspect to this traditional struggle: ideology. The struggle for government in Poland was believed to be a struggle between two irreconcilable ideologies, a struggle between two worlds whose principles were diametrically antagonistic, a struggle toward which nobody in the world would be allowed to remain indifferent. It was just this aspect that made Allied confrontation over Poland a forerunner of the Cold War. But, as will be shown, this second issue was, at least at the outset, nothing but a by-product of the first.

Most people have tended to think that, in a world war in which small powers or local political movements deprived of substantial armed forces are confronted with big powers with gigantic war machineries, only the latter can decide the course of events, to accept which is the only choice left to the former. This notion must now be corrected. The big powers in World War II were not always able to dictate their conditions to local forces. They were often brought into a perplexing situation from which it was difficult to disengage themselves. For this reason, due attention will be paid in the present article to the conduct of the Polish government-in-exile and of opposition movements in Poland, especially the Communists.[4]

Conflict of National Aspirations: June 1941 to February 1943

In 1939, when Poland collapsed following the German attack, it was partitioned between Germany and the Soviet Union. V. M. Molotov, people's commisar for foreign affairs of the Soviet Union, expressed his pleasure at the disappearance of "this ugly offspring of the Versailles Treaty."[5] It was quite natural that the Poles should regard as enemies not only Germany but also the Soviet Union. But in 1941, when the Germans attacked the Soviets, there were obvious reasons for a Soviet-Polish rapprochement. The Soviets wanted to have as many allies as possible against Hitler. On the other hand, it was clear to the Poles that there was no hope for the independence of their country so long as the Germans kept it occupied. There were, however, still many obstacles to be overcome on the way to reconciliation. The most difficult was the problem of the former Polish territories annexed by the Soviets in 1939.

The territories in dispute, constituting 51.7 percent in area and 38.4 percent in population of prewar Poland and inhabited in large part by Ukrainians and Belorussians, had for centuries been an object of aspiration by Russians and Poles. The Bolshevik seizure of power in Russia did not bring an end to the struggle. The Soviet-Polish War of 1920 was a national rather than a class war, as K. Radek, then the leading theoretician of the Russian Bolsheviks, pointedly noted.[6] To the Poles, Bolshevism and Russia appeared as one and the same thing.[7] They fought for their national aims, although they often operated with such high-flown anti-Bolshevik catchwords as "crusade against communist barbarism" or "Poland—the last bulwark of the Western freedom" in order to mobilize Western opinion to their cause. The Russians also fought a national war in which even czarist generals volunteered for service in the Red Army. At that time, a large area claimed by the Russians fell to the Poles. It is not to be wondered at that the Russians should have reclaimed it at the first opportunity that presented itself.

In July 1941, Molotov instructed I. M. Majskij, Soviet ambassador to Great Britain, to approach the Polish government-in-exile with proposals to resume diplomatic relations and to conclude an agreement on common action against Hitler. The Soviet terms specified that (1) an independent Polish state would be established within ethnographical boundaries, including some cities and districts which recently fell into Soviet hands; and (2) the question of the constitution would be regarded as a matter of internal affairs of the Poles themselves. Molotov's instruction referred also to the setting up of a "Polish national committee" and Polish military units on Soviet soil.[8] The Poles could not accept the Soviet proposals. Regarding the frontiers, they wished to see the interwar boundary recognized by the Soviets. But it was only too evident that the Soviets would not agree. Under strong pressures from the British foreign secretary who wanted to bring about a Soviet-Polish agreement as soon as possible, the Poles prepared a compromise formula: the Soviet government was to acknowledge the Soviet-German treaties of 1939 relative to territorial changes in Poland as *nules et non avenus*. This formula seemingly allowed the interpretation that the Soviets recognized the Polish frontiers before the German attack, as the Poles later liked to represent it. But it was nothing more nor less than a compromise. One could interpret it, as the Soviets did, as implying that the German-Soviet treaties were no longer valid, but that the

"referenda," held in the Soviet-occupied areas to justify the an-
nexations, did not lose validity. The practical meaning of the
Polish proposal was to postpone the discussion on the frontiers
to a later date. The Soviets acceded to it in the subsequent negotiations of July 5 and 11. Regarding the other points, the Poles insisted upon the exchange of ambassadors, not the setting up of
a national committee, and that the commander of a Polish army
to be set up on Soviet soil should be appointed by the Polish
government, though in agreement with the Soviet government;
the army should be subordinated only in operational matters to
the Soviet supreme command. The Soviets accepted these conditions. The Poles also insisted upon the release of all Polish citizens
detained in the Soviet Union, but the most that the Poles could
obtain from the Soviets in this matter was an "amnesty" for the
persons in question.[9]

The negotiations with the Soviets gave rise to a serious crisis in
the Polish government. Premier W. Sikorski was inclined to accept
the compromise solution, but President W. Raczkiewicz, Vice
President K. Sosnkowski, Foreign Minister A. Zaleski, and
Justice Minister W. Seyda vehemently opposed all concessions on
the territorial question. But Sikorksi, backed up by the British,
managed to win over the president, while the others resigned in
protest.[10] Although Sikorski's basic political views were not so far
from those of his opponents, as it soon became apparent, the
Soviets highly appreciated his "statesmanly widsom."[11] It seemed
that Stalin did not change this appreciation even after the
rupture of diplomatic relations.[12] It served as a good lesson for the
Soviets that the Soviet-Polish accord could be reached only after
a reshuffle of the Polish government.

The Soviet-Polish agreement of July 30, 1941, was a result of
concessions on both sides. The Soviets were not willing to make
concessions on the territorial question, and the Poles had to give
way by postponing the discussion. In return the Soviets showed
readiness to make concessions on the question of government.
What the Poles managed to secure was considerable: sovereignty
not only in internal affairs but also in affairs that could potentially impinge upon the sovereignty of the Soviet government, namely,
matters concerning Polish armed forces and citizens in the Soviet
Union. In 1939, when the eastern part of Poland was occupied by

the Soviets, about 180,000 soldiers were seized as prisoners of war and over a million civilians were deported into the depths of the Soviet Union.[13] From these prisoners of war and deportees was to be recruited the Polish army in the Soviet Union, and the remaining civil population was to be looked after by the Polish government. Now, the Poles in question were dispersed all over the country. Wherever there were larger colonies of the interned or deported Poles, from Petrozavodsk on the Finnish frontier to Vladivostok on the Japan Sea, and from Archangel'sk in the Arctic to Samarkand on the Afghan frontier, recruit offices were opened, and "embassy delegates" were established, staffed with *hommes de confiance* of the Polish embassy, to engage in welfare activities for Polish citizens.[14] The Polish embassy was permitted to issue an uncensored weekly magazine for distribution among Polish citizens in Russia. That the Soviets showed readiness to tolerate on their territory such activities of a foreign government was unprecedented, and for the time being this deal (frontiers for sovereign government) appeared to promise success. But the sovereignty of the Polish government rested on an insecure foundation, for a sovereign government without clearly defined territories would be impossible. Thus, the question of government necessarily depended on that of the frontiers.

Since 1938 the Polish Communists had found themselves in a most grotesque situation: all party activities were forbidden not only by their government but also by the very headquarters of world communism, the executive committee of the Communist International (ECCI). In that year the Communist Party of Poland (CPP) was dissolved by a decision of the ECCI, and most of the party's leaders were physically liquidated by Soviet security organs.[15] In the next year came another severe blow for the Polish Communists: the proclamation of the Nazi-Soviet friendship on the basis of partitioned Poland, which made it completely hopeless for pro-Soviet groups as represented by the Communists to secure a popular support in the country. Those who remained in the Nazi-occupied country eked out an existence, gathering in various underground organizations such as "Spartacus," the "Union of Peasants and Workers," the "Revolutionary Councils of Workers and Peasants," and the "Association of Friends of the USSR." For the time being their activities were tolerated by the Nazis in view of the need to maintain good relations with the Soviets. But after the war broke out between the Germans and the Soviets, almost all these organizations were swept away by the Gestapo.[16] Those who emigrated to the Soviet Union was by no means better. They often encountered the suspicious eyes of the Soviet authorities.[17] But their situation improved as Nazi-Soviet relations deteriorated. In the fall of 1940 a small group of the Polish Communists, with M. Nowotko in the lead, was sent to the Comintern school for political training. When news of the outbreak of the German-Soviet War reached them, they felt the hour had struck for them.[18] Some Polish Communists in the Soviet Union at once set to work. An appeal they issued to the Poles at home on July 3 revealed their immediate thought: it took no notice of the Polish government in London, but directly called on the Polish people to join the volunteer corps which was to form an integral part of the Red Army.[19]

But the events took a turn that must have been disappointing to the Communists. The Soviets opted for an alliance with the government-in-exile, allowing it to organize an army on Soviet soil. In line with the Soviet decision, the Comintern adopted a new tactics: a national front against the fascist aggressors. Now it was declared the most important task for the Polish Communists to establish a united front with forces supporting the government-in-exile and to try to provide it with more militantly anti-Hitler, and at the same time more militantly pro-Soviet, character. Again, the Polish Communists had to adjust themselves to the requirements of Soviet foreign policy.[20]

On July 9, 1941, in connection with the Anglo-Soviet agreement, Churchill drafted a telegram to Stalin saying, "Territorial frontiers will have to be settled in accordance with the wishes of the people who live there and on general ethnographical lines, and, secondly, that these units, when established, must be free to choose their own form of government and system of life, so long as they do not interfere with the similar rights of neighbouring peoples."[21] Undoubtedly Churchill was concerned with Eastern Europe, particularly Poland. This passage was dropped when the telegram was dispatched, because the war cabinet feared it might cause difficulties for the Poles in their negotiations with the Russians.[22] But Churchill's initial position on postwar settlements was indicative of the extent to which the British were prepared to yield on the Polish question. At the time of the signature of the Soviet-Polish agreement, Eden, anxious to neutralize opposition against it in Sikorski's cabinet, gave assurance that the British did not recognize any territorial changes effected in Poland since August 1939.[23] But, on the same day, Eden declared in the House of Commons that the British were undertaking no guarantee of Polish frontiers as a result of such assurances.[24]

The American position on the Polish question was equivocal. This was caused by the special circumstances of American politics: there were about six million citizens of Polish descent whose majority had always voted for the Democratic party.[25] For fear of losing the votes of Polish Americans, the White House was extremely wary of making any definite statement on the status of Poland. The White House always received with the utmost courtesy delegations of the Polish government-in-exile and seemed to listen attentively to their requests. But the Americans carefully avoided making concrete commitments to them. Relations with the Soviets were more important than those with the Poles. Such circumspection of the American attitude, however, often misled the Poles to think that they could expect help, if not from the British, then at least from the Americans.

On July 14, 1941, Roosevelt mentioned in a telegram to Churchill two principles for peace settlements: (1) to disarm all trouble-makers; and (2) to revive small states through plebiscites. The president asked Churchill to make "no post-war commitments as to territories, populations or economies" prior to the peace conference, and he referred to unfavorable repercussions which such "deals or trades" would have on various ethnic groups in the United States, and to the unfortunate American experience at Versailles with respect to the secret commitments the Allies had made to the Italians.[26] It was understandable against this background that there was no question of an American guarantee of the prewar Polish frontiers. What the Polish ambassador to Washington, J. Ciechanowski, could obtain from the Americans was merely a generalizing statement to the press by a State Department official that the Soviet-Polish agreement was in line with the U.S. policy of nonrecognition of any territory taken by conquest.[27] The famous passage of the Atlantic Charter regarding nonrecognition of any territorial changes without the consent of the peoples concerned did not mean that the Western powers committed themselves to the territorial integrity of prewar Poland, as the Poles often preferred to interpret it.[28] Its implication was rather the opposite: they would not enter into any territorial commitments with the Poles, nor with the Russians, postponing all settlement until after the end of the war when it would be possible to confirm the wishes of the people.

Thus, for the time being there seemed to be no serious discord on the question of government among the parties concerned: the London Poles, the Communist Poles, the British, the Americans, and the Soviets. All of them supported the government-in-exile. Only the American emphasis on plebiscite created a minor dissonance. The advisory committee on postwar foreign policy, set up in the State Department in 1942, pointed out that the return of the exiled European governments in London after the war contradicted American support for self-determination. They feared among other things that it would mean the establishment of a British sphere of influence. As regards the Polish government-in-exile, they thought it did not necessarily represent the people of Poland. But in the end they agreed to its return to Poland on condition that it promise to conform to the strategy and principle of the United Nations and express its commitment to the holding of free elections.[29] On the territorial question, however, there was fundamental disagreement between the London Poles and the Soviets which could be patched over only by postponing the discussion. Although the Western powers were favorably disposed to the Polish standpoint, they failed to meet the repeated requests by the Poles that they intercede on their behalf with the Soviets. The Poles were isolated in their struggle for national aspirations, but they did not recognize the gravity of the situation until it was too late.

From the beginning of December 1941, Soviet-Polish relations had been increasingly strained by the territorial dispute. A Soviet note of December 1, 1941, made it clear that Moscow held to the view that the inhabitants of the former Polish territory annexed by the Soviets in 1939 had become Soviet citizens; that the Soviet Union was showing its "good will and readiness to compromise" by agreeing to recognize as Polish citizens persons of Polish nationality in the area; but that no exception was to be made regarding persons of other nationalities, in particular, Ukrainian, Belorussian, and Jewish.[30] Although the note stressed that the question of frontiers was not yet settled and was susceptible to future discussion, such a decision in effect forejudged it, because the territorial question could not be separated from that of inhabitants. The Soviet note was a warning that unless the matter of frontiers was promptly resolved, the right of the Polish government to govern its own people would be questioned.

Stalin took up the issue directly with Sikorski, who visited the Soviet Union in the beginning of December. Stalin said to him: "We should settle our common frontiers *between ourselves,* and *before the peace conference.* . . . Don't worry, we will not harm you."[31] It seemed that Stalin, understanding the nature of the dispute, prepared a compensation for frustrated Polish national aspirations. He stated to Sikorski that Poland must arise larger and stronger than before, that east Prussia must belong to Poland, and that the Polish western boundary must be based on the Oder river. But Sikorski declined to be involved in any discussion on the frontiers.[32] The British foreign minister who visited the Soviet Union shortly afterward found Stalin demanding that a secret protocol be attached to the proposed Anglo-Soviet treaty in which, *inter alia,* the so-called Curzon line figured as the Soviet-Polish frontier. When Eden pointed out the necessity of consulting the Poles, Stalin agreed to put aside the Polish clause, saying: "The Polish frontier remains an open question and I do not insist upon settling that now. . . . I hope that we shall be able to come to an agreement *between the three of us.*"[33] In the subsequent negotiations the Soviets became increasingly insistent. A Soviet draft of the Anglo-Soviet treaty, handed over to the British side on May 1, 1942, revealed that Moscow now demanded of London *désintéressement* in the question of Polish-Soviet frontiers.[34] Although the treaty was signed without territorial arrangements as a result of American intervention at the last minute, the Soviet position remained unchanged.[35]

Already in the conversations with Stalin in December 1941, Eden had promised to help the Russians in settling the frontier question *before the peace conference.*[36] In a memorandum submitted to the war cabinet shortly after his return home, the foreign secretary urged the necessity to come to an overall settlement of outstanding questions with the Soviets.[37] Though Churchill's first reaction to the Soviet territorial demands was violently negative, he came in the end to support Eden's point of view.[38] It was decided to make an exception of the Soviet-Polish frontiers in view of the strong Polish opposition.[39] But there was no doubt that its turn would soon come.

Washington stuck to the formula: no territorial arrangements prior to the peace conference. But there was a subtle difference between the State Department and the White House on this matter.[40] As a memorandum of Secretary of State C. Hull to the president, dated February 4, 1942, typically showed, the State Department rejected the Soviet demands more from moralistic and even ideological considerations than from realistic calculations of American interests and possibilities.[41] Roosevelt, on the other hand, though deeply concerned about public opinion at home, recognized the necessity to come to terms with the Soviets for the organizing of the postwar world. On March 12, the president received Soviet Ambassador M. M. Litvinov and told him that Stalin should pay due attention to public opinion in the United States, but that he personally anticipated no difficulties in drawing boundaries desirable to the Soviet Union after the war, because there was no essential difference of views on this question between him and the Soviet government.[42]

In view of the fact that their national aspirations evoked no particular sympathy among the Western powers, the Poles resorted to ideological phraseology, although at that time the Soviets were not inclined to justify their claims on Poland in terms of communist ideology. In a conversation with Churchill, Sikorski tried to paint the communist devil on the wall: Stalin, as a staunch communist and first disciple of Lenin, would try to introduce communism in Europe from Norway to Greece.[43] In a memorandom presented to the U.S. government, Sikorski stressed: "There must be a dividing line between the Communist conception of the world as represented by the Soviets and the ideals of the Western Democracies based on individual rights. This demarcation should follow the lines established by the Treaty of Riga [i.e., the interwar Soviet-Polish frontiers]."[44] Though Sikorski's arguments were shrouded in a vocabulary typical of the later Cold War years, they were but a modulation of the old Polish argument against any strong power in the east. It is interesting to see that while Churchill remained unmoved by such arguments,[45] American officials were often sensitive to them.[46]

From the beginning of 1942 the Poles were confronted with growing Soviet pressure. In the international arena it was Moscow's tactics to isolate the Poles and to expose them directly to its pressure. The shift of Moscow's emphasis from a trilateral to a bilateral settlement of the frontier question strongly pointed to the new line of the Soviet diplomacy. Another indication was delivered when Moscow rejected the conception of a Polish-Czechoslovak confederation. Though the conception originated with the British government which considered it a stabilizing factor in postwar Europe,[47] it was Sikorski who enthusiastically embraced and promoted it. His calculations were to create an organism which would be able to assert itself against both Germans and Russians, and in which a dominant position would be occupied by the Poles.[48] In December 1941, when Polish-Czechoslovak negotiations on the confederation were in full progress, the British foreign secretary encountered no objection in Moscow to the encouragement of such a scheme.[49] The negotiators reached agreement on January 23, 1942, but already in the following month the Soviets began to express their doubts.[50] In the course of the Anglo-Soviet treaty negotiations, renewed in May 1942, it became clear that the Soviets had strong reservations about the scheme.[51] Two months later A. E. Bogomolov, Soviet ambassador to the governments-in-exile in London, informed Czechoslovak Foreign Minister J. Masaryk that the Soviet Union definitely opposed it.[52] In the subsequent years, the Soviets were to veto any similar scheme in Eastern Europe, even that of communist countries. Evidently Moscow wanted to deal with the East European countries individually, without any intermediaries and not in blocs.[53] The U.S. attitude toward the confederation scheme was not encouraging either. Roosevelt instructed S. Welles on March 7, 1942: "I think Sikorski should be definitely discouraged on this proposition. This is not time to talk about the post-war position of small nations and it would cause serious trouble with the Russians."[54] Washington's negative attitude was based not only on fears of trouble with Moscow, but also on misgivings that behind such a scheme might be hidden a British ambition to establish its sphere of influence on the European continent.[55] Roosevelt's famous theory of the "four policemen," which was for the first time intimated to the Soviets in May 1942 during Molotov's visit to Washington, and according to which only the Big Four should be responsible for world peace and the other nations disarmed, was not encouraging for a scheme whose main purpose was to strengthen the viability of small nations.[56]

Not only in the international arena, but also in their own country, the Soviets began to exert pressure upon the Poles. In December 1941, Sikorski asked Stalin to evacuate a part of the Polish army from the Soviet Union and take it to the Near East for use on the Western front.[57] Stalin at first reluctantly agreed to it, but soon recognized it as a good opportunity to get rid of the troublesome Poles. Fearing that accelerated evacuations would adversely affect Polish-Russian relations, Sikorski told the commander of the Polish army, W. Anders: "For higher political reasons, the army must remain in the Soviet Union."[58] But Anders, having become a vehement anticommunist after two years of imprisonment in the Soviet Union, and believing that Soviet defeat was imminent, made a single-handed decision to evacuate the entire army together with the soldiers' families from the Soviet Union, to which Stalin willingly gave his consent.[59] By the beginning of August 1942 the evacuation of about 110,000 Poles had been completed. New recruitment was not permitted, and recruit centers were closed.[60] Parallel with the liquidation of the armed forces, the Soviets took one step after another to reduce the scope of activities of the Polish embassy in the Soviet Union. In the course of 1942 most of the Polish delegations were closed. Many members of the embassy as well as the delegations were arrested on the grounds of espionage or other illegal activities.[61] The already sharply curtailed sovereign rights of the Polish government regarding its citizens in the Soviet Union received the final blow by a Soviet note of January 16, 1943. On that day the People's Commissariat for Foreign Affairs informed the Polish embassy that now all the inhabitants of the former Polish territories annexed by the Soviets in 1939, including those of Polish origin, would be treated as Soviet citizens.[62] With

the Polish population declared nonexistent, there would be no
more foundation for Polish claims to the civilians in the Soviet
Union.

Evidently, by the beginning of 1943 Soviet-Polish relations had
reached a point at which either the Poles had to make essential
concessions on the territorial question to save the integrity of their
government, or the Soviets would proceed further to question the
legitimacy of the Polish government. One can argue that whatever
concessions the Poles might have made, the Soviets were determined to introduce a communist regime in Poland.[63] An answer
to this question might be obtained by investigating the Comintern's instructions to the Polish Communists. Shortly after the
German attack on the Soviet Union, the ECCI had decided to
reactivate the Polish party. To this end, an initiative group was
formed out of the Polish trainees of the Comintern school. They
had to decide on the name of the new party. The return to the old
name, the Communist Party of Poland, was out of the question,
because they felt that it had unfortunate associations like "foreign
agency."[64] Through the personal intervention of G. Dimitrov,
general secretary of the Comintern, it was decided to adopt the
term "Polish Workers' party."[65] The name *Polish* Workers' party,
not Workers' Party *of Poland*, stressed the new party's primarily
national, not international, character, in accordance with Dimitrov's concept of a "national workers' party which conducts a
communist policy."[66] The initiative group worked out a completely new program in the form of a declaration: "To Workers,
Peasants and Intellectuals. To All Polish Patriots."[67] This was a
remarkable document. There was no mention of revolution,
socialism, communism, class struggle, dictatorship of the proletariat, nationalization, or collectivization. There were only slogans which would be typical of a social reformist party with
certain nationalistic undertones. The solidarity with the Soviet
Union was presented as the solidarity with a big Slav brother:
"Together with the great Russian nation, we all rise up for the
sacred struggle for the liberation of the Slavs from under the
yoke of the Teutonic Order." The historical significance of the
Polish-Soviet agreement was stressed, as was the need to establish
a national front. It was firmly declared that the PWP had "no
intention to compete with other parties which wholeheartedly

fight for the liberation of the Polish nation. On the contrary, it endeavours to co-operate with them as closely as possible and to fight together with them against the common enemy." The PWP's slogans on social problems were rather modest: eight-hour work day, social insurance, freedom of association, land reform, ban on national discrimination, and free education. Evidently, emphasis was more on national solidarity than on social antagonism. The support for the government-in-exile was unequivocal.[68] An "all-sided and most effective aid" was promised to the Polish army.[69]

The Comintern stood godfather to the PWP in every sense of the word. One cannot attach much importance to the formality that the new party was not a section of the Comintern.[70] Even an official history of the workers' movement in Poland admits that the PWP was tied ideologically, politically, and even organizationally to the Comintern.[71] The new party was even more dependent on the Comintern than its predecessor; it was in fact the creation of the Comintern. After the disbandment of the CPP, the Comintern had made it clear that the reconstruction of the party could take place only at the initiative of the ECCI and warned that any independent attempt to resurrect the party would be judged negatively.[72] Subsequent events showed that the Comintern kept exactly to this line. The nucleus of the PWP was literally selected by organs of the Comintern from among the Polish emigrants in the Soviet Union and elsewhere.[73] Members of the initiative group, some coming straight from Polish prisons and some from the International Brigade in Spain, had for a number of years been cut off from the political life at home.[74] They received full political training at the Comintern school, but lacked contacts with their country,[75] and did not know exactly what was actually happening at home.[76]

Obviously the Comintern intended to retain control over the party about to be established. Dimitrov advised the initiative group not to make haste to convoke a central committee at home, but to conduct party affairs in a troika which should be composed of people smuggled in from the Soviet Union.[77] The Comintern prepared the undertaking so thoroughly that it set up a second echelon which was either to become the local cadre or to take over the central leadership if the first echelon should fail to call the party into being for any reason.[78] The first group could not be parachuted into Poland in September 1941 as scheduled because of an airplane accident immediately after the take-off in which one member was killed. It was only after this accident that the two groups were brought together and given the opportunity to discuss among themselves problems of the new party.[79]

At the end of December 1941, the first group was dropped near Warsaw. They quickly established contacts with various Communist groups in the underground. As early as January 5, 1942, the initiative group succeeded in calling a founding meeting in Warsaw. It turned out, however, that native Communists had strong reservations about the concept of a new party. They were shocked by the apparently noncommunistic character of the PWP.[80] There were even those who listened with distrust to the news of a new party and suspected that it might have been inspired by the government-in-exile.[81] The initiative group argued that it was impossible to make any amendment to the draft declaration because they had left in Moscow a copy which was to be published at once when the Comintern was informed of the party's coming into being.[82] As late as August 12, 1942, Nowotko, general-secretary of the new party, complained in a report to Dimitrov that the greatest trouble was that the party had to break through sectarian tendencies, especially among the former CPP members.[83]

Support for the London government meanwhile underwent a subtle shift of emphasis. An article in the May Day issue of the underground PWP's central organ *Trybuna wolności* (The tribune of freedom)[84] acknowledged the "undoubtedly positive achievements" of Sikorski's government in cultivating relations with Allied nations and setting up Polish armed forces abroad. At the same time, it blamed the London Poles for their tendency to postpone the showdown with the enemy till 1944–45 and for their failure to have the "Polish working class, peasant masses, and toiling intellectuals" represented in the government "in proportion to their specific weight [*ciężar gatunkowy*] and ideological orientation." In a threatening tone, the article concluded that the PWP attitude toward the London government "depended on its actions, not on its words."[85]

The PWP was taciturn and equivocal on the territorial question. The Polish Communists had been among the least pretentious toward the territorial question, in relation not only to the Soviet

Union but also to Germany and Czechoslovakia; this was why they were unpopular among their countrymen. In the fall of 1941, when the first discussion on the frontier question took place at a meeting of the initiative group, one of the participants recommended an annexation of large German territories to Poland. After a heated exchange, the idea was rejected and its exponent blamed for nationalism.[86] Thereafter, until the spring of 1943, the topic did not come up again for discussion and found no mention either in the party press or in any public enunciations. As regards the Polish-Soviet frontier, it is really surprising that the PWP failed to define its position throughout the first year of its existence. An article in *Trybuna wolności* of April 1, 1942 ("New Poland Must Be Strong") vaguely stated, "We believe that the need to coexist with the brotherly Ukrainian and Belorussian nations, as well as the sympathy in the Soviet Union for the Polish cause, will bring the question of our eastern frontiers to a fair solution. But we know also that square kilometers and population numbers are not decisive for the strength of a country."[87] An interesting fact is that until April 1943 the PWP maintained a branch office in Lwów and let its partisan units operate there.[88] Why the Comintern allowed an area claimed by the Soviets to come under the jurisdiction of its *de facto* Polish section is not quite clear. Stalin's general conception of future Polish frontiers was already definite in December 1941. Among the Polish emigrants in the Soviet Union, the frontier conception became increasingly more definitive toward the end of 1942.[89] The PWP's persistent taciturnity and equivocation on this question was thus all the more conspicuous.

During the first half of 1942, the PWP managed to build up a national network of party organization, relying mainly on the former cells of the CPP.[90] According to Nowotko's report to Dimitrov in June 1942, there were 4,000 party members and 3,000 partisans.[91] But PWP influence was still very limited. In the summer of 1942, it tried to organize National Committees for Struggle, a national front from below[92] but was unsuccessful.[93] As for military organization, the PWP suffered from shortage of qualified cadres. The gap was filled partly by veterans of the Spanish Civil War who were brought in from France or the Soviet Union,[94] and partly by Soviet officers who were parachuted into

Poland or who escaped from German prisoner-of-war camps.[95] Though small in number, the people's guard, as the Communist partisans would later call themselves, gained popularity by calling for the launching of an immediate armed struggle against the Germans, whereas the home army of the government-in-exile, in spite of numerical superiority and effective organization, was prepared to stage only limited warfare, fearing that premature struggles would only result in unnecessary losses and frustrate long-term plans.[96] The PWP experienced a serious leadership crisis in November 1942 when Nowotko was assassinated on the instigation of B. Mołojec, one of the troika in charge of military affairs. P. Finder, the last of the troika, became general secretary, while Mołojec was executed by the party organ on grounds of treachery.[97]

It is true that Stalin tried to create in Poland a useful instrument for his policy. But this instrument was employed not to replace the government-in-exile but to put pressure on it so that it would take a more resolutely anti-German and pro-Soviet attitude. There was little evidence that the Soviets were at that time already determined to impose a communist regime on Poland. On the contrary, evidence strongly indicates that they gave preference to the government-in-exile.

The Struggle for Government in Poland: March 1943 to July 1944

In January 1943, J. Ciechanowski, Polish ambassador in Washington, was taken aback when Under Secretary of State Sumner Welles asked, "Am I to understand that the Polish Government is determined not to sacrifice even an inch of its eastern territory?"[98] This was the first time that the Poles heard from an American official a demand, though discreet, that they make territorial concessions to the Soviets. On March 15, when Eden came to Washington, he found Roosevelt quite willing to accept territorial settlements on the Soviet line, though he would not commit himself publicly in view of public opinion.[99] A month later, Churchill told Sikorski that it would be necessary at an appropriate moment to redefine the Polish frontiers in the east for Russian benefit, and in the west for Polish benefit.[100] The Big Three would now proceed with the new frontier settlement whether the Poles liked it or not. But the London Poles adamantly refused to face this reality. They were even desirous of obtaining much German territory in the west.[101] A certain megalomaniac tendency came to the fore among the London Poles. They were privately saying that after the war Russia would be so weakened and Germany so crushed that Poland would emerge as the most powerful state in that part of the world.[102]

In the meantime, the Soviet Union began publicly expressing doubt that the existing Polish leaders represented the true opinion of Poland.[103] In March 1943, Majskij stressed in a conversation with Eden that the future Polish government should be "democratic and friendly to the Soviet Union," and that the Soviets would definitely oppose the revival of the prewar regime or the return to power of émigré politicians in England.[104] Eden got the impression that the Soviets were not disposed to allow the existing exiled group in London to return home.[105] At about the same time Bogomolov, Soviet ambassador to the governments-in-exile in London, suddenly began to show an interest in the internal affairs of the Polish government, asking every person concerned who was against whom on what issue in Sikorski's cabinet.[106] More significant, Moscow took concrete measures to set up on Soviet soil an authority that could eventually replace the government-in-exile. On January 4, 1943, W. Wasilewska, a Communist and a Soviet citizen of Polish origin, and others asked Foreign Commissar Molotov for permission to establish a "center for Polish affairs." This was to take over most of the tasks which had been carried out by the Polish embassy.[107] The Polish leaders apparently wished to see the body recognized as the "Polish governement." But Stalin rejected this request.[108] On March 1, the Soviet government instead gave its blessings to the Union of Polish Patriots (UPP). The latter promptly expressed its readiness to recognize the Soviet claims to the area east of the Curzon line.[109] The Soviet Union also took steps to set up a new Polish army in place of the one which had left the Soviet Union in the preceding year. On February 2, 1943, *Nowe widnokręgi* (New horizons), the organ of the Polish Communists in the Soviet Union, called for the creation of Polish military units.[110] On April 1, *Wolna Polska* (Free Poland), the organ of the UPP, published a similar appeal.[111] A week later, Z. Berling, a colonel of the prewar Polish army who had not left with Anders's army, submitted to the NKVD (People's Commissariat for Internal Affairs) a petition for establishing a Polish division on Soviet soil.[112]

It was at this juncture that the fateful Katyn affair became public. On April 13, the Nazi propaganda machine disseminated news that mass graves of Polish officers were discovered at Katyn near Smolensk, and that the Russians were guilty of the massacre. The news shocked the London Poles, particularly because many of them were related by blood to the murdered officers. But the Katyn affair itself was not as important in Polish-Soviet relations as has generally been supposed. There were already enough factors causing strained relations between the two governments; even without Katyn they would have further deteriorated.[113] The impetuous reaction of the London Poles only showed how completely they had lost touch with reality. They requested the International Red Cross to investigate the case, whereupon the Soviet Union broke off diplomatic relations, accusing them of connivance with the Nazis.[114]

The severance of diplomatic relations immediately brought the question of Polish government to the fore. In a dispatch of April 30, Churchill expressed to Stalin his anxiety that the Soviets would set up a Polish government on Russian soil and deal only with them. He made it clear that the British intended to stand by Sikorski.[115] Evidently the question of government was worrying the British more than anything else about Poland.[116] In reply Stalin demanded that the Big Three should try to "improve the composition of the present Polish Government." Pessimistic about his ability to discipline the London Poles, he approvingly cited words of certain American officials that it was doubtful whether the London Poles would ever be able to return home and remain in power.[117] At the same time Stalin stressed that he desired to see a "strong and independent Poland" after the war, and that Soviet-Polish relations should be based on "solid good neighborly relations and mutual respect" or, "if the Poles wished it, an alliance of mutual assistance against the Germans."[118] What Stalin meant by "strong Poland" was obviously a Poland amply compensated for territorial losses in the east by acqustions in the west. The reference to "solid good neighborly relations and mutual respect" implied that the future Polish government must be definitely pro-Soviet. The trouble was that the concept of "Soviet-friendliness" was difficult to define. For the time being it seemed that the readiness to meet the Soviet territorial demands alone sufficed.

Churchill agreed to a reshuffle of the Polish government-in-exile, but did not want to give the impression that Sikorski was reconstructing his government under foreign pressure.[119] In the beginning of May, Lord Halifax, British ambassador in Washington, discreetly asked Ciechanowski whether he did not think that if Sikorski were to express his readiness to remove from his cabinet some of his ministers who, "rightly or wrongly," were considered by the Soviets as unfriendly to Russia, it would make it easier to bring about the reestablishment of Soviet-Polish relations.[120] Such a soft approach, however, did not have any effect on the ever more self-righteous Poles. The Americans, especially the State Department officials, were more inflexible on the question of government than the British. In spite of repeated recommendations by the U.S. ambassadors to the Soviet Union and the governments-in-exile in London, Secretary of State Hull adamantly refused to exert any pressure upon the London Poles to reorganize the government. He considered it an unpardonable interference in the internal affairs of an allied nation.[121] The result was again continuation of the policy of postponement, that is, the policy of inaction. Thus, the matter was left to take its own course.

In July 1943 Sikorski was killed in an airplane accident in Gibraltar. The loss of a man upon whom the Soviets could also have agreed was a serious setback for Polish as well as Western causes. But it also could have given an opportunity to the Poles to carry out a radical reshuffle of the government through their own efforts. But this opportunity was not taken. Indeed, the new cabinet, headed by S. Mikołajczyk, leader of the Peasant party, looked even more radically democratic than its predecessor,[122] but Raczkiewicz, Sosnkowski, and other politicians who had opposed the conclusion of the Polish-Soviet agreement in July 1941, and whom Moscow was attacking by name as anti-Soviet elements, were either confirmed in office or even renominated to important government posts.[123] The new government soon proved to be no less inflexible than the old one.

It was quite natural that the Anglo-American *démarche* with Stalin in August 1943 for the reestablishment of diplomatic relations between Poland and the Soviet Union should have failed to produce any positive result.[124] The Western powers, provided by the Poles with no trumps in the negotiations with Moscow, were so frustrated that they hesitated to take up the issue at the Moscow Foreign Ministers Conference in October.[125] In view of such an impasse, the Western leaders, particularly the British, came to the conclusion that they must come to terms with the Soviets even without consulting the Poles. The British view on the territorial question was that Poland should be given Danzig, East Prussia, and the Oppeln district of Upper Silesia, and should agree to the Curzon line with an adjustment to include Lwów in Polish territory.[126] President Roosevelt accepted this solution, though the State Department was still hesitating.[127] In a memorandum circulated to the war cabinet in November 1943, Eden stressed that in return for a British undertaking to impose the frontier settlement on the Poles, the Soviets should have to give the British their assurance that they would resume diplomatic relations with the Polish government, that it would be allowed to return home and to submit themselves to the approval of the Polish people, and that the latter should be free to choose their own government without any outside pressure.[128] In a word, government in return for territory.

At the Teheran Conference in November–December 1943, Churchill suggested that the three heads of government might agree on a frontier policy that the British would advise the Poles to accept.[129] Stalin, though reluctant to discuss the Polish issue, gave his consent to Churchill's formula: the home of the Polish state and nation should be between the so-called Curzon line and the line of the Oder, including for Poland East Prussia and Oppeln. In a private meeting with Stalin, Roosevelt agreed to the idea of Poland moving westward, but apologized for his inability to take part publicly in such an arrangement because of the imminent presidential elections.[130] With regard to the question of government, Stalin denounced the London Poles for their collaboration with the Nazis and their fratricidal assault on the "partisans." As proof of their collaborationist behavior, Stalin produced a leaflet which showed a head with two faces—Hitler from one side and Stalin from the other side. This leaflet was allegedly published by pro-London elements in the Polish underground. According to a recent study in Poland, however, it originated from an ultra-rightist group called NSZ (Narodowe Siły Zbrojne, National Armed Forces), which stood outside the government coalition.[131] Also, the internecine murders of which Stalin accused the London Poles might be imputed to the same group. A lieutenant of the home army confirmed with some bitterness that though the underground army of the government-in-exile was strong enough to liquidate the Communist partisans with its own forces, Sikorski did not want to create a Yugoslav situation in Poland and strictly ordered the home army to abstain from hostile action toward the Communists.[132] In any case, Stalin made it clear that he was prepared to enter into negotiation with the London Poles only if they would go along with the "partisans" and sever all connections with the German agents in Poland. As "partisans" could mean only Communist partisans, it was obvious that Stalin made the recognition of the London government dependent on its readiness to work with the Communists. Interestingly, this was exactly the reverse of Stalin's policy toward Yugoslavia: at the time of the Teheran Conference, Stalin still recognized the Yugoslav government-in-exile and demanded Tito's partisans to come to terms with it.[133]

On April 16, 1943, A. Lampe, a leading Polish Communist in the Soviet Union, published an article in the UPP's organ *Wolna Polska* and pleaded for a Polish western frontier on the Oder and northern frontier on the Baltic coast.[134] This was the first time that a Polish Communist publicly advanced such far-reaching territorial claims. It meant a *volte-face* of the Polish Communist position on the territorial question, but it also showed that the Soviet Union had decided to help the Polish Communists come to power. Shortly after the Soviets broke off relations with the London Poles, Stalin let Wasilewska, president of the UPP, broadcast over the radio that the émigré government did not represent the Polish nation.[135] The UPP was then allowed to take over the site and belongings of the closed Polish embassy, recruit a Polish army, and look after the Polish population in the Soviet Union.[136] The first congress of the UPP was held on June 10. The declaration adopted at the congress laid stress on democracy as opposed to the "reactionary character" of the government-in-exile on the territorial question.[137]

The setting up of the new Polish army on Soviet soil was an attempt to create not only a military force against the Germans but also a power base for a future government in Poland. At the end of April 1943, Wasilewska submitted a request to Stalin for creating Polish military units in the Soviet Union, saying that it would be necessary to conduct vigorous political work in those units.[138] On May 6, Stalin granted the request and made public the formation of the Kościuszko division under the command of Colonel Berling.[139] The new army was not a volunteer army like the old one, and its soldiers were conscripted from among the Poles in the Soviet Union.[140] There was, however, a serious shortage of qualified officers. According to Stalin's own revelation to Polish Ambassador S. Kot, he had intended to set up a Polish army as early as 1940, but had had to give up the idea because he could find no appropriate commander for it.[141] The situation became worse as more than 10,000 officers were killed at Katyn and elsewhere, and those few who survived departed for the Near East. In 1943, however, Stalin solved the problem by a simple method of detaching a large contingent of Soviet officers for service in the Polish army. From May 1943 to March 1944, the Red Army detached 1,465 officers to the first Polish corps which had grown out of the Kościuszko division, among them 6 generals, 17 colonels, 54 lieutenant-colonels, and 113 majors.[142] The following table shows the composition of the officer corps of the first Polish corps:[143]

| Date | Service Experience | | No Service | Total |
	in prewar Polish army	in Soviet army	Experience	
October 1, 1943	15.3%	75.8%	8.9%	100%
December 30, 1943	21.6%	63.8%	14.6%	100%
January 1, 1944	21.4%	58.6%	20.0%	100%

Officers with no service experience can be considered Soviet officers, because they became officers only after thoroughgoing training from Soviet instructors.[144] Thus, Soviet officers in the first Polish corps almost amounted to 80 percent. Though the ethnic principle was emphasized in their selection, most of the officers from the Red Army could not speak Polish,[145] and the learning of Polish was therefore encouraged.[146] Even after territories inhabited by Poles came under the Soviet hand, the importance of Soviet officers did not diminish, because there were few Polish officers available at home. The Polish army which grew out of the first Polish corps received, from April to July 1944, an additional 3,221 Soviet officers, among them 4 generals, 49 colonels, 99 lieutenant-colonels, 285 majors.[147] The officer corps of the second Polish army, which was formed at the time of the liberation, was almost completely Russian.[148] The Soviets attached the greatest importance to political education among Polish officers and soldiers, and a special staff of educational officers was established to carry out this task.[149] Officers of the prewar Polish army who wavered at critical moments like the Warsaw uprising were at once removed from responsible posts, as was the case with Z. Berling, supreme commander of the first Polish army.[150] While this army copied the prewar Polish army down to the smallest details, such as uniforms, decorations, and military songs, it had in practice a strong Russian character with respect to its command structure. It was preeminently a political army to serve the pro-Soviet government in Warsaw.

The Polish Communists at home adjusted themselves to the new situation only gradually. A resolution of the first plenum of the PWP's central committee in January 1943 stated that their attitude toward the London government and its agents was dependent on the latter's behavior.[151] On January 15, the PWP addressed an open letter to the home delegate of the government-in-exile, proposing "a national reconciliation and the unification of all healthy national forces for the struggle against the invaders."[152] The authorship of the letter was ascribed to W. Gomułka, future general-secretary of the party. In the course of the ensuing negotiations, the PWP's delegation demanded that the Londoners allow them to take part in government affairs on equal terms with other parties and in proportion to the relative strengths of social-political forces represented by them.[153] On March 1, the PWP published a programmatic declaration entitled "What do we fight for?" It called for the removal of "reactionary elements" from the London government, the establishment of a national united front, and the intensification of armed resistance, but it did not question the legitimacy of the government-in-exile. It also stated that "all Polish lands" should be included in the postwar Polish state according to the principle of national self-determination.[154] This reference was evidently to the eastern frontier, but there was still no hint of the PWP's conception of future northern and western frontiers. The negotiations had been dragging on without any positive result when the Soviets broke off diplomatic relations with the London Poles. A high-handed answer of the home-delegate to the Communists on April 28, demanding that the latter accept the London government's supreme authority, repudiate any connections with the Comintern, and recognize the inviolability of the prewar frontiers, put an end to the only serious attempt to bring about cooperation between the pro-Soviet and anti-Soviet forces in Poland during the war.[155]

On April 17, General Secretary of the PWP Finder communicated in a secret telegram to Dimitrov that the party advocated the strengthening of the Polish position in the west and on the Baltic.[156] This was the first echo of Lampe's *Wolna Polska* article among the Polish Communists at home and marked a radical turn of the party's tactics. But the Communists at home were extremely cautious, and it was only seven months later that they subscribed to the new line publicly. It was not the frontier but the government question that showed the party's drift toward the new line. In May the party's central organ *Trybuna wolności* still stressed "not what divides, but what unites Poles."[157] But in July a new tone became discernible with the arrival of a new party activist, B. Bierut, from Minsk. He at once took a seat in the central committee of the PWP and assumed the editorship of *Trybuna Wolności*.[158] A distinctive mark of the new line was an emphasis on democracy. The July 1 editorial of *Trybuna wolności* ("For a Democratic Poland") declared all laws issued by the government-in-exile invalid because that government had derived its legitimacy from the fascist constitution of 1935.[159] The September 1 editorial ("For the Political Idea of Polish Democracy") pointed out that the urgent task of the moment was for "united democratic forces" to take independent political and military action.[160] Already in July a campaign had been launched for setting up a people's army which was to replace the home army of the London government.[161]

Another campaign should follow for the creation of a political body to replace the London government itself.

In November the PWP came out with a new declaration: "What do we fight for?"[162] The big declaration, as it was called, was noted for its provocative explicitness toward both the government and the frontier questions. The legitimacy of the government-in-exile and its right to take office after the war were flatly denied. Only a democratic national front at home was entitled to govern liberated Poland, it was declared. A new army which pledged allegiance to this front, a people's army, should be called into being. Unmistakably the declaration was a bid for power by the PWP. The evolution from a simple national front to a democratic one was significant. The former was one in which all organizations could take part on equal terms, so long as they fought against the aggressors; the National Committees for Struggle offered an example. They were open to all groups "from the communists to the right-wing nationalists."[163] In contrast, only democratic organizations were entitled to take part in a democratic national front, and only the PWP was authorized to define the requirements of such an organization. Undoubtedly a hegemonic position in a democratic national front would fall on the PWP, and the role allotted to all other organizations would be as junior partners.[164] The big declaration also advocated Poland's westward and northward expansion at the expense of Germany. From now on the Communists would be more nationalistic than any party in Poland insofar as western and northern frontiers were concerned.

The first plenum of the central committee was convoked in January 1943. From then on the native group, with Gomułka as the leader, played an increasingly prominent role in the party's affairs. In May, when the Comintern was dissolved, the PWP welcomed the news, hoping it would create more favorable conditions for their efforts now that they could no longer be accused of being agents of a foreign institution.[165] In November, General Secretary Finder, the last of the troika, was arrested by the Gestapo. M. Fornalska, who, coming from the second initiative group, was to have succeeded the troika,[166] also fell victim to the Gestapo. There was no one left in the cadre group smuggled in from the Soviet Union who would be qualified for the highest post of the party. The way was now opened for Gomułka's accession to power.

The new general secretary at once began carrying out the policies of the big declaration. At the end of November, when the Teheran Conference was held, Gomułka called into being an organization committee for a national council of the homeland (NCH). On December 15, the "Manifesto of democratic social-political and military organizations in Poland" was published, defining the NCH as "a factual political representation of the Polish people, entitled to act in the name of the people, and to guide their destiny until the time of Poland's liberation from foreign occupation."[167] Besides the PWP and its military arm, the people's guard, however, signatories of this *ersatz* constitution were organizations whose existences were little known, such as "Group of Independent Democrats," "Group of Polish Teachers," "Group of Polish Writers," and "Group of Socialist Activists." Evidently the Communists failed to induce organizations of influence to collaborate in this undertaking.[168] Nevertheless, they managed to convene the first meeting of the NCH on the night of December 31. The declaration of the meeting stated that the London government was not qualified to represent the Polish people, and that the NCH had the right to name the provisional government at an appropriate moment.[169] As Gomułka stated on March 7, 1944, in a secret report to Dimitrov, the NCH was to perform governmental functions for a certain period.[170] The declaration proposed new Polish frontiers on an ethnographic basis in the east, on the Oder in the west, and on the Baltic in the north. As regards economic policy, expropriation of large holdings and German-owned lands for distribution among peasants, and nationalization of big industries, were advocated. B. Bierut became president of the NCH, and M. Rola-Żymierski, another member of the PWP, took over command of the people's army which was set up with the people's guard as its core. According to the decree on the formation of the people's army, all Polish armed forces both at home and abroad were to come under his command.[171]

Contemporary Polish historiography tends to emphasize the originality of the PWP's tactics ranging from the issuing of the big declaration to the creation of the NCH.[172] It is clear, however, that the Communists in Poland could never hope to improve their relations with the London Poles. What is worthy of mention is surely not the originality, but the readiness and even boldness of the native group in trying to make the most of their opportunities in the struggle for power with the London Poles and in competition for leadership in liberated Poland.

It was in connection with this competition that first signs of internal discord appeared among the Polish Communists. In October 1943, political instructors of the first Polish corps in the Soviet Union tried to define the UPP program in a document "Theses for the active: what do we fight for?"[173] The document did not attach much importance to the resistance movement at home, or to the problem of social and political systems in future Poland, but it flatly stated that the Polish armed forces in the Soviet Union were the decisive political forces that should introduce a powerful regime in liberated Poland and carry out necessary reforms through "organized democracy." Though these theses were not approved, they were among the guiding ideas of the Polish Communists in the Soviet Union. A certain echo of the theses can be recognized in Berling's words in the spring of 1944, which were a profound shock to the London Poles: "Today we have 100,000 soldiers, but tomorrow we shall have a million of them, and this will be a force which will enable us to shape the internal structure of Poland."[174] The discussions on the theses gave rise to the conception of a Polish national committee (PNC) in the Soviet Union. According to a draft declaration of the PNC, written by A. Lampe, the body was intended as a democratic representation of the Polish people until the formation of a provisional government.[175] The draft declaration called upon all patriotic parties, groups, and organizations at home to rally around the PNC. Evidently the NCH in Warsaw would have faced a strong rival in Moscow if the PNC had been called into being.

On January 12, 1944, Gomułka inquired in a secret message to Moscow as to the representation of the Polish people in the Soviet Union.[176] He stressed that the domestic front would have to play a decisive role in the struggle for liberation and take upon itself the main task of Poland's reconstruction. He suggested that the body to be established in the Soviet Union should function not as a government but only as an external representation of the NCH. The superior role of the domestic over foreign front had always been the PWP argument against the London Poles.

Obviously such a position would be seriously undermined if a pro-Communist government-in-exile were established in Moscow. Gomułka did not oppose the idea of a PNC as such, but he would not accept it as a government. Interestingly, the declaration of the NCH, denying the authority of the London government, recognized the need for a Polish representation abroad.[177] One might say that already in the founding declaration of the NCH a place was being reserved for a body like the PNC.

It is not completely clear why the PNC scheme was suddenly dropped. According to standard interpretation in Poland today, the strange situation in which there would have emerged two representatives of the Polish people, one in Warsaw and the other in Moscow, was brought about by a temporary break in the wireless contact between the two places, an accident caused by the arrest of P. Finder and M. Fornalska by the Gestapo; therefore, the conception of the PNC became irrelevant when the news of the establishment of the NCH in Warsaw reached Moscow.[178] But a more recent monograph disputes this view, suggesting that there always was some means of communication between Moscow and Warsaw, and pointing out that the Polish Communists in Moscow did not stop planning for the PNC and, even after February 1944, when the plan was finally dropped, continued to produce one scheme after another for a provisional Polish government.[179] A. Witos, a Peasant party leader who took part in the UPP, reported later that after the fall of 1943 till the spring of 1944 it had plans to establish a Polish administration composed of emigrants in the Soviet Union, but that Stalin put a stop to them.[180] In any case, a representation not of the Polish people but of the Polish Communists was established in Moscow at the end of January 1944: the central office of the Polish Communists (COPC), headed by A. Zawadzki. According to a Polish historian, the Polish Communists in the Soviet Union reacted to the founding of the NCH in Warsaw with "reservation and anxiety."[181] In February the COPC telegraphed to Warsaw their critical comments on the NCH, expressing doubt that it could issue decrees that could not be put into practice under the conditions of occupation, and pointing out the necessity of broadening the mass basis and withdrawing such radical slogans as the nationalization of industry.[182] These comments reflected Dimitrov's and, in the final analysis, Stalin's views. When O. Lange remarked to Stalin in May 1944 that the Polish Communists were now the right wing of the UPP as compared with the Socialists and the Peasant party and that they objected to the demand for nationalization of big industries, Stalin smiled and said, "That's because I've bawled them out."[183] Gomułka replied to Dimitrov in a letter of March 7 with a sober judgment of the situation at home. In the vehement anti-Soviet and anticommunist atmosphere then prevailing in Poland, any revision of the program as suggested by the comrades in Moscow would have failed to achieve a broadening effect on the political basis of the NCH.[184] This statement sheds light on the real background of the NCH. The decision was dictated by the necessity to call into being a pro-Soviet authority as soon as possible and even without popular support. The result was that a representation of the people which, as Gomułka himself admitted, did not represent the people at least for the moment had to be founded.[185]

The Soviet press, except the Polish-language one, kept conspicuous silence on the NCH for the first five months of its existence.[186] It seemed that Stalin left open the possibility of coming to terms with the London Poles. In December 1943 Czechoslovak President Beneš, in Moscow to sign a Soviet-Czechoslovak treaty, learned that Stalin was ready to resume diplomatic relations with the London government on condition that Mikołajczyk remove a few ministers considered anti-Soviet and recognize the validity of the Curzon line. Beneš's efforts as a mediator, supported by the British, ended in failure, however, when Mikołajczyk proved unable to carry his associates with him.[187]

At the beginning of January 1944, when the Red Army crossed the former Polish-Soviet frontier, the London government promised to instruct the underground authorities in Poland to avoid all conflict with the Soviet armies, but they upheld their claims to territory east of the Curzon line.[188] In a message to Churchill on January 7, Stalin angrily called the London Poles "incorrigible people."[189] The official Soviet reply, a Tass communiqué of January 11, categorically rejected the Polish claims, but for the first time publicly confirmed Soviet readiness to make small-scale changes in the Curzon line and to support Poland's territorial acquisitions in the west and north.[190] Molotov stated to American

Ambassador A. Harriman that the Soviet government envisioned an *entirely new* Polish government, including some of the present members of the London government, prominent Poles in the United States, and Poles now in the Soviet Union.[191] The expression "improvement of the personal composition of the present Polish government" continued to be used in official Soviet language, but it was often coupled with adjectives like "radical" or "thorough." In March Moscow requested that Washington permit two American citizens of Polish origin, Professor O. Lange and Father L. Orlemanski, possible candidates for posts in a new Polish government, to come to Moscow for political discussion.[192]

On February 1, Churchill cabled Stalin that "to advocate changes within a foreign government comes near to interference in internal sovereignty."[193] Stalin rebutted that in May 1943 Churchill had not considered it an interference in internal sovereignty of Poland to advocate an improvement in the Polish government's composition.[194] On February 7, Roosevelt urged that Stalin "leave it to Mikołajczyk himself to make such changes in his Government as may be necessary without any evidence of pressure or dictation from a foreign country."[195] Apparently such a turn of events alarmed State Department officials. In a memorandum submitted to Under Secretary of State E. R. Stettinius on March 15, they reaffirmed their opposition to any departure from the Atlantic Charter.[196]

In the meantime Churchill took it upon himself to exert massive pressure upon the London Poles to accept the Curzon line. Mikołajczyk refused to yield. The most that he would concede was to accept the Curzon line not as a final frontier but as a demarcation line with Lwów and Wilno included on the Polish side.[197] This was still far from meeting the Russian demands, what Eden called a product of a "suicide mind."[198] Czechoslovak Foreign Minister J. Masaryk said that he never had seen a group of politicians who could through every act commit suicide with such professional throughness.[199] But Mikołajczyk's actions were limited by internal Polish politics. Even soldiers of the Polish army who fought side by side with the Red Army were against the surrender of Polish cities like Lwów or Wilno.[200] If Mikołajczyk had accepted the Curzon line, he would certainly have lost the support of his people, as the February 15 resolution of the Council of National Unity, a pro-London underground parliament, explicitly warned.[201] Unable to be decisive, Mikołajczyk took refuge in a world of wishful thinking; he hoped for the liberation of Poland by their own forces just before the arrival of the Soviet army, the dispatch of an Anglo-American military mission to Poland, and more resolute Western, particularly American, intercession after the establishment of the Second Front.[202]

The situation was not an easy one for the British. On February 20, Churchill admitted in a telegram to Stalin that his pressure upon the Poles had failed to produce results, but that the British government itself accepted the Curzon line.[203] He made this position public in a speech in the House of Commons two days later, to the consternation of uninformed circles in London, British as well as Polish.[204] On March 21, Churchill stated to Stalin that all territorial questions must await the armistice or peace conferences, and that in the meantime the British could not recognize forcible transfers of territory.[205] Stalin's reply was harsh and bitter. He accused Churchill of going back on the Teheran agreement.[206] On March 3, Stalin told Harriman that he did not believe Churchill would be able to accomplish anything in negotiations with the London Poles; that the Poles at home were welcoming the Red Army as it advanced and that, therefore, either Mikołajczyk's government would have to change or another government would emerge in Poland: "Poland needs democrats who will look after the interests of the people, not Tory landlords." Upon Harriman's inquiry as to how a democratic government might be established in Poland, Stalin answered that circumstances would show how.[207] What Stalin had in view became clear only two months later. A delegation of the NCH, headed by E. Osóbka-Morawski, a leader of a pro-Communist splinter group of the Workers' Socialist party, which was in its turn a left-wing splinter party of the Socialist party, left Poland in the middle of March, crossed the front line, and arrived in Moscow on May 16.[208] On the following day Stalin told Lange that no Polish government would be formed by the UPP and that the Polish government must emerge out of Poland itself, out of the forces which existed among the Polish underground.[209] Two days later Stalin gave an audience to the delegation of the NCH, an act which the Polish Communists thought amounted to a *de facto* recognition of the NCH.[210] On May 24, the Soviet press for the first time publicly referred to the existence of a national council of the homeland in Warsaw and the arrival of its delegation in Moscow.[211]

Osóbka-Morawski later reported, "I gained at that time the impression that between Stalin and the Soviet government on the one hand and the Comintern [which officially should not have existed after May 1943!] in the persons of Dimitrov and Manuilskij on the other hand no final conception had been formed on many questions out of the fields: (1) Polish-Soviet relations, and (2) the Comintern's policy toward Poland's internal affairs. . . . Marshal Stalin in conversation with us at that time did not represent any uniform, rigid, or minutely worked out line of conduct which should be imposed upon us independently of the situation at home and in the world."[212] On the basis of this report, the historian Kowalski concludes, "The thesis of the Western historiography on the *ingérence* of the Soviet Union in Poland's internal affairs and on its imposition of the system of people's democracy upon Poland does not hold in the face of these facts. Paraphrasing the used terminology, it is possible to turn the thesis the other way around and prove successfully that in the period in question it was the very Soviet Union that was compelled to import political arguments and government conceptions from Poland itself, in order to fill the void in Russia's political program in relation to Poland. This was true first of all of the government question, but also applied to the question of postwar Polish frontiers in terms of its concretization."[213] This seems to be a somewhat one-sided presentation of the story. As indicated above, a general framework for the tactics of the Communists at home had already been set by the Soviet Union. But it is true that many Soviet decisions of direct importance for later developments over Poland were made in the two months following the arrival of the NCH delegation in Moscow.

The Soviets did not at once commit themselves to the NCH. In the first conversations with the NCH delegation, Stalin avoided political discussions, and Molotov added that if the Soviets recognized the NCH, there could be trouble from the Western allies. Stalin invited the delegation to undertake a long inspection tour of Polish army camps in the Soviet Union, saying, "The

NCH has no army, and the Polish army in the Soviet Union has no government."[214] The Soviets in the meantime tried to contact the London Poles with a view to drawing at least some of them into collaboration. Contact was established on May 23, May 31, and June 10 between the Soviet minister to the governments-in-exile in London, V. Z. Lebedev, and the president of the Polish National Council in London, S. Grabski.[215] Czechoslovak President Beneš again took upon himself the mediator's role, intimating to Mikołajczyk that the Russians sincerely desired to reach agreement with the latter before resuming their offensive on the eastern front. Four ministers—K. Sosnkowski, W. Raczkiewicz, S. Kot, and M. Kukiel—should be removed from their posts, and the frontier problem could be dealt with later, Beneš said.[216] On June 1, Ambassador A. A. Gromyko informed the U.S. government that the NCH, whose delegation had recently arrived in Moscow, would be willing to work with Polish officials in London "although they did not like some of them," and that they desired to establish "relations" with the Soviet Union, Great Britain, and the United States.[217] The same views were expressed to Harriman by the NCH delegation who called at the American embassy in Moscow on June 11.[218] Two days later Lange told Mikołajczyk, at that time visiting the United States, that Stalin did not intend to intervene in internal Polish questions, but that he was very interested in the future foreign policy of Poland; his attitude toward the country would depend largely on what shape that policy would take.[219] Mikołajczyk then had two meetings with Lebedev in London. The conversations were friendly, and even the frontier question did not seem to be a serious obstacle. But on June 23 the tone suddenly changed. Lebedev presented the following terms as the preconditions for a resumption of diplomatic relations: (1) resignation of the four ministers; (2) complete reconstruction of the Polish government through participation of representatives of "democratic Poles" from Great Britain, the United States, the Soviet Union, and the NCH in Warsaw; (3) condemnation of the previous administration for their mistake over Katyn; and (4) recognition of the Curzon line. Mikołajczyk rejected these conditions on the spot.[220]

On the previous day Stalin had renewed conversations with the NCH delegation in Moscow. He was now ready for political discussions with the Warsaw Poles. This probably was the background for the sudden turn in Soviet attitude toward the London Poles. Stalin's decision was to authorize the NCH to appoint an administration for the liberated areas of Poland.[221] He had the UPP adopt a resolution to the effect that it repudiated the London government's legitimacy, recognized the NCH as the true representative of the Polish people, and expressed confidence that the NCH would create favorable conditions for the formation of a provisional national government.[222] Stalin's June 24 message to Roosevelt expressing opposition to the latter's suggestion that Mikołajczyk visit Moscow, and proposing a "reorganization" of the London government could only mean that Stalin aimed at the establishment of a completely new government.[223] Obviously he was now determined to pursue his own Polish policy irrespective of the outcome of the negotiations with the London Poles.[224]

In the Polish underground, the PWP continued to make efforts to broaden the mass basis of the NCH. But their efforts bore no great success. At the beginning of 1944, three underground parliaments existed: the NCH, the pro-London Council of National Unity, and the noncommunist leftist Central People's Committee. The PWP tried unsuccessfully to obtain the last group's collaboration with the NCH.[225] On July 1 the party's central organ, *Trybuna wolności*, appealed to the democratic forces *within* the London government for support of such collaboration.[226] The author of the appeal, W. Bienkowski, counted Mikołajczyk and his associates from the Peasant party and the WRN (Wolność, Równość, Niepodległość—Freedom, Equality, Independence, a right-wing group of the Socialist party) among "democratic forces." He advised them to disassociate themselves as quickly as possible from the "reactionary elements," warning that if they continued to be prisoners of those elements in a government based on the fascist constitution of 1935, the democratic camp at home would have no other choice but to resort to "extra-constitutional" means. Half a year later Gomułka confirmed that at that time he had actually placed hope in the democratic elements in the London government.[227] But it would be completely erroneous to argue, as Gomułka's opponents did in 1948 and some Western historians later, that on the eve of the liberation of the country by the Red Army the PWP was trying to liquidate the NCH for the sake of an alliance with the London government.[228] The PWP's tactics did not deviate from Stalin's policy toward Poland.

There were only two groups which the PWP managed to draw into collaboration: the Workers' Socialist party and the "People's Will" group. The former, led by E. Osóbka-Morawski, was not the original Workers' Socialist party but a splinter group which later usurped the name of the parent body. The "People's Will" group was also a left-wing splinter group of the large Peasant party.[229] Neither of these groups possessed great influence in Polish society, much less a "mass basis." Under these circumstances the PWP had to fall back upon their own resources. It is estimated that PWP membership reached about 20,000 in July 1944.[230] During the six months following the establishment of the NCH, this party, relying essentially on its own strength, managed to create a network of "national councils," a pyramid of local representatives with the NCH at the top.[231]

For fear of becoming involved in additional complications at the important time when preparations for the cross-channel operation were in full progress, the Western powers avoided taking any new initiatives in the Polish question. In his talks with Mikołajczyk in June, Roosevelt irresponsibly expressed optimistic views: the eastern frontier should run east of Lwów, Poland should have the whole of East Prussia including Königsberg; and Stalin knew that the U.S. government stood solidly behind Mikołajczyk.[232] In practice, however, Roosevelt merely tried to send Mikołajczyk to Moscow for talks with Stalin without committing the United States to either the Polish or the Soviet side.[233] The British were hesitating, too. At the end of May, the Foreign Office took the view that resumption of Britain's mediation efforts would do more harm than good and that it and the United States could be of more help if they remained in the background.[234] While the Western powers were looking on inactively, the Red Army made rapid advances to the west. The summer offensive of the Red Army on the Belorussian front, launched in the second half of June, proved to be a great success. Within a month Russian soldiers were already standing on the Curzon line.

From the beginning of July, Polish emigrant circles in Moscow worked assiduously for the establishment of Polish administration in the liberated areas.[235] On July 6, the second delegation of the

NCH, headed by General Rola-Żymierski, arrived in Moscow, and meetings were held almost daily between the NCH delegations, the central board of the UPP, the COPC, and various Soviet authorities. In the middle of July a joint committee of the NCH and the UPP worked out a memorandum calling for the creation of a "provisional government" on the basis of the NCH but broadened by participation of representatives of the UPP and other democratic organizations at home and abroad.[236] Stalin, who saw Rola-Żymierski on July 15, appeared to prefer a "committee of national liberation."[237] At a meeting of July 18, the Poles, probably urged on by the Soviets, withdrew the provisional government scheme and decided to establish an "NCH delegation," whose authority was to be limited to the liberated areas of Poland. Stalin approved the idea and proposed an agreement on the demarcation line between the Soviet and the Polish administrations, which would mean a *de jure* recognition of the body by the Soviet government.[238] The first cabinet meeting of the NCH delegation was held on the morning of July 20, but that very afternoon the delegation scheme was abandoned at Molotov's intervention. He suggested instead the setting up of a "national liberation committee" whose authority was to extend to the entire territory of Poland within its new boundaries. He pointed out that this would mean the elevation of the status of the provisional Polish authority and serve to introduce to Polish soil a solution similar to that applied in a number of other occupied countries. The delegation of the NCH was thus changed to the "Polish committee of national liberation" (PCNL). The composition of the PCNL showed a definite predominance of Moscow over Warsaw Poles. Though the post of chairman (premier) was given to the Warsaw Pole Osóbka-Morawski, the two vice chairmen's posts were filled by Moscow Poles, W. Wasilewska and A. Witos. Of the 15 posts in all, 10 went to UPP activists and the rest to NCH members.

The PCNL (the so-called Lublin Committee) was not an improvisation necessitated by a sudden turn of the military situation, but was intended as a permanent institution that claimed exclusive authority in the whole of Poland including areas yet to be liberated from Germany and incorporated into Poland. Although for the moment the Russians did not allow the PCNL to call itself a government, their determination to create out of the PCNL the nucleus of a future Polish government was unequivocal, as Stalin's July 23 message to Churchill demonstrated.[239] The Soviets would henceforth treat the London Poles no longer as a Polish government, but only as individual members, offering them seats in the government to be established in Poland.[240]

On July 22, a manifesto of the PCNL was published.[241] It had been preceded by intensive discussions between the NCH and the PWP on the one hand, and the UPP and the COPC on the other.[242] Keeping faithfully to Stalin's instruction, the Polish Communists in Soviet exile tried to appear as moderate as possible.[243] Generally speaking, the Socialists and the Peasant party were more radical than the Communists, and among the latter, those at home were more radical than those in Russia.[244] The manifesto showed that the conservatism of the Moscow Communists prevailed in the end. It was based not on the declaraction of the NCH, but on A. Lampe's draft declaration of the PNC. The manifesto declared that the émigré government in London and its delegation at home were a usurpatory, illegal authority based on the fascist constitution of 1935, and that the only legal authority was the NCH and the PCNL working on the basis of the constitution of 1921.[245] That is, not the "manifesto of democratic social-political and military organizations in Poland" of December 15, 1943, but the constitution of 1921 was to provide the PCNL with a constitutional basis.[246] The PCNL declaration called for the return of forcibly Germanized territories in the west and north of Poland and for an understanding with neighboring nations in the interest of Slav solidarity against the Germans. All democratic rights were solemnly guaranteed. There was no reference to the dictatorship of the proletariat or the leading role of the communist or workers' parties. At the same time, "The enemies of democracy, however, cannot enjoy democratic liberties." As regards social-economic policy, the document promised to respect private property of all except Germans and traitors. The Catholic Church, the owner of large landed property, could keep its possessions. Landholdings of Germans and traitors and those over 50 ha (100 ha in the areas incorporated into the German Reich during the war) should be confiscated and distributed among landless or small peasants. Big industries should come under temporary control of the provisional state administration, to be later returned to the former owners. The manifesto completely failed to mention socialism, even in a roundabout way.[247]

Significantly, the Soviets made a new decision on the frontier question just at this juncture. Up to that time it had not been clear where exactly the future Polish western frontier should run. The Big Three had agreed generally upon the Oder line, but it had been unclear which one of the tributaries of the Oder should be the final boundary. Apparently it had been accepted as self-evident by all, including the Soviets, that Poland could not move farther west than the Eastern Neisse because the area west of this line was inhabited almost exclusively by Germans.[248] But in the meantime Polish pressures for a frontier on the Western Neisse, the westernmost upper stream of the Oder, had become increasingly strong.[249] This time, however, the London Poles remained rather reserved because they feared that Poland's exaggerated westward expansion would burden it internally with a large German minority and isolate it externally against a possible German irredentism.[250] Even O. Lange, who stood close to the Communists and later became Poland's first ambassador to Washington, expressed concern that such territorial expansion would perpetuate German desires for revenge and make it impossible to integrate Germany into a new European order.[251]

It was the Communist Poles who brought forward claims for the Western Neisse and pressed the Soviets to accede to them. They were tough negotiators even on the eastern frontier.[252] And on July 15 Stalin finally expressed to Rola-Żymierski his readiness to support the Polish position on the Western Neisse.[253] The PCNL chairman reported that in a July 24 conversation "Marshal Stalin admitted that we were right and traced with a thick red pencil the new line on the map laid out on the table, declaring that the Soviet Union would advocate this line as the Polish-German frontier. We felt it was our great victory."[254] The Polish-Soviet agreement of July 26, although it did not distinguish the Western from the Eastern Neisse, mentioned the Neisse river, leaving the impression that the matter still awaited final decision.[255] The frontier arrangement was hidden from Western observers so successfully that it was only at Yalta that the Western heads of government discovered the further expansion westward of Poland.[256] At any rate the slogan of a Polish western frontier on the Oder–Western Neisse line proved to be a valuable weapon for the Communists to rally the people around them and to consolidate their power.[257]

In the last days of July, Russian troops stormed Poland. They dealt heavy blows not only at the retreating Germans, but also at the home army of the London government. The latter was given the alternative either to be disarmed and disbanded, or to join the Polish army under Russian command. This army, united with the people's army emerging out of the underground, developed into a "Polish people's army," which numbered about 100,000 men toward the end of July but grew rapidly as it drafted a large number of recruits in the liberated areas.[258] At repeated urgings of the Western leaders, Stalin finally consented to see Mikołajczyk and the latter arrived in Moscow on July 30. Molotov asked: "Why did you come here? What have you got to say?"[259]

Conclusion

Stalin warned Mikołajczyk that, should he not come to an agreement with the Lublin Poles as soon as possible, the Soviet Union would have no choice but to deal exclusively with them. The margin of choice open to Mikołajczyk was extremely narrow. From his conversations with B. Bierut, president of the NCH, it seemed that the Lublin Poles were prepared to offer the London Poles only 4 out of 18 portfolios in a provisional Polish government.[260] This was what Stalin meant by the PCNL forming the nucleus. Russia's attitude toward the Warsaw uprising revealed beyond any doubt its aims in Poland. It might be that the Red Army encountered certain operational difficulties making it impossible to continue the offensive across the Vistula river, as some Soviet historians argue.[261] But ample evidence exists to show that the Russian failure to give effective aid to the rebels in Warsaw was due not only to military but also to political considerations.[262] The disastrous uprising decisively weakened the pro-London elements in Poland; in the liberated areas of the country, they were severely persecuted by organs of the PCNL and the Red Army. As Gomułka himself later admitted, at that time many Communists thought they were going to introduce a one-party dictatorship immediately.[263] In November 1944 the London Poles dropped Mikołajczyk, whose readiness for compromise was too much for them, as their leader. Since he was one of those few Poles who enjoyed confidence of the Western governments and at the same time were still acceptable to the Soviets, the London Poles were thus finally eliminating themselves from the world of real politics. At the end of 1944 the PCNL was reorganized into a provisional government which the Soviet government promptly recognized.

The Yalta agreement was a definite Soviet victory. On the frontier question the Soviet position was accepted without substantial alterations. Only the western frontier along the Oder–Western Neisse line met with reservations on the side of the Western powers, particularly Great Britain; they agreed to it only as an interim demarcation line for administrative purposes. However, the expulsion of the German population out of the area in question, to which the Western powers did not object, predetermined the case. Their view that the frontier question still awaited a final decision could only anger the Poles and made it easy for the Soviets to appear in the role of sponsor of a Polish national cause. They likewise succeeded in defending their position on the constitution of the new Polish regime. The Lublin Committee was to be reorganized into a provisional government of national unity, with the inclusion of democratic leaders from inside and outside Poland. All that the Western powers could obtain from Russia was the pledge that there would be held "free and unfettered elections" at the earliest possible date. The task of nominating candidates for posts in the new Polish government was entrusted to the committee of the three consisting of Molotov, Harriman, and A. Clark-Kerr, the British ambassador to Moscow. Molotov insisted on his right to veto any candidate, and adamantly refused to accept those suggested by the Western powers, particularly Mikołajczyk. The Soviets went so far as to have all potential Western candidates in the Polish underground arrested. This became known as the case of the sixteen and caused a sensation in the West.[264] Under these circumstances even Roosevelt changed his attitude toward Russia and advocated a harder line on Poland in one of his last messages to Churchill.[265]

This deadlock was to be resolved by H. Hopkins, who was sent on a mission to Moscow in May-June 1945. He arranged a new compromise on the basis of which negotiations were resumed. The representatives of the provisional government as well as the Western candidates were hastily ordered to Moscow.[266] At one of the meetings Gomułka delivered a speech, revealing how determined the Lublin Poles were as they took part in the negotiations:

> Please take no offense, gentlemen, that we offer you only such government posts as we consider expendable. It is because it is we who are in power. . . . We sincerely wish to come to terms with you. But please do not think that our existence will depend on it. We will never surrender the power that we have once seized. . . . If a government of national unity cannot be established, perhaps another several hundred people will be killed, but this will not frighten us. . . . We will ruthlessly destroy all reactionary bandits. You may cry that the blood of the Polish people will flow, that the NKVD is governing Poland, but it will not divert us. You have the choice: Either we will come to an understanding and work together for the reconstruction of Poland, or we will part once and for all.[267]

This statement left no doubt that the Communists were determined not to lose their grip on power and that they would never allow a noncommunist government to emerge out of the promised "free and unfettered elections." At the end of June, a compromise was reached at last, and the provisional government of national unity with Osóbka-Morawski as minister-president and Mikołajczyk and Gomułka as vice-minister-presidents was formed with the blessings of the Soviet as well as the Western governments.

The confrontation over Poland was caused neither by Russia's world revolutionary grand design nor by the West's counterrevolutionary intrigues. In November 1941 Churchill had expressed his views in a message to Stalin: "The fact that Russia is a Communist state and that Britain and the United States are not and do not intend to be is not any obstacle to our making a good plan for our mutual safety and rightful interests." With these views Stalin expressed agreement.[268] He seldom resorted to an ideological argument to justify his claims on Poland. He defined himself rather as a defender of Russian national interests and, in this sense, as a successor to the czars' cause than as an apostle of world revolution. Defending the Curzon line at Yalta, Stalin remarked that he could not return to Moscow and face the people, who would say Stalin and Molotov had been less jealous defenders of Russian interests than Curzon and Clemenceau.[269] One might add that the governments these two politicians represented had been allies of czarist Russia. Churchill and Roosevelt had always a ready ear for such arguments, though the latter had to worry about the ethnic voters and the "anti-Soviet cliques" in the State Department. In other words, as far as the territorial question went, there was no fundamental disagreement among the three powers. In fact, conflict began not between the Soviet Union and the Western powers, but between the former and the Poles, with the Western powers drawn into the dispute against their will. Regarding the government question, however, they were deeply committed to the government-in-exile and very anxious to preserve its integrity. Here, therefore, their readiness for compromise was more limited than in the case of the frontier question. Still, they put pressure on the Polish government to change its composition only to the extent that it would not do damage to the integrity of the government as a whole. Of course, the Western powers always stood for the principle of free elections, but they advocated it only in the hope that the same kind of government as the one then in existence would be elected.

In the meantime it became increasingly evident that the frontier dispute between the Soviets and the Poles could not be resolved. The Poles were determined not to give way, although it was clear that they were fighting a losing battle. The background for such a quixotic position might be sought in the political system of interwar Poland. Most of the leading figures of the London government had come from the old feudal ruling class *szlachta*, and even those of plebeian origin were strongly imbued with the *szlachta* political culture.[270] Their anachronistic life styles and unrealistic views of the world had been reinforced by their experience during the interwar period when they held the reins of government for nearly 20 years; they were subjected to no serious internal challenge and allowed to control large areas inhabited by foreign nationals.

At first the Russians seem to have hoped that they could get the Poles to accept the compromise by compensating them for losses in the east by gains in the west. How serious the Soviets were about their desire to come to terms with the London Poles was indicated by the fact that they offered large-scale territorial acquisitions in the west first to the London Poles, not to the Communists, and that they ordered the latter to cooperate with the former. It was only after they assured themselves that no settlement was possible with the Polish émigrés in London that the Soviets turned to the Communists. The Polish Workers' party was initially created by the Russians to press on the London Poles for a more active struggle against the Germans and a more friendly attitude toward the Soviet Union. The PWP lacked a social revolutionary character and did not aim at a seizure of power in the immediate future. In the spring of 1943, however, the Soviets seem to have decided that this party should emerge as the postwar power. It was not their social but national programs that were to help the Polish Communists come to power. They were allowed to court popularity by putting forward the chauvinistic claim for vast German territories. The PWP in the Polish underground gradually grew from a docile instrument of Soviet foreign policy to a political force in its own right. As the time of liberation drew near, not only the national but also the social program of the PWP tended to radicalize. The Soviets showed readiness to meet the desire for further territorial acquisitions in the west, but insisted on a moderate social program. The manifesto of the PCNL showed that the Soviets had their way. It was, after all, not the political strength of the PWP but the military force of the Soviet Union that brought the Communists to power. But there was little doubt that the Soviets would not and could not in the long run keep under control the dynamics of the Communist regime in Poland.

As the government question was raised, the Western powers inevitably became involved so that the conflict between the Soviets and the Poles developed into one between the Soviets and the Western powers. What made the compromise difficult was the fact that there were practically no political forces besides the London groups and the Communists that would be acceptable to both Russia and the West. Thus, the Western powers had either to continue supporting the government-in-exile or to accept total surrender. When at Yalta they received the promise of "free and unfettered elections" they finally decided to abandon the London government, but this promise turned out to be fraudulent, and the reality of Communist rule seemed to confirm the worst fears. Confrontation over Poland reached its climax. The anticommunist arguments of the émigré Poles which had had their roots in the old Polish hatred of everything Russian and to which Western leaders had turned a deaf ear suddenly began to find wide resonance in public opinion in the West. The Western leaders saw that their hopes for a just and fair peace had been deceived. The Cold War began.

1. See in this connection N. A. Graebner, "Cold War Origins and the Continuing Debates: A Review of the Literature," in *The Conduct of Soviet Foreign Policy*, eds. E. P. Hoffman and F. T. Fleron, Jr. (New York: Aldine Atherton, 1971), pp. 219, 226.
2. R. A. Divine, *Roosevelt and World War II* (Baltimore: Penguin Books, 1970), p. 97.
3. A. B. Ulam, *Expansion and Coexistence: The History of Soviet Foreign Policy, 1917–1967* (New York: Praeger, 1968), p. 378.
4. In this sense I fully agree with the Polish historian S. Zabiełło, when he says, "It would be a *naïveté* to think that after the war Poland could have decided independently on her frontiers and constitution against the will of powers which possessed all material means of decision. But it would be also erroneous to suppose that the same big powers could have moulded the form and structure of Poland to their liking, as if it were a passive matter, not a living organism." S. Zabiełło, *O rząd i granice* (Warsaw: Instytut Wydawniczy 《Pax》, 1965), p. 7.
5. *Documents on Polish-Soviet Relations 1939–1945*, vol. 1 (London: Heinemann, 1961–67), p. 116.
6. K. Radek, *Vojna pol'skich belogvardejcev protiv Sovetskoj Rossii* (Moscow: Gosudarstvennoe Izdatel'stvo, 1920), pp. 17, 20–22.
7. P. S. Wandycz, *Soviet-Polish Relations 1917–1921* (Cambridge: Harvard University Press, 1969), p. 107.
8. *Dokumenty i materialy po isotorii sovetsko-pol'skich otnošenij*, vols. 7–8 (Moscow: Izdatel'stvo "Nauka," 1973–74), vol. 7, pp. 198–99. Cf. *Documents*, vol. 1, p. 116.
9. *Dokumenty*, vol. 7, pp. 202–5, 208; *Documents*, vol. 1, pp. 114–42; I. M. Majskij, *Vospominanija sovetskogo posla. Vojna 1939–1943* (Moscow: Izdatel' stvo "Nauka," 1965), pp. 154–58; E. Raczyński, *W sojuszniczym Londynie* (London: Instytut Polski i Muzeum im. Gen. Sikorskiego, 1974), pp. 119–22.
10. *Documents*, vol. 1, pp. 578–79; W. T. Kowalski, *Walka dyplomatyczna o miejsce Polski w Europie (1939–1945)* (Warsaw: Książka i Wiedza, 1974), pp. 199–201; R. Umiastowski, *Poland, Russia and Great Britain 1941–1945: A Study of Evidence* (London: Hollis & Carter, 1946), pp. 22–23.
11. See A. J. Vyšinskij's comments on the Soviet-Polish agreement, *Dokumenty*, vol. 7, p. 215.
12. M. Djilas, *Conversations with Stalin* (London: Penguin Books, 1962), p. 61.
13. There were conflicting estimates on the number of Polish prisoners of war and deported civilians. See *Documents*, vol. 1, pp. 573–74; Zabiełło, *O rząd*, pp. 69–70.
14. On the scope of activities of the embassy delegates, see *Dokumenty*, vol. 7, pp. 269–71, 276–77; *Documents*, vol. 1, pp. 257–58. Cf. S. Kot, *Listy z Rosji do Gen. Sikorskiego* (London: Jutro Polski, 1955), pp. 25–27.
15. The following description of the Polish Communist movement in the years 1938–42 is mainly based on M. Malinowski, *Geneza PPR* (Warsaw: Książka i Wiedza,

1975). *See also* A. Korbonski, "The Polish Communist Party 1938–1942," *Slavic Review*, no. 3 (1968): 430–44.

16. Malinowski, *Geneza PPR*, pp. 372–73.

17. J. S. Ludwińska, "Wspomnienia o Marcelim Nowotce," in *Marceli Nowotko 1893–1942: Artykuły biograficzne, wspomnienia, dokumenty* (Warsaw: Książka i Wiedza, 1974), pp. 272–73.

18. L. Partyński, "Nasz kochany 'Stary', " in *Marceli Nowotko*, p. 268.

19. *Dokumenty*, vol. 7, pp. 199–202.

20. Malinowski, *Geneza PPR*, pp. 343–50.

21. L. Woodward, *British Foreign Policy during the Second World War*, vol. 2 (London: Her Majesty's Stationery Office, 1970–), p. 12.

22. Ibid., p. 13. Cf. the text of the telegram forwarded to Stalin, *Correspondence between the Chairman of the Council of Ministers of the U.S.S.R. and the Presidents of the U.S.A. and the Prime Ministers of Great Britain during the Great Patriotic War of 1941–1945*, vol. 1 (Moscow: Foreign Language Publishing House, 1957), p. 10.

23. *Documents*, vol. 1, p. 142; Woodward, *British Foreign Policy*, vol. 2, p. 613.

24. *Documents*, vol. 1, pp. 143–44.

25. J. L. Gaddis, *The United States and the Origins of the Cold War 1941–1947* (New York: Columbia University Press, 1972), pp. 139–49

26. Francis L. Loewenheim et al., eds., *Roosevelt and Churchill: Their Secret Wartime Correspondence* (London: Barrie & Jenkins, 1975), pp. 149–51.

27. J. Ciechanowski, *Defeat in Victory* (Garden City: Doubleday, 1947), pp. 39–40. See also *Foreign Relations of the United States, Diplomatic Papers* (henceforth cited *FR*), *General, 1941*, I, 247–48; *Documents*, vol. 1, pp. 576–77.

28. *See* for example *FR, Europe, 1942*, III, 107–8.

29. L. E. Davis, *The Cold War Begins: Soviet-American Conflict over Eastern Europe* (Princeton: Princeton University Press, 1974), pp. 74–75. See also *FR, 1942*, III, 207.

30. *Dokumenty*, vol. 7, pp. 255–56. Cf. *FR, 1942*, III, 191–92.

31. *Documents*, vol. 1, p. 245. Italics added.

32. Ibid., p. 274; *see also* pp. 264–65, 270–71. Cf. *FR, 1942*, III, 124; Ciechanowski, *Defeat in Victory*, pp. 78–79.

33. Woodward, *British Foreign Policy*, vol. 2, p. 232. Italics added.

34. Ibid., p. 247; *FR, 1942*, III, 559. Cf. W. T. Kowalski, *Wielka Koalicja 1941–1945*, vol. 1 (Warsaw: Wydawnictwo MON, 1973–), p. 184.

35. According to the Soviet sources, the main reason why the Soviets lost interest in concluding the treaty in its original form was their failure to get through the demands affecting Poland. Majskij, *Vospominanija*, pp. 241–48. See also *Istorija diplomatii*, vol. 4: *Diplomatija v gody vtoroj mirovoj vojny* (Moscow: Politizdat, 1975), p. 260; V. Issraelian, *Die Anti-Hitler-Koalition: Die diplomatische Zusammenarbeit zwischen der UdSSR, den USA und England während des zweiten Weltkrieges 1941–1945* (Moscow: Verlag Progress, 1975), p. 113. But evidence showed that Poland was not the greatest obstacle. It was one of those demands which the Soviets had withdrawn when a new draft was put forward to them; see *FR, 1942*, III, 559. Not completely clear, on the other hand, is the background of the sudden Soviet decision to accept the British suggestion of an alternative treaty with no reference altogether to territorial arrangements. Western historians incline to suppose that there was a connection between the Soviet acceptance of the alternative treaty and the American promise to establish the second front in 1942. *See*, for example, H. Feis, *Churchill, Roosevelt, Stalin: The War They Waged and the Peace They Sought* (Princeton: Princeton University Press, 1957), p. 62; R. Beitzell, *The Uneasy Alliance: America, Britain and Russia 1941–1943* (New York: Knopf, 1972), pp. 38–39, 367, 371.

36. Woodward, *British Foreign Policy*, vol. 2, p. 232.

37. A. Eden, *The Memoirs*, vol. 2, *The Reckoning* (Boston: Houghton Mifflin, 1965), pp. 318–19; Woodward, *British Foreign Policy*, vol. 2, pp. 236–37; *FR, 1942*, III, 517–18.

38. W. S. Churchill, *The Second World War*, vol. 3, *The Grand Alliance* (Boston:

194   ITŌ TAKAYUKI

Houghton Mifflin, 1950), pp. 630–31, 695–96; vol. 4, *The Hinge of Fate* (1950), p. 327; Woodward, *British Foreign Policy*, vol. 2, pp. 234–35.

39. *FR, 1942,* III, 143.
40. A more detailed analysis of this problem is found in Itō, "Tōō ni kansuru ren-gōkoku no sensō mokuteki 1941–1945, part 1," in *Surabu kenkyū* 21 (1976): 200–210.
41. *FR, 1942,* III, 505–12; C. Hull, *The Memoirs,* vol. 2, (New York: Macmillan, 1948), p. 1169.
42. The record of the conversation has not been found in U.S. archives (see *FR, 1942,* III, 533, footnote 64). But a recent Soviet study brought to light a fragment of the Soviet record from the archives. See *Istorija mirovoj vojny 1939–1945,* vol. 5 (Moscow: Voenizdat, 1975), p. 68. *See also* a fragment of the record handed over to the British by the State Department, cited in Woodward, *British Foreign Policy,* vol. 2, p. 240.
43. *Documents,* vol. 1, p. 275.
44. Ibid., p. 471.
45. Ibid., pp. 275, 298.
46. *See,* for example, *FR, 1942,* III, 542; *FR, The British Commonwealth, Eastern Europe, The Far East, 1943,* III, 337, 470.
47. Zabiełło, *O rząd,* pp. 29–30; Kowalski, *Walka dyplomatyczna,* p. 177. The conception is of Polish origin, according to P. S. Wandycz, *Czechoslovak-Polish Confederation and the Great Powers 1940–43* (Bloomington: Indiana University Publications, 1956), p. 37.
48. *Documents,* vol. 1, p. 471; *FR, 1942,* III, 205; *FR, 1943,* III, 337, 470. Cf. Wandycz, *Czechoslovak-Polish Confederation,* pp. 87–88.
49. *FR, 1942,* III, 500; Churchill, *Second World War,* vol. 3, p. 629; Woodward, *British Foreign Policy,* vol. 2, p. 225.
50. Wandycz, *Czechoslovak-Polish Confederation,* pp. 74–76.
51. Woodward, *British Foreign Policy,* vol. 2, p. 247.
52. E. Taborsky, "Politics in Exile 1939–1945," in *A History of the Czechoslovak Republic 1918–1948,* eds. V. S. Mamatey and R. Luža (Princeton: Princeton University Press, 1973), p. 339.
53. See H. Momose, "Soren-tōō kankei no shiteki kōsatsu," in *Sekai* 295 (May 1970): 61–67, and 296 (June 1970): 178–87.
54. *F. D. Roosevelt: His Personal Letters 1928–1945,* vol. 2 (New York: Duell, Sloan, Pearce, 1950), p. 1290. Cf. *FR, 1943,* III, 137.
55. Eden, *Reckoning,* p. 341.
56. Itō, "Tōō ni kansuru," pp. 211–12.
57. Kot, *Listy,* pp. 197–206; *Documents,* vol. 1, pp. 235–42.
58. W. Anders, *Bez ostatniego rozdziału: Wspomnienia z lat 1939–1946* (London: Gryf, 1959), p. 130. Cf. *Documents,* vol. 1, pp. 369–70, 421–23, 427.
59. Anders, *Bez ostatniego rozdziału,* pp. 130–34. There was serious antagonism between Sikorski and his ambassador to the Soviet Union, Kot, on the one hand and Anders on the other. *See* Kot, *Listy,* pp. 38–59, 64–75.
60. *Dokumenty,* vol. 7, pp. 227–35, 300–301; *Documents,* vol. 1, pp. 351–52, 424–27, 447–52, 460–68.
61. *Dokumenty,* vol. 7, pp. 282–84, 292–93, 301–5, 313–15, 317–19, 321–23, 325–30, 336–37, 340–42; *Documents,* vol. 1, pp. 322–24, 375–76, 378–87, 389–91, 393–96, 401–21, 429–40, 442–47, 452–55, 468–69.
62. *Dokumenty,* vol. 7, pp. 342–43; *Documents,* vol. 1, pp. 473–74.
63. *See,* for example, Umiastowski, *Poland*; B. Kuznierz, *Stalin and Poles: Indictment of the Soviet Leaders* (London: Hollis & Carter, 1949); E. J. Rozek, *Allied Wartime Diplomacy: A Pattern in Poland* (New York: Wiley, 1958); W. Pobóg-Malinowski, *Najnowsza historia polityczna Polski 1864–1945,* vol. 3 (London: B. Świderski, 1960).
64. A record of a meeting of the initiative group in the fall of 1941 tells us: "The new party was not called Communist (1) so that the enemies could not operate with the bogey of communism; (2) there are still a lot of elements even in the working class which take a distrustful attitude toward the Communists as a result of the previous errors and wrong policy of the old CPP; (3) after the event which happened [allusion

to the party's disbandment and purge in 1938], the party, as Comrade Dimitrov remarked, should deserve its name by its work before it will call itself communist; (4) it is necessary that the masses should see in our party an organization closely tied with the Polish nation, with its most vital interests, and that the enemies could not call it an agency of a foreign state; and (5) under the new name it will be easier to rally around the party broad masses of workers, peasants, and intellectuals, and to organize under its leadership a united national front for the struggle against the German fascist occupation." Malinowski, *Geneza PPR*, p. 360, footnote 53.

65. Ibid., pp. 351–52.

66. Ibid., p. 351, footnote 29.

67. *Marceli Nowotko*, pp. 343–47.

68. According to a Polish historian, the Polish Communists in the Soviet Union supported the London government even more strongly than those at home. *See* Zabiełło, *O rząd*, p. 81.

69. In a later version of the declaration, the reference to the Polish army was dropped. The first official documentation of the party's history, *Kształtowanie się podstaw programowych PPR w latach 1942–1945* (Warsaw: Książka i Wiedza, 1958), pp. 11–15, reproduces this version, not the original one.

70. H. Bandō, "Pōrando to dainiji sekaitaisen," in *Gendai Pōrando no seiji to shakai*, ed. H. Bandō (Tokyo: Nihon kokusai mondai kenkyūjo, 1969), tries to find a special meaning in this formality.

71. *Historia polskiego ruchu robotniczego 1864–1964*, vol. 2 (Warsaw: Książka i Wiedza, 1967), p. 99. *See also* Malinowski, *Geneza PPR*, pp. 463–64, 482.

72. Ibid., p. 463.

73. Partyński, "Nasz kochany," p. 266; Ludwińska, "Wspomnienia," pp. 274–77; J. Frey-Bielecki, "Komunista w służbie swego narodu," in *Marceli Nowotko*, p. 300–302.

74. Malinowski, *Geneza PPR*, p. 345.

75. Ibid., p. 355.

76. *See* ibid., p. 348.

77. Ibid., p. 357.

78. Ibid., pp. 358, 482.

79. Ibid., p. 359.

80. Ibid., pp. 364–65, 412, 424–25, 440. *See also* R. Halaba and W. Ważniewski, *Polska Partia Robotnicza 1942–1948* (Warsaw: Wydawnictwo MON, 1972), p. 29.

81. Malinowski, *Geneza PPR*, p. 370.

82. Ibid., p. 365.

83. *Marceli Nowotko*, p. 445.

84. "Nasz stosunek do rządu gen. Sikorskiego," in ibid., pp. 347–48.

85. From the fall of 1942, when Soviet-Polish relations began to deteriorate rapidly, PWP attacks on the London government became increasingly sharper, though they were carefully kept within the general line of a united front. *See* "Oblicze polskiej reakcji," *Trybuna wolności*, 15 October 1942, in *Marceli Nowotko*, pp. 414–14. Cf. Nowotko to Dimitrov, 11 September 1942, in ibid., p. 451. *See* note 69 above.

86. Malinowski, *Geneza PPR*, p. 359.

87. "Nowa Polska musi być silna," in *Publicystyka konspiracyjna PPR 1942–1945. Wybór artykułów*, vol. 1 (Warsaw : Książka i Wiedza, 1962–1967), pp. 27–28.

88. A. Przygoński, *Prasa konspiracyjna PPR. Zarys, katalog, życiorysy* (Warsaw: Książka i Wiedza, 1966), p. 221; Malinowski, *Geneza PPR*, pp. 458–60; *Historia polskiego ruchu robotniczego*, vol. 2, p. 102; *Polski ruch robotniczy w okresie wojny i okupacji hitlerowskiej, wrzesień 1939–styczeń 1945: Zarys historii* (Warsaw: Książka i Wiedza, 1964), pp. 204–5.

89. V. Vierheller, *Polen und die Deutschland-Frage 1939–1949* (Köln: Verlag Wissenschaft und Politik, 1970), p. 68.

90. Malinowski, *Geneza PPR*, pp. 372–460.

91. *Marceli Nowotko*, p. 434.

92. "Narodowe Komitety Walki," *Trybuna wolności*, 1 July 1942, in *Publicystyka*

PPR, vol. 1, pp. 39–41; Nowotko to Dimitrov, 29 July 1942, *Marceli Nowotko*, p. 444. *See also* the resolution of the January 1943 plenum of the central committee of the PWP, *Kształtowanie się*, p. 71.

93. Halaba, Ważniewski, *PPR*, p. 73; Malinowski, *Geneza PPR*, pp. 485–86; *Publicystyka PPR*, vol. 1, pp. 41–42, footnote 1.

94. Malinowski, *Geneza PPR*, pp. 477–78; Halaba, Ważniewski, *PPR*, pp. 32–33.

95. I. D. Kundjuba, *Sovetsko-pol'skie otnošenija (1939–1945 gg.)* (Kiev: Izdatel'stvo Kievskogo Universiteta, 1963), pp. 55–60, 68–69, 71–72, 75; Halaba, Ważniewski, *PPR*, p. 33. Soviet citizens who took part in the Polish partisan movement numbered about 7,000 by the spring of 1944, M. I. Smirjaga, *Sovetskie ljudi v evropejskom soprotivlenii* (Moscow: Izdatel'stvo "Nauka," 1970), p. 37, and about 18,000 by the end of the war, ibid. p. 7. *See also* a more recent estimation in V. S. Parsadanova, "Idejno-političeskaja rabota Pol'skoj Rabočej Partii v Gvardii Ljudovoj i Armii Ljudovoj," in *Boevoe sodružestvo sovetskogo i pol'skogo narodov* (Moscow: Izdatel'stvo "Mysl'," 1973), p. 176.

96. J. M. Ciechanowski, *The Warsaw Rising of 1944* (Cambridge: Cambridge University Press, 1974), pp. 89–92.

97. *Polski ruch robotniczy*, p. 205; Halaba, Ważniewski, *PPR*, p. 30.

98. J. Ciechanowski, *Defeat in Victory*, p. 139.

99. *FR, 1943*, III, 13–18, 34–36; R. Sherwood, *Roosevelt and Hopkins: An Intimate History* (New York: Harper, 1948), pp. 709–10; Eden, *Reckoning*, pp. 431–32; Woodward, *British Foreign Policy*, vol. 2, pp. 622–23; Feis, *Churchill*, pp. 122–23, 192; Rozek, *Allied Wartime Diplomacy*, p. 121.

100. Raczyński, *W Londynie*, p. 170.

101. *FR, 1942*, III, 200–201.

102. Sherwood, *Roosevelt*, p. 710.

103. *Izvestija*, 2 March 1943, in *Dokumenty*, vol. 7, p. 381.

104. Woodward, *British Foreign Policy*, vol. 2, p. 622.

105. Feis, *Churchill*, p. 123.

106. Raczyński, *W Londynie*, p. 170.

107. *Historia polskiego ruchu robotniczego*, vol. 2, pp. 120–21; *Polski ruch robotniczy*, pp. 360–61; Kowalski, *Walka dyplomatyczna*, p. 379.

108. Pobóg-Malinowski, *Najnowsza historia*, vol. 3, p. 562.

109. A. Lampe, "Wolność jest niepodzielna," *Nowe Widnokręgi*, 5 March 1943, in *Publicystyka Związku Patriotów Polskich 1943–1944. Wybór* (Warsaw: Książka i Wiedza, 1963), pp. 26–31.

110. Zabiełło, *O rząd*, p. 110.

111. W. Grosz, "Chcemy walczyć z bronią w ręku," in *Publicystyka ZPP*, pp. 56–59.

112. *Dokumenty*, vol. 7, pp. 352–53.

113. G. Kolko offers a comment on Polish reaction to the Katyn affair which is a little too noncommittal. *See* his *Politics of War: The World and United States Foreign Policy, 1943–1945* (New York: Vintage Books, 1968), pp. 104-6. Even historians of People's Poland whom no one would suspect of "class solidarity" with the murdered officers neither affirm nor deny Russian guilt; *see*, for example, Kowalski, *Wielka koalicja*, vol. 1, pp. 344–46.

114. *Dokumenty*, vol. 7, pp. 356–57.

115. *Correspondence*, vol. 1, pp. 124–25.

116. On Churchill's emphasis on government rather than frontiers, *see* Woodward, *British Foreign Policy*, vol. 2, pp. 635, 648.

117. *Perepiska predsedatelja soveta ministrov SSSR s prezidentami SŠA i prem'er-ministrami Velikobritanii vo vremja Velikoj Otečestvennoj vojny 1941–1945 gg.* (Moscow: Politzdat, 1957), vol. 1, pp. 126–27.

118. *Dokumenty*, vol. 7, p. 413. On the background of the Churchill-Stalin correspondence, *see* Woodward, *British Foreign Policy*, vol. 2, pp. 629–31.

119. *Correspondence*, vol. 1, pp. 129–30.

120. Ciechanowski, *Defeat in Victory*, p. 161. Cf. Pobóg-Malinowski, *Najnowsza historia*, vol. 3, p. 294, footnote 153; Rozek, *Allied Wartime Diplomacy*, p. 122.
121. *FR, 1943*, III, 428–30, 434–37. Cf. Davis, *Cold War*, pp. 50–56.
122. Ciechanowski, *Defeat in Victory*, p. 177.
123. Zabiełło, *O rząd*, pp. 132–33. *See also* Molotov's comments on the new Polish government, *FR, General, 1943*, I, 668.
124. *FR, 1943*, III, 445–46, 451–53, 461–67; *Documents*, vol. 2, pp. 30–31, 56–61; Woodward, *British Foreign Policy*, vol. 2, pp. 635–39. Cf. Beitzell, *Uneasy Alliance*, pp. 158–60.
125. Eden, *Reckoning*, pp. 413; Hull, *Memoirs*, vol. 2, p. 1273; *FR, 1943*, I, 622–23, 667–68.
126. Woodward, *British Foreign Policy*, vol. 2, pp. 638–40.
127. Ibid., vol. 2, pp. 639, 640. So far as the writer knows, there are neither documents nor studies on the American side that refer to the fact that the president had already, before Teheran, intimated to the Soviets his readiness to accept Soviet territorial demands regarding Poland—perhaps as early as March 1942 (*see* note 42, above), but certainly by August 1943.
128. Woodward, *British Foreign Policy*, vol. 2, p. 649.
129. The following description is based on *FR, The Conferences at Cairo and Tehran, 1943*, 511–12, 594–95, 597–600, 603–4, 885; *Tegeran, Jalta, Potsdam. Sbornik dokumentov* (Moscow: Izdatel'stvo "Meždunarodnye otnošenija," 1971), pp. 90–93, 95–96. Churchill, *Second World War*, vol. 5, *Closing the Ring* (1951), pp. 361–62, 394–97, 403; C. E. Bohlen, *Witness to History 1929–1969* (New York: Norton, 1973), pp. 144, 151–53; V. M. Berežkov, *Gody diplomatičeskoj služby* (Moscow: Izdatel'stvo "Meždunarodnye otnošenija," 1972), pp. 201–5.
130. Roosevelt did not inform the State Department about the conversation with Stalin. *See* Beitzell, *Uneasy Alliance*, p. 347.
131. Kowalski, *Wielka koalicja*, vol. 1, p. 707. *See also* Zabiełło, *O rząd*, p. 170.
132. J. Karski's statement to Roosevelt on 28 June 1943 cited in J. Ciechanowski, *Defeat in Victory*, p. 188. This seems to be true. At the time of the Warsaw uprising, when the commander of the home army took into his hands all the reins of power in the liberated city, he did not take any measures against the Communists; *see* T. Bór-Komorowski, *The Secret Army* (London: Victor Gollancz, 1950), p. 242.
133. V. Dedijer, *Tito Speaks: His Self-Portrait And Struggle with Stalin* (London: Weidenfeld and Nicolson, 1953), pp. 207–8.
134. "Miejsce Polski w Europie," *Publicystyka ZPP*, pp. 65–74.
135. *Dokumenty*, vol. 7, pp. 360–61.
136. M. K. Dziewanowski, *The Communist Party of Poland: An Outline of History* (Cambridge: Harvard University Press, 1959), p. 166.
137. *Kształtowanie się*, pp. 449–56; *Stosunki polsko-radzieckie w latach 1917–1945: Dokumenty i materiały* (Warsaw: Książka i Wiedza, 1967), pp. 361–65.
138. *Dokumenty*, vol. 7, pp. 364–65.
139. Ibid., p. 365. *See also* ibid., pp. 370, 374–75.
140. *See* O. Lange's report, *FR, The British Commonwealth and Europe, 1944*, III, 1420; *Documents*, vol. 2, p. 260.
141. S. Kot, *Rozmowy z Kremlem* (London: Jutro Polski, 1959), pp. 128–29.
142. *Polski czyn zbrojny w II wojnie światowej*, vol. 3: *Ludowe Wojsko Polskie 1943–1945* (Warsaw: Wydawnictwo MON, 1973), p. 88.
143. Ibid., p. 93.
144. Ibid., pp. 89–90.
145. *See* O. Lange's report, *Documents*, vol. 2, p. 260.
146. *Polski czyn zbrojny*, vol. 3, pp. 88, 91.
147. Ibid., p. 120.
148. Kundjuba, *Sovetsko-pol'skie otnošenija*, pp. 142–43.
149. *Polski czyn zbrojny*, vol. 3, pp. 45, 97.

150. W. Bronska-Pampuch, *Polen zwischen Hoffnung und Verzweiflung* (Koln: Verlag für Politik und Wirtschaft, 1958), pp. 94–95.

151. *Kształtowanie się*, p. 70.

152. W. Gomułka, *Artykuły i przemówienia*, vol. 1 (Warsaw: Książka i Wiedza, 1962), pp. 7–17.

153. *Polski ruch robotniczy*, p. 264. For general background of the negotiations, *see* ibid., pp. 263–67; *Historia polskiego ruchu robotniczego*, vol. 2, pp. 361–62, 407–8; W. Góra, R. Halaba, *O utworzenie i utrwalenie władzy ludowej 1944–1948. Wybrane zagadnienia* (Warsaw: Książka i Wiedza, 1968), pp. 32–43; N. Bethell, *Gomulka: His Poland and His Communism* (New York: Holt, Rinehart and Winston, 1969), pp. 56–58; Bór-Komorowski, *Secret Army*, p. 124.

154. *Kształtowanie się*, pp. 93–96.

155. *Polski ruch robotniczy*, p. 265.

156. "Perepiska General'nogo sekretarja IKKI G. G. Dimitrova s rukovodstvom Pol'koj Rabočej Partii 1942–1943 gg.," *Novaja i novejšaja istorija* 5 (1964): 122–23.

157. "Zadanie naczelne," *Trybuna wolności*, 15 May 1943, in *Publicystyka PPR*, vol. 2, pp. 167–70.

158. *Polski ruch robotniczy*, p. 305.

159. "O Polskę demokratyczną," *Publicystyka PPR*, vol. 2, pp. 231–33.

160. "O myśl polityczną polskiej demokracji," ibid., pp. 308–17. The authorship of the article is ascribed to Gomułka; *see* Gomułka, *Artykuły*, vol. 1, pp. 18–29.

161. "Od Gwardii to Armii Ludowej," *Gwardista*, 1 July 1943, in *Publicystyka PPR*, vol. 2, pp. 196–98. *See also* related articles in ibid., pp. 243–45, 563–66.

162. *Kształtowanie się*, pp. 140–69.

163. *See* the resolution of the January 1943 plenum of the central committee of the PWP, ibid., p. 71.

164. The last echo of the campaign for National Committees for Struggle is found in "W przededniu rozstrzygających bojów," *Trybuna wolności*, 1 July 1943, in *Publicystyka PPR*, vol. 2, pp. 223–25.

165. "Rozwiązanie Kominternu," *Okólnik KC PPR*, 1 June 1943; "Rozwiązanie Kominternu," *Trybuna wolności*, 1 June 1943, in *Publicystyka PPR*, vol. 2, pp. 189–93, 201–6, respectively. But the PWP continued to receive instructions from and send reports to Dimitrov.

166. Malinowski, *Geneza PPR*, pp. 358, 361.

167. Gomułka, *Artykuły*, vol. 1, pp. 44–51.

168. On the negotiations with various undergound groups, see *Historia polskiego ruchu robotniczego*, vol. 2, pp. 113–20, 126, 130; *Polski ruch robotniczy*, pp. 384–96.

169. *Kształtowanie się*, pp. 469–73.

170. J. Pawłowicz, "Uwagi na temat kształtowania się strategii PPR i międzynarodowego ruchu robotniczego w okresie II wojny światowej," *Z Pola Walki*, no. 1 (1964): 40; F. Zbieniewicz, "U źródeł powstania PKWN i Ludowego Wojska Polskiego," *Z Pola Walki*, no. 4 (1964): 44–46; W. Góra, *Powstanie władzy ludowej w Polsce: Z zagadnień kształtowania się zalązków ludowego aparatu władzy w latach 1943–1944* (Warsaw: Książka i Wiedza, 1972), p. 84.

171. *Stosunki polsko-radzieckie*, pp. 377–78.

172. "The new tactics of the PWP was worked out independently by the party and represented the only possible and correct line under the given conditions" (Góra, Halaba, *O utworzenie*, p. 59). *See also* ibid., p. 67; Góra, *Powstanie*, p. 91; "*The tactics of a democratic national front was the independent and original creation of the PWP*," Pawłowicz, "Uwagi," p. 38. Cf. Bethell, *Gomulka*, pp. 70–72.

173. This document has not yet been made accessible in full but is cited by various Polish writers; *see*, for example, *Polski czyn zbrojny*, vol. 3, pp. 97–98; Góra, Halaba, *O utworzenie*, p. 56; Zabiełło, *O rząd*, pp. 182–83; A. Przygoński, "Z rozważań Alfreda Lampego o nowej Polsce," *Z Pola Walki*, no. 2 (1964): 105.

174. *Documents*, vol. 2, p. 262.

175. *Kształtowanie się*, pp. 474–87. The Soviet press reported in January 1944 that a

certain Dr. Penzik proposed to establish a Polish national liberation committee in the Soviet Union. *See* G. H. Janczewski, "The Origins of the Lublin Government," *The Slavonic and East European Review* (July 1972): 429, footnote 87. It is not clear how this proposal was related to the PNC.

176. Gomułka, *Artykuły*, vol. 1, p. 61–76.

177. *Kształtowanie się*, p. 71.

178. *Polski ruch robotniczy*, p. 369; *Historia polskiego ruchu robotniczego*, vol. 2, p. 125.

179. Góra, *Powstanie*, pp. 81–82.

180. Kowalski, *Walka dyplomatyczna* (1965 editon), p. 390, footnote 92. The citation is dropped in the 1972 edition.

181. Góra, Halaba, *O utworzenie*, p. 67.

182. Ibid., p. 68; Góra, *Powstanie*, p. 83; *Polski ruch robotniczy*, pp. 455–56; Pawłowicz, "Uwagi," p. 39.

183. *Documents*, vol. 2, p. 236.

184. Góra, *Powstanie*, pp. 83–84; *Polski ruch robotniczy*, pp. 456–57; Pawłowicz, "Uwagi," p. 40. P. K. Raina, *Władysław Gomułka. Życiorys polityczny* (London: Polonia Book Fund, 1969), and its modified 1970 German edition (*Gomulka. Politische Biographie*, Köln: Verlag Wissenschaft und Politik), are confusing and unreliable as regards the relations of the PWP, the NCH, the UPP, and the COPC to one another as well as the content of the correspondence between Gomułka and Dimitrov; *see* Itō, "Sengo Pōrando no seiritsu: Soren gaikō to Pōrando rōdōshatō no senjutsu, 1943–1945 nen, *Surabu kenkyū* 18 (1973): 131–32, footnotes 12, 16.

185. According to contemporary Polish historiography, "In this situation the central committee of the PWP perceived the possibility and understood the necessity to create a democratic national front at home under its political leadership by means of the unification of people's masses in the first place." *Polski ruch robotniczy*, p. 377.

186. "Utworzenie Krajowej Rady Narodowej," *Wolna Polska*, 8 February 1944, in *Publicystyka ŻPP*, pp. 270–73. This is the text of an announcement broadcast through the Polish language radio station "Radio Kościuszko" in Moscow on 30 January 1944. An English translation is found in *FR, 1944*, III, 1399–401. On the reference to the NCH in the Russian language press, *see* footnote 211.

187. E. Beneš, *The Memoirs: From Munich to New War and New Victory* (Boston: Houghton Mifflin, 1954), pp. 263–68; Churchill, *Second World War*, vol. 4, p. 400; *Documents*, vol. 2, pp. 129–32; *FR, 1944*, III, 1221–22.

188. *Documents*, vol. 2, pp. 123–24; *FR, 1944*, III, 1218–20.

189. *Perepiska*, vol. 1, p. 182.

190. *Dokumenty*, vol. 8, pp. 21–23; *FR, 1944*, III, 1218–20.

191. Ibid., 1230, *see also* 1265.

192. Ibid., 1231, 1265, 1398–99, 1402.

193. *Correspondence*, vol. 1, pp. 192–95.

194. *Perepiska*, vol. 1, p. 35. Cf. note 119.

195. *Correspondence*, vol. 2, pp. 119–20. On the dating of the telegram, see *FR, 1944*, III, 1242, footnote 65. Cf. Roosevelt to Churchill, 7 February 1944, *Roosevelt and Churchill*, pp. 429–31.

196. *FR, 1944*, III, 1267–68.

197. *See* conversations between Churchill and Mikołajczyk on 20 January and 6 and 16 February, *Documents*, vol. 2, pp. 144–49, 165–71, 180–87. See also *FR, 1944*, III, 1249–57; S. Mikołajczyk, *The Pattern of Soviet Domination* (London: Sampson Low, Marston, 1948), pp. 56–59; Woodward, *British Foreign Policy*, vol. 3, pp. 161–67.

198. *FR, 1944*, III, 1224.

199. Ibid., 1279, footnote 18.

200. *See* O. Lange's report, *Documents*, vol. 2, pp. 238–39; *FR, 1944*, III, 1421. Cf. *Polski czyn zbrojny*, vol. 3, pp. 100–101.

201. *Documents*, vol. 2, pp. 179–80.

202. Kowalski, *Walka dyplomatyczna*, pp. 445–49; Kowalski, *Wielka koalicja*, vol. 2, pp. 41–44.

203. *Correspondence*, vol. 1, pp. 201–4.
204. *Documents*, vol. 2, pp. 194–96; Mikołajczyk, *Pattern*, pp. 59–60.
205. *Correspondence*, vol. 1, pp. 211–12.
206. *Perepiska*, vol. 1, pp. 213–15.
207. *FR, 1944*, III, 1265.
208. J. S. Haneman's report, *Dokumenty*, vol. 8, pp. 162–67; Kowalski, *Wielka koalicja*, vol. 2, pp. 271–75.
209. *Documents*, vol. 2, p. 238. Cf. *FR, 1944*, III, 1409–11, 1419.
210. Bethell, *Gomulka*, pp. 148, 156. Cf. Zbieniewicz, "U źródel," p. 51.
211. *FR, 1944*, III, 1412–13. *See also* "Kraj przewodzi w walce o wolność," *Wolna Polska*, 24 May 1944, in *Publicystyka ŻPP*, pp. 368–71.
212. Kowalski, *Walka dyplomatyczna*, pp. 463–64.
213. Ibid., p. 465.
214. *See* Haneman's report, *Dokumenty*, vol. 8, pp. 168–69.
215. Woodward, *British Foreign Policy*, vol. 3, pp. 189–90; Raczyński, *W Londynie*, p. 269.
216. Woodward, *British Foreign Policy*, vol. 3, pp. 190–91; *Documents*, vol. 2, p. 252.
217. *FR, 1944*, III, 1414.
218. Ibid., 1414–17.
219. Mikołajczyk, *Pattern*, p. 69; *Documents*, vol. 2, pp. 259–60; J. Ciechanowski, *Defeat in Victory*, p. 312.
220. Mikołajczyk, *Pattern*, pp. 71–72; Raczyński, *W Londynie*, p. 268; *FR, 1944*, III, 1292–96; Woodward, *British Foreign Policy*, vol. 2, pp. 192–93.
221. Haneman's report, *Dokumenty*, vol. 8, p. 169; Kowalski, *Walka dyplomatyczna*, p. 478.
222. *Dokumenty*, vol. 8, pp. 117–18; *Publicystyka ŻPP*, pp. 406–8. An incomplete English translation is found in *FR, 1944*, III, 1422–23.
223. *Perepiska*, vol. 2, pp. 147–48.
224. *FR, 1944*, III, 1423.
225. *Polski ruch robotniczy*, pp. 412–16, 452–55.
226. "Nasze stanowisko," *Publicystyka PPR*, vol. 3, pp. 299–309.
227. Gomułka, *Artykuły*, vol. 1, p. 142.
228. Bethell, *Gomulka*, pp. 147–49, 153–56. According to G. Rohde, W. Gomułka allegedly pleaded for a union with the right-wing groups and for a joint parliament with the council of national unity at the May 29, 1944, meeting of the central committee of the PWP. G. Rohde, "Die politische Entwicklung Polens im zweiten Weltkrieg," *Handbuch Polen*, ed. W. Markert (Köln/Wien: Verlag Böhlau, 1959), p. 209. But there is no evidence of such an assertion.
229. *Polski ruch robotniczy*, pp. 416–20, 457–62; *Historia polskiego ruchu robotniczego*, vol. 2, pp. 137–50.
230. *Polski ruch robotniczy*, p. 486.
231. Ibid., pp. 464–74.
232. *Documents*, vol. 2, p. 251; *FR, 1944*, III, 1281, 1285–89; J. Ciechanowski, *Defeat in Victory*, p. 305; Mikołajczyk, *Pattern*, p. 66.
233. *Correspondence*, vol. 2, pp. 146–47.
234. Woodward, *British Foreign Policy*, vol. 3, p. 189.
235. *Dokumenty*, vol. 8, pp. 169–71; Góra, *Powstanie*, pp. 144–46; Kowalski, *Walka dyplomatyczna*, pp. 486–91; Zbeniewicz, "U źródeł," pp. 58–64; N. Kołomejczyk, B. Syzdek, *Polska w latach 1944–1949. Zarys historii politycznej* (Warsaw: Państwowe Zakłady Wydawnictw Szkolnych, 1963), pp. 14–16.
236. *Dokumenty*, vol. 8, pp. 129–31.
237. Marshal Żukov writes in his memoirs: "[On July 8, Stalin said to him at a conference:] 'Tomorrow you will meet Bierut, Osóbka-Morawski, and Rola-Żymierski at my home. They represent a Polish committe of national liberation. Twenty in number, they are going to approach the Polish people with a manifesto. As our rep-

resentative for the Poles we will send Bulganin. . . .' In the evening I was invited to Stalin's villa where there were already Bierut, Osóbka-Morawski, and Rola-Żymierski. . . . Members of the Polish committee of national liberation and the national council of the homeland were dreaming of a quick liberation of their fatherland. As a result of the joint discussion, it was decided that Lublin would be the first city where the national council of the homeland would begin its organizing activities." G. K. Żukov, *Vospominanija i razmyšlenija*, vol. 2 (Moscow: Izdatel'stvo Agentstva pečati Novosti, 1974), p. 262. This report includes some incorrect information. For example, B. Bierut was at that time still in Warsaw, not in Moscow, and it was much later that the name "Polish committee of national liberation" was adopted.

238. A stenogram of the discussion on the draft agreement is found in *Dokumenty*, vol. 8, pp. 135–38.

239. *Perepiska*, vol. 1, pp. 244–45.

240. *Documents*, vol. 2, p. 262.

241. The manifesto is reprinted in *Stosunki polsko-radzieckie*, pp. 384–90; Kołomejczyk, Syzdek, *Polska*, pp. 281–85.

242. Góra, *Powstanie*, pp. 129–30, 134–36; Kowalski, *Wielka koalicja*, vol. 2, p. 276.

243. *Documents*, vol. 2, pp. 235–36; Kowalski, *Walka dyplomatyczna*, p. 482; Góra, *Powstanie*, p. 135–36.

244. *Polski ruch robotniczy*, pp. 456–57.

245. Góra, *Powstanie*, p. 154.

246. Ibid., p. 78.

247. Some historians stress that the PCNL aimed not only at liberating Poland, but also at revolutionizing Polish society, erroneously stating that the manifesto called for the nationalization of all big- and almost all medium-size enterprises. *See*, for example, H. Shimizu, "Reisen no kigen to Soren gaikō: Pōrando mondai o megutte," *Kokusai mondai* 170 (May 1974): 54, 57.

248. In May 1944 Stalin confided to Lange that he was not sure whether the Poles should get Breslau or not. *Documents*, vol. 2, p. 239.

249. Vierheller points out that the conception of the Oder line as the Polish western frontier originated with the Soviets, while that of the Oder–Western Neisse line came from the Poles. Vierheller, *Polen*, p. 77.

250. J. Ciechanowski, *Defeat in Victory*, p. 306. Cf. *FR, 1944*, III, 1286, 1305.

251. *Documents*, vol. 2, p. 237.

252. Kowalski, *Walka dyplomatyczna*, pp. 491–93; Kowalski, *Polityka zagraniczna RP 1944–1947* (Warsaw: Książka i Wiedza, 1971), pp. 3–4.

253. Kowalski, *Walka dyplomatyczna*, p. 486.

254. Ibid., pp. 494–95.

255. *Dokumenty*, vol. 8, pp. 158–59.

256. Feis, *Churchill*, p. 521.

257. Zabiełło, *O rząd*, p. 154.

258. *Polski czyn zbrojny*, vol. 3, p. 181.

259. Mikołajczyk, *Pattern*, p. 78.

260. *Documents*, vol. 2, pp. 309–22, 325–33; Mikołajczyk, *Pattern*, pp. 81–85; *FR, 1944*, III, 1306–15.

261. *See*, for example, P. N. Pospelov, ed., *Istorija Velikoj Otečestvennoj vojny Sovetskogo Sojuza 1941-1945 gg.*, vol. 4 (Moscow: Voenizdat, 1962), p. 243; A. J. Manusevič, I. A. Chrenova, *Očerki istorii Narodnoj Pol'ši* (Moscow: Izdatel'stvo "Nauka," 1965), p. 29.

262. Itō, "Sengo Pōrando no seiritsu," pp. 141–44.

263. Gomułka, *Artykuły*, vol. 1, pp. 278–79.

264. Feis, *Churchill*, pp. 521–29, 571–76.

265. *Roosevelt and Churchill*, p. 705.

266. H. Feis, *Between War and Peace: The Potsdam Conference* (Princeton: Princeton University Press, 1960), pp. 102–10.

267. Gomułka, *Artykuły*, vol. 1, pp. 295–96.

268. Churchill to Stalin, 22 November 1941, *Correspondence*, vol. 1, p. 35; Stalin to Churchill, 23 November 1941, *Perepiska*, vol. 1, p. 34.

269. *FR, The Conferences at Malta and Yalta*, p. 669; *Tegeran, Jalta, Potsdam*, p. 145.

270. A penetrating analysis of the *szlachta* political culture of interwar Poland is provided by Miyajima Naoki, "Senkanki Pōrando to Piłsudski. Seiji ni okeru shinwa," *Hōgaku shimpō* 79 no. 1 (1972): 43–110; no. 2: 29–84; no. 3: 75–112; no. 5: 55–84; no. 12: 61–86; "Piłsudski densetsu to Pōrandojin no kachikan," *Hōgaku shimpō* 81, no. 5 (1974): 1–68.

The Sino-Soviet Confrontation in Historical Perspective

Nakajima Mineo

The Structure of Conflict and the Border Regions

The Sino-Soviet conflict is a composite of four levels of confrontation: nation-to-nation; state-to-state; party-to-party; and government-to-government. The first is a confrontation of two separate nationalisms; the second, one of national interest; the third is ideological, a conflict over doctrinal orthodoxy; and the fourth involves diplomatic relationship.

Nation-to-nation conflict is probably the most deeply rooted and historically inevitable. The meeting of the Russian and Chinese peoples in the last three hundred years has been accompanied by a great deal of friction. At no time has one side ever held complete sway over the other, but both have been conquered by the Mongol Empire, and this shared historical nightmare is a stimulus to their nationalistic emotions. The image of a powerful Russian nation and that of the Mongol Empire seem to overlap in the minds of the Han people, constituting a "threat from the north," while, on the other hand, the Russians have always abhorred the notion of a strongly unified China, calling it the "threat from the southeast."

The second level of conflict, state-to-state, is over borders and territories, and has continued unabated since the Nerchinsk treaty of 1689. This conflict is so tenacious that it quickly overwhelmed the spirit of Leninist internationalism spelled out in the Karakhan manifesto of July 1919. With the subsequent rise of Stalinism

203

and Maoism, the national interest of both nations was provided with ideological justification, making the two nations increasingly more incompatible. The Sino-Soviet rift has escalated from theoretical dispute to confrontation in every phase of relationship between the two socialist states. (As ironic as it may seem, Taipei and Peking are in total agreement as far as border and territorial issues are concerned, paradoxical evidence that the confrontation stems from roots far deeper than the realm of ideology.)

The third level, party-to-party, is a variable factor in the confrontation structure. In the future, the two countries will probably exhibit the same degree of restorative capacity that they have in the past to accommodate their doctrinal differences, but this, of course, will depend on changes in their respective domestic situations. The reason is that Sino-Soviet relations have a high degree of correlation to factional struggles within the parties, particularly in the Chinese Communist party (CCP). This, in turn, means that ideological conflict will be affected one way or the other by the outcome of the intraparty struggle or by changes in leadership.

The fourth level, government-to-government, is a superficial confrontation, and is the level most subject to internal political changes. Following the death of Mao Tse-tung, the possibility of a restoration on this level can be foreseen.

The ideological confrontation between China and the Soviet Union became increasingly more serious, although covert, after the beginning of de-Stalinization in 1956, and by the sixties it was an overt part of the conflict on both the party-to-party and government-to-government levels. Nation-to-nation and state-to-state conflict, however, date back long before the birth of the People's Republic of China. A number of potentially explosive issues began to surface during modern China's formative years—in the process of the Chinese revolution in its broader meaning. The areas bordering on either or both of these two great powers, such as Mongolia, Manchuria (Tungpei or Northeast), and Sinkiang, have often been scenes of collision between Chinese and Soviet nationalism, stages in their power struggle for spheres of influence. In one way the involvement of those smaller nations has been the source of the historical dynamics in Sino-Soviet relations.[1]

Confrontation over the sovereignty of Outer Mongolia began at the time of the 1911 revolution and has continued on until today. The declaration adopted by the second convention of the CCP referred to the "liberation" of Mongolia and the prospect of incorporating Mongolia into a Federal Republic of China. Mao Tse-tung talked about the issue in his interview with Edgar Snow in 1936. The issue survived through the Yalta agreement of 1945, the Chinese-Soviet Friendship and Alliance Pact of the same year between Stalin and Chiang Kai-shek (hereinafter referred to as the Chinese-Soviet Pact), the Sino-Soviet Treaty of Friendship, Alliance and Mutual Assistance of 1950 between Stalin and Mao Tse-tung (hereinafter referred to as Sino-Soviet Treaty), and the Sino-Soviet talks in 1954 during Khrushchev's visit to Peking. After the most dramatic series of strategic interplays between the two powers, the problem is still not settled, insofar as the Mongolians remain divided into the Mongolian People's Republic and, within Chinese territory, the Inner Mongolian Autonomous Region.

The memoirs of Otto Braun, who died recently, contain a startling exposé about his experience as an adviser to the CCP during the latter part of the Comintern era.[2] Braun says that Mao Tse-tung's strategy, involving Mongolia and Sinkiang, toward the Soviet Union in the late 1930s was an ambitious attempt to draw the Soviet Union into the war against Japan. About this time Mao Tse-tung's repulsion of Stalin and the Comintern had taken on clear shape. His anti-Soviet and anti-Stalin attitudes probably deepened through the intense struggles with the Twenty-eight Bolsheviks (including Wang Ming [Ch'en Shao-yü], Po Ku [Chin Pang-hsien], and Lo Fu [Chang Wen-tien], and others), an opposition faction within the CCP during the Yenan period in the early 1940s.[3]

On the fluid historical conditions of Sinkiang, which have now become a focal point for Sino-Soviet border clashes, one need only recall that there was a plan for an "East Turkestan Republic" toward the end of World War II. Historically, however, Manchuria has been the most important stage for the Sino-Soviet conflict. From the Yalta agreement and the Chinese-Soviet Pact of 1945, all the way down to the Sino-Soviet Treaty of 1950, both Chiang Kai-shek and Mao Tse-tung fought against but had to yield to Stalin's demands for ice-free ports—Port Arthur and Dairen, and railways—the East China and Manchurian (later Changchun) railways.

The Korean peninsula, on the other hand, has been the buffer zone for China and the Soviet Union. This was obvious when T. V. Soong (Sung Tzu-wen) was carrying out talks centered on the Chinese-Soviet pact on behalf of the Kuomintang (KMT) government, which had been dumbfounded by the secret deals at Yalta; at that time the Soviet Union and China were quick to agree on the "independence" of Korea, quite unlike England and the United States. By its very nature, however, a buffer zone can easily be sacrificed by the conflicting parties once there is a change in the situation. I am inclined to believe that there was such an aspect to the Korean War.

Sino-Soviet relations, nurtured in this particular historical milieu, have had a highly dynamic background of strategic considerations[4] and been the most important factor in the postwar environment of Asia as well. Following the end of World War II American leaders had some historical insight into the possibilities of conflict between China and the Soviet Union, but they were unable to penetrate the heart of this conflict. The China White Paper was a document containing many logical inconsistencies, but in its introduction Secretary of State Dean Acheson did express a view of China, not as subservient to the Soviet Union, but rather as a potential Yugoslavia. If the United States had followed that view of China and begun serious talks with the new regime after the autumn of 1949, then perhaps the postwar Asian situation might have been radically different. From diplomatic papers recently made public, it seems clear that Mao had favorable feelings toward the United States in the late forties. When we compare them with his ill feelings toward the Soviet Union, we can see that the United States could have realistically chosen such a policy toward China.[5]

The Dilemma in the Yalta System

The Yalta Conference was held in February 1945 by the leaders of Great Britian, the United States, and the Soviet Union to lay out plans for the postwar international order. However, the Yalta system had built into it elements that would bring about its own destruction soon after the conference started. Within the framework of this unstable structure, the secret provisions concerning East Asia were bound to create problems. Even before Japan was defeated, the Soviet Union and the United States began to harbor mutual doubts about the other's intentions, and the postwar conditions of East Asia were decidedly influenced by those provisions. The beginning of the Cold War in Asia is generally considered to coincide with the outbreak of the Korean War, but in actuality the conflict in Korea was more aptly the beginning of hot war in Asia. The Cold War had begun much earlier; even the failure of the United States, Great Britain, and China to inform the Soviet Union of their final ultimatum to Japan and the American insistence on keeping secret the existence of the atomic bomb were part of the Cold War. A great deal of research has provided material showing that although the United States knew Japan was sending out peace feelers through Moscow, the Americans decided to use the atomic bomb as a means to prevent Soviet participation in the war against Japan as agreed upon at Yalta.

The Soviet Union pointed out at the Potsdam Conference that, as indicated at Yalta, it would declare war against Japan after the conclusion of the Chinese-Soviet Pact. Only two days after the bomb was dropped on Hiroshima they sent adequately prepared troops quickly into Manchuria and swept over the Kwantung Army, disregarding the fact that the Russo-Japanese Neutrality Pact was still in effect.[6] Although the Soviet Union had broken its promises on East Germany and Poland that had been made at the Yalta Conference, it kept its word in Asia. That meant that the U.S. decision to use the atomic bomb involved a double miscalculation, and by keeping the promises made at Yalta, the Soviet Union won a dual victory: the country became one of the victors in East Asia after only a week of fighting, and its Asian policy was executed exactly as planned.

The biggest flaw in the Yalta agreement was that it made a sacrificial object of China, which, although one of the victorious powers, suffered most from the war. The agreement also miscalculated the future of China and made no provisions for responding to the rise of Chinese nationalism. The first American who recognized the dangers inherent in this secret agreement was the ambassador to China, Patrick Hurley. However, Hurley failed in his attempts to revise the Yalta agreement, and when the Kuomintang government discovered what the secret agreement was about, they hurriedly dispatched T. V. Soong to Moscow for discussions with the Soviets. Because of the power relations that existed at that time and the East Asian situation brought about by the Yalta agreement, China had no choice but to succumb to Stalin's arrogant attitude and make one compromise after another. This is clearly revealed in Chiang Kai-shek's memoirs, which were released recently.[7]

The Chinese-Soviet Pact was signed on August 14, 1945, one day before the Japanese surrender, just when the Soviet armies had almost completely occupied all of the northeastern provinces. Even though the treaty had been concluded on the basis of the secret Yalta agreement, it was signed in such a hurry because the Soviet Union wanted to carry out its intended Far Eastern strategy without U.S. interference. In the exchange of notes and appended agreement of the treaty, China had to recognize the independence of Outer Mongolia and agree to the 30-year joint operation of the Changchun railway, the joint use of Port Arthur, and the declaration of Dairen as a free port. In short, the Chinese allowed czarist Russian interests in China to be restored more or less intact, sanctioned by the Yalta agreement.

This treaty was the basis for Soviet relations with the Chiang Kai-shek government right up until the establishment of the People's Republic of China. (The Soviet embassy moved each time Chiang moved his capital—from Nanking to Chungking, Chengtu, and finally to his last capital on the continent, Canton.) The Kuomintang government was continually threatened by the possibility that Stalin would extend aid or recognition to the CCP, and in order to prevent that eventuality, they had to concede many rights to the Soviet Union. The Soviet Union was able to skillfully take advantage of the KMT's weak position, and when the People's Liberation Army (PLA) was pressing on to the Yangtze, the Soviet ambassador was applying pressure to the KMT government to concede rights in Sinkiang.[8]

It was perhaps only natural that the Soviet Union placed much importance on the KMT as the organization that would hand over to the Soviet Union everything that had been established or built in the territories occupied by Soviet armies. Within only a few months after the occupation of the Northeast, the Soviet

Union had transported to its own country the industrial facilities left behind by the Japanese as well as a great number of Japanese prisoners. The U.S. economic investigation team led by Edwin W. Paulay estimated that the assets removed totaled U.S. $858,100,000 and if the depreciation and replacement costs were added, the figure would surpass $2 billion. Another estimate brings the figure closer to $3.5 billion.

That Stalin concluded the Chinese-Soviet Pact with Chiang Kai-shek and maintained diplomatic relations was in line with his consistent refusal to recognize the CCP and with his professed view that "all efforts would go into unifying China under Chiang's leadership." There is a great deal of evidence of what Stalin thought of the CCP at that time. It is very interesting, however, that the present Soviet view holds that the many contacts the Soviet Union had with the Chiang regime, including the 1939 commercial treaty, indicate that the USSR has always had a friendly attitude toward China.[9] Not only did Stalin continue to recognize the KMT government, but he also underestimated the capability of the CCP. Even during the civil war, on the ground that the advance of the PLA would cause the United States to openly intervene, he put all sorts of pressure on the CCP until he somewhat modified his attitude in 1948.[10]

Moscow Meeting

It is worthy of note that, given this situation, Mao Tse-tung gave instructions to establish bases in the Northeast and strengthen the party apparatus there as early as December 1945.[11] It even seems probable that Mao was then considering preparations for Soviet intrusion and was being pressed to decide whether or not he would bargain with the United States. It is significant that the report made by Mao at the second plenary session of the seventh central committee of the CCP in March 1949 implicitly pointed to a moderate line of accommodation with the United States.[12] But later, on July 1, Mao declared that China would adopt a "lean-to-one-side" policy in favor of the Soviet Union in his thesis on the people's democratic dictatorship.[13] He abandoned the Titoist alternative once and for all. That decision was very important, and involved more complex issues than simply the idea that "blood is thicker than water." Then why did Mao Tse-tung make that decision, having had bitter experience with Stalin's China policy on both the state-to-state and party-to-party levels?

Just prior to the establishment of the Chinese People's Republic, Mao foresaw that Soviet aid and advice would be necessary for nation-building. In addition to this obvious reason, several points which form the background of the decision must also be mentioned. First, there was a risk in selecting a policy of appeasement toward the United States because of the power relation that existed between the Soviet Union and China. To have taken that course would have created apprehension about what Stalin would do, judging from the way he acted in the past. Second, Mao had to consider the situation within the CCP at that time. According to Ch'i Pen-yü in his article "Patriotism or National Betrayal," written during the cultural revolution,[14] in 1949 Liu Shao-ch'i and his followers were contemplating turning against Mao and were therefore even more inclined to be conciliatory toward the United States than Mao. Third, and probably most important, is that the decision resulted from a tactical consideration by Mao, to build up a strong sense of nationalism vis-à-vis the Soviet Union.

Mao, now in place of Chiang, had the responsibility for the future of China and was worried about what would happen to Manchuria and Sinkiang, seized under the Yalta agreement and the Chinese-Soviet Pact. Leaning to the Soviet Union side can be seen then as a tactical move. Earlier, in July 1949, Stalin invited Kao Kang, chairman of the people's government in Manchuria, to Moscow without consulting the CCP's leadership, and a trade agreement was concluded between Manchuria and the Soviet Union.[15] This was probably an additional factor governing Mao's decision. Incidentally, there is no official mention of this trade agreement in *Jen-min jih-pao,* but an editorial in *Tung-pei jih-pao* concerning this pact was reprinted in the August 9, 1949, issue of the official national daily. By contrast, the details of the agreement were reported in the July 31 issue of *Izvestija.*[16]

Against a background of these events, Mao set out for Moscow at the head of a group visiting the Soviet Union on December 16, 1949, immediately after the establishment of the People's Republic. He probably expected to receive his first warm welcome from Stalin as the leader of the Chinese revolution, but he was also wary, knowing what had happened before, and burning with the desire to totally reform Sino-Soviet relations. He felt that the visit would be the starting point. Officially, the reason to go to Moscow was to celebrate Stalin's seventieth birthday, but it was Mao's first trip abroad. Stalin, at least on the surface, welcomed Mao, but the reception was far colder than that accorded T. V. Soong some four and a half years before.

Mao told a Tass reporter on January 2, 1950, "I expect to be in the Soviet Union for several more weeks. The length of my stay depends on how long it takes to solve the problems confronting Chinese interests."[17] This was an indication that the talks were in trouble almost from the beginning. Mao Tse-tung finally signed the Sino-Soviet Treaty on February 14, and he signed two other agreements and exchange of notes before he returned to Peking on March 4. It is rather unusual for the top leader of a country to stay in another nation for more than two months and a half so soon after establishing his regime. Moreover, Mao was accompanied in Moscow by Ch'en Po-ta, his political secretary, who was extremely proficient in Russian. But by January 20, Mao called to Moscow Chou En-lai, premier of the Government Administration Council and concurrently minister of foreign affairs; Li Fu-ch'un, vice-chairman, Northeast (Tungpei) People's government; Yeh Hsiu-chuang, minister of trade; and Wu Hsiu-lo, director of the USSR and East European Department, Ministry of Foreign Affairs. On January 30, they were joined by Saifudin, vice-chairman, Sinkiang Provincial People's government.

It is clear from the two additional agreements and the protocol that were signed later that in these talks with China, Stalin again demanded concession of rights from the Chinese, including ice-free ports and railways. We can easily surmise from the list of Chinese negotiators who later joined in the talks that the Northeast and Sinkiang had again become important issues. Further, problems seem to have arisen over what to to about the trade agreement concluded by Kao Kang for the Northeast.

China and the Soviet Union flaunted their monolithic unity in the Sino-Soviet Treaty as well as making it an alliance that would defend against any revival of Japanese militarism. It was a military alliance in which the United States and Japan were regarded as potential enemies, but in all of the pending questions between China and the Soviet Union, the Chinese won concessions, at least more than what was gained by the Chinese-Soviet Pact of 1945. The treaty provided for the free return of the Changchun railway to China by the end of 1952, the withdrawal of Soviet troops, and the return of facilities at Port Arthur after the conclusion of peace with Japan or before the end of 1952 (in the case of war, then the port would be used jointly). The problems surrounding the port of Dairen would be left for discussion after the peace treaty with Japan. The talks indicate Mao's strong sense of equality vis-à-vis the Soviet Union and the strong impact of the victorious Chinese revolution on Stalin. However, China had to go along with the Soviets for a joint operation of enterprises to exploit petroleum and nonferrous metals in Sinkiang and to submit to Soviet demands that the independence of Outer Mongolia be recognized.

The 1950 Sino-Soviet talks must have left Mao half-satisfied and half-frustrated, but at the tenth plenum of the eighth central committee in September 1962 he made a confession in which he said that "Stalin did not want to sign, but after two months of further negotiation he finally signed."[18] It is clear today that at private meetings in China as early as 1957 and 1958 Mao Tse-tung revealed what went on in the Sino-Soviet talks. In January 1957, Mao is quoted as saying, "Our opinions differed from Stalin's. We were ready to sign but he was not, and we demanded the Chinese Changchun Railway, but he wouldn't give it back. But one can after all take the meat out of the tiger's mouth."[19] In the speech of March 1958 he said, "Stalin and I argued for two months in Moscow in 1950. Our attitude toward the Sino-Soviet Treaty, the Changchun Railway, the joint-stock companies and border issues was to hear the proposals that Stalin made first and then argue with him over the ones that we did not like. The ones that he would push vigorously, we would accept. We did this in consideration of socialism's overall interest. There remained the problems of the colonial areas, Sinkiang and the Northeast. It was not to be tolerated that foreign nationals live there. This has now been solved."[20]

At any rate dissatisfaction remained with Mao after the Moscow meeting; the establishment of the joint-stock companies in Sinkiang served as a new provocation and deepened Mao's antipathy toward the Soviet Union. It was considered equivalent to a policy of Soviet colonialism and later provided a basis for the criticism of Stalin. Moreover, the total amount of aid loans that the Soviet Union promised China was only U.S. $300 million with interest. At the signing ceremony, the Soviet foreign minister's attitude was like that of an arrogant alms-giver.[21] Khrushchev said in his secret report that "Stalin treated Mao Tse-tung like a beggar."[22] In all probability Mao found the typical chauvinism in Stalin and Vishinsky and felt extremely indignant at heart. Such was the true picture of the Moscow meeting—the meeting projected to the world as the manifestation of brotherly friendship and monolithic unity.

Major Miscalculations in U.S. Asian Policy

While Mao was not totally satisfied with the Moscow meeting, it gave the newly born people's republic heightened prestige abroad and ensured a more stable position for the CCP within the country. To do this, China brandished the unity of socialist nations with the Soviet Union like an elder brother. It also had a decisive effect on Mao's view of the Soviet Union and Stalin and eventually brought about a new phase in Sino-Soviet relations in which China sought to equalize its position vis-à-vis the USSR.

The United States had abundant information on China, which finally resulted in the voluminous China White Paper of August 1949 by the State Department. But the State Department was not allowed to make full use of its wisdom. The White Paper was a kind of self-criticism of the previous one hundred years of U.S.-China relations,[23] but as the lofty introduction (Letter of Transmittal) by Secretary of State Acheson shows, there was a logical conflict between the idea of China as a potential Yugoslavia and the attitude that China was subordinate to the Soviet Union. Acheson expressly charged that "the Communist leaders have foresworn their Chinese heritage and have publicly announced their subservience to a foreign power, Russia. . . ."[24] On this point as well we would have to say that the United States was unable to understand what was behind Mao's declaration of the "lean to one side" policy.

As American leaders witnessed the unfolding of events in China with the establishment of the people's republic and the flight of the Chiang government to Taiwan, they again placed their hopes in the possibility of a new Titoism. By the end of 1949, they already foresaw the fall of Taiwan, but were prepared not to intervene. Then in January 1950 President Truman made a statement calling for nonintervention in the Taiwan problem,[25] followed by the famous Acheson speech at the National Press Club on January 12, in which the secretary stated that the U.S. defense line went through the Aleutians, Japan, Okinawa, and the Philippines, but excluded Taiwan and Korea.[26]

If the United States had maintained that China policy, then the result might have been very good, for a great abyss in thinking between Mao and Stalin was emerging just at that time in Moscow. But the conclusion of the Sino-Soviet Mutual Assistance Treaty was a great shock to the United States. Two days after the treaty was signed, on February 16, Acheson again said, "They [the Chinese] were completely subservient to the Moscow regime," a clear statement of the "loss of China" theory.[27] There is also another way of looking at the shift in policy: the Acheson statement is part of the response made at the beginning of the communist witch hunt by Senator Joseph McCarthy.[28] But basically, what was occurring was the adaptation of part of the logical conflict that existed within the China paper: that part which saw China as subservient to the Soviet Union. The concept of Titoization was maintained as a passive idea, an American hope, and it never developed into any active policy, at least not during the time that Mao and Stalin were locked in serious conflict. Then the Korean War broke out.

The Korean War and China[29]

Hypotheses about the War

It seems that all the possible hypotheses about the origins of the Korean War that could be presented have been, ranging from one extreme that places total blame on Stalin to another that labels the war an act of U.S. aggression. A great deal of study has been conducted to unravel the riddle of how the war started and to analyze U.S. Asian policy and its decision-making process. When it comes to relations between North Korea, the Soviet Union, and China, however, there is almost no empirical research except some simplistic guesswork supporting a Sino-Soviet conspiracy theory and theses on Sino–Soviet–North Korean collaboration.[30] D. Horowitz has taken a view similar to I. F. Stone's[31] in analyzing the causes of the war in terms of American and South Korean motives, and he admits that one can see, to some extent, what was actually going on in Washington and East Asia just before the outbreak of the Korean War because a relatively large volume of information on the situation is available. But as far as Communist motivation is concerned, it is impossible to evaluate what was going on with so little information available.[32]

The most simplistic argument in favor of the Sino-Soviet joint conspiracy thesis is based on the premise that some arrangements must have been made between Stalin and Mao Tse-tung in Moscow several months before the war.[33] But most of this conjecture has been brushed aside by the availability of a clear picture of what went on at the Moscow meeting.

In a book into which much time and effort has gone, *Chōsen sensō no boppatsu* [The Outbreak of the Korean War], Shinobu Seizaburō effectively counters those who claim that the Soviet Union, China, and North Korea conspired to start the war.[34] One possible bit of evidence that might refute Shinobu's view is that during Mao's stay in Moscow, a North Korean mission also visited, led by Mao's friend Kim Du-bong, permanent presidium chairman of the Supreme People's Congress.[35] But when we consider what actually went on at the Moscow meeting, it is difficult to believe that Stalin and Mao had the degree of trust in each other necessary for a "conspiracy" that would start the Korean War.

Some subscribers to the joint conspiracy view also point to the fact that after February 1950, the Korean troops that had participated in the PLA were gradually incorporated into the North Korean armed forces. However, a more persuasive interpretation of this troop movement might just simply be that it was the return of Korean soldiers after the scheduled completion of duties with the PLA.[36] Another common contention among those supporting the Sino-Soviet conspiracy thesis is that a secret decision was made by which the Soviet Union had the responsibility for providing weapons and China was in charge of sending troops.[37] However, this too proves to be groundless given the background of the meeting and what was actually happening at the time. As will be discussed in greater detail later, China today criticizes the Soviet Union for having done nothing in the Korean War except sell weapons. If there had been some sort of agreement between the two on the role that each would play in the war, then China would undoubtedly be in no position to criticize the Soviet Union now.

Another view is that some mention must have been made in Moscow of the connection that the coming war would have with the internationalization of the policy of armed liberation. Such conjectures are taken from the fact that both the Cominform and the CCP criticized the Japan Communist party in January 1950.[38] However, even if Stalin and Mao discussed the problems of strategy for world revolution, they probably did not go beyond getting the Cominform to finally recognize the "Liu Shao-ch'i Thesis" for armed revolution in Asia[39] as part of the "Way of Mao Tse-tung." But we have to keep in mind that the "Way of Mao Tse-tung" entails not only aspects of armed revolution, but also those of cooperation with the national bourgeoisie, as Liu Shao-ch'i points out in his "Internationalism and Nationalism." B. T. Ranadive, secretary-general of the Indian Communist party, and others who criticized the "Way of Mao Tse-tung" and advocated a more radical line were censured by the Cominform in March 1950.[40]

China's Frustration

As shown so far, it would be inaccurate to look at China's involvement in the Korean War in terms of Sino-Soviet conspiracy or an assigned division of roles between the two powers. What then was China's position in the background of the war? This question should be examined as thoroughly as possible, using the evidence that is available.

First, attention must be directed to the fact that China is now criticizing the Soviet Union in public for what happened in their relations during the Korean War. China is clearly indignant. One of the earliest examples of this attitude dates from July 13, 1957, right after the sudden shift was made from the Hundred Flowers campaign to the anti-rightist campaign. At the National People's Congress, leaders of the democratic parties each had to make a self-criticism of their part in free speech during the Hundred Flowers campaign. In criticizing himself for statements made against the "lean to one side" policy, Lung Yün, vice-chairman of the National Defense Council, admitted that he had spoken out fervently against the role of the Soviet Union during the Korean War.[41] Following the self-criticism, Lung was temporarily relieved of his position, but after Sino-Soviet relations had definitely turned for the worse, he was returned to the Defense Council in December 1958, showing that by this time the government had officially endorsed his criticism of the Soviet Union. During the Sino-Soviet dispute of 1963, the Chinese position toward the Soviets was made public in an article in *Jen-min jih-pao*. "We have always made the necessary sacrifices and stood at the front-line in the defense of socialism so that the Soviet Union can be kept at the second line."[42] Then, in the "Letter to the Central Committee of the CPSU from the Central Committee of the CCP" of February 29, 1964, the CCP said that during the Korean War, "We made a tremendous sacrifice and spent enormous sums of money for military purposes. . . . We have paid all principal and interest on loans from the Soviet Union at that time. . . . In aiding the Korean War and fighting against the United States, no free aid was ever offered by the Soviet Union."[43] This is exactly the same kind of idea that Lung Yün voiced against the Soviet Union, but here it is presented in an official context. More recently, in January 1972, officials of the Sino-Japanese Friendship Association told members of a Japanese labor delegation from Sōhyō (General Council of Trade Unions of Japan) and Chūritsurōren (Federation of Independent Unions) that "the Soviet Union is a merchant of death. China sent a volunteer army to Korea which gave both blood and life in battle. All the Soviet Union did was sell weapons. Not only did they take the money for those weapons, they also collected interest."[44]

These Chinese statements are indicative of how strong their displeasure is toward the Soviet Union's conduct during the Korean War. Some idea of what the feelings of Chinese leadership were toward the Soviet Union at that time is shown by the fact that there were high tones of praise for the Kremlin at the August 1, 1950, anniversary of the PLA, but no mention whatsoever of the

Soviet Union at the same event in 1951, after China had entered the war.

According to a 1960 RAND Corporation study on Chinese motives for becoming involved in the Korean War, the Chinese entered the war neither in collusion with North Korea nor from pressure exerted by the Soviet Union.[45] The MacArthur strategy was the trigger for China's participation.[46] Perhaps a more basic reason was that if China did not enter the war during this period of unstable relations with the Soviet Union, the danger existed that Soviet armies would again enter the Northeast, which was under the control of the pro-Stalin Kao Kang.[47] As Edgar Snow says, one result of the participation of Chinese volunteer armies in Korea was China's being branded the aggressor by the UN.[48] It also made the People's Republic much more dependent on the Soviet Union, but more than that, it allowed the USSR to avoid direct intervention and continue its role as a "merchant of death." Both these things were ample reason for the strong Chinese antipathy toward the Soviet Union. One other important point is that during this course of events, the liberation of Taiwan was indefinitely postponed.

The Korean War was a great sacrifice for China. While it was developing a stronger system of preparedness to fight a war of resistance against the United States and to help Korea, the Chinese were also upgrading their level of domestic and national unification. Unification was a by-product of preparations for war.

China and the Korean War

It can be inferred, then, that China, rather than actually playing a part in fomenting the Korean War, was caught totally unaware when the war started. That this was the case is shown by three separate facts.

On June, 30, 1950, just five days after the war had begun, China proclaimed its land reform law. Considering the importance of national reconstruction, particularly the years of effort that the CCP had expended on land reform, leads G. Paloczi-Horvath to conclude that there was almost no reason for China to start a war.[49]

Another fact is that at the second central committee meeting of the seventh CCP congress on June 6, 1950, Mao ordered the mobilization (Mobilization for Production and Construction in Peacetime) of part of the PLA solely for domestic construction.[50] Then two days before the war, on June 23, he gave the opening address to the national committee of the People's Political Consultative Conference. His statement was devoted to the two trials of land reform and war, saying that "the trial called war is something that belongs totally to the past."[51]

The third point is that China at that time considered its most important domestic problem yet to be resolved: the liberation of Tibet and Taiwan. Only with the liberation of these two areas could the Chinese revolution be considered complete. In April 1950, the PLA liberated Hainan Island, and in May the Chusan islands were secured. The next objectives were Tibet and Taiwan. The liberation of Tibet was begun in October after the Korean War was well under way. There is a great deal of evidence, however, to show that the plans for attacking Taiwan had been made so that the invasion would take place during that summer.[52] The November 6 editorial in *Jen-min jih-pao* comments on the entrance of China into the Korean War in late October, saying that there was a great deal of argument within the nation as to whether or not China should participate.[53] Apparently, a number of people opposed the intervention.

Stuart Schram says that it is inconceivable that Mao could have had his nation involved in the war before June 25.[54] Allen S. Whiting says that there is no clear proof that China interfered in planning and preparations for the Korean War.[55] My own research leads me to agree with these views. The outbreak of the Korean War was a great surprise to China. Another important bit of evidence lies in the fact that neither Chinese newspapers nor radio carried any prepared reports on the war on the first day. It was not until two days later that the war was announced in the media.

My hypothesis is that the Korean War was part of Stalin's overall international strategy, especially as it related to Asia and China policy. China had just completed its revolution and was still filled with fresh passion. It participated in the Korean War not only because it confronted an emergency situation of defending the fatherland, but also because it was led by a sense of mission to defend the socialist camp. But it led to China's becoming fully drawn into Stalin's strategy, with which the Chinese grew exceedingly discontented.

In relation to this, it is necessary to look again at the Sino-Soviet meeting in the early part of 1950. Stalin had to confront Mao's fervent nationalism and was not able to get the Chinese to accept all of his demands. Since the United States had not completely abandoned the policy of regarding China as a potential Yugoslavia, Stalin's worries and suspicions increased. In this regard, Mao said of Stalin that "he suspected that after we won the revolution, China would become like Yugoslavia, and I would be another Tito."[56]

If the memoirs of Otto Braun are correct in saying that Mao wanted to draw the Soviet Union into the war against Japan by keeping the situation in northeast Asia in a volatile state of confusion,[57] then it seems that the situation was reversed during the Korean War. Stalin's strategy then was to weaken China through protracted military conflict which would be confined to the Korean peninsula and the Chinese mainland. From the beginning, Stalin predicted that China would enter the Korean War, and he at least knew that the war would make the Mao regime even more dependent on the Soviet Union. With the ability of hindsight, we can see what was going on in Sino-Soviet relations at the time, and it can be quite reasonably surmised that the Soviet Union's boycott of the UN Security Council from January 1950 until after the Korean War began was a strategic move. They calculated to first boycott the council on the pretext of pressing for recognition of China, while knowing that the United States would intervene in the war and the Chinese would send in troops.

The situation in Korea was such that conflict could break out in the form of a war for national liberation,[58] but although the internal situation was an indispensable catalyst, it is very difficult to imagine that North Korea had nothing to do with the Stalinist strategy. After Stalin's death, a ceasefire was obtained through Chinese diplomatic efforts. Right after the ceasefire, Ho Ka-i and others of the Moscow group in North Korea were purged.[59] In China as well, those with close connections to the Soviet strategy in Korea, including Kao Kang, were purged.[60] Taking all these facts into consideration, we can see that, as G. Paloczi-Horvath says, the Korean War was started by Stalin's Soviet Union and ended by Mao's China.[61]

This study of the various events at that time thus crosses the border of conjecture and gives us a fairly adequate glimpse of reality. I believe that the events leading up to the Korean War, where China was unavoidably drawn into Soviet strategy and paid a great price in both lives and money, are important factors in understanding the abrasive criticism that China makes of the Soviet Union today.

1. For Sino-Soviet relationship on frontier areas, see Sakamoto Koretada, Henkyō o meguru Chū-So kankeishi (Tokyo: Ajia keizai kenkyūjo), chaps. 2–4.

2. Otto Braun, Kitajskie zapiski: 1932–1939 (Moscow: Politizdat, 1974) pp. 214–16. See also Otto Braun, "Mōtakutō wa ikani seiken o nigitta ka," Kyokutō no shomondai 3, no. 2 (June 1974).

3. A critical analysis of P. P. Vladimirov's memoirs has revealed important information. See Petr Parfenvič Vladimirov, Osobyj rajon kitaja 1942–1945 (Moscow: Izdatel'stvo Agentstva Pečati Novosti, 1973).

4. For the dynamic background of Sino-Soviet relations, see Nakajima Mineo, "Mosukuwa-Uranbatōru-Pekin," Chūō kōron (March 1975).

5. Ambassador John Leighton Stuart's secret plan to visit Peking was one step toward the possibility of such a policy. See Usami Shigeru, "Stuart taishi no Pekin hōmon keikaku," Kokusai mondai 198 (September 1976).

6. See Yubashi Shigeto, Senji Nisso kōsho shoshi: 1941–45 (Tokyo: Kasumigaseki shuppan, 1974), chaps. 8–10.

7. Sankei Shimbun, ed., Shōkaiseki hiroku, I: Higeki no Chūgoku tairiku (Tokyo: Sankei shuppan, 1975), pp. 22–108.

8. J. M. MacKintosh, Strategy and Tactics of Soviet Foreign Policy (London: Oxford University Press, 1962), p. 41.

9. See, for example, A. M. Dubinsky, The Far East in the Second World War: An Outline History of the International Relations and National Liberation Struggle in East and South-East Asia (Moscow: Izdatel'stvo "Nauka," 1972), p. 59.

10. For discussion on this point, interesting material is found in Khrushchev's memoirs. See Strobe Talbot, tr. and ed., Khrushchev Remembers (Boston: Little, Brown, 1970), chap. 18; and Strobe Talbot, tr. and ed., Khrushchev Remembers: The Last Testament (Boston: Little, Brown, 1974), pp. 235–44.

11. See Yen Chung-chuan's article in Wen hui pao (Hong Kong), 10 May 1969.

12. Mao Tse-tung, "Report to the Second Plenary Session of the Seventh Central Committee of the Communist Party of China" (5 March 1949), Selected Works of Mao Tse-tung (henceforth cited SW), vol. 4 (Peking: Foreign Languages Press, 1961), pp. 370–72.

13. Mao Tse-tung, "On the People's Democratic Dictatorship: In Commemoration of the Twenty-eighth Anniversary of the Communist Party of China" (30 June 1949), SW, vol. 4, p. 415.

14. Ch'i Pen-yü, "Ai-kuo chu-i hai shih mai-kuo chu-i? P'ing fan-tung ying p'ien 'Ch'ing-kung mi-shih', " Hung-chi 5 (1967).

15. For details on the Kao Kang problem and the Soviet Union, see Nakajima Mineo, "Kōkō jiken to Chū-So kankei," Kyōsan shugi to kokusai seiji 1, no. 1 (July–September 1976).

16. Tung-pei jih-pao editorial, "Tui Chung-kuo jen-min ti chen-cheng yu-i: Ch'ing-

chu Tung-pei yü Su-lien i-nien mao-i hsieh-ting," *Jen-min jih-pao*, 9 August 1949. "K voprosu o torgovle Man'čžurii s SSR," *Izvestija*, 31 July 1949.

17.　"Mao chu-hsi tsai Mo-ssŭ-k'o." *Hsin-hua yüeh-pao* 1, no. 3.

18.　Mao Tse-tung, "Tsai pa-chieh shih-chung chuan-hui shang ti chiang-hua" (24 September 1962), *Mao Tse-tung Ssŭ-hsiang Wan-sui* (henceforth cited *Wan-sui*) (August 1969), p. 432.

19.　Mao Tse-tung, "Sheng shih-wei shu-chi hui-i shang ti ch'a-hua" (January 1957), *Wan-sui*, p. 85.

20.　Mao Tse-tung, "Tsai Cheng-tu hui-i shang ti chiang-hua" (March 1958), *Wan-sui*, pp. 163–64.

21.　San Yuan, *Mao Tse-tung Ssŭ-hsian yü Chung-su kuan-hsi* (Hong Kong: Sincere Publishers, 1972), p. 22.

22.　Khrushchev's "secret" speech on Stalin, 25 February 1956 (New York: The Anti-Stalin Campaign and International Communism, 1956).

23.　On this point, *see also* Tang Tsou, *America's Failure in China* (Chicago: University of Chicago Press, 1966), especially chaps. 6 and 12.

24.　Dean Acheson, "Letter of Transmittal," in *The China White Paper, August 1949: United States Relations with China* (Stanford: Stanford University Press, 1967), p. xvi.

25.　"United States Policy Respecting the Status of Formosa (Taiwan): Statement by the President, January 5, 1950," in *American Foreign Policy: Basic Documents, 1950–1955*, ed. Department of State (New York: Arno Press, 1971), vol. 2, pp. 2448–49.

26.　"Review of the Position as of 1950: Address by the Secretary of State: January 12, 1950," in *American Foreign Policy*, vol. 2, pp. 2310–22.

27.　"'Total Diplomacy' to Strengthen United States Leadership for Human Freedom: Summary of Remarks by the Secretary of State, February 16, 1950," in *American Foreign Policy*, vol. 1, p. 7.

28.　David Horowitz, *From Yalta to Vietnam: American Foreign Policy in the Cold War* (Harmondsworth: Penguin Books, 1967), pp. 103–9.

29.　For a more extended analysis of this issue, *see* Nakajima Mineo, "Chōsen sensō to Chūgoku," *Kokusai mondai* 182 (May 1975).

30.　One of the recent exceptions is Robert R. Simmons's book: *The Strained Alliance: Peking, P'yŏngyang, Moscow and the Politics of the Korean Civil War* (New York: Free Press, 1975), especially pp. 48–136. My hypothesis on the origins of the war, however, is not in full agreement with Simmons's view, in particular on the Soviet Union's strategy and China's ignorance of the situation.

31.　I. F. Stone, *The Hidden History of the Korean War* (New York: Monthly Review Press, 1952).

32.　Horowitz, *Yalta to Vietnam*, p. 119.

33.　*See*, for example, Edgar O'Ballance, *Korea: 1950–1953* (London: Faber and Faber, 1969), pp. 59–60; Kim Chum-kom, *The Korean War* (Seoul: Kwangmyong Publishing, 1973), pp. 59–61.

34.　Shinobu Seizaburō, *Chōsen sensō no boppatsu* (Tokyo: Fukumura shoten, 1969).

35.　Kim, *Korean War*, p. 83.

36.　Allen S. Whiting, *China Crosses the Yalu: The Decision to Enter the Korean War* (New York: Macmillan, 1960), p. 44.

37.　O'Ballance, *Korea*, p. 60; Kim, *Korean War*, pp. 47–53; Tamaki Motoi, "Nihon ni okeru Chōsen sensō kan," in *Chōsen sensō shi: Gendai shi no saihakkutsu*, ed. Minzoku mondai kenkyūkai (Tokyo: Koria hyōronsha, 1967), pp. 308–9.

38.　Ibid., p. 307.

39.　For the "Liu Shao-ch'i Thesis," *see* Nakajima Mineo, *Gendai Chūgoku ron: Ideorogī to seiji no naiteki kōsatsu*, rev. ed. (Tokyo: Aoki shoten, 1971), p. 64.

40.　*For a Lasting Peace and for a People's Democracy!* 2 March 1950.

41.　Lung Yün, "Lung Yün tai-piao ti fa-yen," in *Chun-hua jen-min kung-ho-kuo ti i chieh ch'uan-kuo jen-min tai-piao ta-hui ti ssu tz'u hui-i hui-k'an* (Peking: Jen-min chu-pan-she, 1957), pp. 1402–3.

42. "Tsai chan-cheng yü ho-p'ing wen-t'i ti liang-t'iao lu-hsien: Wu p'ing ssu-kung chung-yang ti kung-k'ai-hsin, *Jen-min jih-pao*, 18 November 1963.

43. *Jen-min jih-pao*, 1 March 1964.

44. *Mainichi shimbun*, 26 January 1972.

45. *See* Horowitz, *Yalta to Vietnam*, p. 131.

46. For discussion on the MacArthur strategy, *see* Kamiya Fuji, *Gendai kokusai seiji no shikaku* (Tokyo: Yūhikaku, 1966), chs. 2–3.

47. *See* note 15.

48. Edgar Snow, *The Other Side of the River: Red China Today* (New York: Random House, 1962), pp. 654–55.

49. George Paloczi-Horvath, *Mao Tse-tung: Emperor of the Blue Ants* (London: Secker & Warburg, 1962), p. 279.

50. Mao Tse-tung, "Wei cheng-ch'ü kuo chia ts'ai-cheng ching-chi chuang-k'uang erh tou cheng," *Hsin-hua yüeh-pao* 2, no. 3, p. 488

51. *See* Stuart Schram, *Mao Tse-tung* (Harmondsworth: Penguin Books, 1966), p. 263.

52. Whiting, *Yalu*, pp. 21–22.

53. "Wei shen-me wo-men tui mei-kuo ch'in-lüeh ch'ao-hsien pu neng chih chih pu-li," *Jen-min jih-pao*, 6 November 1950. *See also* Tang Tsou, *America's Failure*, p. 575.

54. Schram, *Mao*, p. 263.

55. Whiting, *Yalu*, p. 45.

56. Mao Tse-tung, "Tsai pa-chieh shih-chung chuan-hui shang ti chiang-hua," *Wan-sui*, p. 432.

57. Otto Braun, *Kitajskie*, pp. 214–16.

58. Okonogi Masao, "Minzoku kaihō sensō to shite no Chōsen sensō," *Kokusai mondai* 182 (May 1975).

59. For the purge of Hŏ-ka-i, *see* Robert A. Scalapino and Chong-sik Lee, *Communism in Korea* (Berkeley: University of California Press, 1972), pp. 440, 509.

60. *See* note 15.

61. Paloczi-Horvath, *Mao Tse-tung*, p. 283.

The Cold War and China

Okabe Tatsumi

This essay is an attempt to analyze the process through which the Chinese Communists, as objects of the Cold War rather than active participants, became drawn into the Cold War structure of the postwar period (1945–49). The emphasis will be on the changing Chinese Communist perception of international relations. Though the Cold War can be defined in several ways, it is here defined as an East-West conflict which had as its basis different social systems and ideologies.

Chinese Communist leaders in the postwar period entertained three different images of international relations. The first image, which they held during the war through mid-1946, was one of cooperation among three (or five) democratic powers. According to this image, best expressed by Mao Tse-tung's "On Coalition Government" (April 1945), the major conflict in the world was one between democratic, antifascist forces and antidemocratic, fascist forces or their remnants in the postwar period. The second image was the so-called intermediate zone theory, which emerged between mid-1946 and early 1947 and continued till the end of 1947. This image envisaged an "American imperialism" which, under the banner of an anti-Soviet offensive, tried to invade and exploit the peoples in the intermediate zone between the United States and the Soviet Union. Since, in this image, the Soviet Union was considered to be outside this major conflict, one researcher has termed it a "three-bloc approach."[1] The third image was a tight East-West bipolar perception of the world, which became a policy of "leaning to one side," as Mao called it. This image divided the world rigidly into two blocs by denying "neutrality" or even the possibility of a "third road." The image first appeared at the end of 1947 and was gradually reinforced through 1948 to become the "lean to one side" policy in 1949. According to our definition of the Cold War, this tight East-West bipolar image is a typical Cold War perception. With it the People's Republic of China under the Chinese Communist party (CCP) leadership was incorporated into the worldwide Cold War structure; it became one of the actors in the Cold War, especially after the outbreak of the Korean War, and accepted the concept of monolithic unity with the Soviet Union.

The analysis below aims at examining the process of successive changes in these images and discovering the conditions which brought about the third image.[2]

The First Image

In his political report to the CCP seventh congress in April 1945, Mao Tse-tung described the relationship among Britain, the United States, and the Soviet Union as the unity of antifascist democratic forces, and advocated that "important problems of international relations must necessarily be solved mainly by the Three Big Powers or the Five Big Powers through negotiations."[3] According to him, although the world was advancing toward democracy, peace, and progress, fascist and antidemocratic forces could be expected to continue to cause trouble. Therefore, Mao foresaw a long-term struggle between democratic forces headed by the Three or the Five Powers and the antidemocratic forces. As for China itself, it would aim at the construction of a new democratic nation which would be independent, free, unified, wealthy, and strong, and establish equal diplomatic relations with other countries. He welcomed foreign investment to contribute to China's industrialization and to make it wealthy and strong.

These statements by Mao are very different from those he expressed toward the end of the civil war in China. With such an image of international relations, the Chinese Communist attitude toward the United States was naturally very favorable. The climax of this favorable attitude toward the United States lasted from 1944 to 1945. For example, a July 4, 1944, editorial of the *Liberation Daily* (*Chieh-fang jih-pao,* the CCP organ newspaper in Yenan), written to commemorate American Independence Day, announced that the United States was one of the most typical democratic nations in the world, and that "together with the Soviet Union, [it] was one of the twin stars of the democratic world." This editorial praised the American tradition of democracy and listed President Franklin D. Roosevelt and Henry Wallace along with George Washington, Thomas Jefferson, Andrew Jackson, and Abraham Lincoln as representatives of this tradition. Not only had the United States already made "immortal contributions" to the war effort in the Pacific, but it would "clearly occupy a very important position in securing world peace and democratization in the postwar period."[4]

In August 1944, Mao Tse-tung, in his interview with John Service, made several favorable comments on the United States: "The hope for preventing civil war in China therefore rests to a very great extent—much more than ever before—on the influence of foreign countries. Among these, by far the most important is the United States"; "Every American soldier in China should be a walking and talking advertisement for democracy . . . we Chinese consider you Americans the ideal of democracy"; "China must industrialize. This can be done—in China—only by free enterprise and with the aid of foreign capital. Chinese and American interests are correlated and similar. They fit together, economically and politically. We can and must work together."[5] Mao repeated similar statements in the following March saying, "America and China complement each other economically. . . . America is not only the most suitable country to assist this economic development of China: she is also the only country fully able to participate"; "Without the help of American influence, real unity and democracy will have to be won by a long and bitter struggle."[6] In January 1945, Mao disclosed his desire to visit Washington.[7] A year later, Chou En-lai told George Marshall that despite the rumors that Mao might be going to Moscow, "he would rather go to the United States, because he thinks that there he can learn lots of things useful to China."[8]

These examples of the Chinese Communists' favorable attitude toward the United States does not necessarily mean that there was a possibility of detaching them from the Soviet Union, or that long-term Chinese Communist–American friendship would have been possible, as some American diplomats expected at that time.[9] First, the Chinese Communists regarded the war against Japan as a means for promoting, rather than suspending, their revolutionary efforts.[10] The war, Mao said, was fought in order to achieve democracy and overthrow fascism in China as well as in the world.[11] Democracy here meant the execution of an "antiimperialistic," "antifeudal" revolution as a prerequisite for the future socialist revolution. In more concrete terms, it meant the termination of one-party dictatorship by the Kuomintang, through the formation of a coalition government ("new democracy"), which, after a period of peaceful or violent struggles, was to be transformed into a proletarian dictatorship. The United States was useful insofar as it was antifascist and anti-Kuomintang. Thus it was questionable how far the Chinese Communists and the Americans could have cooperated. Their different objectives became apparent as early as the fall of 1944, when the Communists grew dissatisfied with Ambassador Patrick J. Hurley's China policy. After the death of Roosevelt, Communist uneasiness accelerated. It was clearly expressed in a *Liberation Daily* editorial about the *Amerasia* incident, in which it was argued that there were two different lines in American China policy, one democratic and the other reactionary. The incident, in this view, was an indication of the struggle between the two factions.[12] The Communists' faith in the "democratic" faction continued to be expressed through the period of Marshall's mediation efforts,[13] but gradually faded in the subsequent period.

Secondly, from the Chinese Communist viewpoint the American role changed with the shift in revolutionary strategy. In 1945, they called for the formation of a coalition government which was to include the Kuomintang and was to continue for decades until material conditions for socialist revolution had matured. In the coalition government or the new-democratic period, economic development was to be promoted by capitalist means, though so restricted as not to give rise to adverse side effects. Socialist construction was to be postponed until after the revolution. It was with this regime that the Communists expected the United States to cooperate economically on a complementary basis. It was also to this regime that they tried to apply the American type of democracy, which would provide maximum room for their own activities. Their favorable attitude toward the United States can be best explained by Mao's statement to Service to the effect that "the Russians have suffered greatly in the war and will have their hands full with their own job of rebuilding. We do not expect Russian help. Furthermore, the KMT because of its anticommunist phobia is anti-Russian. Therefore KMT-Soviet cooperation is impossible. And for us to seek it would only make the situation in China worse. China is disunified enough already!"[14] In other words, in the period of the coalition government the United States would be able to play a role which the Soviet Union could not. But when the Communist strategy shifted from the formation of a coalition government to the overthrow of the KMT and "bureaucratic capitals,"[15] the function of the United States in the eyes of the Chinese Communists necessarily changed. American support of the KMT during the civil war naturally accelerated this change. Viewed in this light, recent Soviet attempts to trace the origins of the Sino-American rapprochement of the 1970s to the Chinese Communists' favorable attitude toward the United States during the 1940s[16] are not tenable, since China today is at a different revolutionary stage from that during the 1940s.

Thirdly, despite discrepancies, conflicts, and dissatisfaction with the Soviet Union and Joseph Stalin, Chinese Communists regarded Russia as the "fatherland of socialism" and the last resort for help in their revolutionary struggle.[17] The Soviet Union was qualitatively different from any other country in the world. However friendly the relations between CCP and America, the latter could never be a match for the Soviet Union, simply because it was not a brotherly socialist country, much less the "fatherland of socialism." Until the Chinese Communists lost every reason to believe that the Soviet Union was qualitatively different from other countries (this came about only after 1958 or, more clearly, after 1964), there was no possibility of alienation between the two.

It is true that, even as early as 1945, Chinese Communists were already having enough unpleasant experiences with the Soviet Union and with Stalin. Moreover, they were relatively independent of Soviet control.[18] To mention only a few examples: (1) In the notes exchanged relating to the Chinese-Soviet Pact of 1945, the Soviet Union recognized the Kuomintang government as the central government of China, as the government to which Russia's moral and material support would be given. This was a great blow to the Communists. One observer contends that it so shook Mao, who had been quite militant toward the Kuomintang before he learned of the contents of the treaty and agreements, that he decided to authorize the Chungking talks.[19] (2) With regard to the status of Outer Mongolia, the Communist leaders had expected its incorporation into a federated China.[20] This expectation was betrayed by the Sino-Soviet exchange of notes on Outer Mongolia. (3) Soviet activities in Manchuria dismayed the Chinese Communists, who were denied military help there. Soviet requisitions of large quantities of Japanese industrial plants and machineries as "war booty" were, to say the least, embarrassing to the Communists.[21] (4) According to Mao, in 1945 the Soviet Union "did not permit China to make revolution. . . . Stalin wanted to prevent China from making revolution, saying that we should not have a civil war and should cooperate with Chiang Kai-shek; otherwise the Chinese nation would perish. But we did not do what he said."[22] (5) Stalin and V. M. Molotov, in their talks with Americans, reportedly degraded the Chinese Communists by saying they "were related to Communism in no way at all."[23]

Despite all this evidence, however, Chinese Communist dissatisfaction with the Soviet Union was not so severe as to bring about their estrangement. The Communists still regarded Russia as the "fatherland of socialism" and its only living model. Even the Chinese-Soviet Pact of 1945 was hailed by the *Liberation Daily*, which declared, "With regard to concluding an alliance of friendship with the Soviet people, we, the Chinese people, heartily feel it a glory."[24] On another occasion in commemorating the first anniversary of the October revolution after the termination of the war, a *Liberation Daily* editorial said, "This is the first occasion that we, the Chinese people, in the capacity of an ally, congratulate the Soviet people on their National Day."[25] These expressions of emotional attachment to the "fatherland of socialism" are indicative of the psychological state of the Chinese Communist leaders. They would have expressed their mood in more businesslike ways if they had felt no such attachment. The latter editorial also men-

Appraisal of the Present International Situation" (April 1946),[31] some people in the CCP, since they had overestimated the strength of the "imperialists" and underestimated the strength of the people, feared the outbreak of world war and hesitated to fight a revolutionary against an antirevolutionary war. Mao criticized these viewpoints by arguing that international settlement could be achieved only through the struggle of democratic against antidemocratic forces, and that international settlement did not require a domestic compromise. At the time of writing, the paper was circulated only among some CCP leaders. It was printed and became an official document of the party only in December 1947 by consent of its members. This shows that throughout 1946 and 1947, there existed considerable disagreement with Mao's analysis, which tried to justify the launching of total civil war by minimizing the risk of instigating a world war.

The pessimistic viewpoints within the CCP apparently reflected Soviet fears of world war. It may be that the Soviet Union, having tacitly agreed that China belonged to the American sphere of influence in postwar Asia, was quite reluctant to provoke possible American military intervention by waging total civil war in China.[32] Lin Piao recollected in 1960 in an article commenting on the publication of volume four of Mao's *Collected Works* that "some well-intentioned friends at home and abroad were worried about us"[33] with regard to the prospects in the civil war. Tang Tsou has inferred that "the friends abroad" were an allusion to Stalin.[34] Mao's 1962 recollection cited above, of the negative Soviet attitude toward the civil war in 1945, supports this interpretation. The immediate driving force behind the birth of the "intermediate zone" theory, therefore, was the necessity to justify the urgency of total civil war despite disagreement within the party and with the Soviet Union. The idea that the major contradiction in the world was one between "American imperialism" and people in the "intermediate zone" served to exclude the Soviet Union from the arena of the worldwide struggle and thus effectively furnished a theoretical basis for justifying the confrontation with the Kuomintang. Since the action taken was against the wishes of the Soviet Union, the Chinese Communists could not expect substantial Soviet assistance. As Chou En-lai stated in February 1947, "the Chinese Communists will henceforth work out their own problems without mediation by the Soviet Union, Great Britain, the U.S. or any other foreign country."[35] The slogan of "self-reliance" appeared frequently in the Chinese press after the emergence of the second image.

Seen in a longer historical perspective, however, the "intermediate zone" image has additional importance. The image is not based on a simple horizontal bipolarization of East and West, or of social systems or ideologies. It is, rather, based on a vertical bipolarization of big powers and smaller nations. To use a more recent terminology, the image is an expression of North-South conflict, one between small nations confronting an overwhelmingly strong enemy. In this sense, the image is anti–big power and therefore potentially anti-Soviet. Historically speaking, the prototype of the "intermediate zone" theory appeared in Mao's "On New State" in 1938. In this report, he argued that because democratic nations, especially Britain, did not want to punish aggressors by force, Japan, Germany, and Italy were able to invade "intermediate nations" such as "China, Abyssinia, Spain, Austria, Czechoslovakia, which are all semi-independent or small nations."[36] Though the Soviet Union was not mentioned in this report, it must have been included among those passive democratic nations. It is to be noted that the slogan of "self-reliance" began to appear quite extensively from about that time on.

The "intermediate zone" theory was revived in 1958, again coupled with the slogan of "self-reliance," under a situation where China confronted overwhelmingly strong "American imperialism," while the Soviet Union was quite reluctant in pushing through active policies. Later, with the deepening split with the Soviet Union and the emergence of the Chinese view that the socialist camp had already disintegrated, the theory was transformed, after 1974, into a "three worlds" theory in which the first world of superpowers was allegedly confronted by the third world (developing nations) and by the second world (smaller developed nations). The Chinese Communists have been motivated not only by the desire to realize a socialist system in China, but to elevate underdeveloped China to the "advanced level of the world." They are both nationalist and communist. They have both horizontal, East-West conflict-oriented views and vertical, North-South (or big nation–small nation) conflict-oriented views. Ideologically speaking, the horizontal views should always take precedence over the latter, but when contradictions between North and South become accelerated, the vertical image tends to rise to the surface.

The "intermediate zone" image in 1946 and 1947 was also an expression of this vertical and non–Cold War (according to our definition) image. If the image had persisted, Chinese Communist involvement in the Cold War might have been different and the Sino-Soviet split might have been hastened. This did not happen, however, due to such factors as the worldwide development of the Cold War; the American policy of supporting the Kuomintang; and the restraints of ideological and security considerations against alienating Moscow. The United States did not even acknowledge the possible schism between the CCP and the Soviet Union; Ambassador Stuart commented on Lu Ting-i's article by saying that "it might well have been written in the Kremlin."[37]

It was during the period of this second image that the Communists' attitude toward the United States became hostile. Until mid-1946, while attacking U.S. policy in China,[38] they seem to have expected that American pressure could still control the Kuomintang.[39] On July 7, however, in their declaration commemorating the ninth anniversary of the "Ch'i-ch'i" incident (July 7, 1937), they criticized the United States severely, saying, "American reactionaries, in collaboration with Chinese reactionaries, are trying to take Japan's place and to change China into a colony of American imperialism."[40] On August 16, a *Liberation Daily* editorial declared that the stage of "peace and democracy" had passed and severely criticized American aid to Chiang Kai-shek.[41] Behind these antagonistic pronouncements was a new perception of American government at that time. Upon Wallace's resignation as secretary of commerce, the *Liberation Daily* contended, "The American government has increasingly become the tool of the 'militaristic thought faction.' " The "democratic faction" headed by Wallace and other New Dealers had been completely expelled from the government by the "militaristic thought faction" and "reactionaries."[42] In spite of this, the Chinese Communists still remained hopeful of the victory of the "American people" and the "democratic faction." According to Ambassador Stuart, Chou

En-lai told him in Nanking that "since American policy must be interpreted as favoring the Central Government, thereby damaging Communist interests, the United States is forcing the Communists into Russian arms and alienating their very considerable sympathy for the United States." Stuart, though uncertain about Chou's real intentions, concluded that "in any case the Chinese Communists would be inclined to friendliness toward the United States only so long as it would prove useful to them, and not conflict with their sense of ideological kinship with Communist groups elsewhere in the world."[43] This seems a correct estimate of the Chinese Communist attitude toward the United States at that time.

Toward the Soviet Union, the Communist attitude during the period of the second image was ambivalent. On one hand, there was dissatisfaction with Soviet reaction to the civil war in China. On the other hand, there still remained the sense that the Soviet Union was qualitatively different from others. One manifestation of Chinese dissatisfaction was that there appeared no comment in the *Liberation Daily* on the first anniversaries of Soviet participation in the Pacific War and of the Chinese-Soviet Pact. These two events, both of which occurred in August 1945, had been applauded by the Chinese press at that time. The first anniversaries, therefore, must have been worth mentioning in the *Liberation Daily*, even if formally. On Soviet participation in the war, a comment by Radio Moscow was carried in the paper, but none by Chinese Communists themselves. There was no mention at all of the pact. It is true that the meaning of the pact had changed with the passing of the "peace and democracy" stage, but the change should have been worth explaining. The silence on these events may suggest Chinese Communist dissatisfaction with the Soviet Union. The existence of this sentiment was also suggested by American sources in Manchuria.[44] It is interesting to note that the Soviet journal *Kommunist* later partly supported the American observations. According to the May 1964 issue of the journal, in July 1946 P'eng Chen and Lin Feng, both of whom were CCP leaders in Manchuria, "maliciously distorted the role of the Soviet army, and spread slander about the USSR," and the central committee of the CCP "was forced to condemn the 'mistakes' of the group. . . ."[45]

Despite such dissatisfaction, which may have contributed to the emergence of the "intermediate zone" theory, it is to be noted that the Soviet Union was still regarded as "the main pillar of the world democratic forces."[46] In an editorial commemorating the twenty-ninth anniversary of the Russian revolution, the *Liberation Daily* said, "All the oppressed peoples and nations in the world and those people who eagerly love peace, democracy and progress, all regard the Soviet Union as the 'hope of the human race.' " The editorial, after praising Soviet contribution to the struggle for liberation in China, stated, "There truly exists a difference of heaven and earth between the Soviet Union's complete equal treatment and brotherly friendship to China and the imperialists' help, under the guise of 'China Aid,' to tyrannical Chiang Kai-shek who oppresses and murders Chinese people."[47] The difference of attitudes toward the Soviet Union and the United States was also observed on the spot by an American, who reported, "The Chinese Communists in some areas of north China inform the recipients of UNRRA supplies from the US that these supplies were contributed by the USSR."[48] Even under the potentially anti-Soviet "intermediate zone" image, the Soviet Union was still qualitatively different from other countries. The "intermediate zone" theory often ignored ideological viewpoints or class components involved in worldwide struggles. One typical example was the attitude toward the independence movements in Indonesia. In 1946 and 1947, there were many favorable comments in the *Liberation Daily* and the *People's Daily,* supporting the Indonesian government under Sukarno and Hatta.[49] This clearly contrasted with the Chinese Communist attitude after 1948. It is true that favorable mention was being made of the Communist party of Indonesia with whom the CCP shared the same ideology, but Sukarno and Hatta were regarded as the leaders of the antiimperialist struggle. In this sense, the Chinese Communists at this stage viewed the colonial struggles in terms of a very broad united front. The same was true of the CCP attitude toward the anti-American movements of the peoples of America and Europe.[50] This attitude was nearly the same as the more clearly anti-Soviet "intermediate zone" theory after 1958 and the "three worlds" theory after 1974.

The Third Image

In 1947, both China's domestic situation and the international environment rapidly progressed toward the Cold War between the two blocs. Internationally, the Truman Doctrine, which was a typical example of the East-West conflict-oriented thinking, was made public in March. In June, the Marshall Plan was formulated. It was perceived by the Communists in the framework of the East-West conflict. Domestically, China's civil war entered a new stage through the declaration of People's Liberation Army of China, published in October. In this declaration, the objective of the revolutionary war was redefined as the overthrow of Chiang Kai-shek. Confiscation of the "bureaucratic capitals" was added to the policy program.[51] This was a milestone in the transformation of the revolutionary plan of the CCP. The form of government to be established changed from a broad coalition government which included the Kuomintang to a narrower one led by the CCP. The nature of the government changed from a dictatorship of the union of revolutionary classes[52] to the people's democratic dictatorship[53] which was later reinterpreted as being the same thing as the proletarian dictatorship. In other words, the revolutionary plan was radicalized in the latter half of 1947.

It was at this juncture that the Cominform was formed. The declaration on the international situation published on the occasion clearly showed the new view of international communism headed by the Soviet Union. It contended that (1) two blocs had appeared in the world, one imperialist and antidemocratic, the other antiimperialist and democratic; (2) American imperialism was enslaving Europe, China, Indonesia, and Latin America; (3) the right-wing social democrats were serving this American policy; (4) in order to resist the American policy of enslavement, communist parties in all countries should struggle to defend democracy and independence; (5) although the imperialists were scheming to launch a war, it could be prevented by the strength of the antiwar forces; (6) communist parties should lead resistance movements everywhere without overestimating their enemies; and (7) communist parties should unite all democratic and patriotic forces around them.[54] Zhdanov's speech, also made on the

same occasion, repeated the same points and added that the
United States was oppressing Europe, China, India, and others
under the guise of defending these nations from a fictitious military threat posed by the Soviet Union.[55]

Most of these ideas were similar to the views the Chinese Communists had expressed in 1946 and 1947. The point added by
Zhdanov was quite similar to the "smoke screen" theory of Mao.
Points (4), (5), and (6) of the declaration were just what Mao
had been trying to emphasize in justifying total civil war in China
despite the risk of a world war. The attack on right-wing social
democrats (point [3] above) coincided with the radicalization of
the revolutionary plan in China. In Chinese eyes, therefore, the
Soviet Union was coming closer to the Chinese Communists. It
was thus quite natural for them to welcome the formation of the
Cominform with its new image of the international situation. The
two-camp theory and the narrower united front policy were
accordingly adopted by the CCP as official doctrine.[56]

Their reaction to the new Cominform thesis was very well expressed in articles by Ch'iao Mu (Ch'iao Kuan-hua), then in
Hong Kong. In an article in the October 23 issue of *Ch'ün-chung*,
he stated that the people of the world under the leadership of the
Soviet Union were resisting American imperialism; however,
although the Soviet Union was the leader, the main force of resistance was the people of the world themselves, in countries such as
China, Vietnam, Indonesia, Greece, France, and Italy. "Viewed
on a surface level [*p'ing-mien-ti k'an*], they are the two camps in
the world situation." The form of the struggle had changed from
upper-level compromises to strife at lower levels, and it was now
time for attack. But the attack would never bring about world
war.[57] Here one detects the influence of the two-camp thesis, but
at the same time there are echoes of the earlier "intermediate
zone" theory. The tone of argument changed in Ch'iao's next article in the November 16 issue of the journal. It praised the Soviet
Union as the main force of antiimperialism, as the banner of people's liberation, and as the stronghold of world peace.[58] The dif-
fident attitude toward the Soviet role in the struggle against imperialism which had been characteristic of the intermediate-zone
image now disappeared. The tone of the article was closer to the
Cominform thesis. Adoption of the two-camp thesis was almost

complete in his third article, which appeared in the January 1, 1948, issue. Ch'iao analyzed the world situation in line with the two-camp thesis and denied the possibility of a middle road or the necessity of compromise. The Cominform declaration had called for massive counterattacks, he insisted; the main form of the counterattacks in the Far East was to be armed struggle. The article concluded that, as the power of the Soviet Union became stronger, the imperialists would not dream of starting a world war; it was the time when every road led to communism.[59]

In the CCP's official statements, too, the change of attitude toward the Soviet Union and the adoption of the two-camp thesis became clear. The New China News Agency editorial commemorating the thirtieth anniversary of the Russian revolution, while still referring to "self-reliance," praised the history of the Soviet struggle against the imperialists and admired the superiority of the Soviet socialist system.[60] Mao Tse-tung adopted the two-camp thesis in his report, "Present Situation and Our Tasks," given on December 25, 1947. He contended that the idea of a "third road" in China was already bankrupt. Although this was stated in the context of China's domestic situation, the influence of the tight bipolar image is clear. As mentioned above, at the conference where this report was presented, Mao's paper, "Some Points in Appraisal of Present International Situation," written in April 1946, was circulated and listed as an official document of the party. It seems that disagreement by "some comrades" had by now disappeared; the Cominform itself was admitting that world war could be prevented by people's active struggles, precisely as Mao had contended.

It is true that the convergence of Soviet and CCP images did not eliminate conflict between the two, and that their interpretations of the two-camp thesis were somewhat different: the Soviet Union viewed the antiimperialist camp as consisting mainly of such states as the Soviet Union, the "New Democracies," Indonesia, and Vietnam, and having the sympathy of some other states, while the Chinese included in the camp the masses in America and other capitalist nations, as well as those in the colonies and semicolonies. On the whole, however, the Chinese Communists became inclined toward East-West conflict-oriented Cold War thinking. Instead of viewing world contradictions vertically, they began to pay more attention to horizontal contradictions between ideologies and class positions.

One of the best examples of the Chinese version of the two-camp thesis was their attitude toward the Indonesian question. Before the adoption of the thesis, the Chinese Communists had supported the struggle for independence by the Indonesian government under Sukarno and Hatta. After the conclusion of the Renville agreement at the end of 1947, however, the Chinese began to attack Sukarno and Hatta as traitors and as puppets of the imperialists.[61] The Chinese Communists referred to the experiences of their own revolution as lessons to the Indonesian people, implying that Sukarno and Hatta were the Chiang Kai-sheks of Indonesia.[62] This attack was accompanied by praise of Indonesian communists, who started the adventuristic Madiun uprising in September 1948. Such an attitude persisted until some time after the establishment of the People's Republic of China. It was a product of the two-camp thesis which denied the possibility of "middle roads" or a "third road," and was reinforced by the progress of the revolution in China. It is true that the Renville agreement was a concession to the Dutch, but, retrospectively speaking, it was no more than an episode in the ups and downs of the struggle for independence. Even the Indonesian communists supported it. The Soviet Union, which later joined the Chinese Communists in attacking Sukarno and Hatta, did not attack them for about a year after the signing of the Renville agreement.[63] It is clear that China's rigid application of the two-camp thesis to Indonesia was caused by its own revolutionary experience. In any case, the Indonesian example seems to show that the transformation in the Chinese Communist perception of world politics had been made quite voluntarily.

The Cold War image of the Chinese Communists was reinforced by the China aid act of the United States, enacted in April 1948. American support of the Kuomintang intensified CCP hostility to the United States and, under the influence of the two-camp thesis, promoted unity with the Soviet Union. As Ch'iao Mu pointed out, the differences between the factions within "American imperialism" had rapidly disappeared; Ch'iao was disappointed to learn that even Clarence Gauss, who had been rather sympathetic to the Communists, had supported the aid act, and was disillusioned with the so-called democratic and progressive faction.[64] Ideological bipolarity became the major criterion separating enemy and friend.

An even more profound impact upon Cold War perceptions was caused by the Cominform resolution to denounce Yugoslavia in June 1948. The Chinese Communists had entertained a very favorable view of the Yugoslavs, often equating the revolutionary experiences of China and Yugoslavia, both of which had been self-reliant.[65] The Cominform resolution was doubly shocking because its criticism of Yugoslavia could be potentially or even explicitly applied to the Chinese Communists. The resolution denounced the Yugoslavs for their anti-Soviet behavior, undue emphasis on peasants and on a people's front and slighting the role of the party, petit-bourgeois nationalism, overconfidence in their capacity for self-reliant construction, and concessive attitudes toward the imperialists.[66] These points could have been translated into denunciation of the Chinese Communist policies of that time or at some time in the past. The Chinese Communists, therefore, may have felt the necessity for an overall reconsideration of their past policies. As a result, they expressed their complete agreement with the Cominform resolution and decided to study it seriously, "thereby to strengthen our education on class, the party, internationalism, self-criticism and discipline."[67] Two articles by Mao and Liu Shao-ch'i, both of which appeared in the *People's Daily* on November 7, 1948,[68] were products of the shock and very good indications of compliance with the Soviet line. They ardently emphasized unity with the Soviet Union and categorically denied any possibility of "middle roads" or the "third road" on a global scale. Thus, it can be concluded that the tight bipolar image had been fully accepted by the Chinese Communists by the end of 1948.

The famous "lean to one side" policy was not a new idea in mid-1949 when it was announced, but a logical conclusion of the two-camp theory first adopted by the Chinese Communists toward the end of 1947 and reinforced throughout 1948.[69] The policy was not tactical in the sense that CCP had to choose the Soviet Union as an ally because the United States refused to offer friendly relations with them. The policy was axiomatic, derived from the ideological stand of the Chinese Communists at that period. One example of the policy of leaning to the Soviet side was the Chinese reaction to the alleged espionage case of Anna Louise Strong. She was arrested in Moscow in February 1949 and later expelled from the Soviet Union on suspicion of being a Western spy. The *People's Daily* parroted the Soviet announcement and accused her of having "pretended to be progressive."[70] Judging from the fact that she had made the historical interview with Mao in August 1946 and been very friendly with the Chinese Communist leaders, that she was about to visit China at the invitation of the Communist leaders when she was arrested, and that she later came to China as a sympathetic observer of the People's Republic of China and died in Peking, the Chinese reaction in 1949 is difficult to understand unless the influence of the two-camp, Cold War image is taken into consideration.

In July 1949, when victory was near at hand, Mao officially declared the "lean to one side" policy in his "On People's Democratic Dictatorship," and denied any possibility of a neutral position or a third road. In this article he praised the Soviet Union by saying, "they have already established a great and bright socialist state. The Communist Party of the Soviet Union is our best teacher. We must learn from them."[71] Some argue that in comparison with this paper, Mao's report to the second central committee plenum of the seventh party congress, held in March 1949, was more conciliatory toward the United States. It is true that the report was more moderate regarding domestic policy, but in foreign policy it shunned all compromise. Mao said he desired to establish diplomatic relations with *all* countries on an equal basis but added, "It is absolutely impossible that the imperialists who have antagonized the Chinese poeple so far will treat us on equal terms."[72] The main theme of this report was the need to transfer the major sphere of revolutionary activity from rural areas to cities. The city-oriented approach to their activities was no other than the Soviet strategy of socialist construction. Thus, the tone of the report was leaning to the Soviet side, just like other documents of the period.[73]

The "lean to one side" policy was born as a logical conclusion of the third image, and both it and American responses were mutually reinforcing. This escalation culminated in the Chinese intervention in the Korean War. The People's Republic of China now became completely involved in the Cold War in Asia and, under the illusion of Sino-Soviet monolithic unity, acted as an active participant in the East-West conflict.

The adoption of the "lean to one side" policy, however, was not without problems. There seem to have been anxiety, opposition, and doubts in and out of the party, perhaps because, even at this final stage of the revolution, there persisted disputes between the Chinese Communists and the Soviet Union. In mid-1948, there was a rumor that at a meeting of the central committee, "Stalin had urged (through Liu Shao-ch'i) that the Chinese communists should continue guerrilla war and refrain from pushing their victory to a decisive conclusion."[74] In April 1949, it was suggested by Kuo Mo-jo that "the Soviet Union favored partition of China along the Yangtze in order not to provoke American intervention."[75] In June 1949, on the occasion of the Czech party congress, "the Chinese delegate felt obliged to reiterate that there was no possibility of Titoism in the CCP."[76] Such indications of conflict continued to appear until after the establishment of the People's Republic of China. There was, for example, a conflict over the ideological legitimacy and originality of the thought of Mao Tse-tung.[77] Arduous negotiations for a Sino-Soviet treaty between Mao and Stalin were another case in point. As Mao later recollected, "After the victory of the revolution he [Stalin] . . . suspected China of being a Yugoslavia, and that I would become a second Tito. Later when I went to Moscow to sign the Sino-Soviet Treaty of Alliance and Mutual Assistance, we had to go through another struggle. He was not willing to sign a treaty. After two months of negotiations he at last signed."[78] These examples occurring after the establishment of the People's Republic seem to reflect the general atmosphere then existing between the Chinese Communists and the Soviet Union.

Anti-Soviet attitudes lingered on in the party. P'eng Chen and Lin Feng, who had been accused of anti-Soviet activities in 1946, were again criticized for the same reason in 1949.[79] It was also reported that on the eve of the victory of the revolution, there were two factions in the party. One, radicals represented by Liu Shao-ch'i, "favor[ed] strict pro-Soviet orientation of the Chinese Communist policy and hostility toward the United States and Britain." The other, moderates represented by Chou En-lai and Lin Piao, "while supporting friendship and general collaboration with Russia, want[ed], nevertheless, to pursue a more independent line and particularly believe[d] that Communist China should seek a working relationship with the United States and Britain in the interest of trade and other dealings of advantage to China."[80] Though even the moderates believed that their view lay within the scope of Mao's "lean to one side" policy,[81] the split was indicative of the moods in the party. Anti-Soviet sentiments can also be inferred from articles purportedly supporting the friendship with the Soviet Union and the "lean to one side" policy. An article in *Ch'ün-chung* listed a series of hypothetical questions: "Will not China lose independence by its relations with the Soviet Union, as the relations resemble those between Kuomintang and America?"; "Why is it that the Soviet Union does not return Port Arthur and Dairen?"; "In international activities, why do the Chinese Communists always support the Soviet views? Why is it that the Chinese Communists always comply with the Soviet Union and never criticize it?"; "Is it not all right if another Tito appears as a result of following independent policies?"; "Is it not wiser to take a neutral position so as not to be involved in the War?"[82] These questions were condemned as indications of "narrow nationalism" and "illusions toward the imperialists."[83]

That the Chinese Communists adopted the "lean to one side" policy despite all these obstacles was due to the factors which had brought about the third image to begin with. Internationally, the Cold War was becoming severer and severer. In the Chinese view, the formation of NATO in March 1949 brought about an actual danger of war, thus posing a security threat to China. In order to cope with this deepening crisis, they could not help but depend on the power of the Soviet Union.[84] The two-camp thesis was spirally reinforced.

On the domestic scene, radicalization of revolutionary plans increased the necessity of turning to the Soviet Union as a teacher of socialist construction and as a source of aid. The city-oriented new policy line of 1949 was clearly modeled after the Soviet Union.[85] The United States as an investor and an aid donor became irrelevant, as Mao suggested in his paper, "On People's Democratic Dictatorship."[86]

The image of the Soviet Union as a model of socialist construction was quite important for the Chinese Communists. Being convinced of ideological affinity with the Soviet Union, Mao advocated learning from the Soviet Union time and again. Even in 1962, when ideological conflicts between the two countries were already evident, and when close copying of the Soviet model had long ceased, Mao was still advising learning from "the good people and good things of the Soviet Union, the good experiences of the Soviet Communist Party."[87] In 1949, the necessity to learn from the Soviet Union was far greater.

In this connection, the speech by Liu Shao-ch'i at the commemoration meeting of the Russian revolution in November 1949 was quite suggestive. He said, "The Chinese people have never lost confidence in the final victory during the process of revolution, no matter how difficult was the situation and how big a failure we met with. It was because the Chinese people could have a very big hope, were full of confidence, and convinced of the victory of revolution by witnessing the powerful existence of the Soviet Union and the rapid development of its construction."[88] Not only for the Chinese Communists, but also for communists throughout the world, at least until the death of Stalin, this view of the Soviet Union as the model of the future ideal society, the only living example of socialism, was their only consolation during the difficult struggles for revolution.

Machiavellian, power-political considerations between the two superpowers, slight and dubious economic advantages of allying with the West—all these considerations were worn to a shadow before this overwhelming attachment to the Soviet Union. Even the economic advantages of leaning to the Soviet side were greatly expected by the Chinese in 1950. The *People's Daily*, after the conclusion of the Sino-Soviet Treaty, contended that economic assistance from the powerful Soviet economy was much more promising than that from the declining and exploiting capitalist economy.[89] The success of postwar economic recovery and construction changed the rather reserved estimate of the Soviet economy in 1945.

Faced with this situation, American reaction to China was split into two major lines. The first emphasized monolithic Sino-Soviet unity and the threat of communism throughout Asia.[90] The second tried to alienate the two communist countries and tried to create another Tito in China.[91] The first line, which was actually taken, only reinforced the Cold War image of the Chinese Communists and promoted Chinese involvement in the Cold War. In this sense, the policy was a self-fulfilling prophecy.

The second line, which was a continuation of attempts to alienate the Chinese Communists from the Soviet Union in 1944–45, was not effective because of the factors which produced the third image held by Chinese Communists: massive U.S. support of the Kuomintang and the radicalization of the CCP revolutionary plan which eliminated the necessity and desirability of economic and political cooperation with the United States and increased the immediate relevance of the Soviet model of socialist construction.

In other words, the triangular relations among the Chinese Communists, the Soviet Union, and the United States were not the same thing as a billiard-ball game. For the Chinese Communists, the Soviet Union was still qualitatively different from the United States. American decision-makers at that time understood the difficult situation. Although they were trying "to prevent China from becoming an adjunct of Soviet power,"[92] they recognized that the task was to be "a long-term proposition" (perhaps 25 years or longer).[93] They also admitted that the possible Sino-Soviet rifts "would be occasioned by Kremlin policy, and that there is little the United States could do initially. . . . "[94] Recent arguments trying to see Sino-Soviet and Sino-American relations at that period as more or less equivalent pay attention only to the "billiard-ball" type of power politics and greatly underestimate the Chinese Communist image of the Soviet Union as the "fatherland of socialism."[95]

The Aftermath

The tight, bipolar East-West conflict image of the Chinese Communists, coupled with the reciprocal American reaction, made the People's Republic of China an actor in the Cold War in Asia. The Chinese image, however, began to disintegrate after the death of Stalin. The famous Bandung diplomacy was a sign of departure from the bipolar image. It was a symptom of a reviving North-South conflict model.

The loss of confidence in the Soviet Union in the mid-1950s

finally broke down the third image. The Chinese image of the Soviet Union as the living model of socialism was shattered by de-Stalinization, by the realities of Soviet society, which the CCP later defined as the "revival of capitalism in the Soviet Union," and by conflicts and tensions in political as well as economic relations with this "brotherly" socialist country. The Chinese image of the Soviet Union as a selfless aid donor also deteriorated after the Korean War and the first five-year plan in China. The image of the Soviet Union as the guarantor of China's national security melted away after the Taiwan Strait crisis in 1958.

With the passing of the factors which had sustained the tight, bipolar East-West conflict image, the potentially anti-Soviet "intermediate zone" image was officially revived, along with slogans such as "self-reliance" and "the Chinese road to socialism." Deepening Sino-Soviet conflicts also revived the anti-Soviet sentiment which had been suppressed by the official policy of leaning to one side. Unhappy experiences of Sino-Soviet relations since 1949 and the sense of betrayal by the "fatherland of socialism" were combined with renewed anti-Soviet feelings and brought about emotional antagonism between the two communist countries in the 1960s and the 1970s. The total disintegration of the tight, bipolar East-West conflict image and the adoption of the North-South conflict-oriented image by the Chinese Communists were factors which transformed the Cold War structure into one of multipolar relations after the early 1960s.

1. John Gittings, *The World and China, 1922–1972* (London: Eyre Methuen, 1974), p. 142.

2. Besides the works cited, the writer is indebted to the following articles: Ishii Akira, "Ryū Shōki hihan ni tsuite no ichi kōsatsu—'heiwa to minshushugi no shindan-kai' ron o megutte," *Gaikokugo gakka kenkyū kiyō* 20, no. 2 (January 1973); Ishii Akira, "Chūgoku kyōsantō wa kakuheiki ni dō tachimukatta ka? 1945–50 nen," *Kyōyō gakka kiyō*, no. 6 (March 1974); Mōri Kazuko, "Chūgoku kakumei to Ajia no 'reisen' kōzō—Chūgoku kyōsantō no 'reisen' ninshiki o chūshin ni," *Rekishigaku kenkyū*, special issue (November 1975); Yamagiwa Akira, "Chūgoku kyōsantō no hanbei rosen no kakuritsu katei," in *Chūgoku o meguru kokusai seiji*, eds. Banno Masataka and Etō Shinkichi (Tokyo: University of Tokyo Press, 1968).

3. Mōtakutō bunkenshiryō kenkyūkai, ed., *Mao Tse-tung chi*, vol. 9 (Tokyo: Hokubōsha, 1971), p. 186.

4. *Chieh-fang jih-pao* editorial, "Chu Mei-kuo kuo-ch'ing-jih—tzu-yu-min-chu-te wei-ta tou-cheng," 4 July 1944.

5. John S. Service, "Interview with Mao Tse-tung," 23 August 1944, in *Foreign Relations of the United States* (henceforth cited *FR*), *1944*, VI, 606, 611, 614.

6. John S. Service, "The Views of Mao Tse-tung: America and China," 13 March 1945, in *FR*, *1945*, VII, 274, 277.

7. Barbara W. Tuchman, "If Mao Had Come to Washington: An Essay in Alternatives," in *Foreign Affairs* 51, no. 1 (October 1972): 44–64.

8. *FR*, *1946*, IX, 152.

9. *See* views by Acheson (*United States Relations with China*, pp. 87–92), Davies (ibid., p. 574), and Clubb (*FR*, *1945*, IX, 336–41). After the Sino-American rapprochement in the 1970s, similar arguments reappeared in academic studies. Some of the examples are: Joseph W. Esherick, ed., *Lost Chance in China, The World War II Despatches of John S. Service* (New York: Random House, 1974); Nakajima Mineo's essay in this volume; Robert R. Simmons, *The Strained Alliance* (New York: Free Press, 1975); Donald S. Zagoria, "Mao's Role in the Sino-Soviet Conflict," *Pacific Affairs* 47–2 (Summer 1974).

10. *See*, for example, Mao Tse-tung, "Lun ch'ih-chiu-chan," *Mao Tse-tung chi*, vol. 6, pp. 93–96.

11. See *Chieh-fang jih-pao* editorials, "K'e-li-mi-ya hui-i-te ch'eng-chiu," 17 February 1945, and "Ch'ing-chu Ou-chou fan-Fa-hsi-ssu chan-cheng sheng-li chieh-shu," 10 May 1945.

12. *Chieh-fang jih-pao* editorial, "Ts'ung liu-jen pei-pu-an k'an Mei-kuo tui-hua cheng-ts'e-te liang-tiao lu-hsien," 25 June 1945.

13. *See*, for example, *Chieh-fang jih-pao* editorial, "Mei-kuo kuo-ch'ing," 4 July 1946.

14. *FR*, *1944*, VI, 613.

15. *See* "Chung-kuo jen-min chieh-fang-chün hsüan-yen," 10 October 1947, *Jen-min jih-pao*, Chin-chi-lu-yü edition.

16. *See*, for example, comments by Kukuškin to "Direktiva ck KPK o diplomatičeskoj rabote," *Problemy Dal'nego Vostoka*, No. 1, 1972 (Japanese translation by Mōri Kazuko is published in *Kokusai mondai*, no. 180, March 1975).

17. Pëtr P. Vladimirov, *Osobyj rajon kitaja 1942–1945* (Moscow: Novosti, 1973) (Japanese translation: *En'an nikki* [Tokyo: Simul, 1975]), vividly illustrates through Soviet eyes how, despite conflicts and tensions with the Soviet Union, Chinese Communist leaders expected Soviet support for their revolutionary cause.

18. *See* dispatches by Service, 23 (March 1945 *FR*, *1945*, VII, 302ff), Kennan, 10 January 1946 (*FR*, *1946*, IX, 116ff), and Emerson, 28 April 1945 (*FR*, *1945*, VII, 369ff)

19. Ōta Katsuhiro, "Chūgoku kyōsantō no kokusai kan—iwayuru 'chūkan chitai ron' no seiritsu o chūshin to shite" in *Chūgoku kakumei no tenkai to dōtai*, eds. Nomura Kōichi and Kobayashi Kōji (Tokyo: Ajia keizai kenkyūjo, 1972), pp. 209–10.

20. Dispatches by Service (16 March 1945) and Emerson (28 April 1945) *FR*, *1945*, VII, 284–85, 371.

21. Gittings, *World and China*, pp. 149–50, and John F. Melby, *Mandate of Heaven: Record of a Civil War, China 1945–49* (London: Chatto & Windus, 1969), p. 25.

22. *Mao Tse-tung ssu-hsiang wan-sui* (Reprint edition, Tokyo: Gendai hyōronsha, 1974), p. 432. Japanese translations were published by San'ichi shobō (Tokyo) and Gendai hyōronsha (Tokyo) in 1975. English quotation is from Stuart Schram, ed., *Mao Tse-tung Unrehearsed* (Harmondsworth: Penguin Books, 1974), p. 191.

23. *United States Relations with China*, pp. 72, 94–95, 97–98.

24. *Chieh-fang jih-pao* editorial, "Yüan-tung ch'ih-chiu ho-p'ing-te chi-shih—ch'ing-chu Chung-Su yu-hao t'ung-meng t'iao-yüeh," 29 August 1945.

25. *Chieh-fang jih-pao* editorial, "Chi-nien shih-yüeh ke-ming ch'ing-chu Chung-Su t'ung-meng," 7 November 1945.

26. Mao Tse-tung, "On Coalition Government" in *Mao Tse-tung chi*, IX, 258–59.

27. One of the earliest expressions of the East-West bipolar image was Mao's "On New Democracy" in ibid., VII, 182. For other examples, *see* Tang Tsou, *America's Failure in China 1941–50* (Chicago: University of Chicago Press, 1963), pp. 209–13.

28. *Mao Tse-tung hsüan-chi*, vol. 4 (Peking: Jen-min ch'u-pan she, 1960), p. 1191.

29. *Chieh-fang jih-pao* editorial, " 'Fan-Su' pu-kuo shih yen-mu," 8 October 1946.

30. Lu Ting-i, "Tui-yü chan-hou kuo-chi hsing-shih-chung chi-ke chi-pen wen-t'i-te chieh-shih" in *Chieh-fang jih-pao*, 4 and 5 January 1947. According to a Red Guard publication, Chou En-lai was reported to have said that the article by Lu had been re-edited by Mao and that Lu had refused to include it in volume 4 of *The Selected Works of Mao Tse-tung* under Mao's name. See *Liu Shao-ch'i wen-t'i chuan-chi* (Taipei: Chung-kung yen-chiu tsa-chih she, 1970), p. 552.

31. *Mao Tse-tung hsüan-chi*, IV, 1182.

32. Gittings, *World and China*, pp. 141–42, Charles B. McLane, *Soviet Policy and the Chinese Communists 1931–1946* (New York: Columbia University Press, 1958), pp. 176, 180–81, 195.

33. Lin Piao, "Chung-kuo jen-min ke-ming chan-cheng-te sheng-li shih Mao Tse-tung ssu-hsiang-te sheng-li," *Jen-min jih-pao*, 30 September 1960.

34. Tsou, *America's Failure*, p. 326.

35. *FR, 1947*, VII, 41.

36. *Mao Tse-tung chi*, VI, 235.

37. Dispatch on 30 January 1947. *FR, 1947*, VII, 30.

38. *FR, 1946*, IX, 952, 1009–10.

39. Ibid., 971, 1486–87.

40. "Chung-kuo Kung-ch'an-tang Chung-yang wei-yüan-hui wei chi-nien 'Ch'i-ch'i' chiu-chou-nien hsüan-yen," *Chieh-fang jih-pao*, 7 July 1946.

41. *Chieh-fang jih-pao* editorial, "Chüan chieh-fang-ch'ü jen-min tung-yüan ch'i-lai, fen-sui Chiang Chieh-shih-te chin-kung," 16 August 1946.

42. *Chieh-fang jih-pao* comment, "Lun Hua-lai-shih shih-chien," 25 September 1946.

43. *FR, 1947*, VII, 7.

44. Ibid., 9, 541.

45. A summary of the article in the *Kommunist* was translated into English in *China Quarterly* 19 (July–September 1964): 191. *See also* John Gittings, *Survey of Sino-Soviet Dispute* (London: Oxford University Press, 1968), p. 41.

46. Lu Ting-i, "Chan-hou kuo-chi hsing-shih."

47. *Chieh-fang jih-pao* editorial, "Ch'ing-chu Su-lien erh-shih-chiu-chieh kuo-ch'ing," 7 November 1946.

48. *FR, 1947*, VII, 747.

49. For example, Shu Han, "Lun Yin-tu-ni-hsi-ya wen-t'i," *Chieh-fang jih-pao* 11–13 February 1946; Hsin-hua-she [New China News Agency] editorial, "Yin-tu-ni-hsi-ya-te tu-li chan-cheng," 8 August 1947; and Chang Shang-ming, "Yin-ni jen-min ying-yung tou-cheng shih," *Jen-min jih-pao*, 14 and 17 October 1947.

50. See *Chieh-fang jih-pao*, "Niu-yüeh liang-ta hui-i-te ch'eng-chiu," 20 December 1946.

51. *See* note 15.

52. Mao Tse-tung, "On New Democracy," *Mao Tse-tung chi*, VII, 163–66.

53. Mao Tse-tung, "On People's Democratic Dictatorship," July 1949, ibid., X, 291–307.

54. The Chinese translation of this declaration was published in *Jen-min jih-pao* (Chih-chi-lu-yü edition), 11 October 1947.

55. The Chinese translation of this speech was published in ibid., 2 November 1947.

56. The actual contents of the united front policies of China and the Soviet Union were different, however. On this point, *see* John H. Kautsky, *Moscow and the Communist Party of India* (New York: Wiley, 1956), ch. 1.

57. Ch'iao Mu, "Lun Ou-chou kung-ch'an-tang hsüan-yen" *Ch'ün-chung*, 23 October 1947.

58. Ch'iao Mu, "Su-lien yü shih-chieh," ibid., 16 November 1947.

59. Ch'iao Mu, "Ying shih-chieh min-chu fan-ti tou-cheng hsin chieh-tuan," ibid., 1 January 1948.

60. Hsin-hua-she editorial, "Hsing-hsing-chih-huo k'e-i liao-yüan—chi-nien shih-yüeh ke-ming san-shih-chou-nien," *Jen-min jih-pao*, 9 November 1947.

61. Hsin-hua-she editorial, "Ch'ing-chu Tung-nan-ya ch'in-nien tai-piao ta-hui

kai-mu," *Jen-min jih-pao*, 17 February 1948; Hsin-hua-she editorial, "Yin-ni tu-li tou-cheng-te hsin chieh-tuan," *Jen-min jih-pao*, 3 March 1948; Chang Shang-ming, "Ha-ta nei-ke-te nei-mu," *Jen-min jih-pao*, 12 April 1948.

62. The most typical one is Sha P'ing, "Yin-ni shih-pien-te chiao-hsün," *Jen-min jih-pao*, 24–26 March 1949.

63. Charles B. McLane, *Soviet Strategies in Southeast Asia* (Princeton: Princeton University Press, 1966), pp. 402ff.

64. Ch'iao Mu, "Fan-tui Mei-ti chün-shih kan-she," *Ch'ün-chung*, 13 April 1948.

65. *See* Liu Ning-yi's reports of his visit to Yugoslavia in *Jen-min jih-pao*, 26 October and 20 December 1947.

66. The Chinese translation of this resolution was published in *Jen-min jih-pao*, 13 July 1948.

67. "Chung-kung chung-yang kuan-yü Nan-kung wen-t'i-te chüeh-i," *Jen-min jih-pao*, 14 July 1948.

68. Mao Tse-tung, "Ch'üan shih-chieh ke-ming li-liang t'uan-chieh ch'i-lai fan-tui ti-kuo-chu-i-te ch'in-lüeh," and Liu Shao-ch'i, "Lun kuo-chi-chu-i yü min-tsu-chu-i."

69. *See* Ch'iao Mu, "Jen-min neng ch'ü-te che-yang-te sheng-li," *Ch'ün-chung*, 23 December 1948.

70. *Jen-min jih-pao*, 22 February 1949.

71. *Mao Tse-tung chi*, X, 306–7.

72. *Mao Tse-tung hsüan-chi*, IV, 1436.

73. A typical example is the *Jen-min jih-pao* editorial, "T'ieh-t'o fan-ke-ming chi-t'uan-te chia-mien-chü ssu-tiao-le," 27 August 1949.

74. Gittings, *Sino-Soviet Dispute*, p. 13.

75. Kuo Mo-jo, " 'Pai-wan-hsiung-shih kuo ta-chiang'—tu Mao chu-hsi hsin fa-piao-te shih-t'zu," *Hung-ch'i*, no. 1 (1964), and Gittings, *Sino-Soviet Dispute*, p. 13.

76. Gittings, *World and China*, pp. 151–52.

77. Philip Bridgham, Arthur Cohen, and Leonard Jaffe, "Mao's Road and Sino-Soviet Relations: A View from Washington, 1953," *China Quarterly*, 52 (October–December 1972), pp. 670–98, and Gittings, *World and China*, pp. 155–62.

78. *Mao Tse-tung ssu-hsiang wan-sui*, p. 432. English translation is from Schram, *Unrehearsed*, p. 191.

79. *See* note 45.

80. Tilman Durbin's report from Hong Kong in *New York Times*, 17 September 1949.

81. In this sense, early American recognition of the People's Republic of China could not have altered the basic East-West bipolar image of the Chinese Communists at that time, though it might have hastened the pace of Sino-Soviet conflicts in the late 1950s.

82. Lin Shih-fu, "Kuan-yü Chung-kuo min-tsu tu-li tzu-chu yü kuo-chi kuan-hsi wen-t'i ta k'e-wen," *Ch'ün-chung*, 31 March 1949. *See also* a similar article in *Hsüeh-hsi* quoted in Gittings, *World and China*, p. 152.

83. Lin Shih-fu, "Lun 'i-pien-tao,' " *Ch'ün-chung*, 25 August 1949, and *Jen-min jih-pao* editorial, "Chung-Su yu-hao ho-tso-te hsin shih-tai," 15 February 1950.

84. Hsin-hua-she editorial, "Ch'üan shih-chien ho-p'ing li-liang tung-yüan ch'i-lai fen-sui chan-cheng t'iao-po-che-te yin-mou," *Jen-min jih-pao*, 19 March 1949.

85. *See* Kobayashi Kōji, *Chūgoku kakumei to toshi no kaihō* (Tokyo: Yūhikaku, 1974), p. 48.

86. *Mao Tse-tung chi*, X, 298–99.

87. *Mao Tse-tung ssu-hsiang wan-sui*, p. 418. English translation is from Schram, *Unrehearsed*, p. 181.

88. *Jen-min jih-pao*, 8 November 1949.

89. *Jen-min jih-pao* editorials, "Kung-ku Chung-Su hsiung-ti t'ung-meng," 16 February 1950, and "Huan-ying yu-li-yü Chung-kuo ching-chi chien-she-te Chung-Su ching-chi ho-tso," 5 April 1950.

90. One example is NSC 48/1, June 1949, *Pentagon Papers*, Senator Gravel edition (Boston: Beacon Press, 1971), I, 82.

91. One example is PPS 39 (NSC 34), 7 September 1948, *FR, 1948*, VIII, 146–55.
92. NSC 34/1, 11 January 1949, *FR, 1949*, IX, 475.
93. NSC 34/2, 28 February 1949, ibid., 494.
94. NSC 41, 28 February 1949, ibid., 830.
95. *See* note 9.

Mao, China, and the Cold War

Allen S. Whiting

Historians correctly focus on Soviet-American relations as the main arena of Cold War confrontation where the two superpowers polarized the international community with mutually antagonistic alliances, subversion, and recurring nuclear brinkmanship. However, Sino-American relations deserve attention as more than a minor component of this confrontation. U.S. intervention in the Chinese civil war, three years of conflict in Korea, the American economic embargo against China, and clandestine CIA activities in Tibet all culminated in 12 years of U.S. combat in Indochina. These developments require treatment separate from the Moscow-Washington struggle.

Moreover, the death of Stalin removed the personalized devil-figure from Cold War politics so far as American propaganda and perceptions of the Soviet Union were concerned. In contrast John Foster Dulles and Dean Rusk as secretaries of state projected images of Chinese communist threat, symbolized by Mao Tse-tung, that equaled and eventually exceeded the threat attributed to Khrushchev and his colleagues.[1] Then during the mid-1960s, Moscow competed with and soon outpassed Washington in its portrayal of Peking as a dangerously aggressive regime dominated by the dogmatic if not lunatic chairman.

Suddenly in February 1972 President Richard M. Nixon, formerly a staunch exponent of the Republican right-wing attack on Harry Truman and Dean Acheson as betrayers of Chiang Kai-shek, shook hands with Mao in Peking to dramatize a *volte-face* in U.S. policy. After that historic meeting, Washington pledged to pursue "normalization of relations" with the People's Republic of China, *inter alia* muting all sounds of alarm over past or prospective Chinese policy.

While this political change of atmosphere seemed to signal an end to previous American assumptions about China and the Cold War, new evidence revealed how Mao Tse-tung and Chou En-lai had probed for a working relationship with the United States from 1944 to 1946.[2] This put a different perspective on a second, more systematic attempt along this line in 1955–57, suggesting a major change in analysis of Chinese Communist policy during the postwar period.[3] No longer was Mao's "lean to one side" posture seen as ideologically predetermined or rigidly preconceived. Instead it resulted from U.S. behavior as well as from ideological predisposition.[4] Similarly Chinese military intervention in Korea (1950) and the border war with India (1962) was now understood primarily as reaction to perceived threat instead of as simple unprovoked aggression.[5]

Unfortunately, the pendulum of public opinion can swing far and fast, particularly where emotions and distance obscure reality as in American perceptions of China. The changes in official policy and articulated perception were too great and came too quickly to provide a solid basis either for understanding the past or for anticipating the future. President Nixon's rhetorical references to "a generation of peace" resulting from his trip to China together with the historical revision of postwar Sino-American relations prompted assurances that whatever the past causes of confrontation between Peking and Washington, détente ended this aspect of the Cold War. Critics of this view, however, stress the ideological and political elements of confrontation manifest in continued competition for influence in third countries as well as in direct opposition over the fate of Taiwan and Korea. They caution against simplistic acceptance of "smiling diplomacy" and recall Lenin's famous "two tactics" together with the more colloquial Chinese admonition to "talk-fight."

It is obviously impossible in a brief essay to do justice to either position, much less choose between them on the basis of a comprehensive examination of all the evidence. Instead this essay has the more modest objective of reviewing newly available material on Mao's unpublished views concerning the United States during the years of Cold War. This material pertains to our topic in two ways. First, it adds a further dimension of understanding to how Mao and presumably his associates perceived Sino-American relations in the period of implacable hostility on the part of Washington. This can help to set the historical record straight. Second, because this material appeared only a few years ago, during the Cultural Revolution, it is part of a textual heritage that Mao has left behind him as possible guidance for his successors. Although not issued officially or openly, the documents appear to be authentic and presumably reflect the tenor if not the actual text of his statements as available for limited circulation and study. After surveying this record of Mao's remarks, we will note the degree of congruity between their sense of the American relationship and that communicated in selected Chinese media directed at domestic audiences during the period of détente, 1971–75.

Before beginning our analysis, a brief bibliographic note is in order. As is well known, Mao's published works are overwhelmingly limited to his pre-1949 statements. Moreover they are heavily edited and revised. Finally, they receive differing emphasis and interpretation depending upon the particular political context in which they are assigned for study. Simple textual exegesis, therefore, is a hazardous undertaking and often of limited utility for contemporary understanding of Chinese policy prospects.

However, in 1973 the Chinese Nationalist authorities on Taiwan made available two volumes printed in the People's Republic in 1967–69 which have won careful study elsewhere and generally been accepted as authentic.[6] Titled *Mao Tse-tung ssu-hsiang wan sui*, they offer a rich collection of unpublished speeches, interviews, memoranda, and essays, mainly from the period 1955–65. These materials are not without their analytical pitfalls.[7] First and foremost, they are highly selective. Foreign policy receives relatively little attention and all the documents on the crucial 1960 developments in Sino-Soviet relations are omitted. Items which are duplicated in the two volumes are sometimes not identical in text, with changes that suggest consistent editorial bias on the part of the compilers.[8] Finally, the absence of any official imprimatur raises questions concerning the sponsorship, distribution, and actual use made of the volumes.

Nonetheless, this material represents a major addition in quantity and quality to the previously available works of Mao. Their contents have a consistency of style which argues for their acceptance as a true approximation of Mao's actual words. Moreover, material which seems to contradict the contemporary line on the Soviet Union by praising the earlier technical assistance program is nonetheless included. Specific deletion of production figures and individual names suggests the authenticity of documents that address sensitive aspects of state policy. In short, these volumes permit a partial reconstruction of Mao's expressed views concerning the United States and the prospects for war and world revolution during these years.

One final caveat is necessary. Like any large body of writing, particularly one derived from a lifetime of adjusting theory to practice, there are internal contradictions and changes of emphasis which leave considerable choice in the interpretation of Mao's views. In addition, the express reliance on dialectical analysis elevates contradiction to a point of principle. Mao does not offer a rationale for virtually any policy one wishes to adopt, but there is no denying the considerable degree of flexibility left to those who would use his words as prescriptive advice.

Nonetheless, Mao remains the official source of inspiration and direction for policy in the People's Republic and must be dealt with as such. Fortunately, the main outlines of his views concerning the United States emerge relatively well defined. This enables us to assess the degree to which they may have mitigated or exacerbated past Cold War confrontation as well as their possible relevance for future Sino-American relations.

Mao on the United States

The volumes' earliest relevant statements concerning the United States appear in the context of the 1955–57 probes for improved relations manifested by the Sino-American ambassadorial talks and accompanying moves such as the release of imprisoned Americans, Chinese invitations to journalists, students, and cultural groups, and some softening of the public propaganda line. However, when these efforts failed to elicit any positive response from

Washington, Mao portrayed the United States as the principal source of trouble in the world and explicitly discounted the desirability or likelihood of significant improvement in Sino-American relations.

Two speeches, in December 1956 and in January 1957, discussed the United States in specific terms. On the first occasion Mao countered the notion, apparently held by some in his audience from the All-China Federation of Industry and Commerce, that China should "take a middle course and be a bridge between the Soviet Union and the U.S."[9] He warned that "on one side is powerful imperialism whose oppression China suffered for a long time. . . . The U.S. is not dependable. She will give you something but not much." In fact, the Bandung Conference "was able to unify the Afro-Asian countries because these countries had been under the oppression of imperialism which, in this case, was the U.S."

The next month Mao told a conference of provincial and municipal secretaries, "It is useful to delay establishing relations with the U.S. for several years. . . . Let the U.S. have no way out internally and internationally. Let its politics and capital plunder and cause trouble, and isolate it. Then later one day we can always establish relations. 101 years from now when they will be powerless relations can be established. . . . Imperialist countries are ill-intentioned. . . . The most important is America."[10] In May 1958 Mao lumped together "Hitler, Chiang Kai-shek, and U.S. imperialism," adding scornfully, "We have always regarded U.S. imperialism as a paper tiger. What a pity there is only one; even if there were ten it would not be worth talking about. Sooner or later it must perish."[11]

In March 1960 his "On the anti-China question" admitted that "the hatred between the U.S. and us is somewhat deeper" than other unnamed sources, by implication meaning elements in Moscow, New Delhi, and elsewhere.[12] Mao added, however, that the Americans "do not engage in anti-China activities daily" because "their listeners will get disgusted with them." Moreover, prospects will improve once "the gross output and per capita output in our main production items approximate or equal theirs. . . . This will compel the Americans to establish diplomatic relations with us and do business with us on an equal basis or else they will be isolated."

As U.S. military activity in Indochina increased, he toughened his tone, remarking in August 1964 that "we are a little afraid of America because America is our enemy. When America is afraid of us, it means that we are her enemy and also a powerful enemy."[13] But this did not imply implacable confrontation. The same month Mao illustrated a general principle with a suggestive reference to the United States: "Speaking from a strategic objective, we must use dialectical materialism to replace idealism and atheism to replace theism. But it would be different tactically speaking. There should be compromises. Did we not compromise with the Americans at the 38th parallel in Korea?"[14] Despite his depicting the Korean settlement as only "tactical," it had lasted 10 years at the time of his remarks and remained operative more than 10 years later.

Mao on War

More central to Chinese perceptions of "U.S. imperialism" was the vital question of war, its likelihood and consequences. Mao's words deserve careful study because of their potential impact on his audiences both at the time and later. Differing definitions of the situation could have widely different impact, either contributing to continuation of Cold War confrontation or lessening tensions. At one extreme, an implacably hostile United States threatening China's destruction would maximize "worst case" expectations and virtually rule out any serious prospect of improved relations. At the opposite extreme, an image of American impotence combined with prospects for favorable changes in Washington's attitude would minimize alarm and raise hopes for an eventual détente, if not complete rapproachement.

One obstacle to analysis, of course, is the rhetorical and polemical distortions which may have deliberately obscured Mao's own view. It is possible that Chinese strategic weakness and vulnerability, even during the heyday of the Sino-Soviet alliance, justified a show of fake bravado in discussing nuclear warfare and its consequences so as to sustain domestic morale in the face of American intervention in the Taiwan Strait. In addition, such a line may have appeared particularly necessary when undertaking initiatives that risked a Sino-American confrontation, as in the 1958 Quemoy blockade and bombardment.

However, regardless of his actual view, Mao's remarks do offer a consistent analysis of war, its probabilities and consequences. This presumably affected his associates and potential successors in their perceptions and policies. To sum up in advance of textual quotations, Mao steadfastly denied the likelihood of "U.S. imperialism" attacking China, relegating the probability of war to a low risk in the near future while nonetheless leaving it a possibility so long as imperialism continued to exist. As a secondary theme, Mao argued against apocalyptic visions which depict atomic warfare as ending China's existence, much less that of the world. On the contrary, he asserted that not only survival but recovery and a higher stage of civilization would follow a future nuclear war.

Thus in January 1956, Mao addressed the CCP central committee on "the question of peace" and asked, "Is there the possibility of our having twelve years' time to basically complete industrialization? It appears so." His rationale specifically denigrated the U.S. threat, claiming "America is basically concerned with making money and they will not risk their interests. If no one is willing to carry them in a sedan chair they are not willing to walk on their own. The present American troop disposition does not appear organized for fighting a war. They go everywhere to set up bases just like tying the ox's tail to a post—how can the ox move?" Then in a cautionary note he added, "However, we still must calculate that there is also the possibility of a sudden attack. There can be a lunatic in the world and we must plan for this. Therefore, the earlier our work can be completed the better it will be."[15]

Two years later, Mao began his remarks to the second session of the eighth party congress with typical bombast designed to shock his audience into attention, "My talk will be a little dark. We must prepare for a great disaster and great difficulty. . . . We prepare to fight a big war. If the war maniacs use atom bombs, what is to be done? Let them use them! So long as war mongers exist this is a possibility." Despite this ominous opening, however, he returned to his more sanguine estimate: "Between war and peace, the possibility of peace is greater than the possibility of war. Now the possibility of peace is greater than in the past. The strength of the socialist camp is greater than before and the possibility of peace is greater than at the time of World War II." In addition to Soviet strength and the nationalist independence movement as "our mighty allied troops," he cited as a favorable factor the unwillingness to fight on the part of "the proletariat" as well as "a part of the bourgeoisie" and "the American people." Then he added his standard caution, "But there is also a possibility of war and we must prepare for [the possibility of] a mad man, of imperialism seeking to escape from economic crisis."[16]

At this point Mao went into one of the only two extended commentaries on the consequence of atomic war contained in this 750-page volume.[17] Essentially his advice might be summarized, "tough it out." First Mao assured his audience that, "if they strike, they strike. We will exterminate imperialism and afterwards once again construct. From that point there cannot again be a world war." However, his damage assessment proved a bit breathtaking. After recounting how many times in China's past "half the population has been wiped out,"[18] Mao disparaged "the deaths from two world wars" as not so great, only ten and twenty million respectively as compared with China's alleged loss of forty million in two different historic periods. He confessed, "We have at present no experience with atomic war. We do not know how many will die. It is best if one-half are left; the second best is one-third. So of 2.9 billion, 900,000,000 will remain. Several five-year plans will be developed and in place of the totally destroyed capitalism we will obtain perpetual peace. This is not a bad thing." Mao repeated essentially the same remarks four months later during the Quemoy crisis, albeit with less detail and more specific reference to China's future.

Mao's reasoning combined an anodyne analysis of America's destructive power with an asinine image of the postwar world emerging from a nuclear holocaust only a short step away from "perpetual peace," implicitly better off materially as well as spiritually for the experience. Were his words meant to be taken as an operational guide for Chinese risk-taking, recurring crisis if not catastrophe would have long ago engulfed Asia and perhaps the world. The fact is, however, that the basic thrust of his analysis focused more on downgrading the U.S. threat than on pressing his colleagues to nuclear brinkmanship.

This choice of emphasis is made clear by Mao's statements during the Quemoy crisis of September 1958, when a sudden confrontation with Washington erupted after surrender ultimatums were broadcast to the beseiged and bombarded Nationalist garrison. The chairman's extensive review of the overall international situation explicitly denied any major hostile intentions toward China on the part of the United States:

> I have always believed they aim at hegemony over the intermediate zone. . . . Only if great disorder breaks out in the socialist camp can they be confident they can seize it. Unless the Soviet Union and China totally collapse I do not believe they will dare come. . . . Do they use the "anti-communist" banner to make gains in these places [in the intermediate zone] or do they really seek anti-communist gains? To be called a real anti-communist would mean taking an army to attack us and the Soviet Union. I say there is no person so stupid. They only have a few troops to send back and forth.[19]

After the crisis ended on the status quo ante, Mao spoke even more disparagingly of the war threat: "All evidence proves that imperialism adopts a defensive stance and has not undertaken the slightest offensive. . . . NATO is attacking its own nationalism and its own communism (the central attack is on the intermediate areas of Asia, Africa, and Latin America) but towards the socialist camp it is on the defensive."[20] In passing comment on a theoretical article at this time, Mao remarked, "Disintegration—this is the situation of the Western world. . . . Comrades, look at today's world. Who is the master of the world?"[21]

Mao's most theoretical and philosophical discussion of war occurs in an 80-page essay, written in 1960–61, criticizing a Soviet text on political economy. In contrast with the more truncated and colorful expositions to live audiences, his comments on the possibility of war and its political undesirability present a systematic analysis which bears quotation in full as more likely to guide the thinking of his associates and successors than verbal remarks offered at large gatherings:

Is it conceivable that war can be abolished completely when the capitalist system still exists in this world? . . . How can we abolish war without eliminating classes? Whether there is going to be a world war or not does not hinge upon us. Even if a no-war agreement is signed, the possibility of war still exists. When the imperialist powers want war, no agreement can be taken seriously. As to whether atomic bombs and hydrogen bombs are used when war begins, that is another question. Although there are chemical weapons, conventional arms have been used in wars instead of the former. Even if there is no war between the two camps, this is no guarantee that there will be no war in the capitalist world. It is quite possible that one imperialist power will fight another imperialist power or that inside an imperialist country the bourgeoisie will battle against the proletariat. . . . War is one method of class conflict. Only through war can we eliminate classes and only through eliminating classes can we abolish war forever. We do not believe that classes can be eliminated without carrying out a revolutionary war. It is just not possible to destroy the weapons of war without eliminating classes. In this history of class society of mankind all classes and all nations have paid attention to positions of strength. To set up positions of strength is in fact an inevitable trend of history. Armies are the concrete manifestations of class struggle. As long as there is class antagonism there are going to be armies. Of course we do not hope for war. We are hoping for peace. We are in favor of making great efforts to prohibit atomic warfare and striving for the signing of a nonaggression pact between the two camps. Very early on we advocated striving for ten or twenty years of peace. If this can materialize, it will be most favorable for the entire socialist camp and to socialist construction in our country.[22]

This dialectical analysis encompasses both the Marxist assumption of war as a necessary concomitant of capitalism and the pragmatic human desire to avoid it to the extent possible. The latter emphasis is more clearly expressed here than in Mao's platform speeches and contrasts with official propaganda, concurrent and subsequent, which presented war as both necessary and beneficial for human progress. It is also worth noting that while Mao denigrates the operational utility of international agreements which limit war and weapons, he nonetheless argues for their achievement, specifically in the prohibition of nuclear arms and a nonaggression pact "between the two camps."

These views contradict depictions of Mao as an irrational or reckless firebrand who fueled the Cold War in hope of triggering a superpower conflict which would leave China the most populous and strongest nation in the world. At the same time Mao's analysis questions the basic premises of "peaceful coexistence" and virtually rejects the possibility of wholly avoiding war, whether nuclear or conventional.

Mao on Revolution

As the foregoing quotation shows, Mao's analysis of war, classes, and armies includes the observation, "We do not believe that classes can be eliminated without carrying out a revolutionary war." However, neither here nor throughout most of these volumes does he specify China's role or relationship to a revolutionary war. Perhaps such remarks were omitted as too sensitive for inclusion or perhaps they were offered in more restricted councils than were addressed by these various statements. One notable exception, however, is a document entitled, "China must become the arsenal for world revolution." Dated July 1967, the piece fits well into the ambiance of the time, when Red Guards literally ran riot with China's foreign relations at home and abroad, beseiging embassies in Peking to the point of sacking and burning the British chancery, and provocatively propagandizing in London, Rangoon, Hanoi, and elsewhere.[23] Inclusion of this item in the 1969 volume, by which point extreme revolutionary rhetoric and radicalism had been officially repudiated as "ultra-left," makes it of more than passing interest both as evidence of

Mao's views during the vaunted "containment policy" of Washington's Cold War period and for its possible effect on post-Mao policy debates and decisions in Peking.

Mao's ebullient mood emerged in his opening remarks. "New weapons—missiles, atom bombs—we are achieving very quickly. The hydrogen bomb came in two years and eight months. Our development is quickly overtaking America, England, France, and the Soviet Union."[24] After praising the progress of the Nagas' "armed struggle" in India and the Indonesian Communist party's having "purged revisionism," he focused on Burma:

> The guerrillas in Burma have had great development and compared with the armed struggle in Thailand still have a foundation. They have been active for several decades. In the past the party was not united (there were Red Flags and White Flags); now it is all one, all in opposition to Ne Win. The area of the armed struggle covers 65% of Burmese territory. The geographical conditions of Burma are even better than Viet Nam. The area suitable for guerrillas is big. Burma rises, Thailand rises, and in this way America is tugged around in Southeast Asia. Naturally we must still keep an eye out for an early or big war on our own soil. It is still better for the Burmese government to oppose us. We hope they will break relations. This way we could more openly support the Burmese Communist Party. . . . We—China—are not only the political center of world revolution but moreover in military matters and technology must also become the center of world revolution. If we give weapons then we should stamp them as Chinese (except for some special places) and then openly support. We must become the arsenal for world revolution.

Mao's frustration at being constrained to conceal material support and his express wish that Rangoon "break relations" provides a unique revelation of the tensions inherent in the dual policy which combines friendly governmental relations with subversive antigovernmental assistance. This tension had erupted openly only two months before he spoke. In May 1967 Red Guards broke into the Ministry of Foreign Affairs, emptying its files on the streets and beseiging its occupants, amidst accusations of betraying China's revolutionary objectives for the sake of bourgeois diplomatic goals.[25] Conversely, those responsible for communicating China's revolutionary image abroad reached such heights of Sinocentric rhetoric as to evoke at least one recorded rebuke from the chairman for exceeding the bounds of propriety.[26] Throughout the summer and fall of 1967 top leaders, particularly Chou En-lai, struggled to limit the damage to China's foreign relations resulting from Red Guard excesses while maintaining Mao's Cultural Revolution impetus to revive a radical spirit in domestic affairs. In this context, Mao's admonition that China become an "arsenal for world revolution" may have added fuel to the fires which literally consumed the British chancery a few weeks later.

To sum up, Mao's articulated position on "U.S. imperialism" and the threat of war clearly falls between the two extremes we initially hypothesized as characterized either by excessive rigidity, hostility, and "worst case" expectations, or by complete flexibility and confidence in permanent coexistence. He portrays America as steadily weakening, endeavoring to control others but doomed in this effort, and posing no military threat to China except *in extremis* or under an insane leader. He advocates that diplomatic relations develop together with trade at some future point and even cites the Korean settlement as an example of good compromise. At the same time Mao maintains the Marxist-Leninist concept of war as an inevitable concomitant of imperialism and capitalism, specifically raising the prospect of conflict involving China in the distant future. Finally he advocates material military support for world revolution in the context of defeating "American imperialism."

This is not a program of total mobilization and constant confrontation pegged to the American enemy. On the contrary, Mao's low-key verbiage and his policy referents sanction eventual détente. He does not, however, abandon the ideological framework which characterizes the relationship in terms of good versus evil nor does he ever wholly erase the possibility of an ultimate war between China and the United States.

Domestic Propaganda and the Dialectic of Détente

We have examined the central thrust of Mao's views on "U.S. imperialism" and war together with the ambiguities and contradictions contained therein. We have also noted the duality of policy which is communist-derived in its commitment to furthering world revolution while operating in a nation-state framework that utilizes diplomatic relations with other governments for traditional foreign-policy objectives. Bureaucratic responsibility for pursuing these two competing and at times conflicting goals complicates policy debate and, as in 1967, can actually cause an open schism in policy implementation. The dynamic of debate and division is enhanced by the acceptance of dialectical analysis with its central role for "contradictions" as inherent in all situations together with the necessity to determine "the key contradiction" in each "historical period."

Under these circumstances, it is not surprising that a policy of détente with the United States initiated by Peking in November 1968 and favorably responded to by Washington in 1969 should exhibit signs of internal differences and inconsistency, particularly since the central problem of Taiwan remained unresolved. However, evidence of such differences and inconsistency manifested in domestic propaganda is worth examination for the degree to which it is compatible with Mao's earlier statements, reprinted in 1969, as well as for the parameters of possible future policy.

One suggestive source in this regard is a series of children's booklets which focus in hero-emulation fashion on the Korean War and the fighting of the "Chinese People's Volunteers" against "U.S. imperialist aggression." Published in Peking and Shanghai between 1971 and 1975, in printings of from one to two million copies each, their graphic drawings and text show "U.S." marked on helmets and tanks and characterize American soldiers as "devils," "plunderers," and "aggressors."[27] Only in one booklet concerning a tank unit, printed in December 1974, is the specific identity of the enemy omitted although the context is clearly the Korean War.[28] Nowhere is the UN mentioned as a sponsor of U.S. intervention.

Particularly vivid advice is given Huang Chi-kuang on leaving his village for the front: "U.S. imperialism is like a mad dog, thrashing about from one side to the other, blindly causing trouble. . . . Don't come back home until you have struck down U.S. imperialism. . . . To beat a wolf you must use a wolf-beating club."[29] Another story portrays the bombing of women and children with their homes burning in the background and asserts, "On June 25, 1950, the U.S. imperialists suddenly began an aggressive attack on Korea with the mad ambition to seize Korea and continue on to attack China."[30] The actual course of events is completely obscured by the text, which omits North Korean victories of June–August and implies that Chinese assistance was forthcoming from the outset because of U.S. aggressive initiatives.[31]

This imagery is in contrast with the downplaying of anti-American themes after the Nixon visit of February 1972 in material more readily available for foreign consumption. Thus from 1971 to 1974 *Jen-min jih-pao* failed to issue an editorial on the official anniversary of the "volunteers' " entry into the war despite the annual appearance of an editorial in Pyongyang's *Nodong sinmun*.[32] Throughout this period Chinese speeches in Peking celebrating the event never characterized the remaining U.S. troops in South Korea as "aggressors" while demanding their withdrawal, although this terminology was ritualistically reiterated in North Korean propaganda and echoed on one occasion by the Chinese ambassador in Pyongyang.[33]

To be sure, these booklets might merely be designed to fulfill the commonplace need for patriotic pride as national cement, developed through the exploitation of past military victories. However, the more obvious source for such material is the 1937–45 war with Japan, which ravaged most of the populace and is so portrayed in similar booklets. The Korean War, by comparison, touched a minute portion of Chinese soil, and less than 3 percent of the households had a member in combat. Thus its exploitation seems clearly designed to foster a negative image of the United States among Chinese youth.

As with Mao, the projected image is more one of a weak enemy than a serious threat. Although the damage inflicted by American aircraft is great, the individual soldiers are inevitably shown as craven and cringing. While the Chinese youth is usually outnumbered and often sacrifices his life, victory is his, whether by automatic rifle, satchel charge, grenade, or hand-to-hand fighting with bayonet and rifle butt. The visual and textual message is clearly one of "good guys" over "bad buys."

A less explicitly anti-American theme evolved out of the Paracel Islands (Hsisha's) clash of January 1974 wherein a small Chinese naval force smashed South Vietnamese efforts to control contested islands in the South China Sea. More than two months later *Jen-min jih-pao* carried a unique epic poem eulogizing the action in unusually militaristic language.[34] The poem linked the territorial clash with oil and the United States in noting, "These despicable Saigon puppets . . . are out to find oil, to grab fresh territory, to loot our resources for their decadent bosses." The brief incident was elevated in symbolic significance by comparison with the fighting "to resist U.S. aggression and aid Korea [and] to win victory at Chenpao [Damansky] Island." Nor could the enemy be mistakenly identified as Saigon alone since "this brief encounter put to shame the puppet lackeys and their imperialist bosses."[35] The poem's closing lines contained militant rhetoric on Taiwan:

> High floats our flag,
> High and proud in the east wind,
> Calling on us to fight on,
> To liberate Taiwan Province.
> Every inch of our land,
> Every drop of our country's water,
> Must be returned
> To our people who have stood up![36]

The anti-American implications of this poem were strengthened by the treatment of the incident in one of the first political textbooks issued in recent years. This volume of nearly two hundred pages published in Shanghai in October 1974, initially in 600,000 copies, offers an updated analysis of Lenin's classic work, "Imperialism, The Highest State of Capitalism."[37] An eight-page chronology of events which exemplify his views has the Paracel Islands affair as its final entry and notes in summary, "From the beginning of the Spanish-American War in 1898 down to 1974, during seventy-six years, imperialism has never stopped provoking or supporting large and small wars and armed intervention. This historical fact fully proves the incontestable truth: imperialism is war."[38]

By linking Saigon's actions with the alleged aggressiveness of Washington on an issue of vital concern to Peking—possession of the Paracels and access to potential off-shore oil—the propaganda implicitly questions the depth or durability of détente, as depicted in official toasts and banquets. Coincidentally the Shanghai textbook struck still another point of contradiction with more public postures in the chronology's uniquely personal identification of "Nixon" as "sending troops to invade Cambodia" in April 1970.[39] In contrast, only one month after the book's publication Foreign Minister Ch'iao Kuan-hua, in welcoming Secretary of State Henry Kissinger to Peking, praised the ex-president.[40]

In sum, the Korean War booklets and treatment of the Paracel Islands incident appear to reinforce Cold War images of "U.S. imperialism" as an enemy to be eliminated. This was consistent with Mao's dialectical approach and could have been designed to immunize domestic audiences against ideological confusion which might result from the more overt posture of friendship with American officials who periodically visited Peking. Alternatively it could have represented a different view of the relationship with the United States advanced by a faction competing with official policy.

Space does not permit systematic exploration of these alternative hypotheses. However, a *prima facie* case exists in support of the factional analysis. After the death of Mao in September 1976, increasing tension between "moderates" and "radicals" climaxed with the purge of Chiang Ch'ing and her three Shanghai associates who had catapulted to power in the Cultural Revolution: Chang Ch'un-ch'iao, deputy premier, chief political commissar of the armed forces and fourth-ranking politburo member; Wang Hung-wen, second-ranking politburo member and publicly active with foreign revolutionary delegations; and Yao Wen-yuan, a principle figure in theoretical and propaganda activity.

All of the materials we have examined on the Paracel Islands and the Korean War were Chiang Ch'ing's responsibility. In particular the Korean War booklets published in Shanghai were more virulently anti-American than those published in Peking. Indeed the edition already cited as having eliminated all visual and textual reference to the "American" enemy came from Peking. Conversely the political textbook which attacked ex-President Nixon for the Cambodian incursion emerged from Shanghai.

In August 1973 Wang Hung-wen signaled his anti-American stance at the tenth party congress when he warned against a "surprise attack by imperialism and social imperialism." By contrast, Chou En-lai only alerted the same audience to the possibility of a "surprise attack by Soviet revisionist social-imperialism." In July 1976 Chang Ch'un-ch'iao shocked American visitors by declaring that "the peaceful liberation of Taiwan" was unfeasible and only the use of force could achieve China's objective. The fourth purge victim, Yao Wen-yuan, did not address foreign policy in public. However, as overseer of China's propaganda apparatus and editor of theoretical journals, he was responsible for implementing Chiang Ch'ing 's views.

Thus the radical faction's stance on the United States suggests a deep division in view compared with that of the moderate coalition headed by Chou En-lai. This policy conflict never became so sharp as to jeopardize Sino-American détente during Mao's lifetime. Nevertheless it sowed the seeds of policy stalemate and potential reversal after his demise. While the radicals were purged primarily for domestic policy reasons, their removal also had implications for future foreign policy, facilitating flexibility and compromise in place of intransigence and confrontation.

In Conclusion

So far as history is concerned, Mao's words, at least as available to date, acquit him of contributing to Cold War confrontation through depicting the United States as either an overriding threat or a permanently implacable enemy. His views on war did not permit relaxation in the assurance of peace, but neither did they heighten anxiety over the near future or over an eventual nuclear conflagration. Finally, even when Mao miscalculated and Sino-American tensions increased because of Chinese initiatives in the Taiwan Strait, he still refused to inflate the image of external threat posed by "U.S. imperialism."[41]

This does not, of course, address public statements attributed to the chairman, particularly during the Indochina War, much less the entire range of propaganda which poured forth from Peking's press and radio between 1949 and 1969. Nor does it consider Chinese military actions and reactions for their contribution to escalation of Cold War perceptions and rhetoric on both ends of the Sino-American relationship.

However, our purpose has been to focus exclusively on the chairman's reported statements in private situations not heretofore open to outside observation so as to assess how that portion of his political legacy might affect Cold War prospects from the vantage point of policy debates and decisions in Peking. We have found a mixed heritage wherein less emphasized aspects, such as the linkage between imperialism and war or China's role in the world revolution, coexist with the major thrust downgrading the power and malevolence of the United States, particularly with respect to China's security. Similarly we have found that amidst a major muting of anti-American propaganda immediately prior to and since the Nixon visit in February 1972, some domestic media continue to develop themes inconsistent with public postures of détente.

At times in the most recent past, these contradictions or inconsistencies have become more prominent. Thus the final dénouement in Indochina was marked by a sudden surge of anti-American propaganda in Peking with rallies of ten thousand applauding denunciations of "U.S. imperialism," editorials in *Jen-min jih-pao* repeating Mao's maxim that "imperialism will never become a Buddha and lay down its butcher knife," and long commentaries focusing on the "U.S. defeat" in "using South Vietnam as a testing-ground for stamping out national liberation war."[42] While Moscow scrupulously avoided such explicit and extensive references out of deference to détente and a prospective Ford-Brezhnev summit meeting, Peking showed no such inhibitions. However, after May 1975 this surge subsided and "U.S. imperialism" was once again relegated to being the less dangerous of "the two superpowers struggling for hegemony."

Similarly "armed struggle" and "national liberation wars" won more pointed attention in 1975 despite the possible conflict with the so-called "third world policy," which stressed mutual support through state-to-state relations. On the one hand, the People's Republic and Thailand signed a joint communiqué on July 1, establishing diplomatic relations, wherein both sides agreed "that all foreign aggression and subversion and all attempts by any country to control any other country or to interfere in its internal affairs are impermissible and are to be condemned."[43] Only six weeks later Peking Radio relayed a broadcast message attributed to the "Voice of the People of Thailand" celebrating "the tenth anniversary of the armed struggle of the Thai people."[44] It declared that despite "large numbers of troops, police, and other reactionary armed forces including U.S. troops and remnants of the Kuomintang 93rd division . . . the revolutionary people under the leadership of the Communist party of Thailand took up arms and set up their own revolutionary armed forces which have grown into today's Thai people's liberation army." An earlier telegram of support, front-paged on *Jen-min jih-pao*, applauded "revolutionary struggle" in Burma despite an identical assurance of nonintervention given to Prime Minister Ne Win in 1971.[45] Against the disavowal by one Chinese official that such support was only "moral and theoretical" because Chinese troops would never become involved, the intermediate step of furnishing weapons to the BCP as advocated by Mao in his July 1967 remarks could exacerbate relations and, in the case of Thailand, might reawaken a residual Cold War potential for American reaction.[46]

The most highly publicized threat to "peaceful coexistence" came with the trip of Kim Il-sung to Peking in May 1975. After a rising crescendo of Pyongyang propaganda which depicted "Japanese militarism and U.S. aggressive imperialism" as "hatching new war plots" in South Korea, his visit triggered a wave of apprehension throughout Asia and the United States.[47] This coincided with publicity for discovery in the South of an incredible system of tunnels under the demilitarized zone which could accommodate a significant number of North Korean troops in the event of an attack.[48] Although Chinese handling of the visit made clear Peking's refusal to support a war of nerves, much less one of weapons, the fact that Moscow refused to admit Kim at all suggested either duality or division in Chinese counsels.[49] In the immediate aftermath of America's total defeat and withdrawal from Cambodia and South Vietnam, the visit inevitably raised questions abroad about Chinese sincerity and intentions with respect to détente.

Beyond this commonplace observation, however, an additional complication cautions against any expectation of uniformity or consistency in Chinese postures. Mao's successors inherit his dialectical, dualistic position revealed in selected utterances and manifest in the conflicting emphases of his chief executive officer, Chou En-lai, as compared with his wife, Chiang Ch'ing. Mao's main thrust clearly aimed for détente with the United States both because of the rising Soviet threat and because of his basic pursuit of businesslike relations with all states so long as this served Chinese interests. His revolutionary, antiimperialist thrust persisted nonetheless in limiting the degree to which compromise was to outweigh confrontation with Washington.

The balance at any given time will be determined by the issues at hand and their immediate context. No simple formula in Mao's works can guide his successors on this matter. The dominant trend of Chinese policy, the imperatives of economic development amidst dependency on foreign technology, and the weight of political interests in the government will mute the harsher aspect of Mao's revolutionary doctrine exemplified by Chiang Ch'ing and her Shanghai associates. However, the revolutionary impulse will still be articulated as a form of ideological conscience in high party councils, with varying effect on policy. Its impact will depend on the internal position of individuals, factions, and coalitions as well as on the external behavior of other countries, in particular the Soviet Union and the United States.

Note: Chinese translation is an art, not a science. Most of the textual quotations may be found in *Miscellany of Mao Tse-tung Thought* (*1949–1968*), Part I, II (Arlington, Virginia: Joint Publications Research Service, 20 February 1974), hereafter cited as JPRS. I have interspersed my own translation with that of JPRS according to my preference for style as well as content, and therefore cite the relevant JPRS pages together with the Chinese original for reference.

1. Foster Rhea Dulles, *American Policy Toward Communist China, 1949–1969* (New York: Crowell, 1972).

2. Donald S. Zagoria, "Mao's Role in the Sino-Soviet Conflict," *Pacific Affairs* (Summer 1974): 139–53.

3. Richard Levy (M.A. thesis, on deposit at the Center for Chinese Studies, The University of Michigan, Ann Arbor, Michigan).

4. This represents a shift of emphasis from Allen S. Whiting, *China Crosses the Yalu* (Stanford: Stanford University Press, 1968), ch. 1.

5. Neville Maxwell, *India's China War* (New York: Pantheon, 1970); *also* Whiting, *China Crosses Yalu* and *The Chinese Calculus of Deterrence* (Ann Arbor: University of Michigan Press, 1975).

6. *Mao Tse-tung ssu-hsiang wan-sui!* (n.p., April 1967) (reprinted in the Republic of China), hereafter cited as *Wan-sui*; only the 1969 edition will be used. In addition to the JPRS translation cited above, which translates most of the documents, a complete two-volume translation has been published in Japan. For a thoughtful analysis of their origin and authenticity by the foremost Western specialist in textual exegesis of Mao's works, *see* Stuart Schram, ed., *Chairman Mao Talks to the People, Talks and Letters: 1956–1971* (New York: Pantheon, 1974), pp. 51–53.

7. A critical review is offered by Stuart Schram, "Mao Tse-tung: A Self-Portrait," *China Quarterly* 57 (January–March 1974), pp. 156–65.

8. In October 1975 the author discussed these volumes with an informed official in Peking who did not challenge their authenticity but cautioned that the texts were variously transcribed and had not been verified or authorized for publication. The official further implied that "a certain faction" was responsible for editing the collection.

9. Second session of first committee of All-China Federation of Industry and Commerce, 8 December 1956. *Wan-sui*, p. 63; JPRS, p. 37.

10. Summary of conference of provincial and municipal committee secretaries, January 1957. *Wan-sui*, p. 83; JPRS, p. 55.

11. Second speech to second session, eighth party congress, 17 May 1958. *Wan-sui*, p. 197; JPRS, p. 99.

12. "On the anti-China question," 22 March, 1960. *Wan-sui*, p. 317; JPRS, p. 226.

13. "Talk on Sakata's article," 24 August 1964. *Wan-sui*, p. 567; JPRS, II, p. 402.

14. "Talk on methods of solidarity," 1964 August. *Wan-sui*, p. 546; JPRS, II, p. 404.

15. Speech at conference on question of intellectuals, at opening session of central committee of Chinese Communist party, 20 January 1956. *Wan-sui*, p. 33.

16. Second speech to second session, eighth party congress, 17 May 1958. *Wan-sui*, pp. 207–8; JPRS, p. 108.

17. The other occurred a few months later during the bombardment-blockade of Quemoy, addressing the Supreme State Council, 5 September 1958. *Wan-sui*, p. 231.

18. According to Mao, "From the time of Emperor Wu in the Han dynasty with fifty million to the Three Kingdoms, the two Chin dynasties, the North and South dynasty, it fell to only ten million. . . . Later by the time of Hsüan Tsung of the T'ang dynasty it reached fifty million. During the rebellion of An Lu-shan, China was divided into Five dynasties and ten countries. Only after one–two hundred years down to the Sun dynasty was China united. Only ten million remained." *Wan-sui*, p. 208; JPRS, p. 108.

19. Speech to Supreme State Council, 8 September 1958. *Wan-sui*, p. 239; *also* John Gittings, *The World and China 1922–1972* (New York: Harper and Row, 1974), p. 232.

20. Speech to co-operative heads, 30 November 1958. *Wan-sui*, p. 254.

21. "On Huan Hsing's comment on the disintegration of the Western world," 25 November 1958. *Wan-sui*, p. 245; JPRS, p. 125.

22. "Reading notes on the Soviet Union's Political Economy" (1961–62). *Wan-sui*, pp. 340–41; JPRS, II, pp. 264–65.

23. For details *see* Edward E. Rice, *Mao's Way* (Berkeley: University of California Press, 1972), ch. 22.

24. "China must be the arsenal of world revolution," 7 July 1967. *Wan-sui*, pp. 679–80.

25. Melvin Gurtov,"The Foreign Ministry and Foreign Affairs During the Cultural Revolution," *The China Quarterly* 40 (October–December 1969): 65–102.

26. "Directive on external propaganda work," June 1967. *Wan-sui*, p. 679; JPRS, II, p. 462. Mao complained that "after the Cultural Revolution we propagandize the 'Thought of Mao Tse-tung' too much. We boast too strongly. . . . We must be modest, especially to the outside."

27. *Ch'iu Hsiao-yüan* (Shanghai: July, August 1971); *Yang Ken-ssu* (Shanghai: March, November 1972); *Huang Chi-kuang* (Peking: August 1972); *Ya-lu Chiang P'an* (Shanghai: March 1973); *Lo Ch'eng-chiao* (Shanghai: July 1973); *Yang Ken-ssu* (Peking: January 1974 and Shanghai: September 1974); *Yang Lien-ti* (Shanghai: May 1975). The author found some of these on sale in bookstores and in commune homes during his visit in October 1975.

28. *Ying-hsiung tan-ke-shou* (Peking: December 1974).

29. *Huang Chi-kuang*, p. 15.

30. *Lo Ch'eng-chiao*, p. 46.

31. North Korean forces attacked on 25 June 1950; Chinese "volunteers" began crossing the Yalu on October 16, although their official entry is celebrated on October 24.

32. The twentieth anniversary of the "volunteers' " entry into the war was noted in a *Jen-min jih-pao* editorial, 24 October 1970 (jointly written with *Chieh-fang chih-pao*). No subsequent editorial appeared on this date down to 1975.

33. New China News Agency (NCNA), 24 October 1974, quoted Ambassador Li Yün-chuan at a banquet in Pyongyang: "The U.S. imperialist aggressive troops still hang on in South Korea. . . . The U.S. imperialist aggressive troops must be completely withdrawn from South Korea." *Survey of the China Mainland Press*, 11 November 1974. While Pyongyang's ambassador to Peking used identical language, Vice-Premier Chen Hsi-lien's reply only referred to "U.S. troops" as had all Chinese speakers on previous occasions, whether in Peking or Pyongyang. Omission of the word "aggressive" therefore seems intentional.

34. "Battle of the Hsisha Archipelago" by Chang Yung-mei appeared first in *Kuang-ming jih-pao*, 10 March 1974, and as "revised" in *Jen-min jih-pao*, 16 March 1974, where it was transmitted over Peking Domestic Service in Mandarin, 22 March 1974, and carried in Foreign Broadcast Information Service (FBIS) Daily Report, People's Republic of China, 22 and 26 March 1974. An official Peking translation appeared in *Chinese Literature* 6 (1974): 1–34. Curiously this last version lost some of the more militant flavor of the original so that the FBIS translation is more accurate a rendition at various points.

35. This point is sharpened in the original Chinese. Whereas *Chinese Literature* reads, "Outmatched in size and outnumbered," FBIS correctly translates the pointed Maoist maxim, "We are the small fighting the big, the weak opposing the strong."

36. Again FBIS more correctly reads, "We are determined to liberate Taiwan Province!"

37. *Ti-kuo-chu-i shih tzu-pen-chu-i te tsui-kao chieh-tuan ch'ien-shuo* (Shanghai: 1 October 1974).

38. Ibid., pp. 168–69; the entry reads, "Saigon puppet troops with imperialism's support, conducted an armed invasion of our Hsisha and Nansha islands, started the Hsisha sea battle."

39. Ibid., p. 168. To my knowledge this is the only explicitly critical Chinese reference to Nixon after his February 1972 visit.

40. Peking NCNA in English, 25 November 1974, in FBIS, Chi-74-229, 26 November 1974, quotes Foreign Minister Ch'iao Kuan-hua, "We ought to mention the pioneering role Mr. Richard Nixon played in this regard" (referring to the development of "friendly relations" between the two peoples).

41. For a fuller discussion of this point, see Allen S. Whiting, "New Light on Mao: Quemoy 1958: Mao's Miscalculations," China Quarterly 62 (June 1975): 265–70.

42. Mass rallies in the Great Hall of the People were held for the Cambodian victory on 19 April and the South Vietnamese victory on 2 May; Jen-min jih-pao editorials attacking "U.S. aggressors" appeared on 1 May and 20 May with commentaries and special articles throughout the month.

43. Peking Review, 4 July 1975, p. 8.

44. Peking, NCNA in English, 15 August 1975, in FBIS, Chi-75-162, 20 August 1975.

45. The Burmese cable concerned the deaths of the BCP chairman and secretary which occurred in mid-March but were not officially acknowledged by the BCP until May 18. Two days later the CCP central committee expressed "condolences" and confidence "that all the members of the Communist party of Burma and commanders and fighters of the People's army will unite closely around the central committee of the Communist party of Burma headed by Chairman Takin Ba Thein Tin and win thorough and complete victory in their revolutionary war." Peking Review, 30 May 1975. The same issue contains a CCP central committee cable of congratulations to the Indonesian Communist party on the fifty-fifth anniversary of its founding, praising "people's armed struggle."

46. According to Hong Kong Agence France Presse in English, 2 July 1975, Chu Mu-chih, NCNA chief, told Thai reporters in Peking, "We have always supported the just struggle of the oppressed people against imperialism" but claimed this was "moral and theoretical" and the sending of troops would constitute "interference." FBIS, Chi-75-129, 3 July 1975.

47. Typical of North Korean propaganda attacks throughout March and April 1975 is a broadcast of 4 April, on "the sinister design of the U.S. imperialists to hasten preparations for a war in Korea and keep hold of South Korea to the end . . . feverishly speeding up preparations for igniting a war in Korea at any moment, hastening the perfection of the combat posture by further reinforcing their aggressive forces occupying South Korea and amassing means of war in South Korea and around Korea. A series of hysterical moves of the U.S. imperialists these days clearly suggest that their new war provocation maneuvers in Korea have actually entered a very grave stage . . . becoming more frantic as the political and economic crises in the U.S. become acute as never before." FBIS, Asia-Pacific 75–70, 10 April 1975.

48. The first tunnel was allegedly found in the summer of 1974 and the second one discovered in April 1975. According to South Korean authorities a captured enemy agent claimed six more were under construction at unknown points. Foreign newspapermen testified to the remarkable depth and length blasted through solid rock; see report in Washington Post, 27 May 1975. North Korean authorities denied UN charges concerning the tunnels.

49. Kim Il-sung declared at the initial banquet, "If the South Korean rulers

continue to suppress at the point of the bayonet the people's discontent and wrath . . .
it will result in a greater revolutionary explosion. If revolution takes place in South
Korea, we as one and the same nation will not just look at it with folded arms but will
strongly support the South Korean people." Teng Hsiao-p'ing's speech, together with
all subsequent PRC statements, made no reference to this contingency, instead reiter-
ating support for "the independent and peaceful reunification" of Korea. FBIS, Chi-
75-77, 21 April and Chi-75-83 29 April 1975, reporting Peking NCNA of 18 April and
27 April respectively.

Korea in American Politics, Strategy, and Diplomacy, 1945–50

John Lewis Gaddis

The policy of the United States toward Korea between 1945 and 1950 has long perplexed analysts in search of a rational basis for decision making. How was it that a country in which the United States became involved almost by accident, a country whose security was more than once deemed not to be among Washington's vital concerns, suddenly became, when subjected to surprise attack, the object of a massive American military commitment, carried out under the auspices of the UN, which in turn brought about a fundamental restructuring of U.S. policy in the Far East and a significant expansion in the scope and substance of the Cold War? One cannot answer this question by looking solely at the roots of the Korean conflict, or by concentrating exclusively on the Korean-American relationship, although fruitful work has been done in both areas recently.[1] Rather, the problem must be seen in the global context of American foreign policy, for the fact is that few events in Korean-American relations happened of their own accord; almost all took place in response to, or in anticipation of, developments in the larger international arena.

Thanks to recent releases, both planned and unplanned, of much previously classified material,[2] it is now possible to describe with greater precision than had been feasible in the past the evolution of early American postwar policy in the Far East. It is on these sources that the following account is primarily based.

The very involvement of the United States in Korean affairs

was the product of events transpiring halfway around the world in the summer of 1945. Military plans for concluding the war against Japan had not called for American troops to conduct operations in Korea; although vague agreements had been made for a four-power trusteeship, Washington officials assumed that the Red Army would occupy all or at least part of that country. As late as July 24, General George C. Marshall assured the Russians at Potsdam that there would be no American landings in Korea until the more important Japanese target of Kyūshū had been taken.[3]

The experience of dealing with the Soviet Union in Eastern and Central Europe, however, had begun to convince some American policy-makers that Moscow would not willingly relinquish territory taken in military operations for the purpose of establishing joint occupation controls. Edwin W. Pauley, Truman's reparations commissioner, advised the president on the basis of his experiences in Germany that "our forces should occupy quickly as much of the industrial areas of Korea and Manchuria as we can." A War Department analysis warned in July that "prevention of a repetition of the 'Polish situation' in Manchuria and Korea is essential to post-war stability." Henry L. Stimson too made the analogy between Poland and Korea, and recommended on the eve of Potsdam that "at least a token force of American soldiers or marines be stationed in Korea during the trusteeship."[4]

It seems unlikely, therefore, that the American proposal to make the 38th parallel the demarcation line in Korea was purely a matter of administrative convenience.[5] Had such considerations been dominant, no line at all would have been drawn; Korea would have been left, as had originally been intended, to Soviet occupation. The decision to establish an American presence in Korea must be viewed in the same context as the decision, taken at the same time, to deny the Russians an occupation zone in Japan. Both were made in the light of experiences in Europe; both were intended to minimize the amount of territory in the Far East to come under Russian control.[6] It would not be the last time that circumstances wholly extraneous to the Korean peninsula influenced events there.

Keeping the Russian out of southern Korea, though, required assuming responsibility for the administration of that area. The resulting policies of American authorities have provoked considerable controversy among scholars. There is general agreement that the avowed objective of the occupation—creation of a unified, democratic Korean state—was not met. The debate focuses on the question of whether this happened by inadvertence or design. The first point of view stresses American ignorance of Korean politics, and the consequent ineptitude of the occupation. The Americans "had no selfish aims," Gregory Henderson writes; "indeed, they did not have aims at all, lacking policy."[7] The second point of view sees not confusion but calculation: "Korea," Joyce and Gabriel Kolko write, "was yet another example of the consistent postwar American policy to counter or, through its direct military occupation, reverse the momentum and accomplishments of revolutionary movements."[8]

It is useful, in evaluating this controversy, to maintain the all-important distinction between intent and effect. Available evidence provides little reason to doubt that American leaders sincerely wanted a unified, independent, and democratic Korea; there was no noticeable gap, on this point, between what they said publicly and privately.[9] That this was so should hardly be surprising. Wilsonian principles still provided the ideological foundations of American diplomacy: basic to them was a belief in the universal applicability of democratic institutions, a conviction that extremism on the Right threatened those institutions as much as extremism on the Left, and an assumption that the interests of American foreign policy would best be served by the maximum possible diffusion of those institutions.[10] It followed from this that the United States should support, in the words of an internal State Department memorandum of early 1946, "a firm progressive program for Korea . . . which will stress the four freedoms and . . . which would appeal to the vast majority of Koreans."[11]

Why, then, did American policy fail? It failed first and most obviously because the Soviet Union refused to accept it as a basis for unifying the country. The Russians too spoke of democracy as their objective in Korea, but as had been the case in Eastern Europe, they defined that term narrowly in terms of subservience to Moscow. At no stage in the long and tedious Joint Commission negotiations of 1946 and 1947 were the Russians prepared to extend authority in an all-Korean government to political elements not under their control.[12] What seems remarkable in retrospect is the Americans' patience in trying to negotiate a joint Soviet-American trusteeship, given the discouraging East European precedents and the very considerable difficulties the unpopular trusteeship concept had caused American occupation authorities.[13] It is not the policy one would have expected had it been Washington's intention, from the first, to establish a separate, rightist, undemocratic regime in the south.

The Americans pushed trusteeship because they saw it as the only possible way to reunite Korea. As in the case of Germany, Washington was genuinely reluctant to accept partition until all possibilities for a negotiated settlement with the Russians had been exhausted. The unforeseen effect, though, was to undermine the position of Korean moderates in the south, leaving the United States with the choice, once unification talks had broken down, of choosing between a South Korean government of either the extreme Right or the extreme Left. That the Americans chose the Right should not be surprising, given the Left's close affiliation with the power whose expanding influence they were seeking so desperately to contain. It should be noted, however, that the Americans came to this position slowly and reluctantly, only after it had become apparent that a moderate base for an independent South Korean government did not exist.[14]

There is, therefore, little to sustain the argument that Rhee Syng-man's government, which took power in 1948, corresponded in any very significant way with what American officials had hoped for when they entered Korea three years earlier. This gap between intentions and consequences can be explained partly by Soviet resistance to unification on the basis of anything other than subservience, partly by an increasing American tendency to shift priorities from self-determination to containment, partly to sheer administrative incompetence. To view it as the product of deliberate planning, however, is to credit American policy-makers with greater intelligence, foresight, and efficiency than they actually possessed.

Meanwhile, officials in Washington had begun evaluating the strategic significance of the American presence in Korea in the light of the emerging Cold War. First impressions were that it was considerable. President Truman in July 1946 endorsed an analysis which viewed that country as "an ideological battleground upon which our entire success in Asia may depend." As late as February 1947, a high-level interdepartmental committee concluded that if southern Korea were to fall under Soviet control, "the loss of U.S. prestige and influence, and the consequent increase in Soviet influence and power, would have prejudicial repercussions not only on U.S. interests in the Far East but on the entire U.S. world position."[15]

And yet by April 1947, Secretary of War Robert Patterson was advocating an American withdrawal from Korea "at an early date." That same month the Joint Strategic Survey Committee placed Korea next to last, after fourteen other countries, in a ranking of states whose security was considered vital to United States national interests.[16] It is ironic that this reversal of policy occurred just as the United States was assuming a public position, through the Truman Doctrine, which implied considerably expanded global obligations. But the language of the Truman Doctrine was deceptive. What actually took place in Washington in the spring of 1947 was not so much a proliferation of commitments as a reordering of priorities which emphasized economic assistance to Western Europe at the expense of interests in the Far East and elsewhere.[17] The shift in policy on Korea was part of that process.

The earlier view that Korea was vital to U.S. security interests had been based on the belief that a firm American policy, combined with negotiations on unification with the Russians, might yet produce a showcase for democracy in Korea which would greatly enhance Washington's prestige in the Far East. It also reflected the fact that the administration had not yet, in the summer of 1946, given up hope of forming a coalition government in China. As long as there remained a possibility of keeping China, and especially Manchuria, free from communist control, it seemed important not to let all of Korea fall under Soviet influence.[18] Finally, the administration had not yet, in 1946, begun to calculate realistically the cost of maintaining its overseas commitments in relation to the nation's capabilities. There still existed in high circles in Washington a belief that the United States could meet all of the global responsibilities with which the war had left it without at the same time placing undue strain on peacetime domestic political and economic arrangements. The task of defining the relative importance of American overseas interests had only just begun.[19]

The situation looked very different in the summer of 1947. Although the Russians had agreed to a second round of negotiations on unification, it quickly became apparent that they would lead nowhere. And even if unification had been in sight, American occupation authorities, under increasing attack from both the Korean Right and Left, were becoming convinced that it could never be accomplished on a democratic basis.[20] The failure of the Marshall mission had persuaded Washington that chances of preserving a noncommunist China were slim; this further lessened South Korea's strategic significance. Finally, and most important, the economic crisis in Western Europe had forced a refocusing of attention and expenditures on that part of the world. The severity of that crisis, together with anticipated congressional parsimony in meeting it, left little room for active policies in other areas.[21]

The State-War-Navy Coordinating Committee concluded in August 1947, that "every effort should be made . . . to liquidate or reduce the U.S. commitment of men and money in Korea as soon as possible without abandoning Korea to Soviet domination." Two months later, a State Department policy review determined that while the American position in Korea was ultimately untenable, any abrupt withdrawal would cause an unacceptable loss of U.S. prestige in the Far East. American policy therefore should be "to effect a settlement of the Korean problem which would enable the US to withdraw from Korea as soon as possible with the minimum of bad effects."[22] The best way to accomplish this objective, Washington officials concluded, would be to refer the entire Korean question to the UN.

American policy-makers did not expect to see a unified Korea come out of the UN deliberations. As early as August 1947, the State-War-Navy Coordinating Committee had raised the possibility that a UN solution might fail, in which case the United States would have to "be prepared for the possible necessity of granting independence to South Korea." President Truman privately acknowledged early in 1948 that the commission the UN had set up to hold elections throughout Korea would probably be forced to confine its operations to the southern half of the country. UN involvement in the Korean question was, therefore, primarily a "damage limitation" operation on Washington's part, designed to counteract the adverse consequences of what was seen as an inevitable American withdrawal from Korea. As Under Secretary of State Robert Lovett put it in May 1948: "the extent to which we may be successful in minimizing the possible ill effects of our withdrawal from Korea will depend in large measure upon the extent to which the authority of the UN is associated with the program."[23]

Washington's decision to withdraw U.S. troops from Korea, and, simultaneously, to involve the UN there, represented an uneasy compromise between the competing claims of economy and prestige. American foreign policy could be successful, it was believed, only if it was selective: the dispersal of resources in areas not vital to American security—of which Korea was considered one—would lead either to unacceptable weakness or unacceptable expenditures.[24] At the same time, though, it is important to note that American officials were at no point prepared to write off Korea from the point of view of prestige. Should an American withdrawal be followed by a Soviet takeover in the south, the National Security Council noted in April 1948, this would be interpreted "as a betrayal by the U.S. of its friends and allies in the Far East and might well lead to a fundamental realignment of forces in favor of the Soviet Union throughout that part of the world."[25] As in the case of Vietnam a quarter century later, what American policy-makers sought in Korea was a graceful exit, followed by a "decent interval" in which the South Korean government could pull itself together as a bulwark against further Soviet expansion. UN involvement was expected to provide this opportunity. Should this policy fail, should the United States be confronted with the prospect of dramatic humiliation in Korea, there was nothing in the decisions of 1947 and 1948 to preclude a sudden and fundamental reassessment of the situation.

In order to understand the position which Korea occupied in American strategic and diplomatic planning following the decision to withdraw U.S. troops, it is necessary to look generally at the Truman administration's Far Eastern policy during 1949 and the first half of 1950. The dominating consideration, of course, was the victory of communism in China. Washington officials saw this as an event which would temporarily, but not permanently, increase Soviet influence in Asia. China, they believed, was too big to remain a satellite indefinitely; Chinese nationalism would, in the end, undermine Soviet imperialism. It followed from this that American policy should be to resist any further expansion of Russian influence in the Far East, but to do so (1) without opposing the spirit of Asian nationalism, which constituted the best long-term weapon against Moscow, and (2) without expending scarce resources in peripheral areas at a time when the main confrontation with Soviet power was still taking place in Europe.[26]

The best way to do this, it was believed, would be to maintain a few secure military positions in the Far East, while simultaneously providing economic aid to remaining noncommunist nations there. Because of the high-technology/low-manpower orientation of the American military, these strategic strong points would almost certainly have to be islands. Both General Douglas MacArthur and the Joint Chiefs of Staff were emphatic on the need to avoid military commitments on the Asian mainland, while at the same time keeping major islands such as Japan, Okinawa, Taiwan, and the Philippines out of hostile hands.[27] Economic assistance would be relied upon to keep such mainland nations as India, Burma, Thailand, Indochina, and South Korea from going communist; the Point Four program can be seen, in this context, as an important adjunct to the "defensive perimeter" concept. Finally, as in South Korea, the UN would be involved to the maximum possible extent in the hope that it would serve to deter Soviet or Chinese aggression.[28]

But there were two great difficulties with this strategy. One was the general problem of basing current policy on future contingencies, however likely these were to come about. Peking's differences with Moscow were anything but overt at this time; its antipathy toward the United States, at least in public, seemed painfully clear.[29] Acheson had to struggle constantly to keep short-term indications of Sino-Soviet solidarity from undermining his long-term goal of promoting a Sino-Soviet split.[30] Explaining his objectives to Congress and the public proved to be especially difficult. Too candid an explanation risked driving the Russians and

Chinese closer together; perversely, though, too superficial an explanation might have the same effect by raising charges that the administration was not doing enough to contain communism in Asia, thereby provoking Congress, or the electorate, into demanding remedial action.

The other great problem with Acheson's Far Eastern strategy was the specific question of Taiwan, an island whose strategic importance no one doubted but which could not be denied to Peking without offending the very sense of Chinese nationalism which was, in the long run, supposed to counter Soviet influence. Acheson was well aware of this dilemma and tried, early in 1949, to escape it by promoting a Taiwan autonomy scheme which would have kept both Communists and Nationalists off the island. This top-secret plan received the approval of the president and the National Security Council, but was never implemented, partly because the Taiwanese showed few signs of being able to organize an independent government, partly because the Nationalists established themselves on the island sooner than expected, partly because Acheson became convinced in the end that no matter how secret the American involvement, there would be no way to keep the island out of Chinese Communist hands without incurring the wrath of Peking. It was these considerations which prompted President Truman to announce, on January 5, 1950, that the United States would not defend Taiwan against a Chinese Communist invasion.[31]

Acheson's famous National Press Club speech a week later represented a belated effort to educate both the Congress and the public to the intricacies of his Far Eastern policy. But the speech had two important and wholly unintended consequences regarding Korea. First, it publicized the exclusion of that country from the American "defensive perimeter," thereby eliminating the element of ambiguity which is desirable when one seeks to match maximum deterrence with limited capabilities.[32] Second, reiteration of Truman's statement that the United States would not defend Taiwan provoked congressmen sympathetic to Chiang Kaishek into rejecting the Korean aid bill when it came before the House of Representatives the following week.[33] With current evidence it is impossible to say precisely what effect these two episodes had on the North Korean decision to attack South Korea. It does seem safe to say, though, that these inadvertent "signals" conveyed impressions very different from those Washington wanted disseminated. Acheson's ambitious attempt to achieve a rational public explanation of his Far Eastern strategy had the paradoxical effect of at least encouraging, and possibly provoking, actions which would forestall implementation of that strategy for years to come.

Although there is vigorous debate now regarding the origins of the Korean War, there does appear to be general agreement at least that the timing and location of the attack came as a surprise to Washington officials.[34] The intelligence breakdown was of the first order, comparable to the American failure to anticipate Pearl Harbor almost a decade earlier. Since the element of surprise did much to shape the U.S. response in Korea, it seems pertinent to inquire into the reasons why Washington was caught unprepared.

Part of the problem, as at Pearl Harbor, was the existence of too much, not too little, information. Rumors of a Soviet-supported North Korean attack, reported periodically since 1945, increased in frequency after the last American troops left South Korea in the summer of 1949.[35] The sheer number of these reports made proper evaluation of them difficult; so too did the division of responsibility between Washington and MacArthur's semiautonomous command in Tokyo. But the intelligence failure cannot be accounted for solely in terms of the familiar problem of distinguishing "signals" from "noise."[36]

Receptivity to intelligence is determined in large part by the context in which decision-makers operate. And the dominant context affecting Washington's strategic thinking in late 1949 and early 1950 was a preoccupation with general war, centered in Europe, in which the Soviet Union would be the main adversary. In such a war, involvement in Korea would be more of a liability than an asset; as the Joint Chiefs of Staff noted in June 1949, "any commitment to United States use of military force in Korea would be ill-advised and impracticable in view of . . . our heavy international obligations as compared with our current military strength." The National Security Council put the principle more broadly six months later: "It is essential that a successful strategic defense in the 'East' be assured with a minimum expenditure of military manpower and material in order that the major effort may be expended in the 'West.' "[37]

It is true that, by the spring of 1950, some thought was being given in Washington to the problem of limited war. NSC 68 noted that the Soviet atomic bomb had placed a premium on "piece-meal aggression" and predicted that the United States would therefore "be confronted more frequently with the dilemma of reacting totally to a limited extension of Soviet control or of not reacting at all." Soviet experts in the Department of State, George Kennan recalls, were in May and June anticipating limited military action somewhere along the periphery of the Soviet sphere of influence. But Korea was considered to be among the least likely targets. As General W. E. Todd, Director of the Joint Chiefs of Staff Joint Intelligence Group, had told the Senate Foreign Relations Committee a year earlier: "We feel that if the Soviets attach any priority to areas in which they would like to move by means of armed aggression, Korea would be at the bottom of that list of priorities."[38]

These assessments were based partly on overly optimistic reports concerning the South Korean army: compared to its counterparts in Taiwan and Indochina, the Rhee government appeared to be capable of defending itself. South Korea's proximity to Japan also encouraged complacency: should an attack come, there were few places in the world outside Europe to which American troops could have been sent more rapidly. Then, too, any invasion of South Korea would constitute a direct challenge to the UN, something which would not be true elsewhere in Asia. Finally, Washington's lack of concern regarding Korea may also have grown out of an unconscious assumption on the part of American officials that since they had declared Korea to be strategically unimportant, this would lower, rather than raise, its strategic significance in the eyes of the Russians. To treat seriously recurrent rumors of a North Korean attack would require reassessing current estimates regarding Soviet intentions and, even more difficult, American plans for responding to them. It was easier to disregard the rumors.[39]

It is significant that all of the estimates U.S. officials made concerning the possibility of war on the Korean peninsula were based on the assumption that Moscow controlled all North Korean actions, an assumption which recent scholarship has brought very much into doubt.[40] There is considerable irony in this, in the light of the fact that Acheson's overall strategy in the Far East had been based on the anticipated inability of the Russians to dominate their Asian clients. Had this long-range view been applied to the immediate situation in the summer of 1950, the North Korean attack might not have come as such a shock to Washington, and the American response might not have been so sweeping. As it was, the fighting in Korea was seen as a new and dangerous manifestation of Soviet expansionism; the result was to trigger a chain of events whose effects would spread far beyond the limited area in which the fighting was taking place.

Historians, political scientists, journalists, and participants have devoted so much time and energy to examining the reasons for American intervention in the Korean conflict that there seems little to add, at this late date.[41] Certainly "lessons" of history—the desire not to repeat the mistakes of Manchuria in 1931 and Munich in 1938—played a role, as did defense of the UN, a consideration whose importance to President Truman, if not to all of his subordinates, would be difficult to exaggerate. American credibility was also at stake: while the United States had written off Korea from the military standpoint, it had never done so from the point of view of prestige. Whether so intended or not, the North Korean invasion could not have been better calculated to deny Washington the graceful disengagement from the Korean peninsula which it had so carefully sought.

What has not been given sufficient attention is the question of why, once it had decided to intervene, the Truman administration chose to fight the Korean War in such a way as to encourage, rather than impede, Sino-Soviet solidarity. The extent to which Washington's pre–Korean War strategy had been based on promoting differences between Moscow and Peking has only recently become clear.[42] Other recent research has confirmed the acuity of this approach: disagreements between Russia and China were already apparently substantial at the time the war broke out.[43] Why, then, did the administration not take advantage of them, in line with its previously agreed-upon policy? Why did it choose, through such measures as dispatching the Seventh Fleet to the Taiwan Strait and allowing MacArthur to cross the 38th parallel, to alienate Peking, thereby undercutting its own long-range strategy and, in the end, provoking expansion of a war it had sought to keep limited?

One reason, of course, is the very fact that Washington saw the Sino-Soviet split as a relatively distant prospect. There was little sense of how far disagreements between the two nations had already proceeded, and certainly no strategy for taking immediate advantage of them. Even those officials most firmly convinced that Peking would eventually reject Moscow's leadership tended, during 1949 and 1950, to use the terms "Russian," "Chinese," and "communist" almost interchangeably.[44] The outbreak of fighting in Korea further obscured these distinctions by elevating considerations of military security above all others in policy-makers' minds. It was within this context that the Taiwan Strait decision was made.

This decision has been viewed variously as an effort to contain the Chinese Communists, the Chinese Nationalists, or even the Republicans.[45] Recently declassified documents provide yet another explanation. It now appears that contingency plans for general war with the Soviet Union, while anticipating an overall "strategic defensive" in the Far East, did provide for the neutralization of Taiwan, not so much for the purpose of denying it to the Chinese Communists as to keep the Soviet Union from establishing air and naval bases there.[46] Such bases, General MacArthur claimed, would have given the Russians the equivalent in the Pacific of from 10 to 20 aircraft carriers, with supporting forces.[47] Knowing what we now know about the Moscow-Peking relationship in 1950, the prospect of the Chinese Communists seizing Taiwan and then granting the Russians bases there seems remote, even ludicrous. But policy-makers in moments of crisis rarely enjoy the vision afforded historians years afterward. Given the difficulty of knowing, in the first days of the war, whether Korea was the prelude to a more general conflict, given the tendency, once contingencies have arisen, to implement plans which anticipate, or appear to anticipate, them, the Taiwan Strait decision may well have been directed as much against the Russians as anyone else.

If so, this might explain why Truman and Acheson did not see that decision as undercutting their long-term strategy of promoting a Sino-Soviet split. Washington officials tended during this period to assume a close correspondence between their own intentions and the way in which other nations would perceive them; Peking's hostile reaction to the Taiwan Strait move genuinely surprised them.[48] But even had the full consequences of this action, or the far more provocative decision on the 38th parallel several months later, been realized, this is still no guarantee that they would not have been taken. In any competition between short-term military considerations and long-term political ones, the former have a definite advantage. Restraint on Taiwan or at the parallel would have meant, in the eyes of American officials, risking immediate battlefield security on contingencies which, while anticipated, could hardly be assured. Truman and Acheson had been prepared to take comparable chances in peacetime; it was much more difficult to do so in the very different context of limited war.

American public opinion also restricted the administration's ability to exploit Sino-Soviet antagonism. Acheson's Far Eastern strategy required making subtle distinctions between Moscow and Peking, something which was not easy to do, given the fact that both were communist and, for the moment, hostile. The administration's own imprecision in explaining its policy, together with politically motivated attacks on it, did not make the task any simpler.[49] With foreign policy experts themselves uncertain as to when Sino-Soviet hostility would begin to manifest itself, it was difficult to argue against military operations which might encourage Sino-Soviet solidarity, especially if such restraint would be politically unpopular at home. Considerations of this nature had much to do with both the Taiwan Strait and 38th parallel decisions.[50]

Moreover, the administration had discovered by this time that generalization in the public definition of threats to the national security more often led to popular and congressional support than did precision.[51] The Korean War provided a valuable opportunity to institutionalize the proposals of NSC 68; it also added credibility to arguments for stationing American troops in Europe and rearming West Germany.[52] This is not to say that the administration instigated, or even welcomed, the Korean War for these purposes.[53] It is to say that once it had become clear that the conflict was not going to lead to war with the Soviet Union, American policy-makers took full advantage of it to implement their new strategic concepts. The resulting atmosphere was hardly conducive to differentiating between adversaries.

Nevertheless, despite ample warning, Chinese intervention late in November was almost as great a surprise to Washington officials as had been the initial North Korean attack. Until it occurred, hopes had still remained alive within the administration of eventually playing the Russians off against the Chinese.[54] The visit of British Prime Minister Clement Attlee to Washington early in December provided the occasion for a post-mortem: it is one of the few instances on record in which President Truman and Acheson talked frankly about their Sino-Soviet strategy, and why it had failed.

Attlee initiated the discussion by venturing the suggestion that, despite Chinese intervention, significant differences remained between Moscow and Peking which would, in time, produce hostility between them. The United States was making a mistake, he implied, by treating China in such a way as to leave Russia as its only friend. Acheson replied that the prime minister would not find much disagreement among the president's advisers with his analysis. Indeed he himself had probably been more "bloodied" than anyone else in trying to articulate this argument. "The question was not whether this was a correct analysis but whether it was possible to act on it."

One difficulty, Acheson explained, was that the Sino-Soviet split was still a long-range prospect, while military problems in the Far East were immediate. "Perhaps in ten or fifteen years we might see a change in the Chinese attitude but we do not have that time available. . . . If in taking a chance on the long future of China we affect the security of the United States at once, that is a bad bargain." Moreover, the attitude of the American people had to be taken into account. No administration could expect support for a policy of resisting aggression in one part of the world and accepting it in another. "The public mind was not delicate enough to understand such opposing attitudes." Finally, events in the Far East could not be separated from those taking place in other parts of the world. European rearmament was lagging,

Franco-German differences remained unresolved, NATO needed a supreme commander and troops in formation. Chinese intervention "would provide a better chance to get our people behind the effort and to draw on the power from the United States which is actually the only source of power. It is vitally important to hold the United States in this effort."[55]

Truman made the same argument, but with characteristic brevity. The Chinese, he told Attlee, "are satellites of Russia and will be satellites as long as the present Peiping regime is in power. . . . The Chinese do, of course, have national feelings. The Russians cannot dominate them forever, but that is a long-range view and does not help us just now."[56]

More than a century earlier, the great Prussian strategist Karl von Clausewitz had written that the first principle of war was "to trace the weight of the enemy's power back to as few centers of gravity as possible, . . . to confine the attack against these centers, . . . to the minimum possible number of principal undertakings, . . . [and] to keep all secondary undertakings as subordinate as possible."[57] The Truman administration's failure to follow this rule emerges, in retrospect, as its greatest single mistake in fighting the Korean War. Despite its determination to keep the war limited, despite its success, indeed, in confining hostilities to the Korean peninsula, the administration nonetheless took actions which unnecessarily expanded the number of adversaries it had to face. As a result, men who had set out to exploit a Sino-Soviet split wound up instead encouraging Sino-Soviet unity.[58] Rarely in recent history have short-term considerations exerted such dominance over more distant ones; rarely have preoccupations of the present so tyrannized the future.

What strikes one in looking at American policy toward Korea between 1945 and 1950 is the chronic inability of the policymakers involved to estimate accurately the consequences of their own actions. Whether one considers the original decision to send troops to Korea after World War II, the formulation of occupation policy, the decision to withdraw troops in 1947–48, the shaping of the "defensive perimeter" strategy, the intelligence failure preceeding the North Korean attack, or the conduct of strategy and diplomacy following it, the gap in each case between intentions and results is startling. Nor was the problem unique to the Americans, as the North Korean and Soviet failure to anticipate Washington's reaction to the events of June 1950 illustrates. The recurring pattern of miscalculation which characterizes big-power involvement in Korea during the early postwar years provides a sobering commentary on the impact of inadvertance in human affairs. One hopes it is an impact contemporary statesmen have in mind more firmly than their predecessors of a quarter century ago.

1. I have in mind here especially the work of S( )n Sung Cno, Bruce Cumings, Okonogi Masao, and Robert Simmons cited below.

2. The most important new sources for United States Far Eastern policy in the 1945–50 period include the appropriate volumes in the Department of State series *Foreign Relations of the United States* (henceforth cited *FR*), complete for the Far East through 1948, with several volumes on 1949 also available; the Department of Defense study *U.S.-Vietnam Relations, 1945–1967* (Washington: 1971) (henceforth cited *Pentagon Papers*); volumes in the Senate Foreign Relations Committee's "Historical Series" and the Department of the Army's official history of the Korean War, cited individually; and, finally, important documents released either through routine declassification or under the provisions of the Freedom of Information Act, conveniently accessible through the *Declassified Documents Reference System* (henceforth cited *DDRS*).

3. Joint Chiefs of Staff memorandum, meeting of the American, British, and Soviet chiefs of staff, 24 July 1945, *FR, Potsdam*, II, 351–52. *See also* State Department paper, "An Estimate of Conditions in Asia and the Pacific at the Close of the War . . . ," 22 June 1945, *FR, 1945*, VI, 563; and JCS 1388, as read by Marshall at a Joint Chiefs of Staff meeting with Truman, 18 June 1945, *FR, Potsdam*, I, 905.

4. Harry S. Truman, *Year of Decisions* (New York: Doubleday, 1955), p. 433; summary by Peabody of a report on "The Chinese Communist Movement," 5 July 1945, in Lyman P. Van Slyke, ed., *The Chinese Communist Movement* (Stanford: Stanford University Press, 1968), pp. 266–67; Stimson to Truman, 16 July 1945, *FR, Potsdam*, II, 631. *See also* a briefing book paper, prepared for Truman's use at Potsdam, which concluded that "it is considered politically inadvisable for any one of the interested countries alone to invade Korea for the purpose of driving out the Japanese" (Ibid., I, 926).

5. *See*, on this point, a memorandum by Rusk, 12 July 1950, *FR, 1945*, VI, 1039; and James F. Schnabel, *Policy and Direction: The First Year* (Washington: 1972), pp. 9–10. Rusk's memorandum stresses a conflict between the State Department's desire to accept the Japanese surrender as far north as possible and the War Department's concern to avoid overextending military operations. Schnabel's account makes it clear, however, that War Department officials also shared State's concern to keep the Russians as far north on the peninsula as possible.

6. Soon Sung Cho, *Korea in World Politics, 1940–1950: An Evaluation of American Responsibility* (Berkeley: University of California Press, 1967), p. 56. Both Gabriel Kolko *The Politics of War: The World and United States Foreign Policy, 1943–1945* (New York: Random House, 1968), pp. 602–4, and Bruce Cumings, "American Policy and Korean Liberation," in *Without Parallel: The American-Korean Relationship Since 1945*, ed. Frank Baldwin (New York: Pantheon, 1974), pp. 46–48, stress the political motives behind the 38th parallel decision, but fail to relate it, as Cho does, to the situation in Central and Eastern Europe.

294   JOHN LEWIS GADDIS

7. Gregory Henderson, *Korea: The Politics of the Vortex* (Cambridge: Harvard University Press, 1968), p. 121. Other examples of this point of view include Schnabel, *Policy and Direction*, pp. 18–19; and Cho, *Korea in World Politics*, pp. 90–92.

8. Joyce and Gabriel Kolko, *The Limits of Power: The World and United States Foreign Policy, 1945–1954* (New York: Harper and Row, 1972), p. 277. Other examples of this point of view include Cumings, "American Policy and Korean Liberation," pp. 85–88; and Jon Halliday, "The United Nations and Korea," in *Without Parallel*, ed. Baldwin, pp. 109–10.

9. *See*, for example, SWNCC 176/18, "Political Policy for Korea," 28 January 1946: "The persons chosen [to participate in a provisional Korean government] should be the leaders of all the democratic political parties and social organizations which have sufficient political strength and popular backing to warrant representation. . . . Special efforts should be made to find and select a definite majority of strong competent leaders who are not extremists of either right or left. Care should be taken that the Korean leaders chosen are true Koreans and not puppets of foreign powers" (*FR, 1946*, VIII, 625).

10. The Wilsonian ideology is most clearly set out in N. Gordon Levin, *Woodrow Wilson and World Politics: America's Response to War and Revolution* (New York: Oxford University Press, 1968); but *see also* the discussion in Franz Schurmann, *The Logic of World Power: An Inquiry into the Origins, Currents, and Contradictions of World Politics* (New York: Pantheon, 1974), pp. 62–76. Both works stress the fact, often obscured in New Left accounts, that in the eyes of American liberal internationalists, autocracy on the Right posed as much of a threat to Wilsonian ideals as autocracy on the Left.

11. Proposed message to MacArthur, 28 February 1946, drafted in Department of State, *FR, 1946*, VIII, 645. *See also* State Department policy statement, "Policy for Korea," concurred in by the War and Navy Departments and transmitted to MacArthur for Hodge, 7 June 1946, ibid., p. 697.

12. Cho, *Korea in World Politics*, pp. 155–58.

13. Ibid., pp. 105–13; Cumings, "American Policy and Korean Liberation," pp. 75–76.

14. "It is unfortunate," political adviser Joseph E. Jacobs noted in July 1947, "that events are forcing us into a position where we may be compelled for reasons of expediency (opposition to the Soviets) to support extreme rightist leaders such as Rhee and Kim Koo." (Jacobs to Marshall, 21 July 1947, *FR, 1947*, VI, 711.) For other examples of the hostile relationship which existed between Rhee and American officials in 1947, *see* ibid., 645–47, 653, 682–84, 745–46. It might be argued that the American relationship with Rhee in Korea parallels a pattern which occurred elsewhere, notably with de Gaulle in France, Franco in Spain, Perón in Argentina, and Chiang Kai-shek in China. In all of these situations, the initial American attitude was one of suspicion and even hostility, based on the suspected rightist orientation of the leaders involved. As concern over communism intensified, however, leaders on the Right came to seem less sinister, and accommodations were made.

15. Truman to Pauley, 16 July 1946, *FR, 1946*, VIII, 713–14; Report of a Special Inter-Departmental Committee on Korea, 25 February 1947, *FR, 1947*, VI, 612. *See also* draft letter from Truman to Patterson, 1 August 1946, prepared in Department of State, *FR, 1946*, VII, 721–22.

16. Patterson to Acheson, 4 April 1947, *FR, 1947*, VI, 626; JCS 1769/1, "United States Assistance to Other Countries From the Standpoint of National Security," 29 April 1947, ibid., I, 737–38.

17. *See*, on this point, the argument in John Lewis Gaddis, "Was the Truman Doctrine a Real Turning Point?" *Foreign Affairs* 52 (January 1974): 390–93. Rhee, for one, interpreted the Truman Doctrine as implying an expanded commitment to Korea. In a letter to Truman written the day after the president's speech to Congress on aid to Greece and Turkey, Rhee congratulated him on "this courageous stand against communism" and requested that he "instruct the American military authorities in Korea to follow your policy and abandon their efforts to bring about coalition

and cooperation between nationalists and communists." On the recommendation of John M. Allison, assistant chief of the State Department's Division of Japanese Affairs, the letter was not answered (Rhee to Truman, 13 March 1947, *FR, 1947*, VI, 620).

18. Truman to Pauley, 16 July 1946, *FR, 1946*, VIII, 713–14; State Department policy statement, "Policy for Korea," 7 June 1946, ibid., 697. Pauley had reported to the president after a trip to the Far East that Korea under Soviet control could be used as an arm in two potential pincers—one, with Outer Mongolia, directed against Manchuria and north China; the other, with the Kuriles, Sakhalin, and Vladivostok, directed against Japan. (Pauley to Truman, 22 June 1946, ibid., 707–9.) *See also* the assessment in Ernest R. May, *"Lessons" of the Past: The Use and Misuse of History in American Foreign Policy* (New York: Oxford University Press, 1973), p. 57.

19. For example, Clark Clifford's famous memorandum to Truman on relations with the Soviet Union, dated September 1946, concluded that "all nations not now within the Soviet sphere should be given generous economic assistance and political support in their opposition to Soviet penetration" (quoted in Arthur Krock, *Memoirs: Sixty Years on the Firing Line* [New York: 1968], p. 482).

20. See *FR, 1947*, VI, 644–47, 673, 682–84. Political adviser Jacobs reported in September that Americans would likely find themselves increasingly "in the unenviable position of being shot at by both the leftists and the rightists. The only safe alternative would be to arrange with the Soviet Union for mutual withdrawal and let nature take its course which will eventually mean another Soviet satellite state in Korea." Two weeks later, he observed pessimistically: "We cannot give democracy, as we know it, to any people or cram it down their throats. . . . Money cannot buy it; outside force and presure [*sic*] cannot nurture it" (Jacobs to Marshall, 8 and 19 September 1947, ibid., 783, 806).

21. Secretary of War Patterson warned Acheson in April that, given the existing congressional mood, any request for economic aid to Korea might well backfire and result in a net reduction in appropriations (Patterson to Acheson, 4 April 1947, ibid., 627).

22. SWNCC 176/30, "United States Policy in Korea," 4 August 1947, *FR, 1947*, VI, 738; Butterworth to Lovett, "Presentation of Korean Problem to the United Nations," 1 October 1947, ibid., 820–21. The full course of the 1947 policy review on Korea can be traced in ibid., 738–818. Its conclusions were ultimately ratified in NSC 8, "The Position of the United States With Respect to Korea," approved by Truman on 8 April 1948 (*FR, 1948*, VI, 1163–69).

23. SWNCC 176/30, 4 August 1947, *FR, 1947*, VI, 740; Truman to Mackenzie King, 5 January 1948, *FR, 1948*, VI, 1082; Lovett to Draper, Jr., 19 May 1948, ibid., 1201. *See also* the analyses in Leland M. Goodrich, *Korea: A Study of U.S. Policy in the United Nations* (New York: Council on Foreign Relations, 1956), pp. 207–8; James A. Field, Jr., *History of United States Naval Operations: Korea* (Washington: 1962), p. 19; and Denis Stairs, *The Diplomacy of Constraint: Canada, the Korean War, and the United States* (Toronto: University of Toronto Press, 1974), pp. 17–18.

24. Secretary of State Marshall stated this principle succinctly in a speech at Berkeley, California, on 19 March 1948: "Rich and powerful as we are, we cannot afford to disperse our efforts to a degree which would render all ineffective. Every region has its claims and its proponents, and it is therefore necessary to decide on a general strategy to be employed, having in mind the entire world situation" *Department of State Bulletin* 18 (28 March 1948), 423. *See also* Marshall's speech in Bogota, Colombia, 1 April 1948, ibid. 18 (11 April 1948), 472; and Waltar Millis, ed., *The Forrestal Diaries* (New York: Viking, 1951), pp. 369–70, 376, 431–32.

25. NSC 8, 2 April 1948, *FR, 1948*, VI, 1167.

26. For the most comprehensive expressions of this point of view, *see* NSC 48/1, 23 December 1949, *Pentagon Papers*, VIII, 225–64; NSC 48/2, 30 December 1949, ibid., 265–72; Acheson memorandum of conversation with Joint Chiefs of Staff, 29 December 1949, *FR, 1949*, IX, 463–67; and Acheson's executive session testimony be-

fore the Senate Foreign Relations Committee, 29 March 1950, U.S. Congress, Senate Committee on Foreign Relations, *Reviews of the World Situation, 1949–1950* (Washington: 1974), pp. 272–77. The best public statement is Acheson's National Press Club speech, 12 January 1950, *Department of State Bulletin* 22 (23 January 1950), 111–18. For two revealing comments by Truman on this strategy, see *The Journals of David E. Lilienthal* (New York: Harper and Row, 1964), II, 525; and Arthur H. Vandenberg, Jr., ed., *The Private Papers of Senator Vandenberg* (Boston: Houghton Mifflin, 1952), pp. 559–60.

27. Kennan notes, conversations with MacArthur, 5 and 21 March 1948, *FR, 1948*, VI, 700–701, 709; Flexner memorandum, conversation with MacArthur, 6 December 1948, *FR, 1949*, IX, 263–65; Denfield to Forrestal, 10 February 1949, ibid., 285; NSC 48/1, 23 December 1949, *Pentagon Papers*, VIII, 256–57; Acheson executive session testimony, Senate Foreign Relations Committee, 10 January 1950, *Reviews of the World Situation*, p. 162; Acheson National Press Club speech, 12 January 1950, *Department of State Bulletin* 22 (23 January 1950), 115–16; Joint Chiefs of Staff paper, "Military Objectives in Military Aid Programs," 26 January 1950, *Pentagon Papers*, VIII, 274. It is important to note that while both MacArthur and the Joint Chiefs of Staff considered it vital to deny Taiwan to hostile forces, neither advocated stationing American troops there.

28. NSC 48/1, 23 December 1949, ibid., 257–64; Acheson speech, *Department of State Bulletin* 22 (23 January 1950), 116–18.

29. On this point, *see* Richard P. Stebbins, *The United States in World Affairs, 1949* (New York: Harper, 1950), pp. 53–54; Allen S. Whiting, *China Crosses the Yalu: The Decision to Enter the Korean War* (New York: Macmillan, 1960), pp. 6–13; Tang Tsou, *America's Failure in China, 1941–1949* (Chicago: University of Chicago Press, 1963), pp. 504–6. For a new interpretation which distinguishes between the public and private positions of the Chinese government on Sino-American relations in 1949, *see* Robert R. Simmons, *The Strained Alliance: Peking, Pyongyang, Moscow and the Politics of the Korean Civil War* (New York: Free Press, 1975), pp. 59–65.

30. *See*, for example, Acheson's often acrimonious exchanges with members of the Senate Foreign Relations Committee in executive session, 10 and 13 January 1950, *Reviews of the World Situation*, pp. 105–92.

31. For documentation on the evolution of U.S. policy on Taiwan during 1949, see *FR, 1949*, IX, 261–471.

32. *See*, on this point, Coral Bell, *Negotiation From Strength: A Study in the Politics of Power* (New York: Knopf, 1963), p. 92; Alexander L. George and Richard Smoke, *Deterrence in American Foreign Policy: Theory and Practice* (New York: Columbia University Press, 1974), pp. 160–61, 245–47, 562–65.

33. For the debate on the Korean aid bill, which the House defeated by a vote of 192 to 191, see *Congressional Record*, 19 January 1950, pp. 631–57. *See also* H. Bradford Westerfield, *Foreign Policy and Party Politics: From Pearl Harbor to Korea* (New Haven: Yale University Press, 1955), pp. 353–54, 366–67. The bill was eventually passed, but only after the administration agreed to add to it aid for Nationalist China. For Acheson's assessment of the impact of the House vote, *see* his *Present at the Creation: My Years in the State Department* (New York: Norton, 1969), p. 358.

34. *See*, especially, Kolko and Kolko, *The Limits of Power*, pp. 565–99; William Stueck, "An Exchange of Opinion: Cold War Revisionism and the Origins of the Korean Conflict: The Kolko Thesis," *Pacific Historical Review* 42 (November 1973): 537–75; Helene Carrere d'Encausse, "Corée, 1950–1952: aux origines du conflit," *Revue française de science politique* 20 (December 1970): 1181–98; Alfred Crofts, "The Start of the Korean War Reconsidered," *Rocky Mountain Social Science Journal* (April 1970): 109–17; Karunakar Gupta, "How Did the Korean War Begin?" *China Quarterly* 52 (October–December 1972): 700–716, and an exchange of correspondence on the above article, ibid., 54 (April–June 1973), 354–68; Simmons, *Strained Alliance*; Robert R. Simmons, "The Korean Civil War," in *Without Parallel*, ed. Baldwin, pp. 143–78; and Okonogi Masao, "The Korean War as a War of National Liberation," article ab-

stract in *Basic Studies on the International Environment, 1973–1975* (Tokyo: Tokyo Institute of Technology, 1975), pp. 37–39.

35. *See,* for example, Hodge to MacArthur, 2 November 1945, *FR, 1945,* VI, 1106; Hodge to MacArthur, 28 October 1946, *FR, 1946,* VIII, 750; Jacobs to Marshall, 22 October 1947, *FR, 1947,* VI, 845–46; JCS 1483/50, Joint Strategic Survey Committee report to the Joint Chiefs of Staff, 30 January 1948, *DDRS,* 75: 11A; Muccio to Marshall, 12 November 1948, *FR, 1948,* VI, 1325–26; JCS 1776/4, Bradley to Joint Chiefs of Staff, 20 June 1949, cited in Schnabel, *Policy and Direction,* p. 50. *See also* the summary of intelligence reports on the eve of the war in ibid., pp. 61–65.

36. I employ here the terminology of Roberta Wohlstetter, whose book, *Pearl Harbor: Warning and Decision* (Stanford: Stanford University Press, 1962), is a classic case study on the interpretation of intelligence. For the problem of divided responsibility between Tokyo and Washington, *see* J. Lawton Collins, *War in Peacetime: The History and Lessons of Korea* (Boston: Houghton Mifflin, 1969), pp. 42–43, 76.

37. JCS 1776/4, 23 June 1949, quoted in Schnabel, *Policy and Direction,* p. 50 (for the full text, see *DDRS,* 75:11B); NSC 48/1, 23 December 1949, *Pentagon Papers,* VIII, 256. *See also* George and Smoke, *Deterrence in American Foreign Policy,* p. 146; and Martin Lichterman, "Korea: Problem in Limited War," in *National Security in the Nuclear Age,* eds. Gordon B. Turner and Richard D. Challener (London: Stevens, 1960), p. 31.

38. NSC 68, 14 April 1950, *Naval War College Review* 27 (May–June 1975): 80, 93; George F. Kennan, *Memoirs: 1925–1950* (Boston: Little, Brown, 1967), pp. 484–85; U.S. Congress, Senate, Committee on Foreign Relations, *Economic Assistance to China and Korea: 1949–50* (Washington: 1974), p. 176. *See also* Robert R. Simmons, "The Korean War: Containment on Trial" (paper delivered at the annual meeting of the American Political Science Association, Washington, D.C., 5–9 September 1972), pp. 16–17.

39. George and Smoke, *Deterrence in American Foreign Policy,* pp. 170–71. *See also* Kennan, *Memoirs: 1925–1950,* p. 485; Collins, *War in Peacetime,* p. 4; Schnabel, *Policy and Direction,* p. 63; and *Economic Assistance to China and Korea,* pp. 170, 182.

40. Simmons, *Strained Alliance. See also* Gaddis Smith, "After 25 Years—The Parallel," *New York Times Magazine,* 22 June 1975.

41. The fullest account is in Glenn D. Paige, *The Korean Decision (June 24–30, 1950)* (New York: Free Press, 1968), but this should be supplemented by the accounts in Acheson, *Present at the Creation,* pp. 402–13; Schnabel, *Policy and Direction,* pp. 65–79; Collins, *War in Peacetime,* pp. 1–44; May, "*Lessons,*" pp. 52–86; and Gaddis Smith, *Dean Acheson* (New York: Cooper Square Pubs., 1972), pp. 172–201. *See also* Richard W. Leopold's recent survey of literature on the Korean War, "The Historian's Task" (paper delivered at the Harry S. Truman Library, 3 May 1975).

42. *See* the sources cited in note 26, above.

43. Simmons, *Strained Alliance,* pp. 55–102. *See also* Donand S. Zagoria, "Containment and China," in *Caging the Bear: Containment and the Cold War,* ed. Charles Gati (Indianapolis: Bobbs-Merrill, 1974), pp. 109–27; and Zagoria, "Mao's Role in the Sino-Soviet Conflict," *Pacific Affairs* 47 (Summer 1974): 139–53.

44. This tendency is clearly evident in Acheson's "letter of transmittal," accompanying the China White Paper, published in U.S. Department of State, *United States Relations With China, With Special Reference to the Period 1944–1949* (Washington: 1949), pp. iii–xvii. *See also* Johnson to the executive secretary of the National Security Council, 10 June 1949, *Pentagon Papers,* VIII, 218; Acheson to Jessup, 18 July 1949, quoted in Philip C. Jessup, *The Birth of Nations* (New York: Columbia University Press, 1974), p. 29; and Acheson's public statements on the matter on 12 January, 16 February, and 15 March 1950, *Department of State Bulletin* 22 (23 January, 20 March, and 27 March 1950), 115, 428, 468–69. Jessup acknowledged in executive session before the Senate Foreign Relations Committee on 29 March 1950 that, while a Sino-Soviet split would eventually develop, Russian influence might well be dominant in China "for a number of years" (*Reviews of the World Situation,* pp. 283–84).

45. Tsou, *America's Failure,* pp. 558–61; Smith, *Acheson,* pp. 191–92; John W. Spanier,

The Truman-MacArthur Controversy and the Korean War (New York: Norton, 1965), pp. 41–64; Foster Rhea Dulles, *American Foreign Policy Toward Communist China, 1949–1969* (New York: Crowell, 1972), pp. 94–97.

46. *See* Bolte to Pace, 28 June 1950, *DDRS*, 75: 64D: "The emergency war plan provides that in the Far East the primary task is to 'defend Japan, Okinawa, and the Philippines.' Additionally, the emergency war plan provides that Formosa will be denied to the Soviets as a base for offensive operations." Schnabel, *Policy and Direction*, pp. 75–76, closely summarizes this document, but without reference to the sentence on Formosa.

47. MacArthur letter of 14 June 1950 read to Truman and advisers at Blair House on the evening of 25 June 1950, *DDRS*, 75:28E.

48. Smith, *Acheson*, pp. 201, 219–20; David S. McLellan, "Dean Acheson and the Korean War," *Political Science Quarterly* 73 (March 1968): 21; John G. Stoessinger, *Nations in Darkness: China, Russia, and America* (New York: Random House, 1971), p. 52.

49. *See* Gaddis, "Was the Truman Doctrine a Real Turning Point?" pp. 394–95.

50. Spanier, *Truman-MacArthur Controversy*, pp. 62–63; Louis J. Halle, *The Cold War as History* (New York: Harper and Row, 1967), pp. 218–20; Martin Lichterman, "To the Yalu and Back," in *American Civil-Military Decisions*, ed. Harold Stein (Birmingham: University of Alabama Press, 1963), pp. 596–97.

51. *See*, on this point, the argument in Richard M. Freeland, *The Truman Doctrine and the Origins of McCarthyism* (New York: Knopf, 1972), especially pp. 93–94, 101, 196–97, 286–87; *also* Kennan, *Memoirs, 1925–1950*, pp. 322–24; and Gaddis, "Was the Truman Doctrine a Real Turning Point?" pp. 399–400.

52. Simmons, "Korean Civil War," pp. 153–57; Halle, *Cold War as History*, pp. 237–47; Walter LaFeber, "Crossing the 38th: The Cold War in Microcosm," in *Reflections on the Cold War: A Quarter Century of American Foreign Policy*, eds. Lynn H. Miller and Ronald W. Pruessen (Philadelphia: Temple University Press, 1974), pp. 77–79.

53. The administration could not expect to use the Korean conflict as an instrument with which to accomplish its reorientation of national security policy until it was clear that the conflict would not erupt into general war with the Soviet Union. In this connection, *see* executive session colloquy between Acheson and Senator R. Alexander Smith on 24 July 1950, *Reviews of the World Situation*, p. 323.

54. Smith, *Acheson*, pp. 219–20; Spanier, *Truman-MacArthur Controversy*, pp. 97–98.

55. Minutes, Truman-Attlee, Acheson conversation, 5 December 1950, *DDRS*, 75: 29F.

56. Minutes, Truman-Attlee meeting of 4 December 1950, *ibid.*, 75: 29E. A "sanitized" but nonetheless revealing account of these conversations appears in Harry S. Truman, *Years of Trial and Hope, 1946–1952* (New York: Doubleday, 1956), pp. 396–413. Acheson's account in *Present at the Creation*, pp. 480–85, is briefer and, in places, misleading.

57. Karl von Clausewitz, *On War*, trans. and ed. Edward M. Collins (Chicago: Regnery, 1962), p. 279.

58. *See*, on this point, Schurmann, *Logic of World Power*, p. 242; and Raymond Aron, *The Imperial Republic: The United States and the World, 1945–1973* (Englewood Cliffs, N.J.: Prentice-Hall, 1974), pp. 60–61.

The Domestic Roots of the Korean War

Okonogi Masao

The political processes that were set in motion in and around the Korean peninsula in 1945 reveal how far the Korean War, while complex, was basically a domestic conflict over the legitimacy of political power. The conflict developed in the course of Korea's quest for independence. The geopolitical position of the peninsula, however, and the international character of Korean liberation itself, rendered what was purely internal conflict particularly vulnerable to external pressures, thereby expanding its scope and adding to its complexity. The domestic power struggle became "internationalized" when the waves of the Cold War reached the shores of Korea in the late forties.

The "internationalization" of the Korean conflict, however, because it was *ex post facto*, does not justify the popular view that domestic factors were largely irrelevant and war was imposed from outside. A balanced understanding of the Korean War can be achieved only by analyzing, on the one hand, the way in which world events impinged upon the Korean peninsula to "internationalize" the domestic independence struggle and, on the other, the way domestic political forces drew in, or "internalized," the international environment in the course of pursuing their goals. Furthermore, both internal and external factors in the struggle shifted in quality and relative significance as the influence of the Cold War grew stronger. In Korea immediately following liberation, for example, a domestic confrontation that anticipated the structure of the Cold War was already in existence. Also, the outbreak of the Korean War itself implied abrogation of the U.S.-Soviet agreement, based on the Cairo declaration of 1943 and the Moscow agreement of 1945, to the effect that neither side would unilaterally attempt to incorporate the Korean peninsula into its sphere of influence.[1]

In this essay I will expand upon the above thesis in an analysis of the domestic roots of the Korean War and attempt to unravel some of the war's complexity by focusing on the linkage between domestic and international political factors. The most important assumptions underlying this approach are that the Korean War was a complex struggle in which domestic and international elements were intertwined, that it was the consequence of historical processes both inside and outside Korea that emerged in the summer of 1945, and that the Korean War arose out of a vicious circle of escalation between domestic and international forces, whereby domestic politics were "internationalized" and international politics "internalized."

The International Framework of Domestic Confrontation

Antecedents of the Cold War

The Moscow agreement of December 27, 1945, proposed that the Korean peninsula be placed under a four-power trusteeship for a period of up to five years. This formula, based on a mutual understanding between the United States and the Soviet Union beginning with the Cairo declaration, was presented to the Korean people as the only choice compatible with "international reality." Within Korea at that time, however, there were already two distinct movements to establish autonomously a unified Korean government. One was the Korean People's Republic set up in Seoul on September 6, the day before the American troops were scheduled to land. The other was the provisional government of the Republic of Korea based in Chungking, which boasted of a history extending all the way back to the March First independence movement of 1919. The former was a coalition between the Korean communists headed by Pak Hon-yong and the left-wing nationalists. The latter was supported by such prominent nationalists as Rhee Syng-man (Syngman Rhee), who had returned to Korea from the United States in October, and Kim Koo and Kim Kyu-sik, who had returned from China a few weeks later.

The two "governments" engaged in a short negotiating session to explore the possibility of merging, but the talks failed. Each insisted on an exclusive title to legitimacy, so that by the time the Moscow accords were announced at the end of December there was no room for compromise. It was quite obvious by November, in fact, that a merger would be impossible.[2] From December on each sought to discredit the other through epithets such as "exile politicians" who could not shake "the inertia of their royal, despotic life style" or "subversive elements" attempting to "destroy the country and put it under foreign influence."[3] The two groups did not limit their fight to Korea proper. Each asked for international recognition as the government of a unified Korea, thus colliding with both the United States and the Soviet Union. The Korean People's Republic persisted in acting as though it possessed governmental authority within South Korea despite two American military government declarations of non-recognition.[4] By the same token, Rhee Syng-man was not content to oppose communist activity in Korea, but went further to criticize the "conciliatory" American attitude toward the Soviet Union.[5]

In retrospect, what the Moscow agreement meant was quite obvious: the United States and the Soviet Union were forcing the Korean people to choose between trusteeship and partition. As indicated above, however, Korea at that time was already seeing the disintegration of the kind of national solidarity that would have been necessary to effectively meet such an ultimatum. Song Chin-u and Rhee Syng-man, who were among the few leaders able to comprehend the true intent of the agreement, were diametrically opposed: Song chose trusteeship, and Rhee partition.[6] Kim Koo was strongly against a trusteeship initially, but as trends toward partition became more pronounced, he made an about-face. Centrist leaders such as Kim Kyu-sik and Lyuh Woon-hyung vacillated like a pendulum between the two alternatives. As a result, both governments disappeared, and a free-for-all ensued, with a variety of political participants ranging from communists to right-wing nationalists vying for power, each against all others.

Finally, as conflict among the various left- and right-wing factions went out of control, the trusteeship proposal became merely an instrument of domestic power struggle.[7]

Between that initial chaos and the outbreak of the Korean War in June 1950, domestic and international politics intertwined in a complicated manner. As they groped for a new order on the peninsula, external forces clashed over such matters as the establishment of a provisional government under the Soviet-American joint commission, general elections under the supervision of the UN, and withdrawal of Soviet and American troops, in addition to the problem of trusteeship. Each external force sought domestic allies to look after its interests on the peninsula, and domestic groups in turn looked for international aid and sponsorship for their own causes in the power struggle.[8] This cycle of "internationalization" and "internalization," combined with the traditional tendency of Korean politics to isolate moderates while extremists decided the political course of the nation, induced a pattern of political instability which later would be reproduced on a larger scale in the context of the Cold War. From another angle, this was a period of resistance by Korean radical groups against Soviet-American cooperation, which had been effective since the Cairo declaration. That aspect is evident both in Rhee's insistence on an independent government for South Korea and in the strong resistance by Pak Hon-yong and other left-wing radicals against American military government.

Rhee's advocacy of an independent South Korean government was revealed during a speech at Chongup, Chollapuko, on June 3, 1946.[9] It was very clear that, through the anti-trusteeship movement which had gained the overwhelming support of the Korean people, Rhee intended to isolate the American military government from all domestic groups. This would, he hoped, force the United States to renounce the Moscow agreement, which was the product and symbol of Soviet-American cooperation. Because he was confident that relations between the United States and the Soviet Union would inevitably decline anyway, he was not worried about the partition of Korea that would result from the renunciation of the agreement. To him, cooperation with the communists was nothing but a "sweet illusion," and he believed that Korea could be unified only through military force.[10] In this sense, his demand for the establishment of an independent government in South Korea was a "lean to one side" policy in its assumption that the United States eventually would become anti-Soviet.

By the same token, South Korean communists such as Pak Hon-yong, who failed in establishing the Korean People's Republic and were being expelled from the mainstream of the Korean communist movement, acted in advance of Soviet policy, much as Rhee did with the Americans. The National Council of Korean Labor Unions called a general strike on September 24, 1946, and that was followed by a series of incidents called the October people's resistance, which centered in Taegu. These events marked a departure from the earlier strategy of indirectly attacking the American military government and heralded a new line of "terror for terror" and "blood for blood."[11] The South Korean communist objective was "to make it difficult for American troops to remain in Korea and to erode Korean confidence in them."[12] At about that time, Kim Il-sung was saying that "the fundamental enemy of the Korean people is the group of reactionaries around Kim Koo and Rhee Syng-man."[13] His continued reluctance to directly criticize the American military government shows that the radical policies of the South Korean communists did not have the consent of the Soviet Union and North Korea.[14]

To recapitulate, in 1946 groups of radical Korean nationalists and communists stood opposed to Soviet-American cooperation and in favor of a much stronger anti-Soviet and anti-American policy, respectively, than either the United States or the Soviet Union ever would have advocated against each other. Of no less importance is the fact that the radical political lines found their origins and rationale in the vortex of domestic politics, where a power struggle of "each against all" was underway. The highest goal of each group was to control a unified government.[15]

Domestic Confrontation during the Cold War

Sandwiched between the political struggles of domestic factions in 1946 and the political turmoil caused by the UN-supervised elections for a South Korean government held in 1948, the first half of 1947 was relatively quiet in Korea. That short-lived stability was contingent upon the preservation of the framework of Soviet-American cooperation through the convening of the joint commission and some success by the American military government in their efforts to set up a moderate coalition government, as well as upon concentration by South Korean communists on rebuilding their strength after the debacle of the October people's resistance.[16]

Stability did not last. The second meeting of the Soviet-American joint commission, which had been expected to make steady progress, broke up. The United States and the Soviet Union now stood in unmediated confrontation, with the former urging that the Korean problem be entrusted to the UN, and the latter demanding the immediate withdrawal of Soviet and American troops from Korea. Soviet-American cooperation collapsed, and domestic strife spread with heightened intensity. Conflict reached its climax with the UN-supervised general elections for a South Korean government held in May 1948.

Trouble started on February 7, shortly after the arrival in Seoul of the UN commission (UNTCOK) in charge of observing the election. The anti-election campaign, which included strikes, blocking of communication and transportation, assaults on police stations, anti-rightist terror, and propaganda against the election, lasted for over three months. Fifty locomotives were destroyed overnight; more than 100 people, including 33 policemen, were killed within the month; and 8,000 people were arrested.[17] The situation rapidly deteriorated thereafter. It is confirmed that by May 27 the number of deaths had mounted to 330 protesters, 150 members of right-wing local defense corps, 18 election officials, 2 national assembly candidates, and 73 policemen or members of policemen's families.[18]

The greater intensity and violence of the confrontation in the first half of 1948 than in the latter half of 1946 provides some measure of the effects of the Cold War on domestic conflict. In the first place, the struggle in 1946 had strong overtones of resistance against Soviet-American cooperation by radical groups which were excluded from the scope of both American and Soviet policies toward Korea. The confrontation of 1948, on the other hand, took place as Cold War influence closed in. The clear support of Rhee by the United States, and the Soviet and North Korean move toward the radical Pak Hon-yong line, are the most obvious indications that the 1948 conflict was more than local. It was without question much more of a bipolar confrontation than that of 1946. Secondly, the contending forces in Korea regarded the 1948 confrontation as a decisive struggle over "unification or partition," "revolution or counterrevolution," because the framework of Soviet-American cooperation had collapsed and Korea was about to be severed in two. For this reason, conflict was blown up to maximum scale.[19] Just as significantly, however, the 1948 conflict was limited to confrontation among domestic groups. The South Korean communist struggle against the election had to be carried out independently; the United States and the Soviet Union still respected each other's spheres of influence on either side of the 38th parallel, sharing a concern for the status quo on the peninsula, albeit in partitioned form.

Deterrent Effects of the International Environment

Deterrence through Cooperation

As pointed out above, domestic and international issues were closely intertwined in the unfolding of Korean politics following liberation. Despite the multiple combinations formed by internal and external forces, however, a fundamental pattern seems to pervade the Korean political process, with the exception of a short period just before the outbreak of the Korean War. I refer to the tendency of conflict among domestic forces for political legitimacy to move in advance of international confrontation between the United States and the Soviet Union, and to exert thereby continuous pressure outward onto the international environment.

Neither the United States nor the Soviet Union had ever demanded that Korea be placed under its exclusive influence throughout several wartime meetings and the tripartite (U.S., Great Britain, USSR) Moscow Conference of Foreign Ministers. While they failed in jointly administering Korea as called for in the Moscow accords, it did not necessarily mean that either side wanted to exchange the framework of mutual cooperation for one of confrontation by military force. Until July 1947, when the Cold War in Europe spread to the Korean peninsula, the United States and the Soviet Union had tried to forestall a confrontation on the peninsula by maintaining a framework of cooperation through the joint commission. With that in mind, it is difficult to explain away the Moscow agreement, which advocated a trusteeship and the establishment of a unified provisional government by the Korean people, as merely a temporary expedient designed to meet an immediate need. Certainly the basic policy of the United States toward Korea at that time was to search for a moderate political force within Korea that the Soviet Union would accept and to establish a provisional government at the earliest date. The Soviet Union did not discard the policy of cooperating with the United States through the joint commission until October 1947. The attitudes of the United States and the Soviet Union were fully reflected in their respective Korean policies.

American policy at that time emphasized the early establishment of a provisional government based on agreement with the Soviet Union and support for a middle-of-the-road force within Korea to achieve that.[20] Reaching an agreement with the Soviet Union was at least as important to the United States as the matter of what forces would comprise such a government. Consequently, following the fruitless joint commission meeting on May 6, 1946, the United States found itself completely isolated from domestic forces. The nationalists demanded that the United States renounce the Moscow agreement and immediately recognize Korea's independence; the communists criticized the United States from the other direction for conspiring with reactionaries and planning to renounce that very same "sacred" document. Such hostility put the United States in an extremely difficult situation.[21]

Even then, however, American policy did not fundamentally change. On June 30, U.S. occupation forces commander John R. Hodge disclosed, on order from the State Department, the American intention to support a moderate coalition composed of right-wing moderates led by Kim Kyu-sik and left-wing moderates led by Lyuh Woon-hyung.[22] On September 9, he announced plans for a legislative assembly led by those two groups.[23] This plan amounted to a form of collaboration between the American military regime and South Korean moderates. The intention was to establish a firm foundation within South Korea from which to negotiate with the Soviet Union.[24] Efforts to group moderate factions into a coalition progressed despite opposition by right- and left-wing radical groups. On October 8, the seven principles of union worked out between right-wing and left-wing moderates were announced. On December 12, the South Korean interim legislative assembly was finally organized with Kim Kyu-sik as chairman. An Chae-hong, a moderate right-winger, was appointed the first Korean civil administrator on February 10 the following year.

Soviet policy toward Korea at that time incorporated the intention to build a strong system under Soviet leadership in the northern half of Korea.[25] But that did not imply diametrical opposition to the policy of cooperation with the United States. On February 4, 1946, a Provisional People's Committee for North Korea was established with Kim Il-sung at its head. Prior to the opening of the first Soviet-American joint commission meeting, the People's Committee announced a platform consisting of 20 articles to serve as the basic policy for a provisional government of all Korea, and began to carry out its policy of land reform. The primary objective of these actions, however, was to give the Soviet Union the initiative in negotiations with the United States toward the establishment of a unified Korean government.[26]

After the collapse of the first Soviet-American joint commission meeting, the North Korean side repeatedly announced that "North Korea, which is advancing toward true democracy, and South Korea, which is again being dragged back toward a reactionary, antidemocratic, and antinational course under the despotism of reactionary elements," were "moving in opposite directions."[27] The brunt of their criticism was directed at "reactionary elements such as Kim Koo and Rhee Syng-man," however, and they carefully avoided direct criticism of the United States. As for relations between the Soviet Union and South Korean communists, no evidence exists to suggest that the Soviet Union supported the attempted establishment of the Korean People's Republic or the adventuristic struggles that took place in the fall of 1946.[28]

The Soviet Union continued steady efforts to establish a pro-Soviet regime in North Korea. These efforts materialized in the establishment in February 1947 of a *de facto* state composed of party, government, and a people's assembly. Even at this stage, however, mutual cooperation between the United States and the

Soviet Union had not been abandoned completely. The joint commission was reconvened on May 21. It may be seen as a last-ditch
effort toward cooperation between the two countries. At first it
seemed to go smoothly enough, and the statement issued in
Washington on July 2 by Military Governor Archer L. Lerch
augured well for successful negotiations.[29] By July 8, however, the
Soviet Union had reverted to a rigid stance when encountering
the problem of selecting Korean organizations with which to
discuss the establishment of a provisional government. On July 10,
the conference virtually stalemated. This sudden Soviet change
of attitude corresponded to changes in the European situation.
When the Kremlin opposed the Marshall Plan and decided on a
policy of "refusing any accommodation to the West, any cooperation with it,"[30] they had no choice but to apply the same policy
to Korea. With the expansion of the Cold War, the formulation of
policy toward Korea had been raised to the level of world strategy.

Deterrence through Partition

Since political conflict on the Korean peninsula had, to some
extent, been deterred by Soviet-American cooperation centering
on the joint commission, the collapse of the commission caused
far-reaching changes in the framework of Korean politics. In the
period between the collapse of the commission and the spring of
1948, both the United States and the Soviet Union moved much
closer to meeting the demands of radical groups on right and
left. As the Cold War developed, the confrontation between right-
and left-wingers in Korea was accepted internationally as an established fact, creating a double bipolarity—within Korea itself
and in the worldwide confrontation between two ideological
systems.

The moderate coalition, whose activities had achieved a measure of success, suddenly began to collapse following the assassi-
nation of one of its leaders, Lyuh Woon-hyung, on July 19. On
October 18, the United States referred the Korean question to the
UN, and there on November 14 it was decided that general elections be held throughout Korea under the supervision of the
international body. The United States began to throw whole-
hearted support behind Rhee Syng-man. The final reconciliation
between Rhee and the Americans took place at the end of the year.

Commander Hodge made a special announcement on December 17 warning the Korean people of a communist threat, and Rhee responded the next day by saying that Hodge's statement "dispelled, once and for all, the doubts which had been created by statements and official documents issued previously by the American military government."[31] From then on, no nationalist movements except those which were anticommunist, anti-trusteeship, and pro-partition could avoid frustration due to the rigid solidarity which grew up between the United States and Rhee Syng-man.

The Cold War favored extremists in North Korea as well. It is clear that the radical struggles carried out in the spring of 1948 by South Korean communists against the elections in South Korea resulted from Soviet and North Korean endorsement of the Pak Hon-yong line. By the same token, Kim Il-sung's report to the second conference of the North Korean Workers' party, held in March 1948, was filled with vitriolic criticism of American imperialism. He declared that the northern half of the peninsula had now become "a solid base for the democratization of the homeland" and "headquarters for democratic forces which will save the homeland from the American imperialists' policy of colonial subordination."[32] In the summer of 1948, two governments were formed, each of which regarded itself as the only lawful government of all Korea: the Republic of Korea in the south, and the Democratic People's Republic of Korea in the north.

However, despite the close approximation of Soviet and American policies with those of the radical groups in Korea, and the antithetical nature of their ideologies as expressed in the Cold War, there was no sign that either the United States or the Soviet Union desired direct confrontation in Korea. They still preferred, in other words, not to abrogate their agreement at Yalta. Contrary to the tendency on the part of Koreans to criticize the 38th parallel demarcation line as an injustice, the United States and the Soviet Union proceeded further to define their respective zones of influence—which amounted to the freezing of partition—and seemed tacitly to recognize the need to avoid direct confrontation. In this sense, the fundamental reason why the United States and the Soviet Union favored the division of Korea from the summer of 1947 onward was that they wanted to avoid direct confrontation between the two systems, not because cooperation had collapsed.

It is obvious, however, that their attempt to prevent conflict between North and South Korea by dividing the country contained an inherent contradiction: their scheme of preserving the ideology of Cold War confrontation while containing actual conflict within Korea was internally contradictory. As a result, after the summer of 1948 there reappeared a tendency for the heated domestic conflict to intensify international confrontation. That tendency subjected the framework of deterrence through partition to continuing strain. It was under such circumstances that the withdrawal of both Soviet and American troops from Korea was carried out.

Maturing Conditions for Civil War

Localization of Conflict

Many unanswered questions remain with regard to the withdrawal of Soviet and American troops from Korea in October–December 1948 and June 1949, respectively. Nevertheless, it may be noted that the Soviet proposal of September 26, 1947, for simultaneous early withdrawal, made in an apparent attempt to counter American referral of the Korea question to the UN, was less concerned with partition per se than with the conditions of partition. Despite the clash of opinions on the surface, the interests of both the United States and the Soviet Union coincided to the extent that they wanted to partition Korea in such a way that they would not become involved in direct military confrontation. In 1947 and 1948 neither country intended to build a strong military power on its own side of the 38th parallel and thereby challenge the other, but they each worried that the other side planned such a move. Not only the Soviet Union, which later made such a proposal, but also the United States was already actively examining simultaneous withdrawal plans.[33]

The simultaneous withdrawal of troops can be interpreted as part of a Soviet-American policy of reducing their presence in Korea. It is well known that the United States, which, since the trusteeship issue first arose, had been plagued by political and economic difficulties in dealing with the Korean question, had a low estimation of Korea's strategic value.[34] Therefore, the United

States wished to keep American involvement to a minimum. In the context of a worldwide Cold War strategy of containing communism, however, there was a limit beyond which the ideal of minimal involvement could not be realized. Risking oversimplification, it may be said, therefore, that the United States was faced with contradictory demands and attempted to satisfy both through a small-scale version of "Vietnamization": simultaneous withdrawal of troops.[35]

It was not apparently the United States alone that found a policy of reduced commitment necessary. In fact, both the steady construction of a friendly system in North Korea following liberation and the timely proposal for the simultaneous withdrawal of troops imply that the Soviet Union was more anxious to disengage than the United States. The reason for this was quite complicated. Apparently, Soviet policy at that time combined its earlier aim of preventing the establishment of a unified Korea under an anti-Soviet government, with the later goal of supporting a movement to unify Korea under a pro-Soviet government, the latter to be achieved without direct confrontation with the United States.[36]

Discussion within Korea on withdrawal, on the other hand, tended to be influenced by domestic political considerations. Rhee Syng-man himself, when he opposed American support for the Moscow pact, had demanded the immediate withdrawal of both American and Russian troops.[37] It is apparent, therefore, that withdrawal of foreign troops was usually demanded by anyone who, at that time, was being excluded from association with external forces. When the withdrawal of Soviet troops was announced in September 1948, anti-Rhee elements within South Korea equaled the communists in calling for immediate American withdrawal in response.[38] This is because they all believed that the external forces alone prevented them from acquiring political power and that the Korean people were on their side. Indeed, Rhee's belief that American withdrawal was inevitable undoubtedly arose from that sort of behavior on the part of his opponents. However, Rhee's relatively early retraction of his opposition to an American withdrawal was not premised solely on such objective factors. In addition, as evidenced in the diplomatic efforts in the United States of Rhee's special envoy, Cho Pyong-ok, Rhee saw in the withdrawal of American troops a good opportunity to negotiate for American military aid.[39] American military withdrawal offered a way to replace the "weak Republic of Korean troops" under the U.S. occupation troops with "strong Republic of Korean troops" who would take over from the Americans. In fact, it is clear from a letter which Rhee Syng-man sent to Cho on April 10, 1949, that the American supply of weapons to South Korea which he demanded in exchange for American withdrawal was a basic prerequisite for the execution of his plan: to unify Korea by attacking the north.[40]

As for North Korea, a formal Korean people's army consisting of two complete divisions and an independent brigade had already been organized in February 1948, prior to the establishment of the Democratic People's Republic of Korea. In September, it was announced that the withdrawal of Soviet troops had been executed on time at the behest of North Korea.[41] A review of subsequent developments reveals no evidence of factors that might have motivated the North Koreans to oppose Soviet withdrawal.

In Korea following the withdrawal of the troops of both sides, then, a former big-power strategy of deterrence of conflict through partition was gradually superseded by a process of "localization of conflict." The attempt to deter conflict through partition while endorsing the ideology of North-South confrontation, and the effort to decrease big-power commitment while a bitter confrontation went on inside the country, could not be expected to tone down the intensity of that conflict. Rather, it amounted to transferring the initiative to the Korean leaders. D. F. Fleming has pointed out that "a balance of power conflict is likely to transfer the power of decision from the major power to small allies who may be entirely irresponsible, or worse, but gain the power to commit their principles."[42] If this is correct, then it can be said that the structure of deterrence in Korea had already begun to turn in that direction.

In the latter half of 1949, neither Rhee Syng-man nor Kim Il-sung concealed his intention to unify Korea by force. Each repeatedly maintained that armed unification was a domestic issue. In the course of their campaign for American weapons, Rhee and Cho had already assured the United States, where many feared that supplying weapons to South Korean troops might ultimately embroil the United States in an international military conflict, that "the Republic of Korea requires only logistical support," and that "if a war becomes necessary, we will fight it ourselves."[43] They repeatedly asserted that their march to the Yalu river was purely a domestic matter. Kim Il-sung's views on this point were even clearer. His theory of North Korea as a "democratic base" derived from the belief that the south could be liberated and a unified Korea attained without outside participation.[44] According to Khrushchev's memoirs, Kim Il-sung's scheme for liberating the south appealed strongly to Stalin because it was presented as "an internal problem for the Korean people themselves to solve."[45]

Rhee and Kim held such views not only because they themselves sought armed unification, but also because they were forced into extremist action by their involvement in ideological battles with other domestic factions. Post-liberation strife between northern and southern communists over the leadership of the Korean communist movement had developed favorably for Kim Il-sung,[46] but the legitimacy of his postulation of the north as a "democratic base" was continually threatened by the theory of "South Korean revolution" advocated by Pak Hon-yong and others, who pushed for immediate, forced unification. Rhee's strategy of "unification by northward advance" was also under constant pressure from opponents who supported unification through a North-South entente. In the Cold War atmosphere, which tends to sanction even the most extreme positions, radical policies served both Kim Il-sung and Rhee well in gaining domestic power and legitimacy.

Asymmetrical Development of Conflict

In the summer of 1949, for the first time in many decades, the Korean people experienced peace with no foreign troops in their homeland. The communists' desire to liberate the southern half of the Korean peninsula had not waned, but for the present it was offset by Rhee's lusty call for a northern campaign. A great deal of ammunition that American forces had left behind at the time of their withdrawal was put under the strict supervision of 500 American military advisers. Washington also imposed definite limitations on the type of weapons supplied to Korean troops[47] and repeatedly warned Rhee that if his troops went north, American military aid would cease entirely.[48] With that, it seemed that the Soviet-American agreement on "deterrence through partition" remained effective.

Rhee's slogan of marching north was certainly not a bluff when he formed his own government. It still had a basis in fact during arms negotiations with the United States, and there is a good possibility that an American decision to supply Rhee with heavy weapons would have allowed him to put his idea into practice. However, Rhee's continued claims following his failure to get any more arms cannot be taken at face value. As Lee Ho-jae rightly points out, Rhee's policy at that point degenerated into virtual blackmail to force a change in U.S. policy; it was no longer preparation for the northern campaign.[49] His biting criticism of American "appeasement," his call for a Pacific alliance with Chiang Kai-shek, and his exaggerated claims concerning South Korean military power—he said he could "occupy Pyongyang within three days"—all indicate that the realistic basis of his "march north" slogan had evaporated.[50]

In North Korea, in the meantime, several covert initiatives were under way to dissolve the big-power "deterrence through partition": one officially encouraged movement sought donations for the purchase of Soviet planes, tanks, and ships; the Korean volunteer corps was brought back from China and incorporated into the North Korean army; and guerrilla squads were sent across the 38th parallel into South Korea. All these activities suggest that the conflict between north and south was losing its symmetry in terms of both intention and capability. Based on a mid-October decision to buy planes, tanks, and ships, the movement to procure modern arms from the Soviet Union was vigorously promoted through an "association of supporters for maintaining and defending the fatherland," which was begun on July 15. A ceremony for the presentation of funds donated was held at the People's Army Art Theater on January 25, 1950.[51] By the spring of that year, the Soviet Union had delivered to North Korean troops a large volume of heavy arms, including aircraft, warships, and the T-34 tanks which made possible the large-scale advance into South Korea on June 25.[52] As for the return of the Korean volunteer corps from China, the 166th division under Pang Ho-san returned in July 1949, the 164th division commanded by Kim Chang-dok returned in August, and in the following March those Korean soldiers who had served in two divisions of the Chinese People's Liberation Army also came back. The total number of Korean volunteer corps soldiers was estimated at about 50,000, which constituted one-third of the entire North Korean regular army.[53] Guerrilla groups composed of communists from the South Korean Workers' party were sent south in 10 different waves beginning in the summer of 1949, and by the spring of the next year a total of more than 2,000 had been sent.[54]

Of these three initiatives, the gathering of donations was undoubtedly based on a prior Soviet decision to supply North Korean troops with a large volume of the latest weapons. In view of the trends in relations between the Soviet Union and North Korea at that time, it is also difficult to conceive of the assignment of the volunteer corps back to the North Korean Army as having nothing to do with a Soviet policy of reinforcing North Korean troops. The dispatch of guerrilla bands to the south is difficult to evaluate. But, in view of the fact that, in late 1949 and early 1950, the Soviet Union praised guerrilla activities in South Korea and that the initiation of guerrilla activities coincided with a Soviet reexamination of Asian people's liberation movements following the Chinese revolution, we may surmise that the Soviet Union was favorably disposed toward North Korean guerrilla activity.[55] On the other hand, this should perhaps be interpreted as reflecting a strong desire for war on the part of North Korea, particularly the communists of South Korean origin.[56]

Of course, nothing mentioned above constitutes positive proof that the Soviet Union at that stage approved or agreed to a war in Korea. By putting together several pieces of circumstantial evidence, it is possible to conclude that the final Soviet decision on the war was made in the spring of 1950. Nevertheless, it is impossible to deny that the above-mentioned initiatives were in direct contravention of the tacit agreement between the United States and the Soviet Union not to build up a dominant military power on the peninsula. Therefore, those initiatives attacked from within and destroyed the framework of "deterrence through partition." At that point, the international environment began to cease functioning in its role as deterrent.[57]

Conclusion

The most remarkable aspect of the entire political process leading up to the outbreak of the Korean War is that domestic Korean
forces were always more inclined toward armed unification than
were external forces. Therefore, the role of the international
environment throughout was to deter rather than foment war,
with the exception of the period just before the war's outbreak. As
sketched above, before the influence of the Cold War reached the
Korean peninsula, both rightist and leftist radicals strongly resisted Soviet-American cooperation. The United States and the
Soviet Union, on the other hand, rejected the radicals and culti-
vated the moderates. Even after the advent of the Cold War, the
big powers attempted to hold conflict in Korea to a minimal level
by clarifying their own respective spheres of influence. Meanwhile,
Korean radicals violently opposed the freezing of the partition and
insisted on removing the barrier at the 38th parallel by force.
There was obviously a qualitative difference between the Soviet-
American intentions and those of the Korean radicals. Evidence
for such a difference was clearly offered during the later truce
negotiations when it was the extremist Korean leaders such as
Rhee Syng-man and Pak Hon-yong who were the most anxious to
continue the war.[58]

Since the Korean conflict was fundamentally concerned with
the legitimacy of a unified government, perhaps it is natural that
there was a strong inclination toward war. Nevertheless, although
conditions for an outbreak of war had matured within Korea, the
war, when it came, did not occur independently of the intentions
of the great powers. The events which took place in North Korea,
beginning in the latter half of 1949, show that in the international
environment the framework of "deterrence through partition"
was being discarded. In this sense, the Korean War stemmed from
a combination of two elements: domestic developments which
made war possible and an international situation in which the
great powers attempted to take advantage of domestic developments in order to achieve their own ends. This essay does not seek
to analyze Soviet motives, but it is clear that the Soviet Union
tried to use the Korean situation to attain its own international
objectives.[59] There is a strong possibility that the change in Soviet

policy was based not on a misunderstanding of American policy but, rather, on the optimistic miscalculation that the United States would allow hostilities to remain a civil war.

The above interpretation of the war indicates that it resulted both from the "internationalization" of the Korean problem by the United States and the Soviet Union, and from the concurrent "internalization" of international issues by political forces on the Korean peninsula. This was vividly evident, as the Cold War progressed, in the tendencies of big-power policies to develop in tandem with the struggle between domestic forces, as that struggle grew progressively more heated, and to use that struggle to reach self-serving objectives. The immediate cause of the war's outbreak was the Soviet military aid to North Korea which broke the symmetry of the conflict, but this too may be interpreted as only a transitional phase in the development of a completely bipolar system on the Korean peninsula.[60]

    1. The only agreement with regard to Korea that existed between the United States and the Soviet Union from the Cairo declaration until the Moscow Conference was the informal one that the peninsula should be placed under a trusteeship. See Kamiya Fuji, *Gendai kokusai seiji no shikaku* (Tokyo: Yūhikaku, 1966), p. 38. Put another way, throughout a series of wartime conferences, the two powers shared the opinion that Korea should not belong exclusively to the sphere of influence of either. See Akira Iriye, *The Cold War in Asia* (Englewood Cliffs, N.J.: Prentice-Hall, 1974), pp. 126–27; Lee Yong-hui, "38 dosŏn hoekchŏng singo—Soryŏn taeiljŏng ch'amjŏn-sa e chŭmhayŏ," *Asea hakpo*, vol. 1, pp. 461–63.
    2. The split between the two powers had become evident at the beginning of November. It was decisively revealed by Rhee Syng-man's speech broadcast on 7 November and by the official announcement of the "People's Republic central committee" on 9 November.
    3. *Seoul sinmun*, 13 and 21 December 1945.
    4. The jurisdiction of the Korean People's Republic was to extend to the north as well as the south. A number of delegates from North Korea, especially from Hwanghaedo and Hamgyongdo, attended a national convention of people's committee representatives held in Seoul from 20 to 25 November 1945. At an enlarged executive committee meeting, northern delegates presented reports on the situation in their respective provinces. See *Chŏn'guk immin ŭiwŏnhoe taep'yoja taehoe ŭisalok* (Seoul: Convention Secretariat, 1946).On the conflict between the government of the Korean People's Republic and the American military government, see author's article, "Minzoku kaihō sensō to shite no Chōsen sensō—Kakumei to sensō no kōsaku," *Kokusai mondai* 182: 38–48.
    5. See Lee Ho-jae, *Han'guk woegyo chŏngchek ŭi isang kwa hyŏnsil* (1945–53)—*Yi Sŭngman woegyo wa miguk* (Seoul: Pangmunsa, 1969), p. 119.

6. Koha Sŏnseng Chŏngi P'yŏnch'an Wiwŏnhoe, ed., *Koha Song Jin-u sŏnseng jŏn* (Seoul: Donga-Ilbo Publishing Bureau, 1965), p. 335.

7. Lee, *Han'guk waegyo*, pp. 137–38.

8. Ibid., p. 77.

9. *Seoul sinmun*, 10 June 1946.

10. Lee, *Han'guk waegyo*, pp. 190–92.

11. For details *see* Kim Nam-sik, *Sillok Namnodang* (Seoul: Sinhyŏnsilsa, 1975), pp. 277–78.

12. Special announcement by U.S. Military Commander John R. Hodge concerning the September general stike, in *Chosun ilbo*, 2 October 1946. *See also* author's article (note 4, above), p. 44.

13. Kim Il-sung, "8.15 isshūnen no tame ni," *Kin Nissei senshū*, vol. 1 (Tokyo: San'ichi shobō, 1952), p. 144.

14. Pak Hon-yong's radical policy points out the struggle for leadership between the northern and southern communists. It is evident that the anti-Pak group, which advocated a "legitimate struggle," had expected North Korean support. For details, *see* Ko Jun-sok, *Chōsen 1945–1950: Kakumeishi eno shōgen* (Tokyo: San'ichi shobō, 1972), pp. 148–54. The general strike of September seems to have been carried out by Pak Hon-yong without consultation with the North Koreans. *See* Kim, *Sillok Namnodang*, pp. 303–9.

15. Gregory Henderson finds, in the loss of political cohesiveness which characterized post-liberation Korean, "an old theme under the new form: continued and almost exclusive concentration on central power." Gregory Henderson, *Korea: The Politics of the Vortex* (Cambridge: Harvard University Press, 1968) p. 57.

16. On the activities of communists in South Korea, *see* Kim, *Sillok Namnodang*.

17. See *Foreign Relations of the United States* (henceforth cited *FR*), *1948*, VI, 1097–98; Henderson, *Korea*, p. 155.

18. *See also* the damage reports by Police Director Cho Pyong-ok in *Seoul sinmun*, 3, 4, 5, and 6 June 1946.

19. The National Democratic Front proposed a "great struggle in defense of the fatherland" to "smash the puppet independent elections and government, kick the imperialist lackey UN commision on Korea out of the country, force both the United States and the Soviet Union to withdraw their troops, and protect the sovereignty, unity, freedom, and independence of the fatherland." *See* Kim, *Sillok Namnodang*, p. 359.

20. *See*, for example, SWNCC 176–18, "Political Policy for Korea" (28 January 1946) in *FR*, *1946*, VIII, 623–27.

21. Lee, *Han'guk waegyo*, pp. 169–72.

22. Statement by Hodge supporting the formation of the conference to promote unity between Left and Right (Kim Kyu-sik and Lyuh Woon-hyung) in *Seoul sinmun*, 2 July 1946.

23. Announcement by Hodge concerning the establishment of a legislative assembly in *Donga ilbo*, 10 July 1946.

24. On Rhee Syng-man's isolation during the formation of moderate alliance and the legislative assembly, *see* Son Se-il, *Yi Sung-man kwa Kim Ku* (Seoul: Ilchokak, 1970), pp. 237–50. Rhee visited the United States at the beginning of September to establish direct diplomatic ties. It is obvious that his aim was to criticize "the appeasement policy" of the State Department and the military government. *See* Lee, *Han'guk waegyo*, pp. 193–98.

25. On the preparation of a communist party organization in North Korea during

this period, *see* Pang In-hu, *Puk'han Chosŏn Nodongdang ŭi hyŏngsŏng kwa paljŏn* (Seoul: Asiatic Research Center, Korea University, 1969).

26. At the beginning Soviet policy toward Korea aimed at preventing the establishment of an anti-Soviet government in a unified Korea. This was explicitly stated by T. F. Shtykov, representative of the Soviet Union at the opening of the first Soviet-American joint commission meeting.

27. Kim Il-sung, "Subete o minshu seiryoku kesshū no tame ni," *Kin Nissei senshū*, pp. 78–79.

28. The "October People's Resistance" was strongly criticized by North Korean communists as "having consciously betrayed the Marxist-Leninist doctrine regarding armed riots." See *Kŭlloja* (February 1954).

29. *Seoul sinmun*, 4 July 1947.

30. *See* Louis J. Halle, *The Cold War as History* (London: Chatto and Windus, 1970), p. 134.

31. *Donga ilbo*, 19 December 1947.

32. Kim Il-sung's address to the second congress of the Korean Workers' Party, in *Kin Nissei senshū*, supplement, p. 35.

33. Kamiya, *Kokusai seiji*, pp. 54–55.

34. Ibid., pp. 56–57.

35. The National Security Council decision of 2 April 1948 (NSC 8) indicates that the United States was caught on the horns of a dilemma due to the inherent conflict between the realities of international politics and fundamental policy aims. *See* NSC 8 in *FR, 1948*, VI, 1164–69. *See also* A. C. Wedemeyer's report to the president (19 September 1947), in *Wedemeyer Reports!* (New York: Devin-Adair, 1958).

36. This scheme was based on the Soviet analysis of the Korea situation. They felt that "the progressive forces which could assume responsibility for the fate of this nation [Korea] had already emerged." E. M. Zhukov, ed., *Meždunarodnye otnošenija na dal'nem vostoke 1840–1949* (Moscow: Politizdat, 1956), p. 693. In addition, the Soviets might have seen that the withdrawal of foreign troops would leave the North Korean–Soviet partnership in a stronger position against the troubled U.S.–South Korea partnership. The net effect of withdrawal would, in any case, mean the localization of the conflict and an increase of Soviet influence in the Korean peninsula.

37. Lee, *Han'guk waegyo*, p. 192.

38. The issue of withdrawal of foreign troops was one of the most important questions during both the first and second congresses. Both in October 1948 and February 1949, anti-Rhee congressmen introduced a resolution for the withdrawal of foreign troops.

39. Lee, *Han'guk waegyo*, p. 242–43.

40. "Letter from Rhee Syng-man to Special Presidential Emissary Cho Pyong-ok," in *Fijitsu wa kataru* (Pyongyang: Foreign Language Press, 1960), pp. 14–18.

41. Statement of the Ministry of Foreign Affairs of the USSR on the evacuation of Soviet troops from Korea, 20 September 1948, in *The Soviet Union and the Korean Question* (Moscow: 1948; reprinted in London: Soviet News, 1950), pp. 61–62.

42. D. F. Flemming, *The Cold War and its Origins 1917–1960*, vol. 2 (London: George Allen & Unwin, 1961), p. 608.

43. Rhee Syng-man's speech on 2 November 1949, *Taet'ongnyŏng Yi Sung-man paksa tamwhajip*, vol. 1 (Seoul: Government Printing Office), p. 24.

44. *See* author's article (note 4, above), pp. 45–46.

45. *Khrushchev Remembers* (Boston: Little, Brown, 1970), p. 368.

46. On the conflict between them, *see* Dae-sook Suh, *The Korean Communist Movement 1918–1948* (Princeton: Princeton University Press, 1967), ch. 10.

47. *Military Situation in the Far East, part 1* (Washington, D.C.: U.S. Government Printing Office, 1951), p. 243.

48. Lee, *Han'guk waegyo*, pp. 258, 307.

49. In the final analysis, Rhee's call for a northern campaign resulted in (1) the Americans strictly limiting the weapons supplied to Korea, (2) miscalculations of the quality of South Korean troops both within Korea and abroad, and (3) stimulating an armament buildup in North Korea. The "march to the north" campaign's real significance lies not in actual military preparations but in creating these conditions. *See* Lee, *Han'guk waegyo*, pp. 311–12.

50. Up to the very last moment, Rhee could not be sure of U.S. military support for his march north. He admitted as much in a speech broadcast to the North Korean people on 6 May 1950 by saying that the biggest barrier to launching the campaign was the international situation. A similar statement appeared in a letter to Cho Pyong-ok, written a year prior to the speech. *See* War History Editorial Committee, ed., *Han'guk chŏllan illyŏnji* (Seoul: Korean Department of Defense, 1951), p. c-1.

51. Wire service from the Korean Central News Agency to Construction News Agency in Tokyo, 4 and 26 January 1950. According to the same source, the "weapon dedication movement" involved three million people. Three hundred million *won* was raised for arms.

52. *See* Roy E. Appleman, *United States in the Korean War: South to the Naktong, North to the Yalu (June–November 1950)* (Washington, D.C.: Office of the Chief of Military History, U.S. Department of the Army, 1961), pp. 11–12.

53. Ibid., pp. 9–10. *See also* War History Editorial Committee, ed., *Han'guk chŏnjeng-sa*, vol. 1 (Seoul: Korean Department of Defense, 1967), pp. 689–90.

54. On partisan activities in South Korea, *see* Kim, *Sillok Namnodang*, and Kim Chum-kon, *Han'guk chŏnjeng kwa Nodongdang chŏllyak* (Seoul: Pakyŏngsa, 1973).

55. From 28 June 1949, guerrilla activities in South Korea were carried out under the leadership of the Democratic Front for the Unification of the Fatherland. For Soviet evaluation of South Korean guerrilla activities, *see* F. I. Shabshina, "Koreja posle Vtoroj mirovoj vojny," in *Krizis kolonial'noj sistemy: nacional'no-osvoboditel'naja bor'ba narodov Vostočnoj Azii*, ed. E. M. Zhukov (Moscow: Izdatel'stvo Akademii nauk SSSR, 1949). Russia's favorable attitude reached its peak with the publication in *Pravda* on 27 March 1950 of the essay by Pak Hon-yong on the heroic struggles of the South Korean people.

56. *See* Lee Sung-yop, "Choguk t'ogilŭl wihan nambanbu immin yugyŏk t'u-jaeng," *Gunloja* (January 1950), along with the previous paper by Pak Hon-yong.

57. This is not to deny the possibility of similar moves on the U.S. side. More research is needed on the relationship between Rhee and MacArthur.

58. On Pak Hon-yong's advocacy of continued war, *see* Kim Hak-chun, "Han'guk chŏnjeng kwa puk'han chŏnch'i," *Seoul pyŏngnon* 33: 13–14.

59. It seems that there was a prior understanding between the Soviet Union and North Korea to the effect that the war should be waged as a civil war. In this respect, the Soviet attitude was consistent. North Korea did not request Chinese and Soviet support until after UN troops had pushed north of the 38th parallel. *See* Robert R. Simmons, *The Strained Alliance: Peking, Pyongyang, Moscow and the Politics of the Korean Civil War* (New York: Free Press, 1974), pp. 176–79.

60. I question the theory that Korean conflict was the ultimate result of the U.S.-Soviet confrontation on the Korean peninsula. The creation of a completely bipolar system in Korea was the result of the Korean War, not the cause of it.

Who Set the Stage for the Cold War in Southeast Asia ?

Yano Tōru

One object of this essay is to determine how Japan's historical inroad into Southeast Asia and the "power vacuum" created there by Japan's defeat in World War II encouraged stability or instability in the region in the postwar period. The Cold War in Southeast Asia had peculiar characteristics that could not be attributes in Europe. For one thing, the Cold War became hot in Southeast Asia. This fundamental paradox may be due to the unique political environment into which the classic pattern of conflict between West and East was brought. What is important in any study of the Cold War in Southeast Asia is to pay attention not only to the rivalry of different actors but also to the nature of the environment.

Another aim of this essay is to clarify the basic logic of political dynamism among different actors that shaped the Cold War in Southeast Asia. The Cold War in this region can be defined as a polarized ideological conflict among major powers with a certain degree of military tension which was imported from the European scene into the Asian climate in the process of the disintegration of the Yalta accord.

Japan's Involvement in the South and Its Political Legacy

If broadly defined in terms of "involvement in the south," the relationship between Japan and Southeast Asia goes back to the early Meiji era.[1] Japan's involvement in the region from the Meiji era to around 1935 was not a matter of official policy, and Japanese influence was not substantial. This "involvement" lacked overall purpose and direction, consisting solely of the spontaneous southward flow of private individuals and groups. Suddenly, however, around 1936, involvement in the south became the object of official attention, and the government policy of "southward advance" began to take shape.

Japan made a commitment to a policy of southward advance soon after the formation of the second Konoe cabinet on July 22, 1940. "The principles of basic national policy" and "The principles of policy for coping with the situation in accordance with world developments," which were approved soon after the cabinet was organized, marked a turning point of epochal significance. The first document stated, "Should the China War not be cleared up, a decision on shifting emphasis to southern policy will be made with full consideration of the domestic and international situation" and "We will make every effort to seize the right moment in the changing situation in carrying out policy toward the south." With regard to Indochina, it clearly stated, "Depending upon circumstances, military force may be employed."[2]

It was not much later that government officials publicly aired the policy slogan of the new era, the "Greater East Asia co-prosperity sphere." The first public use of the term was by Foreign Minister Matsuoka Yōsuke during a press conference on August 1, 1940. He referred to Japan, China, and Manchukuo as "part of the Greater East Asia co-prosperity sphere." The co-prosperity sphere scheme served as a blanket concept, covering, and thereby superficially legitimizing, anything deemed in the interest of Japanese "self-reliance and self-defense." Rather than a "grand design" polished to the last detail, it was a hollow shell, devoid of content. Nor, of course, was it in any way based on consultation with other Asian peoples. As a writer noted in 1944, "Construction of a new East Asia developed as the cumulative result of consecutive ad hoc moves 'in conformity with inexorable necessity.' As a result, it was erratic and generally unplanned. . . . Events from the Manchurian incident onward represented merely piecemeal responses to the exigencies of the moment rather than the unfolding of a consistent plan."[3]

The co-prosperity sphere idea gradually took concrete shape

following the outbreak of the Pacific War. On November 1, 1942, the Greater East Asia Ministry was established, and the Greater East Asia conference was held on November 5 and 6, 1943. Meanwhile, a large number of pro-government ideologues were competing to develop a coherent and theoretical rationale for the co-prosperity sphere. Their products were all fanciful and fallacious. Nevertheless, the four years between 1941 and 1945 constitute a perplexing period in Japanese history. The Japanese had so thoroughly reversed their earlier desire to "leave Asia and join the West" that now, according to Tōjō Hideki, "Imperial diplomacy consists of 90-percent Greater East Asia sphere matters and only 10-percent other."[4] They suddenly plunged single-mindedly into pursuits in which they had had no experience. It was a very curious and confused historical period indeed. For instance, there was the "boom phenomenon" whereby the entire intellectual community was, overnight, extremely enthusiastic about prospects in the "south." The strangely shallow intellectualism associated with co-prosperity sphere policy can be traced to that sort of psychology.[5]

Japan's initial military victories effectively undermined the legitimacy of colonial authorities. When colonial governments returned after the war, they were unable to wield effective power. The vacuum was then filled by either "Japanized" or "European-ized," immature, and inexperienced native nationalist leaders. Since these leaders lacked a sense of international politics, the Southeast Asian region was left in the hands of scattered, unstable, and disunited regimes which failed to form a coherent international system. But the fatal mistake of the colonial governments was in their failure to protect the colonies from the Japanese. The British author, Maurice Collis, includes in his book, *Last and First in Burma*, a chapter entitled "Implications of the British Defeat." There he searchingly explores British responsibility. He says Great Britain received a mortal wound by submitting to ignominious defeat and leaving the Burmese to be trampled upon by Japanese forces. "The tragedy was that not the most loving friend, nor the greatest saint, could relieve the wound. There was no anodyne but farewell."[6] Aside from the issue of moral responsibility, however, the British deprived their colonial rule of much of its legitimacy by involving the Burmese in the war and therefore alerting them to the dangers inherent in affiliation with a big power, by abdicating for three-odd years and allowing Burmese nationalism to expand rapidly, the Thakins to grasp *de facto* power, and the Burmese to obtain experience in self-government. The extent of that loss during the war is revealed in the attempted arrest of Aung San. Bewildered by the strengh of the Anti-Fascist People's Freedom League (AFPFL), the returned British colonial government tried to arrest as a war criminal the leader of AFPFL, Aung San. Through Aung San's trial, the government sought to reduce the power of Burmese nationalism. The plan failed before it even got under way, however, and in effect only contributed to enhancing Aung San's prestige.

Military governments established by Japan in the region contributed to the latent strength of local national independence movements. But rather than reinforcing national solidarity in occupied areas, Japanese involvement exacerbated social schisms, thereby planting the seeds of instability following independence. A typical incident can be found in the discriminatory policy taken by the Japanese military in Indonesia.[7] Not all the Indonesian nationalist leaders were originally from Java. Some were from Sumatra's Minankabao, Batak, and elsewhere; some were from Banjarmasin on Borneo; others were from Minahasa on Celebes; and several were from Ambon. For these, Japanese policy came as a great shock. Christians among them found themselves looked down upon by Japanese as "pro-Dutch elements." In setting up military administration, the Japanese discriminated by choosing only Javanese leaders, such as Sukarno and the sultans of Solo and Jogjakarta, for responsible positions. This contributed, in turn, to bad feelings among Indonesia's ethnic groups. Javanese officials were shunned by the people of Celebes and Borneo, while in Sumatra, Minahasans and those from Ambon were mistreated. Minahasans were comparatively well treated in Celebes, but in Java, Borneo, and Sumatra they were violently rejected as "pro-Dutch" Christians. Discriminatory treatment of the ethnic groups created an atmosphere which heightened ostracism among them. This tendency had considerable effect politically and administratively, hindering the realization of a unified state, the ideal pursued by nationalist leaders.

Japan's occupation policy and administration were typically

colonialist in the single-minded emphasis on the exploitation of resources and only served to heighten the anticolonialist and antiimperialist sentiment of the nationalists. By the end of the war, they were bursting with emotional energy. In extreme cases, these emotions were conducive to the rise of communism in Southeast Asia, a result which cannot be ignored when tracing the origins of the Cold War.

On November 20, 1941, the Imperial headquarters–government liaison conference approved "Guidelines for administration of occupied areas in the south," and six days later it passed "Central army-navy agreement on the establishment of military government in the occupied areas." These documents provided the basic scheme for government administration of the southern region.[8] The former document included "three guiding principles for government administration," one of which called for "rapid acquisition of essential natural resources for national defense." Policy measures such as the following were instituted to carry out the establishment of military government and achieve this objective:

> (1) To the extent that it does not interfere with military operations, occupation forces should devise means of obtaining and exploiting resources essential to national defense;
>
> (2) Local residents will have to bear whatever burden is necessary to secure resources for national defense and establish self-sufficiency for occupation forces, and the need to pacify local residents should not be allowed to interfere with acquisition of resources.

The overriding objective of the southward advance was to secure resources, particularly oil, and, through them, to create a system of self-sufficiency required in the formation of a new order in Asia. For that reason, the military governments put great emphasis on economic policy. It was the "Principles of economic policy towards the south" which filled in the details of policy for military administration. The document stated: "With emphasis on satisfying the demand for essential resources and thereby contributing to the immediate war effort, we also plan to establish a system of self-sufficiency for the Greater East Asia co-prosperity sphere, in order to complete rapidly the strengthening of the economic power of the empire." The southern region was divided into two groups according to the degree of their importance as sources of raw materials. Group A included the Netherlands East Indies, British Malaya and Borneo, and the Philippines. Group B included French Indochina and Thailand. Policy toward Group A was to center on strong measures to acquire needed resources and to prevent their outflow from the country. The development of petroleum resources was particularly important; according to "Principles of economic policy toward the south," "in resource development, primary emphasis is to be placed on petroleum resources," and "petroleum enterprises are to be placed under direct military management and control in the early stages of military rule." The latter directive was carried out for both the oil and coal industries. With regard to currency, extreme caution in the use of military payment certificates was dictated by the bitter experience on the China mainland, where inept currency management invited extreme inflation, causing suffering and resentment among the people. Wages were to be kept extremely low in order to control prices, and this allowed the cheapest possible exploitation of the local labor force.

In the final analysis, Japan's southward advance, and the power vacuum left in its wake, can be judged to have been detrimental to the creation of stable political structures.

The Yalta System and Asia

The so-called Yalta system evolved out of a series of discussions held among the United States, Britain, and the Soviet Union at the Yalta Conference in February 1945, discussions that were directed toward conceptualizing a postwar settlement through the creation of an international political system. Although the focus was on the Far East, the talks did cover the place of Asia as a whole within the system. The three powers, deferring to prevailing circumstances, tacitly agreed upon the division of Asia into spheres: the United States would bear responsibility for the Pacific area, while the Soviet Union would become the caretaker for Northeast

Asia, and responsibility for Southeast Asia would fall on Britain.[9]

Some historians see a strong isolationist trend in early postwar American history, but President Franklin D. Roosevelt's positive determination to take on the burden of the Pacific area after the inception of the Yalta system seems, rather, to suggest just the opposite. What is important is exactly what place Southeast Asia held in the conceptual structure of the Yalta system and its proportionate weight as a region. Its place was actually diminutive, and there is no evidence of any sustained, serious discussion on Southeast Asia at Yalta.[10] It is probably fair to assume, however, that Britain, as the dominant colonial power in the region, quite naturally took on the responsibility for Southeast Asia, without giving it much thought. Once the war was over, however, and a settlement imposed, the pattern of thinking at Yalta which automatically related Britain with Southeast Asia became completely bankrupt. In the first place, indigenous movements toward independence among the peoples of Southeast Asia had crystallized, and the struggle was gaining violent momentum. Most of them were forging their way to national sovereignty, and all were plagued by chronic political instability. Their subsequent history was one of unilateral intervention by the United States in a progression of events that represented a course of action directly counter to the plans and spirit of Yalta.

What can explain the direction taken by the United States after the collapse of the Yalta concept? It is necessary first of all to understand how China originally fit into the overall scheme envisioned at Yalta.[11] At the time, in 1945, the three powers assigned China the status of the "weak fellow," and the Soviet Union took the role of a guardian for China. It had been tacitly agreed, furthermore, that northeast China (then Manchuria) also fell within the Soviet sphere of influence. It seemed that China would not move out of the weak semicolonial status it occupied in 1941 unless somone acted to support it. There was therefore no opposition to the understanding that the Soviet Union would bear that responsibility. Also at Yalta, however, was established the superficial agreement that the powers would recognize China's sovereignty, uphold the principle of nonintervention in the internal political and economic affairs of China, and recognize Chiang Kai-shek as the representative of the Chinese people.

The Yalta concept as it related to Asia could not possibly have been sustained, however, in the face of the emergence of conflicting policies of the powers toward China. The same was also true in Europe, and that reality demolished the Yalta idea soon after the war ended. If one were to define the cause of its collapse in a word, it would be "unilateralism."[12] What the world saw after 1945 was not concerted progress toward joint international decision making and mutual agreement based on cooperation, or at least the spirit of cooperation as outlined at Yalta, but rather a fast-rising wave of autonomous action by each of the three powers moving in directions independent of one another.

From a certain vantage point, it may be possible to assign responsibility for the emergence of unilateralism to the Soviet Union. Having obtained recognition that Manchuria fell within its own sphere of influence, the USSR began a concentrated effort to plunder the area of its natural resources. Further, despite the agreement that Chiang Kai-shek would be accepted as head of the Chinese government, Stalin continued to supply assistance to the Chinese Red Army. Just about the same time that the Soviet Union began moving away from the other powers, Britain, also, was showing the same tendency. The country was exhausted and financially near ruin. Prime Minister Winston S. Churchill was aware that the power position of his country was, in the long run, quite different from that of either the United States or the Soviet Union, and that for that reason Britain would have to find its own way back to national recovery. England was left three assets, he said in April 1945: superior statecraft, experience, and the unity of the British Commonwealth of Nations. Those were left, and no more, so they must utilize them to the maximum, he declared.[13] Britain came to place priority on economic rather than political or diplomatic matters, and this impelled it to abandon deliberately the Yalta concept and swerve off onto a unilateral course. As a result, the United States and the Soviet Union were left to uphold what remained of the ideal of Yalta, but that became impossible because the American response to independent Soviet moves was in itself unilateral. At that point there emerged in American thinking the idea that a "united China" had to be maintained, and that the United States bore part of the responsibility. Thus, in the process of collapse of the Yalta system soon after World War II, the United

States reacted to the wave of unilateralism sweeping the other countries but, at the same time, went off onto its own unilateral course; in American thinking, there was no other way to proceed. If it did not, nothing would be accomplished.

All through American thinking ran the extremely legalistic, moralistic conviction that it was the Soviet Union, not the United States, that was to blame, because the USSR had gone "unilateral" first. This was the emergence of the " 'violation of Yalta accord' theory," which Americans handled with moral righteousness. American unilateralism was perhaps most succinctly stated by the one-time head of the CIA, Allen Dulles; the United States could, he said, without approval from other countries concerned, make independent judgment and intervene in the internal affairs of others.[14] It seemed as though the significance and importance of the Yalta concept had become a fixation in American thinking. Their moralism and legalism attached greater importance to the Yalta system than did the other Yalta powers. In addition, because the United States was the only country left with anything approaching national power or economic viability in the early postwar years, it showed a marked inclination to underestimate the economic needs and anxieties of the others. Americans had no idea why the other powers had to suffer what they did not; thus they neither understood nor appreciated the economic motives of Britain or the reasons for the Soviet plunder of Manchuria. Bound by a set idea of what Yalta demanded, America persisted in the conviction that if the others upheld the system, it could be preserved. In this way, in Asia, and probably in other areas as well, the Yalta system split into three unilateral thrusts, all completely different, causing the final collapse of the system.

The Initial Stage of American Commitment to Southeast Asia

As early as the fall of 1948, the Office of Intelligence Research of the State Department made a survey of communist influence in Southeast Asia and concluded that "evidence of Kremlin-directed conspiracy was found in virtually all countries except Vietnam."[15] This analysis did not reflect the reality of Southeast Asia; rather, a stereotypical preoccupation about the universal presence of the "Kremlin-directed conspiracy" apparently dominated the whole judgment. However, it must be noted that American interest in Southeast Asia at this stage varied from country to country. At the time, its attitude toward Indochina was a reserved one.

It was by force of the events in China in 1948 and 1949 that the United States was brought to a new perception of the nature of communism in Asia and also to a total approach to Southeast Asia as region of common political destiny. The transition of American policy toward Southeast Asia can be read in the series of National Security Council papers, the most important of which were disclosed to the public in the Pentagon Papers.

NSC 48/1 was probably one of the few earliest official documents of the United States that discussed the danger of communism in Southeast Asia.[16] There are a few remarkable points to be noted in this document. First of all, it declared explicitly that "southeast Asia is the target of a coordinated offensive directed by the Kremlin. In seeking to gain control of southeast Asia, the Kremlin is motivated in part by a desire to acquire southeast Asia's resources and communication lines, and to deny them to us." Secondly, the pattern of thought similar to the so-called Domino theory was present long before President Eisenhower's famous press conference on April 7, 1954. "If southeast Asia also is swept by communism we shall have suffered a major political rout the repercussions of which will be felt throughout the rest of the world, especially in the Middle East and in a then critically exposed Australia." NSC 48/2, approved on December 30, 1949, contained a set of strategies by which to block further communist expansion in Asia: by regional associations of noncommunist states of the various Asian areas, by collective security which would be consonant with the purposes of those regional associations, and also by collaboration with major European allies and commonwealth nations.[17]

A new turning point in the American posture toward Southeast Asia came after both the Chinese and Soviet governments recognized the Ho Chi Minh movement as the legal government of Vietnam. The United States, in its turn, recognized the Bao Dai government on February 1, 1950. This move was followed by another series of official statements which included NSC 64 of

February 27 and Dean Rusk's note addressed to General James H. Burns. In those documents, there were salient new features in the way the United States perceived the current situation in Southeast Asia. First, Rusk's note contained the following sentence: "Southeast Asia is in grave danger of Communist domination as a consequence of aggression from Communist China and of internal subversive activities."[18] Here was a new implication that the source of danger was now Peking rather than Moscow. Second, according to Rusk, "Indochina is the most strategically important area of Southeast Asia"—this looming up of Indochina as the key to Southeast Asia was totally new in American security consideration. This line of thought was consolidated after June 1950 to give ample substance to anticommunistic hysteria in America. For instance, the statement of policy by the National Security Council on "United States objectives and courses of action with respect to Southeast Asia" (NSC 124/2) contained all the embryonic thoughts which would eventually culminate in the course of the Vietnam War.[19]

The advent of the Republican administration in 1953 marked the start of a new policy orientation on the part of the United States. Instead of unilateralism, which had been the dominant theme of American foreign policy, the "united action" concept was adopted by Secretary of State John Foster Dulles. While the announcement of this united action proposal was, on the one hand, to offer the French an alternative to surrender at the negotiation table, it was also to reinforce the American position at the international forum by forming a collective defense of plural nations. This strategy included even the possibility of military action. Moreover, the united action scheme was necessitated by the pressure from within the United States which tended to negate any possibility of an American unilateral intervention into Indochina.[20]

In this connection, the Southeast Asia Treaty Organization (SEATO) was, in retrospect, a creation of ambivalent public feelings. Certainly, it was a version of the united action concept. The membership comprised eight countries including three from Asia: the Philippines, Thailand, and Pakistan. However, the SEATO treaty carried a few strange stipulations. First, the word "communist" did not appear in the treaty, so that the United

States had to file a separate statement clarifying that its commitment applied only in the case of communist aggressions.[21] Second,
the area covered by the treaty was defined as the "general area of
Southeast Asia" including the entire territories of the Asian member states as well as the "general area of the Southwest Pacific."
Interestingly enough, by a protocol to the treaty, Cambodia, Laos,
and South Vietnam were included in the area to be covered by the
treaty.[22] It is easy to imagine that the lack of clear-cut stipulations
must have been frustrating for Dulles.[23] The half-finished nature of
the treaty was partly due to the Joint Chiefs of Staff, who were not
too enthusiastic about earmarking forces for the SEATO.[24] Another reason was British reluctance to hastily implement the united action formula in Southeast Asia. When the idea of forming
the new organization became actual, British reaction, though basically congenial, was that the basis of affiliation with the organization should be as broad as possible and that nations adjacent to
Indochina, such as Thailand or Burma, or even neutral states like
India or Ceylon, must be permitted to participate or cooperate
actively.[25] The British conception of the treaty was thus not
anticommunist. The British were also reluctant to enhance the risk
of Chinese intervention in Southeast Asia.[26] Nor did the British
accept the Domino theory. The member states of the British Commonwealth were reluctant to show a sense of dedication to Dulles's concepts.

However, the most significant aspect of the SEATO treaty was
that, under the cloak of the united action gesture, it was still a
product of the postwar American tradition of unilateralism, a
product of the Dullesian sense of mission that all tricky ventures
by communists must be contained through America's unilateral
commitment. Therefore, it was more than natural that some
Americans should have thought of the treaty as a justification for
legitimately intervening in Vietnam, which was seen as a target of
communist aggression.[27]

It is by now well known that Dulles once made an assertion that
neutralism was "immoral."[28] Such a view on neutralism was not
his monopoly but the prevailing sentiment of the American people
in the Cold War period. The much-heralded Asian-African Conference held at Bandung in April 1955, where Afro-Asian neutrals

representing nearly 1.5 billion people of the world gathered together in the brotherly spirit of Bandung was, from the American
point of view, merely an occasion for the United States to have its
policy in the defense of Quemoy and Matsu justified by participants
from the Afro-Asian nations.[29] The United States was totally
indifferent to the spirit of Bandung.

Soviet Interest in Southeast Asia, 1945–50

At the outset, Southeast Asia, including Indochina, was not an
object of serious concern to the Soviet Union, as it was primarily
absorbed in European affairs for the sake of its own national security. Concurrently, the task of coping with domestic problems
was urgent. Moreover, there was a tendency in the Soviet way of
thinking to presume that revolutionary maneuvers should be the
responsibility of the communist parties of the metropolitan countries. Hence, Indochinese affairs were thought to be basically affairs of the French Communists.[30] By the same logic, there are no
notable signs that the Soviets paid serious attention to communist
activities in Malaya, Burma, or the Philippines.

The formation of the Cominform (the Communist Information
Bureau) in 1947 provided a new momentum by which Soviet policy shifted toward a more positive concern with Southeast Asia.
Zhdanov's famous speech at the founding meeting of the Cominform touched on the "crisis of the colonial system" only in an
abstract way:[31] "The peoples of the colonies no longer wish to live
in the old way. The ruling classes of the metropolitan countries
can no longer govern the colonies on the old lines." Such an
abstract message had to be more systematically interpreted so as
to be applicable to Asia. E. M. Zhukov's article in *Bol'shevik* in
December 1947 ("The sharpening crisis of the colonial system")
was perhaps one of the most authoritative efforts to apply Zhdanov's doctrine to Asia;[32] in it he apparently propounded the
"united national front" formula. In this article, mention was made
of Vietnam and Indonesia as well as China. While Zhukov's
theory left many ambiguous points yet to be defined, and while
lack of precision in terminology was remarkable, ambiguity was

welcome from the point of view of the local communist elements,
as many of them seized upon Zhdanov's or Zhukov's pronouncements as if they were political messages of a specific nature.

In this second phase of Soviet concern with Southeast Asia,
Russian policy was motivated by new necessities. Allan W. Cameron rightly points out, "Soviet policy shifted further toward
active support of the Vietminh during the balance of 1947 and in
1948. Part of the change is attributable to a general hardening of
Soviet policy toward the Western powers, part probably to the
changing internal situation in France, notably the isolation of the
FCP in opposition to the government. The increasing success of
the Chinese Communists may also have helped attract Soviet
attention to Indochina. Often overlooked as an additional contributing factor is the increasing amount of open and direct contact
between the Vietnamese Communists and the international
Communist Movement."[33] However, it must not be overlooked
that most of the new necessities were still related to Europe, where
the American offensive was creating an unprecedentedly tense
atmosphere. In contrast, Soviet attitude toward colonial or Asian
affairs tended to be sluggish. Certainly, the Soviets were by now
anti-French, anti-American, and antiimperialist, but there were no
elaborate prescriptions for directing revolutionary trends in
Southeast Asia.[34]

"The conference of youth and students of Southeast Asia
fighting for freedom and independence," held in Calcutta in February 1948, was a significant event in this context. There exist different interpretations concerning this Calcutta Conference. One
school maintains that the conference provided an opportune setting where "instruction" for armed revolts was conveyed from
Moscow to the local communists in Southeast Asia.[35] The other
school argues that the conference was not a setting for receiving
orders from Moscow.[36] Judging from Moscow's premature interest in Southeast Asian affairs, the latter interpretation appears
correct. "At most, the conference could be said to have broadcast
to wider circles the Zhdanov two-camp message. While different
speakers sounded divergent themes and there was no general
endorsement of armed struggle nor unambiguous condemnation
of 'neutralist' governments, the dominant themes were praise for
the military successes of the Chinese, Indonesian, and Indochinese

struggles and hostility toward the national bourgeoisie."[37] Although there is presumably no valid basis for alleging Moscow's use of the Calcutta Conference, it must be noted that the meeting, with its agitational character, "quickened perceptibly the tempo of all revolutionary movements in Southeast Asia."[38] The political situation all over Southeast Asia then was so unstable that even a minimum input of the agitational factor could easily lead to rebellious movements. Moreover, by force of the unexpected effects of the agitational inputs, Moscow's diplomatic interest gradually shifted from Europe to Asia, and its legitimate line of policy in Asia was altered from the moderate and half-baked "united national front" formula to the more militant line put forth by Zhdanov.

The third phase of the postwar Russian concern with Southeast Asia came in the period after the victory of the Chinese Communist party in the fall of 1949. This phase can be characterized as a gradual convergence of the Soviet Union's interests upon affairs in Indochina. This localization might be deduced from the fact that, in almost all other countries in the region, communist uprisings turned out to be unsuccessful. The communist insurrections that erupted in 1948 in Malaya, Burma, the Philippines, and Indonesia were defeated partly because they were not in tune with the proper course of action prescribed by Moscow for colonial communist parties. Their failure did not reinforce Moscow's faith in the united national front scheme.

The shift in Soviet colonial strategies in 1949 was accompanied by an endorsement of Chinese revolutionary doctrine. For instance, Liu Shao-ch'i's statements in November 1949 that "armed struggle is the main form of struggle in the national liberation struggle in many colonies and semicolonies" and that "this is the main path followed in China by the Chinese people" were explicitly endorsed by Moscow in January 1950.[39] Now that the validity of the Chinese formulation was verified, prospects for communist victories following the Chinese pattern seemed to have become better in Asia. Although Chinese militancy was something Russia did not find very comfortable, it was sufficient to give a new impetus to Russian thinking on Asian revolutionary movements. The Russians were reminded anew of the importance of the communist leadership in a national liberation movement. In this third

phase, the communists were no longer mere participants in a national liberation movement.
All these new policy orientations resulted in intensified Soviet interest in Indochina. In January 1950, Moscow formally recognized the newborn Democratic Republic of Vietnam. "Since then the Democratic Republic of Vietnam has officially sided with the socialist camp headed by the Soviet Union," wrote Ho Chi Minh.[40] The convergence of Soviet interest on Indochina implied that Zhdanovism completed its own logical development and that the Russians now engaged in a Cold War venture in Southeast Asia in their own way.

1. For more details on the history of Japan's involvement in the Southeast Asian region, see Yano Tōru, *Nanshin no keifu* (Tokyo: Chūō kōron, 1975).
2. Japan Ministry of Foreign Affairs, ed., *Nihon gaikō nempyō narabi ni shuyō bunsho* (Tokyo: 1966), II, 437.
3. Matsushita Masatoshi, "Daitōa kensetsu no kihon seishin," in *Daitōa no kensetsu*, ed. Daitōa Sensō Chōsakai (Tokyo: Mainichi shimbun, 1944).
4. See Japan Ministry of Foreign Affairs, ed., *Gaimushō no hyakunen* (Tokyo: Hara shobō, 1969), II, 752.
5. Yano, *Nanshin*, pp. 164–71.
6. Maurice Collis, *Last and First in Burma* (London: Faber & Faber, 1956), p. 249.
7. Waseda University Ōkuma Memorial Social Science Research Center, ed., *Indoneshia ni okeru Nihon gunsei no kenkyū* (Tokyo: Kinokuniya, 1959) provides ample information on Japanese military rule in Indonesia.
8. *Nihon gaikō nempyō*, II, 562–63.
9. Akira Iriye, "The United States as an Asian-Pacific Power," in *Sino-American Detente and Its Policy Implications*, ed. Gene T. Hsiao (New York: Praeger, 1974), p. 9.
10. However, it is true that much mention was made of the colonial questions, which logically included Southeast Asia.
11. Iriye, "United States as Asian-Pacific Power," pp. 11–13.
12. Richard H. Rovere and Arthur M. Schlesinger, Jr., *The General and the President: The Future of American Foreign Policy* (New York: Straus and Young, 1951), pp. 234–35.
13. Iriye, "United States as Asian-Pacific Power," p. 14.
14. Allen Dulles, *The Craft of Intelligence* (New York: Harper and Row, 1963), p. 217.
15. *Pentagon Papers*, Senator Gravel edition (Boston: Beacon, 1971), I, 34.
16. Ibid., pp. 37–38.
17. Ibid., pp. 38–40.
18. Ibid., p. 363.
19. Ibid., pp. 384–90.
20. Ibid., pp. 100–101.
21. Kenneth T. Young, Jr., "The Southeast Asia Crisis" (Background Papers and Proceedings of the Eighth Hammarskjold Forum, 1966), pp. 57–58.
22. Russell H. Fifield, *The Diplomacy of Southeast Asia: 1945–1958* (New York: Harper, 1958), p. 102.
23. Townsend Hoopes, *The Devil and John Foster Dulles* (Boston: Little, Brown, 1973), p. 243.
24. *Pentagon Papers*, I, 212.

25. Anthony Eden, *Full Circle* (Boston: Houghton Mifflin, 1960), pp. 158–59.

26. *Pentagon Papers*, I, 102.

27. George M. Kahin and John W. Lewis, *The United States in Vietnam* (New York: Dial, 1967), pp. 61–63.

28. *Department of State Bulletin* 34 (18 June 1956), 999–1000.

29. Hoopes, *Devil*, pp. 282–83.

30. Allan W. Cameron, "The Soviet Union and Vietnam: The Origins of Involvement," in *Soviet Policy in Developing Countries*, ed. W. Raymond Duncan (New York: Wiley, 1970), p. 173.

31. Allan W. Cameron, ed., *Viet-Nam Crisis: A Documentary History*, vol. I, 1940–1956 (Ithaca: Cornell University Press, 1970), pp. 114–15.

32. Robert H. Donaldson, *Soviet Policy toward India: Ideology and Strategy* (Cambridge: Harvard University Press, 1974), p. 75.

33. Cameron, "Soviet Union," p. 75.

34. For the evolution of Soviet ideology concerning the colonial question in Asia in the postwar period, *see* Charles B. McLane, *Soviet Strategies in Southeast Asia: An Exploration of Eastern Policy under Lenin and Stalin* (Princeton: Princeton University Press, 1966), pp. 250–60.

35. *See* J. H. Brimmel, *Communism in South East Asia: A Political Analysis* (New York: Oxford University Press, 1959), pp. 255–63. Brimmel admits that, by the time of the Calcutta Conference, "the stage was prepared for the wave of violence which swept through India and Southeast Asia." Lucian W. Pye's *Guerilla Communism in Malaya, Its Social and Political Meaning* (Princeton: Princeton University Press, 1956) is also of the view that instructions were conveyed. A most interesting exchange of contrasting views is available in Michael Stenson, "The 1948 Communist Revolt in Malaya: A Note on Historical Sources and Interpretation" (Occasional paper 9, Institute of Southeat Asian Studies, 1971), in which Gerald de Cruz fervently insists that there were concrete instructions. *See also* Yeoh Kim Wah's letter which was published in *Journal of Southeast Asian Studies* 1, no. 2 (September 1970).

36. Ruth McVey's widely quoted piece, "The Calcutta Conference and the Southeast Asian Uprisings" (1958), convincingly demonstrates that the conference was not the scene for "orders from Moscow." McLane says, "the insurrections in Southeast Asia had their own logic and need not be explained solely in terms of Moscow's strategies or of some secret Soviet "instruction." Stenson (*see* note 35, above) asserts that the view that insurrections were dictated from outside is doubtful in the extreme.

37. Donaldson, *Soviet Policy*, p. 77.

38. McLane, *Soviet Strategies*, p. 360.

39. The text of Liu Shao-ch'i's speech is excerpted in Cameron, *Vietnam Crisis*, pp. 130–33.

40. Ho Chi Minh, *Selected Works*, III (Hanoi: Foreign Languages Publishing House, 1969), 191n.

The United States and the Anticolonial Revolutions in Southeast Asia, 1945–50

George McT. Kahin

American policy toward the anticolonial revolutions in Indonesia and Indochina during the Truman administration has often been regarded as ambiguous and inconsistent. It is my object to identify, and briefly assess, several of the principal factors that shaped those policies in the hope that thereby some of the areas of ambiguity may be reduced and the character of the American role in postwar Southeast Asia during this formative period may become a little clearer. But it should be emphasized that this essay is meant to be no more than a brief reconnaissance; it does not pretend to be comprehensive, and primary attention is given to the more controversial aspects and to factors that I believe have been slighted in previous accounts.

The period up to early 1947 was the one when American policies toward the Franco-Vietminh and Dutch-Indonesian disputes were marked by the greatest ambiguity. Thereafter the posture of the United States began to be clarified, especially with regard to Vietnam; but in neither of them can one discern reasonably clear-cut and coherent policies before early 1949. Although at the most fundamental level the ambiguity was actually more apparent than real, it was sufficient to help make plausible the assertion of American officials that the U.S. position in these disputes was one of neutrality.

Two sets of circumstances made it much easier for the United States to maintain an apparently neutral position during the early postwar years. First, for the initial part of this period, the British and Chinese Kuomintang (KMT) governments were the Allied agents charged with liquidating the Japanese occupation through-out Southeast Asia except for the Philippines. Thus, in nearly all of the area responsibility for actions taken in the name of the Allies was out of American hands, and consequently the United States could more easily remain aloof from the controversies surrounding the contest between the colonial powers and indigenous national-ist independence movements. Second, until mid-1948 the United States did not have to face any significant Soviet competition in Southeast Asia. While the Cold War did affect that part of the world indirectly via Europe, stemming from the priority accorded by the United States to support of the colonial metropoles there, it did not impinge directly as a consequence of any palpable Soviet intervention or even clear-cut Soviet ideological prescriptions. This was primarily a consequence of two factors: first, the lag in adjust-ment of Soviet policy toward colonial areas in general; and sec-ond, the high degree of independence from outside direction of both the communist movement in Vietnam and what was the most influential of several competing communist leaderships in Indonesia.

Initial British and Chinese Responsibility

With the expectation that American forces would have to be husbanded for the invasion of the Japanese home islands and for subsequent heavy occupation duties there and in Korea, it had been decided at the Potsdam Conference of July 1945 to reduce General Douglas MacArthur's area of operations and to expand the British Southeast Asian command under Admiral Louis Mountbatten. Thus, except for the Philippines and the areas of Vietnam and Laos above the 16th parallel, all of Southeast Asia became a British area of responsibility, with occupation authority north of the 16th parallel in Indochina vested in Generalissimo Chiang Kai-shek's government. These assignments and the par-ticular political casts of mind of some of Mountbatten's local com-manders had an important influence on the course of the inde-pendence struggles in Indochina and Indonesia. By the time the Allied occupation was officially terminated and Allied forces had withdrawn—from Indochina by early March and from Indonesia by November 30, 1946—a substantial amount of external political force had been injected into these disputes in ways which substantially favored the colonial powers.[1]

The impact of British and Chinese interventions on the military and political situations in Cambodia, Indonesia, and Vietnam went well beyond official Allied policy, and they highlight the important role played by the Allied military commanders on the scene. The influence of these men was not transitory; their actions had ongoing consequences that significantly shaped the course of events in the region for many years after their departure from the scene.

Within the context of the broad directives of Admiral Louis Mountbatten, commander in chief of Allied forces in Southeast Asia, some local British commanders took initiatives of their own that sometimes went well beyond the orders under which they operated. Most partisan and interventionist of all was General Douglas Gracey, commander of British forces in southern Vietnam and in Cambodia. Departing clearly from the generally modest bounds of Mountbatten's directives, he presented him and the British government with several *faits accomplis*[2] that heavily weighted the scales in favor of the French.

In Cambodia Gracey promptly moved to oust an apparently popular anti-French prime minister and paved the way for a reassertion of French control in alliance with the Cambodian royal house. In Saigon he armed French troops interned seven months earlier by the Japanese and arranged for them to stage a coup against the Vietminh administration which, in effect, he outlawed. He expanded his right to exercise authority beyond Saigon to all of southern Vietnam, helping the French to reestablish their control over as wide an area as possible. When short of troops of his own, he rearmed Japanese units and forced them to support his operation. By the time he left Saigon a large French expeditionary force had taken over from him and occupied most strategic centers of southern Vietnam.[3]

The impact of British power on the military and political balance in Indonesia, though significant, was less than in southern Vietnam and Cambodia; and this was so even though considerably greater power was actually applied (and with much heavier

British combat losses). One reason was that the British generals in Java appear to have been somewhat less partisan in favor of the colonial power than was General Gracey in Indochina. But undoubtedly also very important was the much heavier military force that the Indonesian revolutionaries were initially able to marshal—a factor which, of course, reflected major differences in both Japanese occupation policies and surrender procedures in Vietnam and Java.[4] Because the military power of the Indonesian insurgents was so considerable, the British were obliged to rearm a considerable number of Japanese troops to help "maintain public order," and were unable to pull out of Indonesia until almost nine months later than in southern Vietnam. However, when they did, numerous well-armed Dutch forces had been positioned in many of the most strategic positions just as had been the case with the French in the southern half of Indochina.[5]

Although the devastating economic effect of the KMT 150,000-man occupation of northern Vietnam is well known, the extent of its impact on the course of political events there does not appear to be widely appreciated. The KMT generals brought along their own Vietnamese protégés (VNQDD and Dong Minh Hoi) who they expected would displace the Vietminh leaders and cooperate, on KMT terms, with the large Chinese occupation force. Indeed, as the Chinese troops crossed the frontier into the Vietnamese border areas, they immediately began to disarm or eliminate local Vietminh people's committees and replace them by administrative bodies made up of the Vietnamese that they brought in their train. A number of border towns were so invested, but apparently the Vietminh's popular support was too strong for this aspect of the occupation to be spread very far or endure very long.[6] Thereafter, the KMT commanders' efforts at political control were limited to securing positions of secondary importance for their Vietnamese wards and subordinated to the objective of squeezing as much economic profit as possible from the occupation.

Despite their numbers and superior arms, the Chinese were not spoiling for a fight with the Vietminh. Once its leaders met their minimum economic demands and agreed to a face-saving political formula whereby the VNQDD and Dong Minh Hoi were granted nominal political representation in the government of the Democratic Republic of Vietnam, the KMT commanders were eventually satisfied to leave the Vietminh pretty much alone. But achievement of such a *modus vivendi* required tact and skill on the part of Ho Chi Minh and other Vietminh leaders.

However, these arrangements broke down when Chiang Kai-shek, needing his troops elsewhere because of the exigencies of China's civil war, found it profitable to make a deal with the French. In the accord of February 28, 1946, France granted Chiang substantial economic advantages[7] conditional upon the withdrawal of Chinese forces from Vietnam by a stipulated time and the Vietminh's assent to the entry of a limited number of French troops into northern Vietnam to replace the departing Chinese. Consequently, Chiang ordered his generals to help pressure Ho's government into an agreement with France, finally signed on March 6, that granted the French both political and military advantages greater than their power alone could have then exacted. Had the Vietminh refused to sign, it would probably have found itself confronting the KMT and French forces concurrently rather than in sequence.

Thus by the time that British and Chinese power had been removed from Indochina and Indonesia, the stage had been set in a manner highly favorable to France and the Netherlands. Not only were the armies and supplies of both colonial powers ensconced in favorable positions behind an initial Allied shield, but Allied actions, particularly by the British, had significantly altered the political as well as military balance in these areas. In view of the U.S. acquiescence to these interventions, the stated American policy of "neutrality" toward the independence struggles there in effect signified tacit support for actions highly advantageous to France and the Netherlands. However, the division of Allied areas of occupation set at the Potsdam Conference made it easy for Washington to avoid responsibility.

Lack of Soviet Competition

Soviet policies also made it easier for the United States to avoid any really forthright confrontation of the issues raised in the struggles between the revolutionary nationalists and the colonial powers

in Southeast Asia. The first few years of American postwar policy toward this area were characterized by an absence of competition with the Soviet Union. During this period Soviet policy was every bit as Europe-centric as that of the United States, and Moscow was no more responsive than Washington to the hopes of Southeast Asian nationalist leaders.

For more than two years after the end of the war Moscow paid little attention to the anticolonial struggles in Asia, and even during the period 1948–50 its role was almost exclusively rhetorical, with the prescriptions it did advance vague and restrained in tone.[8] For those Asian communists who looked for Soviet guidance there was until the end of September 1947 little more than the clearly outmoded Dmitrov doctrine of a decade before—a policy attuned to collective international antifascism and support of popular-front governments. In conformity with this objective, communist parties in colonial countries had been urged to shelve their struggles for independence and work with the European colonial powers against Japanese and Nazi imperialism. The lag in Soviet policy helps explain why just after World War II in Indonesia the Soviet-oriented communists stood to the right in the nationalist political spectrum, favoring a high degree of autonomy but opposed to severing all political ties with Holland. Thus, in April 1946 we find the Dutch government assigning high military priority to flying out to Indonesia known Indonesian communists who had been active in the anti-Nazi underground in Holland. They were sent out because within the context of the Indonesian revolution they were regarded as moderates—men who the Dutch expected would pull the Indonesian nationalist movement to the right and prevent a full break with the Netherlands.

Tanigawa Yoshihiko's recent assessment of Andrei Zhdanov's September 1947 address at the opening meeting of the Cominform and E.M. Zhukov's subsequent major article strikes me as very sound.[9] If these statements reflect any watershed in Soviet policy toward Southeast Asia, it was a rather modest one, with at most only a slight influence on communist parties in the area.[10] Their emphasis was on Europe, and although they presumably can be seen as a Soviet riposte to American policies there, and perhaps in Japan, I believe that there has been a tendency to exaggerate their importance for Southeast Asia. They were, it seems to me, primarily attempts to analyze what it was thought had been happening there rather than calls to action.[11]

I have seen no evidence that these new departures in Soviet policy affected the action of either the Vietminh in Vietnam or Tan Malaka and his followers in Indonesia; their policies remained unchanged. As for the communist-led armed uprising that broke out in Indonesia in September 1948, I am in full accord with Tanigawa's conclusion that "the basic cause was internal." The decision of late August 1948 by Sjarifuddin and several other radical socialist Indonesian nationalists to merge their substantial political organization with the smaller pro-Stalinist Communist party was, I believe, primarily a consequence of a keen disillusionment with U.S. policy stemming from the American failure to enforce implementation of the UN's compromise Renville solution.[12] This disillusionment was aggravated by the harsh material conditions resulting from the strict economic blockade that the Dutch maintained in defiance of the UN.[13] Whatever the long-term strategy of Musso, Sjarifuddin, and other top leaders of the newly enlarged Indonesian Communist party, it is clear that the Madiun rebellion of mid-September caught them by surprise and that it was launched by second- and third-echelon leaders panicked by the erosion of procommunist strength in the Indonesian army as a consequence of the rationalization policy of the Hatta-Sukarno government.

Charles McLane has, I believe, correctly concluded that "Moscow's reluctance to indicate full approval of Ho Chi Minh's course in Indochina did not dissipate until the spring of 1948."[14] And it was only considerably later that Ho's government received anything more than verbal encouragement. Moscow appears to have taken no initiative to accord diplomatic recognition to the Democratic Republic of Vietnam until January 30, 1950, two weeks after the DRV had made a global appeal for diplomatic relations with all countries, whatever their political system. Indeed, Soviet recognition of the DRV came only some three months before Moscow established diplomatic ties with the same Indonesian leadership that had so recently crushed Indonesia's Soviet-oriented Communist party in the aftermath of the Madiun rebellion.

It was not only Soviet Southeast Asia policy—or perhaps more

accurately the lack thereof—that helped the United States avoid direct confrontation of the issues raised during the early postwar years by the struggles of France and the Netherlands against the revolutionary nationalists in Indochina and Indonesia. The actions of the communist parties in the two metropoles had the same effect. At this time neither the French nor Dutch parties followed policies that were likely to spread the Cold War from Europe to Southeast Asia. For both of them, the French Communist party especially, calculations of advantage in domestic politics militated against supporting strongly anticolonial policies. Both favored increased self-government for their countries' Southeast Asian possessions, but within the context of continuing political ties with the metropole. In France until at least early 1948, communists as well as socialists followed policies that were on balance supportive of a reassertion of French political control over Indochina.[15]

It would, I believe, be very difficult to establish that from 1945 to 1949 the United States was subject to any real pressure to abandon its official stance of "neutrality" in Southeast Asia because of any significant Soviet attempts to influence political developments there—either directly or via the communist parties of France and the Netherlands. This made it that much easier for American officials to avoid any substantial degree of direct American involvement, while at the same time adhering to policies that remained just as Europe-centric as those of the Soviet Union.[16]

Although the United States was initially under little pressure to confront the issues raised by these disputes because of the circumstances just described, it eventually had to face up to them. It is, therefore, now appropriate to look at those factors that in a more positive sense gave shape to the American policies that ultimately emerged.

Anticolonialism

Wartime American support of the principle of self-determination, as evidenced in the Atlantic Charter and in U.S. Office of War Information trans-Pacific broadcasts, had combined with the clear-cut promise of independence for the Philippines to raise high hopes among leaders of the independence movements in Indochina and Indonesia that the United States would oppose any reimposition of colonial authority. However, these expectations were soon disappointed, and within a few months references to the American revolution and constitution that had been painted on the walls of buildings in Jakarta and Hanoi yielded place to more realistic slogans.

Soon after the proclamations of Indonesian and Vietnamese independence it became clear that the United States would provide no tangible support to revolutionary nationalists anywhere in Southeast Asia and was prepared to go little further than politely urging the colonial powers to pledge eventual self-government— with no minimum period of time even being suggested. The disillusionment of nationalist leaders obliged to fight for their independence mounted as it became increasingly evident that the Truman administration was unwilling to follow policies that actually accorded with the principle of self-determination.

Neverthless, the French and the Dutch were initially acutely worried about American intentions. Uneasy over Franklin Roosevelt's known opposition to the reestablishment of colonial regimes in Southeast Asia, numerous European colonial officials continued for more than a year after his death to nurture the suspicion that the real objective of the United States was to elbow France and the Netherlands out of Indochina and Indonesia in order to take over their economic stakes there. The French presumably had some knowledge of Ho Chi Minh's requests to U.S. officials during 1945–46 for American capital investment as well as economic and technical aid to help rebuild Vietnam's shattered economy.[17] And they were undoubtedly alarmed over the openly friendly attitude of several American OSS and army officers toward the Vietminh and its aim of independence.

However, the Americans who stood on the rostrum with Ho Chi Minh on September 2, 1945, when he declared Vietnam's independence were out of touch and out of phase with American policy—not only Truman's, but Roosevelt's as well. There is no evidence that Roosevelt's anticolonial feelings and his bitterness toward France over Vichy's accommodation with Japanese occupation forces had moderated before he died. But his evaluation of American strategic interests in Europe and the western Pacific (retention of islands previously held by Japan) had apparently come to outweigh his opposition to the reestablishment of French control over Indochina and his earlier plan of replacing it by a UN trusteeship. Moreover, opposition to France's return appeared a less feasible policy in view of Roosevelt's well-founded, if belated, disenchantment with Chiang Kai-shek's capacity to serve as America's partner in East Asia.[18]

Anticolonial sentiment in the United States did not, of course, die with Franklin Roosevelt. It retained a broad base in Congress and the populace as well as being represented among some, if by no means all, American foreign policy officials. Yet anticolonialism did not play a major role in shaping American policies toward the French and Dutch colonies in Southeast Asia. Never did it exert a really substantial influence on U.S. policies in Vietnam, and not until 1949 did it begin to approach that dimension in Indonesia. Some of the reasons for this, of course, transcended American interest in Southeast Asia as such.

Europe-centricity

There was constant tension between American anticolonial sentiment and the U.S. objectives in Europe. Increasingly the most influential American policy-makers were convinced that attainment of those objectives was incompatible with any substantial pressure on France and the Netherlands to abandon their effort to reassert control over their Southeast Asian colonies. Until the rise to power of the Communists in China in 1949, European concerns dominated American policy toward both Indonesia and Indochina, and in Vietnam they continued to exert an important influence right through the 1954 Geneva conference. Between 1946 and 1949, as the United States became more deeply involved in providing for the economic reconstruction of the countries of Western Europe and in shoring up their defense capabilities against Soviet power, the priority assigned to these programs heavily overshadowed considerations regarding American interest in Southeast Asia. The preeminence of Western Europe in American global strategy left the United States unwilling to challenge France and the Netherlands over Southeast Asia even if this meant

abandoning any effective support of the principles of anticolonialism and self-determination there.

In both economic and political terms these two European states
were viewed as too weak and unstable for the United States to risk
sufficient pressure on them to promote independence for their
Southeast Asian colonies. Such an attempt, it was argued, might
result in upsetting the political balance within them, especially
France, in ways that could strengthen their communist parties.
Moreover, influential voices in Washington argued that as the
Dutch home economy had been so heavily dependent upon the
colonial economic relationship with the East Indies in the prewar
years, its postwar health could only be restored if the Dutch resumed control over Indonesia's economic resources. And French
national pride, smarting from the ignominy of defeat and occupation by the Nazis, was seen as too sensitive to sustain a further blow
such as would attend France's forced withdrawal from Indochina.
(The plausibility of this consideration can be seen from the role it
played in inducing the French Communist party to hold back
from pressing for prompt independence for the countries of Indochina because of its expectation that such a policy would lose it
votes in the French elections.)

But certainly by 1947 the argument most frequently employed
in Washington against supporting Southeast Asian nationalist
movements centered on U.S. strategic objectives in offsetting
Soviet power in Europe. It was held that the willingness of France
and the Netherlands to cooperate in building up Western Europe's
military defenses would be seriously undermined by the antagonism that it was believed would be engendered by any strong
American pressure aimed at inducing them to grant full independence to their Southeast Asian colonies. It is evident that this
factor outweighed the concern of some American military leaders
that plans for the collective defense of Western Europe were being
undermined by the draining of the best troops of France and the
Netherlands to Southeast Asia.[19]

Consequently, for those charged with the conduct of U.S.
foreign policy, objectives in Europe overshadowed American anticolonial sentiment. This same priority also came to take precedence over pursuit of more effective policies for combating indigenous communist movements in Southeast Asia (a consideration of

evidently greater weight in the judgment of some U.S. officials than opposition to colonial rule).[20]

Anticommunism

From the very beginning of the postwar period one of the constants in the shaping of American policy toward Southeast Asia was opposition to the growth of communism. Although initially relatively restrained, this influence was given successive fillips by the development of the Cold War in Europe, the rise of the Communists to ascendancy in China, and the Korean War. Despite general agreement that the growth of communism in Southeast Asia was inimical to U.S. interests, there was, however, an evident lack of consensus among American policy-makers with regard to the character of the revolutionary nationalist movements in the area and whether or not they were, or were likely to become, communist dominated. Only a very few American officials, whose influence did not extend beyond 1946, believed that if not frustrated by Western military power these movements might serve as a countervailing force against the spread of Soviet-controlled communism into Southeast Asia.[21] Apart from this small group, until 1949 there were two major official schools of thought in Washington, one holding that the anticolonial nationalist movements would inevitably pass under communist control, and the other arguing that this was not necessarily so.[22] But it is my impression that all senior American policy-makers proceeded from the assumption that in the colonial areas there was a strict dichotomy between nationalism and communism, that the two could never genuinely fuse, and that in any alliance between them the communist element would be unchallengeably dominant. If any contemporary European example was regarded as relevant to Southeast Asia, it was Czechoslovakia and not Yugoslavia.

From the outset the Truman administration saw Ho Chi Minh as more a communist than a nationalist, and it soon took the position—despite an acknowledged lack of real evidence—that he was acting in behalf of the Soviet Union. (This accorded, of course, with the conventional American official wisdom of the time that *all* communist parties were controlled by the Kremlin.) By the beginning of 1947 the United States had pulled back from any earlier disposition to argue for a compromise settlement between France and the Vietminh, and, while admitting that it could propose no feasible alternative, the State Department concluded, "We do not lose sight of the fact that Ho Chi Minh had direct Communist connections and it should be obvious that we are not interested in seeing colonial empire administrations supplanted by philosophy and political organization emanating from and controlled by Kremlin."[23] In view of this assessment, it is perhaps understandable how American policy-makers, abandoning their own initial better judgment, had by mid-1949 become proponents of France's abortive "Bao Dai solution."

With regard to Indonesia, most officials in the American foreign policy community were apparently unwilling to give credence to Dutch allegations that the leadership of the Indonesian revolution was actually procommunist, but they were continually worried about the possibility of an existing and potential communist influence on those leaders.[24] By crushing the communists' Madiun rebellion in October 1948, the leadership of the Indonesian Republic temporarily dissipated this concern. Indeed, soon after it had become clear that Sukarno and Hatta were moving energetically to confront this communist challenge, the CIA dispatched its first regular agent to the capital of the Indonesian Republic at Jogjakarta in a role that it presumably regarded as supportive of their noncommunist leadership.[25] However, by the spring of 1949 the fear of the communist potential in Indonesia was beginning to revive among U.S. officials. Because of the military stalemate and the continuing refusal of the Dutch to release Sukarno, Hatta, and other top anticommunist leaders,[26] and against the backdrop of Communist success in China, there was a growing belief in Washington that further frustration of the independence struggle might bring many Indonesians to look sympathetically on communism— at least the strongly nationalist variant associated with the name of Tan Malaka.[27] Such an outcome seemed all the more likely in early 1949 as the embittered Indonesian guerrillas became increasingly convinced that the United States stood behind the Dutch.

Economic Interest

The influence of any American Southeast Asian economic interest on U.S. policies on these disputes is difficult to establish, and I believe that the importance of this factor was probably relatively minor and subsidiary to the others described in this paper. Despite the lack of direct evidence, there is, I think, sufficient circumstantial evidence to conclude that local economic interest probably exerted some influence on United States policy in the dispute between the Indonesians and the Netherlands; but I have seen no evidence that it was operative with regard to American policy toward the struggle between France and the Vietminh.

While the United States had practically no economic stake in Vietnam—with respect to either investment or trade—it had a considerable, if in worldwide terms relatively modest, direct economic stake in Indonesia, capital investment as well as commerce. French colonial policy had shut out American capital from Indochina, and the French gave no sign that they were going to reverse this policy.[28] The Dutch, on the other hand, had permitted considerable American investment before the war, particularly in oil and rubber, and they appear to have given no indication that they would cease doing so after the war. Thus, in Vietnam there was no direct economic incentive for American intervention on either side.[29] Such an incentive did exist in Indonesia, but it appears to have affected American policy differently during the course of the Dutch-Indonesian struggle, depending upon the relative strength of the contestants.

During the early period, when the Dutch seemed to be militarily ascendant, this economic factor probably worked in their favor. It was then possible to argue—as the Dutch did—that a continuing application of the maximum available Dutch power would bring an early end to the fighting and thus reduce the extent of destruction and damage to American as well as Dutch properties. However, beginning in early 1949 the argument commenced to run increasingly in the other direction. By then the Indonesian Republic was achieving greater military success and

Dutch forces were being pushed progressively on the defensive, becoming largely isolated in major towns and cities. Mounting Dutch inability to contain Indonesian scorched-earth tactics, particularly in the areas of the great plantations, finally changed the attitudes of a large number of Dutch businessmen. They then became aligned with liberal sentiment in Holland in favor of the compromise settlement recommended by the UN, one entailing an end not only to the physical destruction of Dutch properties but also to their protection after the envisaged transfer of sovereignty to the Indonesians. It seems reasonable to assume that this consideration was also operative among American business interests so far as their existing investments and expectations for trade and investment following a political settlement were concerned.

As noted above, European economic considerations clearly did exert influence on American policy toward these disputes, particularly with respect to the viability of the Dutch economy, which before the war had been much more dependent on Indonesia than the French economy had been on Indochina. But once it became clear that the Dutch could not impose a political settlement of their own choosing, even the more pro-Dutch American foreign policy officials came to recognize that an early end to the fighting was desirable—not only to protect Dutch investments in Indonesia but to stanch the flow of the metropole's economic assets into its very expensive overseas military campaign. Moreover, their knowledge that the proposed UN settlement provided for a substantial recoupment of Dutch expenditures in Indonesia presumably strengthened their belief that such a settlement would be beneficial to the Dutch home economy. Indonesia finally did in fact have to shoulder $1.13 billion of the Netherlands East Indies debt, of which approximately 70 percent constituted the entire internal debt of the colonial government. American support of the Netherlands in its demand that Indonesia assume the whole of this internal debt provided one of the most controversial issues in the final settlement arrived at in the Hague Conference of December 1949. Since the Indonesians held that 42 percent of this amount had been incurred by Dutch military operations in Indonesia, they argued that they were being saddled with a substantial proportion of the costs of the Dutch military effort to block Indonesian independence.

The UN Factor

France's power of veto in the Security Council insured that no UN spotlight ever shone on Vietnam to illuminate the facts and issues there for a worldwide audience. This obstacle probably deterred some states sympathetic to the Vietminh from trying to put its case on the UN agenda; and neither the French Communist party nor the Soviet Union itself appeared to be interested in raising the matter in that forum. The UN never gave any support to the Vietnamese independence struggle, and indeed until 1950 the Vietminh received virtually no backing from members of the international community.

But the UN ultimately came to play an influential role in Indonesia's independence struggle, which early in the history of the world organization precipitated a major test of its peace-keeping capacity. The Netherlands held no power of veto on the Security Council, and though several council members had some sympathy for the Dutch position, none was willing to go so far as to veto consideration of the issue by the UN. Thanks to insistent efforts by Australia and India, usually supported by the Soviet Union, the Security Council had by August 1948 become seized by the Dutch-Indonesia dispute. From that time many adherents of the UN, both in the United States and elsewhere, saw the future of the organization intertwined with the question of Indonesian independence.

Within the context provided by the UN, it was much more difficult for the United States to remain publicly uncommitted with regard to the Indonesian independence struggle. In effect, it found itself in a position whereby it could not remain aloof from the Indonesian-Dutch dispute without at the same time disassociating itself from the UN.[30]

Although Dean Acheson and other Department of State officials were unable to keep the UN out of Indonesia, they were successful in helping insure that it played a more modest part in the dispute than was advocated by Australia, India, and the Soviet Union. The role of the UN's Committee of Good Offices was limited to that of merely suggesting compromise solutions, with no actual power of arbitration; and appropriately enough, an American representative occupied the middle, moderating position on the three-man UN committee that in October 1947 began to explore the possibilities for a viable compromise solution.

The Truman administration would have probably continued on a middle-of-the-road course, without seriously challenging the Netherlands position, if the Dutch had not so flagrantly flouted the UN-monitored truce in Indonesia and refused to abide by the UN's prescription for a compromise solution.[31] It was predictable that in this situation the broadly based American hopes for the success of that newly launched organization would fuse with American anticolonial sentiment in condemning Dutch actions. As a result of the adverse congressional reaction to this Dutch defiance of the UN, the administration was finally forced in the early months of 1949 to endorse a position more critical of the Netherlands than it would otherwise have taken. Moreover, the executive branch's resistance to this pressure began to erode as even some of those American officials who had been most partial to the Dutch recognized that the issue in Indonesia had escalated beyond the dispute itself into the question of whether or not the UN would become simply another impotent League of Nations. Particularly with the pointed Dutch disregard of the UN during and after the all-out attack against the Republic of Indonesia of December 19, 1948—launched in the face of a UN-monitored ceasefire—the lines were drawn in a way that insured much stronger American criticism of the Dutch position. In addition, since this attack came less than two months after the Indonesian Republic had demonstrated its anticommunist character by quelling the communist-led Madiun rebellion, some of the less anticolonial U.S. officials and congressmen were much more disposed to criticize the Dutch for flouting the UN than would otherwise have been the case.

Though initially the influence of the UN factor on American policy in the Indonesian-Dutch dispute was neither persistent nor very great, it became increasingly so beginning in January 1949. Acheson and other members of the top echelon of the administration's foreign policy management for a time dug in their heels against a mounting congressional insistence on economic sanctions against the Dutch, but by the late spring of 1949 congressional and public pressure became sufficiently strong to bring them to talk more sternly to the Dutch than ever before. They then made clear to The Hague that if it continued to defy the UN,

Congress would indeed cut off Marshall Plan assistance to the Netherlands. This pressure was propitiously timed to help end Dutch intransigence. It came just as they were beginning to acknowledge that they lacked the power to enforce a political decision in Indonesia by military means, and after Dutch business interests had come to appreciate that continuation of the scorched-earth tactics being carried out on an ever wider scale by Indonesian guerrillas would rapidly erode what remained of the Dutch economic stake there.

Whatever the relative weight of the factors described above in shaping American policy toward the independence struggles in Indonesia and Vietnam, the influence exerted by the United States on the course of these conflicts was not limited to the levels of diplomacy and political pressure. Any full evaluation of its role must also involve an assessment of the impact of American actions in providing the material means with which the scales were weighted in favor of the colonial powers.

Material Means

The United States provided France and the Netherlands with the essential material resources for the massive military efforts they mounted to reassert control over their Southeast Asian colonies. However insensitive some officials of the Truman administration may have been to the consequences, the United States in fact supplied both countries with most of the arms and economic resources that made possible their antirevolutionary efforts in Indochina and Indonesia.

In the first place, both European states had received from the United States without cost under lend-lease authorization large amounts of modern arms—including planes, tanks, and infantry weapons—for use by their forces in the projected Allied assault on the Japanese home islands. These arms were never, of course, so employed; but no effort was made to recall them, and both colonial powers were permitted to use them as they saw fit.

Secondly, after the war had ended both France and the Netherlands were permitted to purchase additional weapons from the

United States, with Washington directly advancing the necessary credits in some instances.[32] Moreover, it was unnecessary for either colonial power to rely on U.S. credits specifically earmarked for the purchase of arms. Both before and after the inception of the European recovery program (Marshall Plan) they were able to utilize—either directly or indirectly—a considerable part of the U.S. financial aid provided for the rebuilding of their shattered domestic economies for purchasing additional weapons and meeting the costs of their military campaigns in Southeast Asia. Despite official denials, U.S. policy-makers were quite aware of this situation.[33] Whatever system of bookkeeping one wishes to apply, it is abundantly clear that neither France nor the Netherlands could have afforded military efforts of the magnitude they mounted in Southeast Asia without drawing heavily on the postwar rehabilitation funds received from the United States through the Marshall Plan and earlier credits.[34]

Publicly, however, the Truman administration disassociated itself from any appearance of supporting the two colonial powers. In January 1946 it refused to transport troops, arms, or ammunition "to or from the Netherlands East Indies or French Indochina,"[35] and as early as October 1945 Secretary of State James Byrnes ordered all U.S. insignia removed from American equipment. (This request was so often ignored by the Dutch in Indonesia as to give rise to the suspicion that they were trying to appear as if they enjoyed fuller American backing than was in fact the case.)[36] Officially the American government took the position that no arms could be sold to France "in cases which appear to relate to Indochina."[37] However, as the Department of State was quite aware, no such limitation was enforced. Thus, in a secret policy statement of September 27, 1948, the department observed that in fact American arms being exported to France were "available for reshipment to Indochina or for releasing stocks from reserves to be forwarded to Indochina."[38] Presumably a similar policy was operative in the Dutch-Indonesian dispute.

Whatever the public statements of American officials, the leaders of the Indonesian and Vietnamese independence struggles and the guerrillas who did the fighting were understandably inclined to see the United States as standing behind the Dutch and French military forces that they confronted.

Some Concluding Observations

One must, I believe, conclude that on balance for almost three and a half years after the end of the war American policy was partial to and heavily supportive of both France and the Netherlands in their efforts to reassert control over their Southeast Asian colonies. Whatever the official position described by American spokesmen, U.S. actions were hardly neutral. Indirectly, via the European metropoles, American power was at the most fundamental level ranged against the revolutionary nationalists.

To assign relative weight to the elements that shape a country's foreign policy is bound to be somewhat arbitrary. However, I am convinced that by far the most powerful and enduring factor that influenced U.S. policy toward the Dutch-Indonesian and French-Vietnamese conflicts is what I have termed "Europe-centricity." There were, as we have seen, subordinate elements that supported or detracted from its salience, but until the beginning of 1949 with respect to both Indonesia and Vietnam American anticolonialism was the only major factor ranged in opposition. In Vietnam nothing happened to change this situation; but in Indonesia an unexpected development in the fall of 1948 led to a considerable alteration in the balance of factors bearing on American policy. Indeed, if there was any clear watershed in the circumstances that influenced U.S. policy toward Indonesia, it was the communists' abortive Madiun rebellion and its suppression by the government of Hatta and Sukarno. As a consequence of these events the thrust of the anticommunist factor in American policy began to operate differently with regard to Indonesia, by early 1949 no longer working to offset either American anticolonialism or the more recently introduced UN factor; and by that time the influence of economic interest worked against rather than for any continuing Dutch attempt to secure a solution by military means. With this change in alignment, the still powerful factor of Europe-centricity had to yield and accommodate.

But Vietnam was not so fortunate. There the priority of U.S. objectives in Europe never came under serious challenge. American anticommunism continued to check American anticolonialism; no UN factor was ever operative, and there was no significant economic interest to exert influence on policy in either direction.

Thus, in early 1949, the Truman administration began to move toward a more even-handed policy in the Dutch-Indonesian dispute, while becoming more strongly and overtly supportive of the French in Vietnam. By the summer of 1949, the United States was finally putting sufficient pressure on the Dutch to help expedite their relinquishment of sovereignty over Indonesia, while in Vietnam it had moved to support France's futile Bao Dai solution even though American officials privately acknowledged that Ho Chi Minh represented the main thrust of Vietnamese nationalism.

1. There is, of course, no certainty that Douglas MacArthur would have been less supportive of the Dutch and the French had he remained in charge of areas turned over to the British at Potsdam. Indeed, with respect to Indonesia, the available indications are that he would have insisted upon an initial reestablishment of Dutch authority.

2. Vice-Admiral The Earl Mountbatten of Burma, *Report to the Combined Chiefs of Staff: Section E, Post Surrender Tasks* (London: 1969), pp. 286, 288, 293.

3. Ibid., pp. 287–89. *See also* Philippe Devillers, *Histoire du Vietnam de 1940 à 1952* (Paris: Seuil, 1952), and George Rosie, *The British in Vietnam* (London: Panther, 1970).

4. In most of Java and in some parts of Sumatra it was easier for revolutionary nationalists to have access to Japanese military equipment than was the case in Vietnam; moreover, the regroupment of Japanese army units in the crucial period between Japan's capitulation and the arrival of Allied forces was more favorable to the revolutionaries on Java and Sumatra than to those in Vietnam.

5. *See* Mountbatten, *Report*, pp. 289–98, 308–12.

6. Of those few accounts of the KMT occupation available in English, Mai Elliott's translation of and introduction to Vo Nguyen Giap's *Unforgettable Months and Years* (Ithaca: Southeast Asia Program, 1975) is especially useful. (*See also* the extensive bibliographical references in her introduction.)

7. In addition to France's relinquishment of extraterritorial privileges in China and the French concessions in Chinese cities, Haiphong was to become a special port for the duty-free transit of goods from or to China. Chinese goods were to have duty-free passage over the Yünnan-Haiphong railroad, and the portion of that line running through China was to be turned over to China. Moreover, Chinese nationals would continue to exercise the rights and privileges in Vietnam that the French had previously granted them.

8. For the period 1945–48, *see* Charles B. McLane, *Soviet Strategies in Southeast Asia* (Princeton: Princeton University Press, 1966), pp. 249–60. The most substantial scholarly treatment focusing on Soviet policy toward the Indonesian revolution remains Ruth T. McVey's *The Soviet View of the Indonesian Revolution* (Ithaca: Cornell University Press, 1957). I have found no comparable study of Soviet policy toward the Vietnamese revolution.

9. *See* Tanigawa Yoshihiko's essay in this volume.

10. Ruth T. McVey has found that the Soviet press was generally supportive of the noncommunist Indonesian revolutionary leadership for almost two years before and nearly a year after Andrei Zhdanov's pronouncement of the "two camps doctrine" at the opening meeting of the Cominform. She notes that on Mohammed Hatta's succession as prime minister following Sjarifuddin's resignation there was between Febru-

ary 2 and 29, 1948, some unfavorable criticism in the Soviet press of the new cabinet (it being initially regarded as pro-American), but that thereafter until August 25 there was no indication that Moscow was not supportive of Hatta's government. Indeed, as late as August 4, 1948, in *The New Times* in an article entitled "The Struggle of the Colonial Peoples," Hatta's government is described as "courageously defending" Indonesia's independence "against encroachments by the Dutch behind whom loom the monopolists of Wall Street. . . ." McVey, *Soviet View*, pp. 38, 71, 73.

11. One gets the impression either that Soviet knowledge of developments in Indonesia was very meager or that wishful thinking or efforts at ideological tidiness were responsible for distorting what information was available. Both E. M. Zhukov in his substantial monograph in the December 1947 issue of *Bol'shevik* and V. Vasil'eva (a Soviet specialist on Indonesia) in the first issue of *Voprosy ekonomiki* for 1948 bracket the Indonesian and Vietnamese revolutionary governments together as "peoples' democratic republics." Ibid., pp. 34–35.

12. Prime Minister Sjarifuddin had staked his political prestige and career on U.S. assurances that the concessions made by the Indonesians in the U.S.-sponsored Renville agreement of January 1948 would be balanced by Dutch concessions, and that the United States could be relied upon to insure that the Netherlands would live up to its part of the agreement. Because the United States failed to do so, even after the Indonesians had implemented their major concession, and the Dutch were able to violate the agreement with impunity, Sjarifuddin felt betrayed by the United States and was particularly distrustful of the Truman administration. (Frank Graham, the U.S. representative on the UN Good Offices Committee, who in good faith had negotiated the agreement with the expectation that the United States would honor its pledge, also—as he once indicated to me—had reason to feel betrayed.) When I talked with Sjarifuddin on August 29, 1948, two days before he decided to merge his powerful Socialist party with the Communist party, his principal preoccupation was the 1948 U.S. presidential elections. Dewey didn't look any better to him than Truman, and he kept returning to the question of when progressive forces in the United States such as he associated with Roosevelt's New Deal could be expected to return to power. When I acknowledged that it was unlikely for another four years, he indicated that this was his own judgment too and said, "That will be too long."

13. The Dutch blockade kept all medicines as well as food from entering the densely populated, heavily food-deficit areas still held by the Indonesian Republic in Java, and into them approximately a million refugees had streamed from areas overrun by the Dutch army. Serious malnutrition and disease were widespread.

14. McLane, *Soviet Strategies*, p. 432. He also points out that "until the outcome of the Communist struggle for power in France was known, a clear cut policy in Indochina was blocked." Ibid., p. 271.

15. In March 1947 the communist members of the French cabinet voted credits for supporting the war against the Vietminh. They left the cabinet in May 1947, but their posture toward the Indochina issue continued for at least another year to be strongly influenced by calculations of political advantage in domestic elections, and communist-dominated labor unions continued to load ships carrying military supplies to French forces in Vietnam.

16. This is not to say that these officials abandoned their intense suspicion of Moscow's intentions toward Southeast Asia and their exaggerated estimate of its capacity to influence the course of political events there.

17. Details of these requests can be found on pp. 11–13 of "Ho Chi Minh and the United States," a report prepared by Robert M. Blum as part of a staff study for the Senate Foreign Relations Committee, entitled *The United States and Vietnam: 1944–1947* (Washington: 1972).

18. These conclusions are persuasively argued by Walter LaFeber in his article, "Roosevelt, Churchill, and Indochina: 1942–1945," *The American Historical Review* 80, no. 5 (December 1975): 1277–95.

19. With respect to this concern over the absence of these troops *see* statement of General George C. Marshall (then of the American Red Cross) before the meeting held under the aegis of the Department of State, 8 October 1949, *Transcript of Proceedings, Meeting on U.S.-China Problems,* Department of State, division of central services, mimeo., 1949, p. 405.

20. This proposition is set forth with unusual clarity in the "Department of State Policy Statement on Indochina, September 27, 1948." *Foreign Relations of the United States* (henceforth cited *FR*), *The Far East and Australasia, 1948,* VI, 48–49.

21. These were mostly to be found in the newly established Southeast Asia division of the Department of State, and the majority of them were individuals temporarily seconded from academic life.

22. For a clear statement of this division, *see* Robert Lovett's reply of 30 December 1948, to the position paper of the U.S. Moscow embassy dispatched in its telegram of 17 December 1948, in *FR, 1948,* VI, 613–16.

23. Marshall to U.S. embassy in Paris, 3 February 1947, *U.S.-Vietnam Relations,* vol. 2, pp. 98–99, cited in *The United States and Vietnam, 1944–47,* U.S. Senate Foreign Relations Committee, Staff Study, 3 April 1973 (Washington: 1972), p. 20.

24. The Dutch consistently tried to persuade American officials that procommunist sentiment in the Republic of Indonesia was strong and a long-term danger; they argued that to accede to the republic's demand for full independence would open the whole archipelago to communist influence. Even after the Madiun rebellion they argued in this vein, without differentiating between the Soviet-oriented communists who were involved in that rebellion and Tan Malaka's more strongly nationalist communist group which had helped Sukarno and Hatta put it down. A good example of this is provided in the Dutch embassy's note to the Department of State of 17 January 1949. See *FR, The Far East and Australasia, Part I, 1949,* VII, 160.

25. During his brief stay in Jogjakarta this agent managed to antagonize the leaders of an anticommunist political party by his offer of financial support, but he succeeded in securing agreement for sending a number of officers of the mobile police brigade to U.S. bases for special training.

26. Most of the major political leaders in the republic's capital had been captured in the Dutch blitz attack of 19 December 1948.

27. This was a view also held by the British. *See* letter of 5 January 1949 from Franks to Lovett, in *FR, The Far East: China, 1949,* IX, 10.

28. The Vietminh, apparently wishing to develop multilateral economic relations, indicated that it welcomed American investment. *See* note 17, above.

29. One could, of course, argue that American interest in the rehabilitation of France, as with the Netherlands, called for an end of the fighting and a diversion of the metropole's economic assets away from crushing the colonial independence movement in favor of rehabilitation and strengthening of the home economy. This was, in fact, a point sometimes raised in discussions by American officials, but does not appear to have had great influence on the policies they pursued toward the two colonial powers.

30. For a discerning treatment of the influence of the UN factor on U.S. policy, *see* Evelyn Colbert, "The Road Not Taken: Decolonization and Independence in Indonesia and Indochina," *Foreign Affairs* (April 1973): 608–28. The most comprehensive coverage of the UN's role in Indonesia is Alastair M. Taylor, *Indonesian Independence and the United Nations* (Ithaca: Cornell University Press, 1960).

31. A good example of the views dominant in the Department of State shortly before the development of pressure in the Senate for such sanctions is represented by Acting Secretary of State Lovett's cable to Philip Jessup, the U.S. representative to the UN, on 23 December 1948. *FR, 1948,* VI, 597–601.

32. The *Pentagon Papers* note that in late 1946 Washington extended Paris a credit of $160 million for the purchase of "vehicles and industrial equipment for use in Indochina." Senator Gravel edition (Boston: Beacon, 1971), I, 51.

33. *See* GPO edition of the *Pentagon Papers,* I (IV. A. 2.), 1.

34. According to figures made available to me at the time, the cost of maintaining Dutch army and air force elements in Indonesia for the year 1948 was $436,297,874 (cost of the navy was additional). In the 1948 fiscal year the United States allotted $402,800,000 in economic aid (ECA) to the Netherlands directly and an additional $68 million to the Dutch administration in Indonesia. Three-quarters of this ECA aid was on a grant basis. For the next fiscal year the total was $506 million, with the provision that $84 million could be directly allocated to the Netherlands administration in Indonesia.

35. Department of State circular to certain American diplomatic and consular officers, 23 January 1946. Cited in GPO edition of the *Pentagon Papers*, I (IV. A. 2.), 1, 20.

36. In the all-out attack against the Indonesian Republic of 19 December 1948, I saw that some of the Dutch planes still bore the U.S. white star, and as late as February 1949 I encountered Dutch officers up to the rank of major wearing U.S. battle fatigues with the words "U.S. Marines" highly visible above their breast pockets.

37. Gravel edition, *Pentagon Papers*, I, 30.

38. *FR, 1948*, VI, 45.

The Cominform and Southeast Asia

Tanigawa Yoshihiko

This paper seeks, first, to clarify the nature of the Calcutta Conference—that conference sponsored by communist student and youth organizations in February 1948; and, second, to analyze and explain the relationship between the Calcutta Conference, the Cominform, which had been established under Soviet direction the previous September, and the communist-led armed insurrections which broke out in various Southeast Asian countries immediately after the conference. The Calcutta Conference was a subject of intensive study in the West, particularly the United States, during the 1950s and 1960s, for it related to the origins of the Cold War in Asia and to the Korean and Vietnam wars. In the Soviet Union and the Eastern Bloc, on the other hand, the Calcutta Conference has been completely ignored, perhaps because the significance of this kind of problem is not acknowledged there.

Western interpretations of the Calcutta Conference and of the interrelationship between the conference, the Cominform, and the Southeast Asian armed uprisings can be divided into two general groups. The first group holds that with the establishment of the Cominform, the Soviet Union switched its policy from cooperation to confrontation with the West; during the Calcutta Conference, it issued a directive to the communist forces of the participating countries to launch armed revolts and thereby caused the series of uprisings in Southeast Asia. Extending this argument, the group views the Korean War as the culmination of the Soviet policy. This type of interpretation, which may be called a "Soviet conspiracy" or "Soviet-directed revolution" theory, has been put forward by scholars who generally support U.S. policy, such as Walt W. Rostow, A. Doak Barnett, and Frank N. Trager. Barnett, for example, states: "In February 1948 two important Communist gatherings, attended by representatives of Communist parties throughout South and Southeast Asia, were held at Calcutta; the Southeast Asia Youth Conference, and the Second Congress of the Indian Communist party. Apparently the new Cominform 'line' was pressed home at these meetings, for almost immediately there-after the Communist parties of Southeast Asia either adopted or intensified the strategy of militant insurrection."[1] Taking the same position, Rostow expresses his view quite clearly: "Stalin, working through the Cominform, launched an offensive in the East, which can roughly be dated from Zhdanov's speech of September, 1947. It involved guerrilla warfare in Indochina, Burma, Malaya, Indonesia, and the Philippines. And after the Chinese Communists came to power in . . . 1949, the offensive in Asia reached its climax in the invasion of South Korea."[2]

However, there are non-Marxist scholars in the West who criticize or reject this theory. They base their views on solid historical research on Soviet foreign policy and Southeast Asian communist movements. Leading representatives of this group are Ruth T. McVey, well known for her research on the Indonesian Communist party; Charles B. McLane, author of a brilliant study on Soviet policy toward colonial areas and developing countries; and John H. Kautsky, who has carried out extensive research on the relationship between Moscow and the Indian Communist party. On the basis of their research, they emphasize two main points: first, although the Calcutta Conference was a forum for the propagation of Soviet policy, it would be inappropriate to view it as a place where a "directive for revolution" was issued; and, second, while Southeast Asian armed uprisings were influenced by the Calcutta Conference in some fashion, the fundamental causes of these uprisings were inherent in the conditions existing in the region at the time.

This essay will examine these two opposing interpretations. Let us begin with a look at the foreign—especially Asian—policies of the Cominform and its leading member, the Soviet Union.

Asian Policies of the Soviet Union and the Cominform

Though explanations of the origins of the Cold War differ extensively, there seems to be general agreement on two points: first, that the cooperative relations that existed between the United States and the Soviet Union during World War II had collapsed by 1947; and, second, that President Harry Truman's declaration in March of that year relating to the Greek civil war was an important first step in American Cold War policy. This declaration, known as the Truman Doctrine, was aimed at helping the Greek government and containing foreign and domestic communist forces there. The Truman Doctrine was derived from a particular view of foreign affairs which later came to be called the Domino theory, and it became the foundation stone of the U.S. policy of containing communism on a global scale. Guided by this doctrine, the Truman administration decided in June 1947 to give aid to Greece and Turkey, and in July drew up the Marshall Plan which involved economic aid to 16 Western European countries. The Soviet Union, in response to this American activity, organized a conference for the purpose of exchanging and coordinating information among the communist forces of Europe. At the conference, held in September 1947, at Wiliza Gora, Poland, the Communist Information Bureau (Cominform) was created and its establishment officially announced on October 5. It should be noted that representatives of the communist parties of only nine European countries—the Soviet Union, Bulgaria, Yugoslavia, Hungary, Rumania, Poland, Czechoslovakia, France, and Italy— participated in the formation of the Cominform. Not a single representative from any Asian country was present at the conference.[3] This fact shows that at the time of the Cominform's creation the Soviet Union's active concern was with Europe and that it had not yet been extended to Asia and other regions. Behind this Soviet preoccupation with Europe lay such problems as Russia's postwar reconstruction and the defense and reconstruction of the Eastern European countries it had liberated.

This attitude of the Soviet Union was evident in the keynote speech delivered by Andrei Zhdanov, the Soviet delegate to the Cominform's organizational conference. Since Zhdanov was considered to be Stalin's heir-apparent, his speech drew a great deal of attention in the West and was translated into many languages. The speech was seen as marking a watershed in Soviet foreign policy because it heralded a change in Soviet policy from cooperation to confrontation with the West and a shift of focus from Europe to Asia. Zhdanov first emphasized that World War II had been instrumental in creating great changes in the international situation. On the one hand, Japan, Italy, and Germany had been effectively eliminated from the pre-1945 group of six great imperialist powers, and, on the other hand, beginning in 1945, the liberation struggles of the colonial peoples of the world had escalated, bringing the colonial system itself to a point of crisis.

Zhdanov also argued that the postwar world had become divided into two large camps—the "imperialist and antidemocratic camp," led by the United States, and the "democratic and antiimperialist camp," led by the Soviet Union. He emphasized, however, that socialist and capitalist systems could coexist and that Soviet foreign policy was based on this assumption. In his analysis of the world situation, Zhdanov stated that the former colonies of Vietnam and Indonesia were "associated" with, and India, Egypt, and Syria were in "sympathy" with, the antiimperialist camp.[4] Zhdanov argued, in other words, that the age of the antifascist united front—the "united front from above"—had passed and that a new doctrinal line was necessary. Since the world was in a transitional stage, however, a clear and concrete new line had not yet been established for the communist forces in Asia and the colonial world. This was due to the fact, though Zhdanov did not say it, that the Soviet Union, which was planning to discard the strategy of the antifascist united front, was facing the problem of choosing between two strategies. These were, first, the strategy of the "united front from below," adopted at the sixth Comintern congress in 1928 and upheld until the seventh congress in 1935; and, second, the strategy of the national united front—the "Chinese formula"—led by the working class but also including the national bourgeoisie. Later, when the victory of the Chinese revolution became a reality, the Soviet Union came to advocate this "Chinese formula," but until then its position was difficult to ascertain. Let us say that the Soviet Union leaned more toward the "united front from below" line. If, in fact, this was the case, then the Soviet Union's policy was particularly problematic in two important strategic and tactical areas. First, it was unclear whether the "national bourgeoisie" who led anticolonial movements should be considered part of the imperialist camp or members of the antiimperialist camp. Second, it was uncertain whether strikes, parliamentary struggles, or even armed uprisings should be given emphasis as tactics of anticolonial struggles.

The distinctive feature of Zhdanov's speech was the evidence it gave that the Soviet Union and the Cominform did not possess a strong interest in the anticolonial struggles taking place in Asia and the rest of the world. In his book, *Moscow and the Communist Party of India*, John H. Kautsky states: "The composition of the Cominform, the reports made at its establishment . . . and the contents of its newpaper are clear evidence of the lack of attention devoted to Asian affairs by Moscow, an attitude of which disbelief in total Communist victory in China must have been a part."[5] This fact is also revealed in the October 5, 1947, announcement of the creation of the Cominform, and in the article by E. M. Zhukov published in the magazine *Bol'shevik* in December 1947. As Charles B. McLane has pointed out, Zhukov attempted in this article to apply systematically and concretely Zhdanov's speech to the problems of Asia and the colonial areas. Since Zhukov was a leading Soviet Orientalist, his article attracted wide attention. While he criticized neutralism—the "so-called theory of a third force"—from the standpoint of the two-camp thesis and acknowledged the success of the armed struggles taking place in China and Vietnam, he never urged the communist forces in Asia to use military force in their struggles against foreign imperialism and national governments.

Thus it can be seen that the Soviet Union and the Cominform were then completely preoccupied with European problems and did not indicate any positive concern with the problems of Asia and the colonial areas. Nor did they possess concrete strategy or tactics to deal with these problems. It would seem correct to assume, therefore, that the Soviet Union and the Cominform were in no position to direct or order armed struggle by communist forces in Asia. It was under these conditions that the Calcutta Conference took place.

The Calcutta Conference

Officially called "The conference of youth and students of Southeast Asia fighting for freedom and independence," the Calcutta Conference was held during February 19–25, 1948. It was sponsored by the World Federation of Democratic Youth (WFDY) and the International Union of Students (IUS). Since both of these organizations were under communist leadership, they were able to determine the political course of the conference proceedings. McLane has pointed out, however, that these groups were mass front organizations and were not delegated any revolutionary function by Moscow as were the youth and student organizations of the Comintern era.[6]

Several years before the Calcutta Conference, the WFDY had decided to investigate the state of affairs of youth in the colonial areas of Asia and to establish relations with youth organizations there. A WFDY mission was scheduled to leave Paris in November 1946, but then war broke out between Ho Chi Minh's Democratic Republic of Vietnam and France, which was attempting to regain its control over Indochina. France refused to grant permission to the WFDY mission to enter Indochina, thus delaying its departure. The mission decided to cross India first and there wait for the permit. Because of all this trouble, the mission, which finally left Paris for India in early February 1947, was decidedly smaller than that originally planned, and consisted of only four members—one representative each from the Soviet Union, France, Yugoslavia, and Denmark.[7]

Following its arrival in India, the mission was able to meet with younger representatives from Southeast Asian countries who had gathered in New Delhi for the Asian relations conference. They discussed the idea of convening a conference of youth and student groups active in promoting democratic and antiimperialist movements in Southeast Asia. The Indonesian delegation volunteered to play host to such a conference, and so it was decided to hold the Southeast Asian youth conference in Indonesia in November of that year. Invitations to the conference were sent by the WFDY and IUS in June 1947 to youth and student groups in Asian countries. It should be noted that this was prior to the creation of the Cominform. In the sponsoring country of Indonesia preparations for the conference were energetically carried out, led by the Indonesian Youth Congress (BKPRS)—the largest youth organization in Indonesia which included nationalists as well as communists. President Sukarno, Vice President Mohammed Hatta, and Prime Minister Soetan Sjahrir were asked to become honorary members of the Indonesian preparatory committee.[8] Such activity by Indonesians was motivated by a desire to gain international recognition for their recently created Republic of Indonesia through the sponsorship of the first international conference to be held in that new nation. However, the Netherlands at this time began its "police action" against the republic in an attempt to force Indonesia to resubmit to colonial rule. Indonesia was in a state of war from July 1947, so the youth conference planned for November could not be held in that country. The WFDY decided to hold the conference in Calcutta at the beginning of 1948.

After two years of complications, the Southeast Asian youth conference was finally held in Calcutta in February 1948, under the joint sponsorship of the WFDY and IUS. It was attended by official delegates representing 39 groups from the Southeast Asian countries of Indonesia, Vietnam, Burma, the Philippines, and Malaya, and from the South Asian countries of India, Pakistan, Ceylon, and Nepal. China was invited as an observer, but the conferees acceded to the demands of China's six representatives and granted them official status as delegates. Observers and guests from Korea, Mongolia, Australia, Yugoslavia, France, Canada, Czechoslovakia, and the Soviet Union were also present at the conference.[9] Although the exact number of the participants is not known (one account gives 900), it is certain that it was very large.[10]

The political ideologies of the participants were as varied as their number—nationalists and democrats as well as communists were at the conference. Ruth T. McVey gives two major reasons for this situation. First, the invitations had been issued before the Soviet Union began its attacks on neutralism and nationalism, based on its two-camp doctrine. Second, the nationalists hoped that it would be possible to enlist the cooperation of the communists in their anticolonial struggles.[11] Nationalists and communists, of course, did not talk and act in total agreement. Parts of the Indian and Burmese delegations withdrew midway through the conference over differences of opinion, and the Philippine delegation, on its return home, criticized the conference for being dominated by the Soviet Union.[12] In reality, communists did control the Calcutta Conference—the Burmese delegate Than Tun and representatives of the WFDY and IUS played important roles by controlling the agenda and the seating arrangements. Nevertheless, there were no important communist leaders—other than Than Tun—among the delegates, observers, and guests at the conference. The lone Soviet delegate was an unknown communist from Soviet Central Asia who sat as an observer.[13]

Though communists controlled the conference, it would seem that it was not a very favorable place for the discussion of a secret directive for armed insurrection—even if the Soviet Union had issued one—because it was held on such a large scale and composed of so many political ideologies. Furthermore, the confrontation between the Indian government and communist forces had intensified, and the government had become very nervous about internal and external communist influences. Such a political atmosphere would have made it even more difficult to conspire about an armed struggle. The Soviet Union and the Cominform, as we have seen, placed greater emphasis on using the conference as a forum for thorough propagation of the Soviet line concerning the international situation rather than as a conduit for orders for an insurrection. This is also clear from the statements and discussions made at the conference. Although not much is known about the exact progress of the week-long conference, we do know something about its discussions and prouncements thanks to McVey's study of WFDY and IUS publications.[14] Following the two-camp doctrine, the conference, like the Cominform, attacked American imperialism as the "greatest enemy" of the people. At the same time, it singled out for criticism "junior partners" of American imperialism—Britain, the Netherlands, and France— for their imperialism and oppression of colonies. The conference based its specific evaluation of the national bourgeoisie in each country on different criteria, but it also displayed a critical attitude toward this class in general, stating, "Afraid of the revolutionary mass movement, [they] have compromised with imperialism." The conference criticized national bourgeois governments that had adopted a neutral stance because they profited from imperialism.

Even though the Calcutta Conference had theoretical coherence, no clear position on the problem of the antiimperialist, united front line was taken. But it did favor the strategy of the "united front from below." While the delegations from China, on the verge of victory in its revolution, and from Vietnam, which was in the midst of its war for independence, were greeted enthusiastically by the conferees, the line advocated by China and Vietnam—the national united front, or "Maoist formula"—was only a minority view at the conference due to a very strong distrust of national bourgeoisies among the participants. For the majority at the conference, it was the very success of China's revolution, rather than the methods employed by the Chinese revolutionaries to bring about this success, that was important in providing confidence and incentive to colonial liberation struggles and communist movements. Furthermore, Ho Chi Minh, who was following a national united front policy in Vietnam, was attacked by the Yugoslavian delegation for giving priority to national interests above class interests. Tito himself, ironically, was later expelled by Stalin from the Cominform for this very same reason.

Though the Calcutta Conference was thus inclined to support the "united front from below" line, various controversies developed when attempts were made to apply this strategy to specific cases. For example, the conference majority ruled that the independent countries of India and Burma were areas for further struggles because they were products of compromise between national bourgeoisies and British imperialism and, therefore, their independence was merely an imperialist sham. The Vietnamese delegation opposed this view and praised these countries as partners in the national united front movement. In discussions concerning armed uprising as tactics, the Chinese and Vietnamese delegations argued for an antiimperialist struggle by a national united front and for the importance of an armed struggle as a means in this effort. The majority did not agree, and the matter was dealt with only indirectly. No resolution whatsoever was made concerning the problem of armed insurrection.

The Calcutta Conference provided a favorable opportunity for the Soviet Union and the Cominform to propagate and to win acceptance of their policy and doctrinal line. The hypothesis that the conference was the place where a directive was issued for armed insurrection—the "Soviet conspiracy" theory of American scholars—cannot be supported by an examination of the Calcutta Conference or by the logic of Soviet and Cominform policy. Nevertheless, a series of military uprisings did take place in Burma, Indonesia, Malaya, and the Philippines immediately following the conference. Let us next examine the causes of these uprisings.

Southeast Asian Armed Insurrections

The first armed insurrection following the Calcutta Conference took place in Burma in March 1948. In 1946 the communist forces in Burma had split into the Trotskyist "Red Flag" faction and the Stalinist "White Flag" faction. Following this division, the Red Flag faction had no connection with either the Cominform or the Calcutta Conference, and continued its armed struggle against the Burmese government. The White Flag faction advocated immediate and complete independence from Britain and, therefore, opposed the nationalist regime which accepted a compromise independence as unavoidable. This movement further intensified when Burma gained its independence at the beginning of January 1948. The Burmese government in turn suppressed the Communist party, and this was the immediate reason for the White Flag communists to launch their own armed insurrection. Minority peoples such as the Kachins and the Karens who had become dissatisfied with the Burmese government began their antigovernment struggles at about the same time. These struggles of the Burmese minorities continue today.[15]

The armed uprisings in Burma were complicated in terms of timing and character, a fact which makes understanding difficult. The fundamental causes, common to these struggles, however, were neither external directives nor influence. They were clearly caused by the confrontation between government and antigovernment forces in Burma over national independence and other domestic matters. Still, we should not completely ignore the doctrinal influence of the Communist Party of India (CPI) and the Calcutta Conference on the White Flag communist faction in Burma. It should be noted, for instance, that communist-led peasant armed insurrections had begun in the Indian state of Hyderabad in

1946. Subsequently, at a meeting in December 1947, the CPI central committee had adopted an extremely critical and uncooperative resolution against the Nehru government, but not a call for armed insurrection, following Zhdanov's speech.[16] Attending this conference was H. N. Ghoshal, a member of the CPI and a leader of the White Flag faction of Burmese communists. Upon his return to Burma, Ghoshal, along with Than Tun, who had just returned from the Calcutta Conference, is said to have played an important role in the Burmese Communist party.[17] Only in this sense can we say that the antigovernment armed uprisings in Burma received external influence.

Armed insurrection next occurred in colonial Malaya under the leadership of the Malayan Communist party. As in the Burmese case, the basic cause of the Malayan struggle cannot be found in any external "directive" as argued by the "Soviet conspiracy" theorists, but rather lies in the indigenous independence movement itself. The general desire for freedom from Britain lay behind the development of the struggles, led by communist-related labor unions, for national independence and reform of labor conditions. Faced with this development, the colonial government used repressive measures to deprive the communists of their legality. As a result, the Communist party was no longer able to influence labor or the people and was forced to resort to the tactics of armed insurrection.[18]

Next, let us examine the armed uprising which took place in Indonesia at Madiun on Java in September 1948. As mentioned previously, Indonesia entered a state of war with the Netherlands from July 1947 onward, and it received very high praise from the Soviet Union, the Cominform, and the Calcutta Conference for pursuing this antiimperialist struggle. In February 1948, however, a truce known as the Renville agreement was signed by Indonesia and the Netherlands through the mediation of the United States. The socialist cabinet of Amir Sjarifuddin was replaced at this time by one headed by Mohammed Hatta, former vice president, and as a result Indonesia's political situation and attitude toward the Soviet Union underwent a great change. The Hatta government leaned toward the United States in its policy and adopted an attitude of compromise toward the Netherlands, which, even after the truce agreement, was still maintaining an economic blockade of

Indonesia. In reaction to this shift in Indonesian policy, the Communist party and communist-related labor, youth, and peasant organizations, along with the left wing of Sjarifuddin's Socialist party, formed the people's democratic front in February 1948 and began a movement against the government.

As this confrontation was intensifying, Manovar Musso, the former leader of the Indonesian Communist party, returned from Moscow after an absence of 20 years. He resumed leadership of the party and urged the need for a "people's democratic revolution" on the basis of his own experience in Eastern Europe. As the first step toward this goal, Musso brought about a union of socialists and established a reformed and enlarged new Communist party. The leadership of this new party set out on a speaking tour throughout Java in order to publicize and gain adherents to the communist cause. Midway through the tour, however, armed forces and labor unions under the influence of the Communist party rose in revolt against the government at Madiun in eastern Java. They defeated the government forces there and captured the city. According to George McT. Kahin, this uprising was caused by local, lower-level members of the Communist party who were intent on escalating the confrontation between the government forces and the Trotskyists, and not by the senior leadership of the party who had not entertained any immediate plans for armed insurrection. Though the Madiun uprising deviated from the communist leadership's plans, the leaders, when presented with the *fait accompli*, nevertheless quickly made their way to Madiun and assumed control of the rebellion. Perhaps they were prompted by the feeling that it was "better to act than to sit watching its collapse." The Madiun rebellion was quickly suppressed by government troops and ended in defeat. A great many communist leaders, including Sjarifuddin and Musso, were shot to death.[19] The progress of this incident clearly shows that the armed uprisings in Indonesia were not the result of any influence of the Cominform or the Calcutta Conference. Rather, they were the result of divisions within Indonesia itself concerning the methods for promoting the struggle for national liberation.

The same can be said of the Philippines. The Communist party of the Philippines decided in May 1948 to begin an armed struggle against the government and, as a result, a guerrilla war broke out under the leadership of the Hukbalahap in August. Clearly, this situation in the Philippines had nothing to do with the Calcutta Conference. As has already been mentioned, the Philippine delegates to the conference were noncommunist nationalists who, on their return home, criticized the conference for being dominated by communists.

Among the Philippine communist documents at the Hoover Institution at Stanford University there are valuable collections of directives and statements issued by the Philippine Communist party and the Huks.[20] An examination of these documents fails to uncover any evidence of a connection between a Calcutta Conference "directive" or "secret order" and the party or the Huks. The basic causes of this armed insurrection are to be found in conditions existing within the Philippines, more specifically, in such things as the political system, the search for national independence, and other social and political problems.

Finally, let us consider the case of Vietnam. It is a well-known fact that France, prompted by its desire to force Vietnam to submit to colonial rule, attacked the newly created Democratic Republic of Vietnam in November 1946, and that this war continued until 1954. If there was any kind of relationship between the Vietnamese war of national independence and the Calcutta Conference, it was in the stimulating influence of the Vietnamese delegates, who were mature, experienced revolutionaries, on the other conference participants. Moreover, there were no diplomatic relations between Vietnam and the Soviet Union until the latter decided to recognize the Democratic Republic in January 1950. It is even said that until 1950 the Democratic Republic of Vietnam did not appear on any Soviet map. This Soviet lack of interest in the Vietnamese national revolution is similar to its attitude toward the Chinese revolution and also holds true for the national liberation movements and armed insurrections in other Southeast Asian countries. McLane has studied Soviet attitudes toward the armed uprisings in Southeast Asia which followed the Calcutta Conference through a careful analysis of Soviet newspapers and magazines. He draws three conclusions: first, the Soviet Union did not provide any doctrinal leadership in the armed uprisings; second, no clear formula was adopted concerning the problem of a national united front which included the national bourgeoisie; and third, no definite theory of colonies and developing countries was developed by Soviet policy-makers beyond the ideas contained in Zhdanov's speech, Zhukov's article, and the general discussion at the Calcutta Conference.[21]

The three main conclusions of this essay are: (1) The Soviet Union and the Cominform were too preoccupied with the situation in Europe to have any active interest in the direction of armed insurrection in Asia. Moreover, neither the theory nor the logic of Soviet and Cominform policy supports the idea that a directive was issued for armed insurrection in Southeast Asia. (2) The Calcutta Conference provided an opportunity for the Soviet Union and the Cominform to propagate their doctrinal line and win acceptance of their policy. The conference was not a very appropriate forum for the discussion of an order for armed insurrection, even if the Soviet Union had issued one, in view of the large number of participants, their differing political ideologies, and the special situation existing in India, the host nation. There is no evidence that such a directive was ever discussed. (3) It would not be right, however, to ignore the influence of the conference in terms of the stimulus or incentive it provided to the armed uprisings which followed in Southeast Asia. Still, the fundamental causes of these uprisings existed within each country.

If these conclusions are correct, the "Soviet conspiracy" or "Soviet-directed revolution" theory is an extremely inaccurate historical explanation; it considers only external factors as primary causes in Southeast Asian national liberation movements and armed uprisings, and disregards the basic internal causes. This is an example of a one-track historical viewpoint which seems to give precedence to "politics" rather than to the study of politics or history. Such a viewpoint hinders the search for historical truth.

I would like to touch briefly on a related subject, the role of China in the national liberation movements and armed struggles in Southeast Asia and the response of the United States to this activity. This subject has great significance for the history of the Cold War in Asia. The "Soviet conspiracy" theory gives too little attention to the influence and role of China. Not only did China receive a telegram of congratulations from the Calcutta Conference, but the Chinese delegation to the conference was also praised for developing an armed struggle based on a national united front. The New China News Agency unceasingly broadcast revolutionary propaganda to Southeast Asia from Shensi province.[22] Furthermore, a conference was held immediately following the victory of the Chinese revolution in Peking in November 1949, attended by representatives of labor unions from Asia and the Pacific. Liu Shao-ch'i gave a speech in which he lauded the success of the Chinese revolution and stressed the importance of waging armed struggles through a national united front which was to include the national bourgeoisie but to be led by the working class.[23] These events surely had a great influence on the revolutionary forces in Southeast Asia. The success of the Chinese revolution in fact quickly forced the Soviet Union to adopt the "Chinese formula."

Though the United States seems to have supported the European countries in their disputes with their colonies such as those between Vietnam and France, and between Indonesia and the Netherlands, at least on the surface, it professed neutrality.[24] Confronted with the success of the Communist forces in the Chinese civil war, however, the United States government came to fear that the influence of China would spread to Southeast Asia, a fear generated by the so-called Domino theory. To prevent this from taking place, the United States decided to base its Cold War policy of containing China and suppressing communist forces in the surrounding Asian countries on the strategically and economically important Indochina peninsula. Decisions by the National Security Council in December 1948 and in the following February make this clear.[25] Following an expression of congratulations to the Bao Dai government set up by France in Vietnam in June 1949, the U.S. government sent its ambassador-at-large, Philip Jessup, to Vietnam in January 1950, with a promise of support for the new government. The Seventh Fleet conducted a demonstration near Saigon that same January. In February the United States recognized the three countries of Indochina in response to the recognition of Ho Chi Minh's government by the Soviet Union and China. In May the U.S. government extended military aid to France to help carry out the war in Indochina. Thus it was in Indochina that the United States took its first active steps of the Cold War in Asia.

1. A. Doak Barnett, *Communist China and Asia: Challenge to American Policy* (New York: Harper, 1960), p. 152.

2. Walt W. Rostow, speech at University of Leeds, 23 February 1967, in *Viet Report* 3, no. 3 (June–July 1967), p. 31. *See also* his *The Diffusion of Power: An Essay in Recent History* (New York: Macmillan, 1972), p. 13.

3. Charles B. McLane, *Soviet Strategies in Southeast Asia: An Exploration of Eastern Policy under Lenin and Stalin* (Princeton: Princeton University Press, 1966), p. 354; Isaac Deutscher, *Stalin* (Harmondsworth: Penguin Books, 1966), p. 570.

4. Andrei Zhdanov, *International Situation* (Moscow: Foreign Language Publishing House, 1947), excerpts in Alvin Z. Rubinstein, ed., *The Foreign Policy of the Soviet Union* (New York: Random House, 1960), pp. 236–39.

5. John H. Kautsky, *Moscow and the Communist Party of India: A Study in the Postwar Evolution of International Communist Strategy* (New York: Wiley, 1956), p. 27.

6. McLane, *Soviet Strategies*, p. 359.

7. Ruth T. McVey, *The Calcutta Conference and the Southeast Asian Uprising* (Ithaca: Southeast Asia Program, Department of Far Eastern Studies, Cornell University, 1958), pp. 1–2.

8. Ibid., pp. 2–4.

9. McLane, *Soviet Strategies*, pp. 357–58.

10. John Gittings, "The Great Asian Conspiracy," in *America's Asia: Dissenting Essays on Asian-American Relations*, ed. Mark Selden (New York: Random House, 1969), p. 117.

11. McVey, *Calcutta Conference*, p. 9.

12. Ibid.

13. McLane, *Soviet Strategies*, pp. 359–60.

14. McVey, *Calcutta Conference*, pp. 11–19.

15. John F. Cady, *A History of Modern Burma* (Ithaca: Cornell University Press, 1958), pp. 578ff; Gushima Kanesaburō, "Biruma dokuritsu ron," *Hōsei Kenkyū* 19, nos. 2–4 (1952): 291ff.

16. Kautsky, *Moscow and Communist Party of India*, pp. 33–34.

17. Cady, *History of Modern Burma*, pp. 582–83.

18. Gene Z. Hanrahan, *The Communist Struggle in Malaya* (New York: Institute of Pacific Relations, 1954), pp. 49ff; Tanigawa Yoshihiko, "Dainiji sekaitaisengo no Maraya minzoku dokuritsu undō," *Hō to seiji no kenkyū* (Tokyo: Yūhikaku, 1957), pp. 168ff; Michael Stenson and Gerald de Cruz, *The 1948 Communist Revolt in Malaya: A Note on Historical Sources and Interpretation* (Singapore: Institute of Southeast Asian Studies, 1971).

19. George McT. Kahin, *Nationalism and Revolution in Indonesia* (Ithaca: Cornell University Press, 1952), ch. 9; Ruth T. McVey, *The Soviet View of the Indonesian Revolution* (Ithaca: Southeast Asia Program, Department of Far Eastern Studies, Cornell University, 1957), p. 38ff; Tanigawa Yoshihiko, "Majiun no hōki," *Hōsei kenkyū* 23 (September 1953): 207–24.

20. Hoover Institution, ed., *Philippine Communist Documents 1925–1955*.

21. McLane, *Soviet Strategies*, pp. 360–64.

22. Harold C. Hinton, *Communist China in World Politics* (Boston: Houghton Mifflin, 1966), p. 69.

23. *Ryū Shōki chosaku shū*, (Tokyo: San'ichi shobō, 1952), pp. 223–33.

24. *See* George McT. Kahin's essay in this volume, and Tanigawa Yoshihiko, "Amerika no tōnan ajia seisaku 1945–50—G. M. Kahin kyōju no shoron o megutte," *Hōsei Kenkyū* 42 (December 1975): 147–63.

25. *Pentagon Papers*, Senator Gravel edition (Boston: Beacon Press, 1971), I.

Continuities in U.S.-Japanese Relations, 1941–49

Akira Iriye

The great reversal in U.S. policy in East Asia, from an alliance with China in the war against Japan to a security pact with the latter in the postwar confrontation with the former, has generally been attributed to the impact of the European Cold War upon American diplomacy in Asia and the Pacific. The United States and Japan, in the usual interpretative framework, were so fundamentally opposed to each other, militarily, economically, and intellectually, that war in the Pacific became all but inevitable in 1941. Their bloody conflict was also a cultural confrontation in that the two countries championed contradictory visions of international relations, Japan espousing the cause of pan-Asianism and the United States that of internationalism as expressed in the Atlantic Charter. China, the key to the success of Japan's anti-Western strategy, actually chose America as an ally and even as an ideological partner in the joint struggle against Axis imperialism. Japan's defeat, in such a perspective, was to have been a catalyst to eradicate once and for all its ambitions and harmful doctrines so that a new Asian order of peace and stability would be constructed. The United States and China were to have emerged as the principal architects of that order, which they would try to preserve with the cooperation of other countries, especially the Soviet Union and Great Britain. Instead, within a few years after the end of World War II, the United States and the Soviet Union opposed each other in Europe and the Middle East as the two superpowers, and here again their confrontation was defined not only militarily but ideologically as well. In order to incorporate Asia and the Pacific into such a scheme of global affairs, both America and Russia needed allies in the region. Thus it was quite natural, according to most accounts, for the former to turn to Japan as a security partner and for the latter to assist the Communists in China. The result, so it is often argued, was the extension of the Cold War to Asia, variously dated by writers from 1947, 1949, or 1950.

A close examination of available American documents during the war indicates, however, that policy-makers and bureaucrats in Washington were making assumptions during 1941–45 which broadly defined the nature of postwar U.S.-Japanese relations in a way that anticipated the actual course of these relations. If this was in fact the case, as this essay will try to demonstrate, then it logically follows that the groundwork for U.S.-Japanese relations after 1945 had been laid during the war, i.e., before the extension of the Cold War to Asia. In other words, the initial postwar shape of these relations had little to do with the American-Soviet Cold War. It was in fact a pre–Cold War definition. To examine this definition is to understand the continuities in U.S. policy toward East Asia, which in retrospect seem to have been more pronounced than discontinuities. For at the bottom was the question of how the United States, Japan, China, Russia, and other nations might develop an equilibrating relationship with one another in a situation where they represented extremely diverse historical and cultural traditions as well as different stages of economic development. Because these factors changed little during the 1940s, it was not particularly surprising that the seeming reversal of U.S. policy in postwar Asia masked an underlying pattern of continuity in American-Asian relations. This accounted for the differences between the Cold War in Europe and the Middle East and that in Asia. An examination of U.S. policy toward Japan during and immediately following the war provides a clue to the understanding of these differences.

The point becomes clearer when one compares wartime American thinking toward the future of Germany and Japan. The United States, of course, was guided by broad generalities such as the principles enunciated by the Atlantic Charter and reiterated from time to time at various wartime conferences of the Allies. Planning for Germany, however, was a most laborious process, not only

because the United States had always to consult the British and
Soviet allies, but also, and most fundamentally, because a clear-
cut perception of what role, if any, America would play in postwar
Europe was excruciatingly slow to develop. Thus while American
and British officials began exchanging ideas about the treatment of
defeated Germany at the beginning of 1943, and while the Moscow Foreign Ministers Conference later that year established a
European advisory commission to discuss the postwar German
boundaries, no firm conclusion was reached on any significant
issue. The Morgenthau plan for pastoralization of the German
economy made its appearance as late as the fall of 1944, when the
war was all but over, and it managed to influence President
Franklin D. Roosevelt as much as it did because neither he nor his
advisers had, even at this point, established a clearly defined
formula for dealing with a defeated Germany. This was a reflec-
tion of the confusion and uncertainty that still plagued the
administration's perception of postwar Europe. The president and
the State Department were often divided on the advisability of
continued cooperation with the Soviet Union or with Great Britain. It was only at the Yalta Conference of February 1945 that
these three powers were able to come to some understanding on
the division of Germany into zones of occupation, the reparations
payments due the victors, and the outlines of the new Soviet-
Polish and Polish-German boundaries. Even so, much remained
uncertain about America's role in postwar Europe, the more so
as Roosevelt insisted on taking out U.S. forces two years after the
end of the war.[1]

Compared with the delay in formulating a policy toward Germany, wartime American perception of the future of Japan was
remarkably coherent. In part this was because in the Asia-Pacific
region the United States did not have to consult its allies regarding
strategic decisions, and because the nation was expected to emerge
as the definer of the postwar international system in the area.
Equally important, the State Department was able to make a head
start in postwar planning with little initial interference by the
White House or the Joint Chiefs of Staff. The establishment, in
February 1942, of an advisory committee on postwar foreign
policy, within the State Department, enabled the department's
Japan specialists to undertake extensive studies of all imaginable

problems that were expected to arise at the end of the war. These men became members of various subcommittees that dealt with specific questions such as postwar security, territorial dispositions, and economic relations. While the studies carried out by such bodies were not policy papers and their researchers were lower-ranking and middle-echelon foreign service officers and academic specialists recruited to assist them, many of them stayed with this work when the advisory committee was restructured at the beginning of 1944 to turn it into a more explicitly policy-oriented body. The newly organized postwar programs committee, together with the policy committee of the State Department which was created at the same time, became the major instrument for coordinating all departmental recommendations and decision making on postwar planning. In the meantime, a number of "country and area committees" had been set up in mid-1943 to provide policy-makers with expert advice and information, and Japan and China experts had been grouped together under Stanley K. Hornbeck, chairman, and George Blakeslee, his alternate, as the Far East area committee. Then, in December 1944, the State-War-Navy Coordinating Committee was established to bring civilian and military specialists together for formulating specific policy guidelines for the occupation and administration of the defeated Axis countries. Through all such transitions, a core of Japan specialists—including career foreign service officers as well as academic figures—held to certain ideas and assumptions with a remarkable degree of consistency.[2] It was this consensus, and the fact that they held strategic positions in these various committees, that accounted for continuities in American policy toward Japan during and immediately after the war.

Japan specialists, to be sure, had to work with officials and experts who were interested in China, the Pacific islands, and other parts of Asia, some of whom held rather extreme views on the future of Japan. There were several, for example, who considered it sufficient to crush Japan militarily: what role that country would play after the war was an insignificant problem that might not arise in view of its anticipated near-annihilation by the Allied powers. At a security subcommittee meeting of May 1943, Captain H. L. Pence of the Navy Department insisted that "Japan should be bombed so that there was little left of its civilization, so that the country could not begin to recuperate for fifty years."[3] Stanley K. Hornbeck, although less extreme, echoed the same sentiment when he remarked later in the year, "It will be possible for us to get along without Japan in the postwar world."[4] "It would be quite possible for us to let the Japanese nation disappear," he repeated in December.[5] Hornbeck was far more interested in the future of China than that of Japan and believed that only through cooperation with a strong China could the United States hope to maintain peace and order in postwar Asia. What might happen to Japan or to U.S.-Japanese relations was of decisively minor importance.

These, however, were minority views. Already by the end of 1943 a group of Japan and Asia specialists within the State Department had succeeded in developing a fairly well-defined approach to postwar Japan. They all accepted the territorial decisions made at the Cairo Conference—that Japan would be deprived of its overseas colonies and territories and confined to the four main islands with a teeming population and scarce resources. Such a Japan, they believed, would never again be a menace to peace. As Hugh Borton pointed out, he could not "conceive of a country with the limited resources of Japan becoming a serious menace if outside controls were completed."[6] The danger lay rather in Japan's becoming so destitute economically that it might create complicated problems for the victorious powers. Social and political instability would accompany economic impoverishment and militate against the development of democracy and liberalism. Such a situation would not be desirable from the American point of view. As Joseph Ballantine noted, the Japanese "desire for revenge would be enhanced if they felt they could not sell their products or get access to raw materials."[7] That would leave a dangerous condition, and the Allied powers would not have attained their aims of eliminating Japanese militarism and aggression. The best hope for the United States, these officials believed, lay in encouraging the growth of a liberal Japan that depended on external economic transactions and in turn contributed to the welfare and prosperity of the neighboring countries. It would then be able to transform itself into a peaceful nation, while at the same time maintaining political stability. In time it would be permitted reentry into the community of peace-loving countries. This was a more desirable alternative than a Japan treated harshly by the victors and given no chance for postwar recovery and readmission into the family of nations.

The minutes of numerous committee meetings as well as the voluminous amount of study papers prepared in the State Department indicate that by the end of 1943 these perceptions were becoming well established. The vision of a liberal postwar Japan had two important implications. First, Japan must be given an open-door treatment in its economic activities after the war. One of the earliest and best expositions on this theme was written by Robert Feary for the territorial problems subcommittee in June 1943. As he said, "Loss of political and monopoly control over any or all of her present dependencies would not seriously interfere with the normal peacetime operation of the Japanese economy—provided, of course, opportunity to trade freely with those areas and the rest of the world is granted Japan." The country's peaceful future depended on "normal, profitable trading relations with the rest of the world," and Feary believed such an opportunity should be granted to Japan as part of the postwar world order that was to be built upon the principles of liberal economic internationalism.[8] Likewise, at the end of the year, George Blakeslee wrote in a memorandum that "economic and financial conditions in the postwar world, so far as they may be controlled by the United Nations, should ultimately permit Japan, within the framework of the restrictions necessary for international security, to share in the development of a world economy on a non-discriminatory basis, looking toward a progressively higher standard of living."[9]

Second, the prospective emergence of a peaceful Japan presupposed the existence of those in the country who would be predisposed to accept the vision and carry out the task of reconstruction along liberal lines. Here the most influential idea within the U.S. government was the notion that despite totalitarian politics and aggressive foreign policy, Japan still contained many liberals who were at bottom opposed to them. For instance, in October 1943 Hugh Borton wrote a 22-page memorandum for the territorial subcommittee and stated, "There seems evidence . . . to warrant a hope that sufficient moderate or liberal elements in Japan may exist to operate a reformed government, providing a situation will be established which will be conducive to the development of liberalism . . . and will make feasible the inauguration of effective checks on the power of the military." As possible candidates for leading such a reformist government, Borton mentioned Matsudaira Tsuneo, Kido Kōichi, Wakatsuki Reijirō, and Konoe Fumimaro, all prewar leaders who had been close to the throne. The naming of these men reflected Borton's belief, shared by most though not all of the Japan specialists in the State Department, that the emperor system could become an important nucleus of postwar reconstruction in Japan. As he said, "The institution of the Emperor is likely to be one of the more stable elements of postwar Japan. As such, it may be a valuable factor in the establishment of a stable and moderate postwar government."[10] The idea that the institution should be utilized, not destroyed, to effect desired changes within the country had by this time become an article of faith on the part of most American officials knowledgeable about Japan. When Hamilton Fish Armstrong argued at a State Department meeting that "the emperor was nothing more than an impotent and dangerous symbol," Joseph Ballantine, Borton, and others insisted that "the Japanese people [were] relatively easy to influence," and were likely to accept military defeat and the necessity for reform if the emperor gave his endorsement.[11]

These central concepts, expressed in disparate memoranda and at subcommittee meetings throughout 1943, were given more formal and elevated status in 1944 as the U.S. government began making preparations for the occupation of liberated areas and enemy lands in Asia and the Pacific. In February the State Department was requested by the War and the Navy departments to make suggestions for "the planning, training and organization for civil affairs administration in Japan Proper, the Mandates Islands, and the countries occupied by Japan." For instance, which territories should be occupied, and by whom? Should the administration of occupied territory be "punitive, mild, or primarily to safeguard reparations?" With respect to Japan proper, the key questions were whether all or parts of the country were to be occupied, what countries should participate in the occupation, whether it should be "by zones or by one supreme council of interested United Nations membership," and how long it should

last. In addition, should the existing political parties and organizations in Japan be dissolved? "What will be the status of the
Emperor? Will he be removed both as an individual and as an
institution? . . . Will both remain? If so, under what measure
of control?"[12]

The State Department was thus given an opportunity to make
a contribution to the formulation of occupation policy, spelling
out in clear outline the ideas its officials had developed since the
beginning of the war. In response to the War-Navy query the
committee produced a large body of papers, of which the most
important was PWC-111, a document drafted by H. Borton, D. C.
Blaisdell, E. R. Dickover, and E. H. Dooman and approved by
the whole committee on March 13. It dealt with the composition
of forces to occupy Japan and recommended three basic guidelines. First, these forces should be multinational, representing the
countries that had had a role in fighting Japan. Second, Japan
proper should not be divided into distinctive zones as was being
contemplated for Germany. In a statement which was to survive
numerous revisions, the paper asserted that "[the] occupation of
Japan should be organized on the principle of centralized administration, avoiding the division of the country into zones administered separately by the different national contingents composing
the occupational force." Third, Allied participation in the occupation should not "be so large as to prejudice the dominantly
American character" of the military government which, it was
assumed, would be set up under the American field commander.[13]
Another memorandum written at this time underscored the basically moderate character of the occupation regime by stating,
"The military government will naturally take such action as may
be found necessary to safeguard the security of the occupying
forces. Otherwise, its measures should not aim to be punitive in
character or needlessly humiliating to the Japanese people."[14]

Such a principle had the effect of sanctioning a lenient treatment of the emperor after Japanese surrender. In April and May
the State Department's Japan specialists worked assiduously to
finalize their views of the matter. Two position papers were prepared, one by Borton and the other by Dickover, arguing contrasting cases. Borton's memorandum recommended that the
occupation regime suspend most of the emperor's functions but

permit him to delegate administrative duties to subordinate officials. Such a procedure, it was pointed out, "would tend to assure the good behavior of the Japanese people and to keep in office the maximum number of Japanese officials who would be willing to serve directly under the supervision of [Allied] civil affairs officers." Dickover, alone among the Japan specialists, advocated more extreme measures. He argued that "peace and security in the Pacific can best be assured by creating a truly democratic Japan," and that democracy could never gain a firm foothold in the country "unless and until a more or less clean break with the past is made." He would suggest, therefore, that the emperor should not be allowed to issue edicts in his name at all, and that "[if] any considerable section of the Japanese people indicate a desire to abolish the institution of the emperor, the occupation authorities should give that section their support and encouragement."[15]

The differences between these two papers had somehow to be ironed out before the postwar committee could make a recommendation to the military. Accordingly, the area committee on the Far East went over the two documents and voted overwhelmingly to endorse the Borton draft. Explaining this preference, Ballantine remarked that Dickover's paper had been based on a simplistic assumption that by getting rid of the emperor system, the Allied powers would have effectively destroyed Japanese militarism. "We do not believe," he said, "that Japanese militarism has its roots in the emperor or in any other single institution. . . . We believe that it is grounded in a habit of thought and in an [ideology] which have persisted among the Japanese for many centuries which can be eradicated only by the sufferings of defeat and by long drawn-out and gradual processes." He concluded that if the Japanese could "evolve along the same democratic political lines as have the British . . . an emperor could be a source of stability and reform."[16] Agreeing with Ballantine, Joseph Grew, director of the office of Far Eastern affairs, asserted that "the institution of the Throne will offer a measure for the constructive development of Japan in the ways of peace and for the regeneration of the Japanese people in a direction which would conduce to the security of the United States." He believed that during the 1920s the emperor institution had in fact been "turned toward peaceful international cooperation," and that the same thing could happen again once the military caste and cult had been discredited by thorough defeat.[17]

While disagreement arose over the question of the emperor system, it is to be noted that all these officials assumed the existence of "liberal-minded Japanese," as Dickover called them. According to Borton, "there exists a fairly substantial body of moderate political influence which has been rigidly suppressed and silenced since 1931 but which it is believed can be encouraged and made the nucleus of a liberal movement." It was to these men, State Department officials thought, that the Allied powers must turn to demilitarize and democratize Japan.[18] The postwar programs committee agreed with such an analysis, and on May 9 it adopted a paper (PWC 116d) on the treatment of the emperor which aimed at encouraging the growth of liberal, democratic forces in postwar Japan. The emperor, the paper said, was to be placed under protective custody but permitted to exercise functions which related to the delegation of administrative duties to subordinate officials. At the same time, the occupation authorities were to "refrain from any action which would imply recognition of or support for the Japanese concept that the Japanese emperor is different from and superior to other temporal rulers, that he is of divine origin and capacities, that he is sacrosanct or that he is indispensable."[19]

By the spring of 1944, then, Washington's Asia specialists had succeeded in developing a fairly concrete blueprint for postwar Japan and U.S.-Japanese relations. Unconditional surrender still remained the stated objective, but its content had become clearer: the surrender of Japan and the subsequent establishment of a military government would not mean the annihilation or enslavement of the country. While Japanese life after the war would be regulated and in some cases severely controlled by the forces of occupation, every effort would be made to foster conditions in which political and economic liberalism would develop. Instead of subjugating the Japanese to total military occupation and alien rule, the United Nations would work in cooperation with individual Japanese who were opposed to militarism. While the country's overseas territories would be taken away, Japan proper would retain its territorial and administrative integrity, and its economy would in time be reintegrated into the postwar system of multi-lateral economic relations. In contrast to the ambiguities that still plagued U.S. policy toward postwar Germany, there was, a year before the end of the war, a remarkably well articulated vision of what the country wanted in and of Japan after the latter's defeat.

This fact is even more impressive when contrasted to wartime British thinking. The government in London, when it considered the future of Asia during 1942–44, was almost entirely preoccupied with India and Southeast Asia.[20] The war against Japan was seen basically as an American undertaking, and hardly any thought was given to the question of surrender terms or of the postwar administration of defeated Japan. The Foreign Office was interested in the growing number of publications in the United States which speculated about these problems, but it took no initiative before 1945 to consider systematically various alternatives or to start making plans for the occupation of Japan. The Far Eastern department had men whose knowledge of Japan was substantial: A. J. de la Mare, L. H. Foulds, D. F. McDermot, and others. The British embassy in Washington had George Sansom, probably the world's leading authority on Japan at that time. But these men were kept completely in the dark about the plans being developed and ideas expressed in the State Department. While a Far Eastern committee was organized within the war cabinet in late 1944 to look into postwar problems, its concerns were almost always with Southeast Asia.

Thus, in contrast to thinking within the U.S. government, it would be correct to say that the British government had no conception of what to do with Japan after its defeat. Typical was a comment by McDermot in October 1944 that "the beneficent participation of Japan in the world order will require so immensely long a period of reeducation—in most difficult circumstances—as to seem beyond the range of useful speculation in connexion with the post-war settlement. . . . It would probably be wise to limit our immediate post-war objective to finding for Japan a place in a regional economic scheme which would allow her just enough of a living to keep social discontent in check; and to review her long term destiny during the succeeding decades, during which the decisive factor will no doubt be what happens to China."[21] British officials were aware of the controversy in the United States, both within and outside the government, on the future treatment of the emperor, but they formulated no systematic approach at this time. Foulds thought it conceivable, for instance, that only through "revolution following crushing defeat" would it be possible to "purge Japan of the virus of military aggression," and that "[the] question of whether or not it is desirable, from the Allied point of view, that the Japanese monarchy should survive, seems to me to be subsidiary to the accomplishment of this purpose."[22]

The United States and Great Britain had never cooperated fully in East Asia, but at least during the 1930s the two governments had consulted one another regularly and frequently to cope with the mounting crisis in China and Southeast Asia. After Pearl Harbor, however, there was only a minimum of strategic and policy coordination. To the extent that serious discussion was held, it dealt with India, Indochina, or the Australia–New Zealand initiatives regarding the southwestern Pacific. The question of Japan was left more or less entirely in American hands. With the Soviet Union maintaining an uneasy neutrality toward Japan, and China increasingly estranged from the United States, it was not surprising that the latter should, even during the war, be recognized as the controlling power over postwar Japan. But the situation became more complicated in 1945 as the war approached its end, and as other United Nations began to be interested in the future of Japan.

As far as the United States was concerned, there was little departure from the basic guidelines established in the spring of 1944. Planning for the surrender and occupation arrangements for Japan was now principally carried on by the State-War-Navy Coordinating Committee, of which there was created a subcommittee on the Pacific and Far East consisting of Eugene Dooman (State), George V. Strong (War), and Harold C. Train (Navy). Between February and July 1945, the subcommittee prepared a number of papers, among the most important of which were SWNCC 21 (February 7) and SWNCC 150 (June 11). The former spelled out how the emperor should proclaim Japan's unconditional surrender and what the Allied supreme commander should do to accept the surrender. The latter document stated the basic objectives of the post-surrender military government in Japan. They included the "creation of conditions which will insure that Japan will not again become a menace to the peace and security of the world," "[the] eventual emergence of a government in Japan which will respect the rights of other states and Japan's international obligations," and "[the] eventual participation of Japan in a world economic system on a reasonable basis."[23]

Both these documents went through various revisions until they were finally adopted as official policy: SWNCC 21/3 (August 10) and SWNCC 150/2 (August 12). It would be tedious to trace these revisions in detail, nor should it be necessary to cite other, equally pertinent documents which were daily issuing from various agencies of the U.S. government. Certain key facts must be mentioned, however. First, the basic objectives of U.S. policy toward postwar Japan remained the same. It was assumed that Japan's unconditional surrender would be followed by the implementation of measures designed to encourage the growth of a peaceful, democratic, liberal nation. There was some serious debate, to be sure, among American officials about the advisability of announcing these objectives in order to induce Japan's early surrender. The joint staff planners, for instance, recommended on May 3 that the president issue a public statement explaining to the Japanese that unconditional surrender meant "the termination of the influence of the military leaders who have brought Japan to the present brink of disaster" but that it "does not mean the extermination or enslavement of the Japanese people. On the contrary, it does mean that the people of Japan, after eliminating the burdens of militarism, can begin to earn their way back into the fellowship of peace-loving and law-abiding nations."[24] Five days later, when Germany surrendered, President Harry S. Truman called on the Japanese people to capitulate, assuring them that surrender was not the same thing as extermination or enslavement. Not satisfied with such vague assurances, Acting Secretary of State Grew sought to persuade Truman to declare that the Japanese people would "be permitted to determine their own future political structure."[25] This reflected Grew's continued belief that the emperor system could be utilized for reforming Japanese politics after the war. Nothing came of this suggestion at this time, primarily because the top military leaders were anxious first to wait for the completion of the Manhattan Project, but they were all in agreement with the objectives of postwar U.S. policy in Japan.[26]

Second, the military occupation of Japan was considered essential to carry out these objectives. But it would not entail complete seizure of Japanese administrative functions. In the language of SWNCC 150, "Military government should utilize the Japanese administrative machinery and . . . Japanese public officials, making these officials responsible for the carrying out of the policies and directives of the military government." Even more important, Japan proper would be governed as one unit. As Dooman wrote in May, Japan "was basically a single geographic, ethnic, sociological, economic and political unit." Consequently, he saw no reason to depart from the formula presented in PWC-111 (March 1944) that the post-surrender military government should be "organized on the principle of central administration avoiding the division of the country into zones administered separately" by the various occupying forces.[27]

Third, the United States would play the predominant role in the occupation and governing of Japan. It would name and provide the supreme commander of the Allied forces occupying the country, and those forces, while internationally constituted, would be overwhelmingly American. According to Dooman, "[the] representation of countries other than the United States in the forces to occupy Japan and therefore in the military government of Japan should not be so large as to prejudice the predominantly American character of that Military Government." The State-War-Navy Coordinating Committee accepted these ideas as axiomatic, and started work on occupation planning on the basis of the assumption that "our paramount interest in and responsibility for the peace and security of the Pacific area is generally recognized by all of the United Nations," and that "it is militarily desirable that we deny to any other nation control of the occupation of the main Japanese islands."[28]

Fourth, as a corollary of this insistence on American predominance, the tendency toward unilateral planning and action vis-à-vis Japan was even more pronounced than earlier. There was virtually no consulatation with the Soviet Union on these matters. By early May the Joint Chiefs of Staff had concluded that "early Russian entry into the war against Japan . . . is no longer necessary" as the United States prepared for a final assault upon the home islands.[29] Even so, the American leaders assumed that the Soviet Union would enter the war on its own initiative to capture the prizes promised at Cairo and Yalta. Russian forces would surely seek to occupy Sakhalin, and for this reason the coordinating committee decided to exclude the island from the centralized administration envisaged for the military government of occupied Japan. Before the Potsdam Conference, moreover, there was no exchange of views between Washington and Moscow regarding the nature of that government, or about the implementation of Allied policy in Japan.

British officials were somewhat better acquainted with American planning, but their input into occupation policy was minimal before Potsdam. In February, the Foreign Office belatedly began the study of the "occupation and control of Japan," but before Germany's defeat Prime Minister Winston Churchill had not even indicated if Britain was to participate in the occupation and military government of Japan.[30] Efforts to find out something about United States plans were to no avail. In Washington Sansom was told by Dooman on May 3 that "he did not see how we and the United States authorities could usefully discuss policy" toward postwar Japan until the British government had undertaken as extensive a study of the problem as the American. The report of this conversation prompted J. C. Sterndale Bennett, chief of the Far Eastern department, to comment, "This shows a most uncooperative spirit. . . . What this letter does show is that planning as regards the occupation and control of Japan appears to have reached a more advanced stage than we had hitherto supposed."[31] On May 29, however, Sansom was finally shown, "at Grew's instance," a copy of SWNCC 150, which gave the impression that "the United States expected to take the lead and run the show."[32] Sansom's telegraphing, from memory, of the content of SWNCC 150 immediately evoked a response by Foulds that "the document . . . sounds like the production of a group of doctrinaires who have been planning a new Japan in accordance with their pet theories without any regard for the realities of the situation which is likely to exist at the end of the War."[33]

Pet theories or not, the document warranted scrutinizing by the Foreign Office, and Sansom was ordered home to formulate Britain's response to what appeared to be the final U.S. policy. There was a basic misunderstanding in that the British officials thought the United States was contemplating a protracted and total occupation of Japan, entailing the assumption of all functions of government. Foulds did not think this would work; the Japanese "are a proud, stubborn race who have never known any non-Japanese control since the beginning of their history." Instead of such drastic measures, Foulds believed that economic control would sufficiently and effectively ensure Japan's demilitarization. As he said, "Japan deprived of her overseas territories is so poor in natural resources that it should be a fairly straightforward matter . . . to keep her in order by means of economic controls." Thus he did not think an extensive occupation of the country would be required. Instead, he would recommend such things as "a triumphal march through Tokyo . . . the long-term occupation of four or five easily held key points . . . the presence of Allied war vessels at ports and . . . occasional demonstration flights of manned aircraft." Sansom fully agreed with Foulds's analysis, and together they drafted a memorandum on June 20, adding to the above points a historical perspective derived from the experiences of the late nineteenth century, when the Japanese were eager to behave well in the international community in order to have the unequal treaties removed. Likewise, Sansom, Foulds, and other Japan specialists argued that through exercising "the positive power of controlling trade and the negative power of withholding treaties, the Allies should be able . . . to induce Japan herself to introduce such reforms in her institutions and the working thereof as will justify confidence in her future good behaviour."[34]

These ideas and assumptions were similar to those which Feary, Borton, Grew, and others in the United States had expressed for over two years. There was, however, a crucial disparity between the American and British formulations. The U.S. government contemplated the military occupation of the Japan homeland during the initial post-surrender period when Allied personnel would work with liberal-minded Japanese civilians to effect various reform measures. Given the predominant role of the United States in the occupation and military government, such a project was tantamount to perpetuating American control over postwar policy in Japan. The British conception, on the other hand, sought to minimize the need for military occupation and instead to turn to economic measures which were to be undertaken through inter-Allied cooperation. Obviously this was designed to challenge the American monopoly of power and allow Britain and others to retain a modicum of influence. Otherwise, Britain would not be able to match American manpower in providing occupation forces and government personnel to undertake the democratization of Japan. There was real danger, as Sansom pointed out, that the United States might go ahead with a unilateral occupation and administration of Japan, with the consequent loss of British prestige both in America and in Asia.

The British government scored a small victory at the Potsdam Conference when Foulds, accompanying the official delegation, was able to influence the drafting of the final declaration. As originally presented by the United States, it had talked of the military occupation of "Japanese territory . . . to the extent necessary to secure the achievement of the basic objective" of the Allied powers. This was changed, in the Potsdam declaration, to the occupation of "points in Japanese territory to be designated by the Allies"— a modification which, Foulds noted, committed the victors to "something less than total occupation of Japan." In addition, whereas the American draft had been designed as a call to the Japanese people to reject their militaristic leaders and terminate the senseless war, in the final version all references to "the Japanese people" were changed to "Japan" or "the Government of Japan." This redrafting was a result of Foulds's view that it was unrealistic to address the Japanese people over the head of the government; as he wrote Churchill, "the mass of the people are loyal to the Emperor and therefore obedient to the lawfully constituted administration."[35] The implications of these revisions were that the Allied powers would deal with a government of Japan in effecting the latter's surrender and carrying out the occupation of the country, and that military occupation and administration would be confined to unspecified "points in Japanese territory." The Potsdam declaration assumed, however, that the government of Japan would undergo change until there emerged "in accordance with the freely expressed will of the Japanese people a peacefully inclined and responsible government." When this was attained, the forces of occupation were to be withdrawn.

To the extent that Britain was capable of influencing the phrasing of the declaration, it contributed to the making of Allied powers policy toward Japan. This was more than could be said of China, whose government was shown the text of the statement at the very last moment, or of the Soviet Union, which was not consulted at all about it. Nevertheless, the degree of American-British cooperation was very limited. The United States, after all, had never visualized total and direct control over post-surrender Japan, and it had looked to collaboration on the part of non-militaristic Japanese civilians. The basic objectives enumerated in the Potsdam declaration—Japanese demilitarization, democratization, and eventual incorporation into the world economic system—had long been established by the State Department. The implementation of these objectives would necessitate extensive military occupation, something that could not be achieved by merely seizing "points" of Japanese territory. This was a contradiction in the Potsdam declaration, as the State Department was quick to point out.[36] It should be noted, however, that the Joint Chiefs of Staff had adopted a paper, just prior to the Potsdam Conference, on the postwar occupation of Japan, which, while endorsing the principle of U.S. preponderance, stated that the American show of force "may well be accomplished by air forces located in perimeter areas and fleets in adjacent waters."[37] This principle was formally approved by the State-War-Navy Coordinating Committee on August 11 and by President Truman seven days later.[38] It may be said, therefore, that the British amendment was in agreement with the thinking of the American military.

Even more important, the Joint Chiefs of Staff proceeded to make concrete plans for the occupation of Japan as if the Potsdam provisions had never existed.[39] There was no consultation with the Allies as to which "points" were to be occupied, or as to the number of divisions each country would contribute. British authorities were kept completely in the dark about these matters. Nor was there inter-Allied discussion regarding the initial Japanese response to the Potsdam declaration. The Foreign Office regarded Prime Minister Suzuki Kantarō's statement about "ignoring" it as something intended for domestic consumption, not a rejection of the Allied terms for surrender.[40] But the United States so interpreted it, decided to use the atomic bomb, and, when Japanese peace overtures were finally received on August 10, acted unilaterally to bring about Japan's surrender. As Assistant Secretary of State James Dunn told John Balfour, British minister, on August 13, "the United States government was not in a position to consult their Allies about the act of surrender." He continued, "The unwillingness of the United States Government to enter into formal consultation with [Britain] arose from the fact that they had no intention of inviting the comments of the Soviet and Chinese Governments on the text."[41] The British government had no choice but to acquiesce in the American initiatives and accept whatever the United States carried out in the name of the Allies.[42]

Japanese surrender left Asia divided. The Soviet Union was now the supreme power in northeastern Asia, its troops fast occupying Sakhalin and Manchuria, while in Southeast Asia Britain and its European allies carried out their plans for reestablishing authority over the colonial regions. The United States did not interfere with these activities, leaving Russia and Britain more or less free to do what they pleased in their respective spheres of power. In Japan proper, however, there was no doubt that the United States meant to place occupation policy under its more or less total control.

The occupation of Japan lies beyond the scope of this paper, but as an example of American unilateralism in the immediate post-surrender period, one may recall the complications attending the birth of the Far Eastern Commission. The State-War-Navy Coordinating Committee had, in the spring of 1945, proposed the setting up of a Far Eastern advisory council, patterned after the European Advisory Council, which would consist of the United States, Britain, China, and the Soviet Union (in case the latter entered the war against Japan before the end of hostilities).[43] It was felt that such a council would be an expression of United Nations solidarity and serve to perpetuate wartime cooperation among the big powers. But the American officials had never contemplated yielding the virtual monopoly of power to be enjoyed by the United States in the postwar occupation and administration of Japan. A formal proposal for the establishment of a Far Eastern advisory commission was communicated to Britain, China, and Russia on August 21. Subsequently, the United States invited France, the Philippines, Australia, New Zealand, Canada, and the Netherlands to become members of the commission. Its first meeting took place in Washington on October 30.

The setting up of such a machinery, and the way the American government brought it about, were profoundly disturbing to Britain and the Soviet Union. Both of them wanted an Allied control council, not just an advisory body of so many states. The Foreign Office in London insisted, as early as August 18, that a control council over Japan should have the authority "to guide [the supreme Allied commander] in political, economic, and financial matters." It was clear, Secretary Ernest Bevin told the embassy in Washington, "that the Americans intend to act as independently as possible in controlling Japan," but it was desirable that "we should have an equal say with the Russians and the Chinese and that our share in any control machinery should not . . . be linked too closely with our contribution to the forces of occupation but should be exerted at the highest level."[44] From London's point of view, the American proposal for a purely advisory commission was unacceptable. The Far Eastern department expressed how it felt about the matter in a memorandum of September 11: "What His Majesty's Government cannot accept is the assumption which the Americans appear to be making that we have given them an unlimited power of attorney to act on our behalf in all matters relating to Japan. . . . The position of the Supreme Commander should not imply any derogation from the principle of collective responsibility for policy of the Governments on whose behalf he is acting. This is in accordance with democratic principles. We suffered even more than the Americans did from Japanese treachery; our contribution to the defeat of Japan has been, proportionately to our resources, as great as theirs. . . ."[45] By late September Foreign Office patience was wearing thin. "One is driven to the conclusion," Foulds wrote, "that the Americans desire a Far Eastern Advisory Commission mainly to serve as a moral umbrella for the conduct of their own policy toward Japan." Sterndale Bennett agreed. The Americans, he said, "are behaving with singular arrogance, lack of frankness and disregard for anyone but themselves."[46]

The Soviet Union, in contrast, had initially accepted the American proposal, as did China, for setting up a Far Eastern advisory commission. It concentrated on consolidating its position in Manchuria and North Korea, leaving Japan to the United States. After the London Conference of Foreign Ministers in September, however, Moscow stiffened its stand and, like Britain, began insisting on a control commission for Japan. Reasons for this change can only be speculated on, but it is likely that it was connected with the general atmosphere of distrust among the powers which pervaded the London conference. Given America's growingly stringent criticism of Soviet policies in Eastern Europe and the Balkans, the Russian government could plausibly point to Japan as a case of even more blatant unilateralism by the United States. Or, as a British diplomat in Moscow suggested, a point of view shared by the American ambassador, Averell Harriman, Russia was interested in the continuation of wartime cooperation among the great powers and viewed American policy in Japan as a major hindrance, indicating the lack of interest in Washington to work together with its allies.[47] Whatever the explanation, there seems little doubt that the Soviet Union soon gave up insisting on an equal voice in the occupation of Japan. There never was even a pretense of American-British-Soviet cooperation in postwar Japan comparable to that which obtained in Germany or Austria.

One complaint which both London and Moscow harbored at this time was that General MacArthur and his aides were not being thorough enough in eradicating "feudal," militaristic elements in Japan. While not quite fair, such criticism did point to an important phenomenon emerging immediately after the war: collaboration of Japanese "liberals" with the American occupation authorities. As a paper prepared by the joint intelligence committee in Washington noted in mid-October, Japanese leaders "appear to be convinced that their long-term interests may best be promoted by cooperation with the occupation authorities. . . . [The] Japanese will attempt to cultivate American friendship by representing themselves as the bulwark against Communism and as a stabilizing influence in the Far East. They will make every effort to foster a revival of trade and will encourage cultural exchange with America."[48] This was exactly as had been predicted by State Department officials during the war. Although MacArthur's headquarters did gradually institute stringent measures to purge Japanese politics and society of militaristic influences, occupation measures were carried out through willingly cooperative Japanese bureaucrats, businessmen, intellectuals, and assorted prewar liberals. As General MacArthur reported to the Joint Chiefs in May 1946, he had tried to "give moral support and encouragement to the liberal forces struggling in Japan for reform against tradition, prejudice and reaction." It was his view that these liberals, along with "well over 95 percent of the Japanese people," were disposed to retain the emperor institution in some reformed fashion, and it would be contrary to the spirit of the Potsdam declaration for the outside powers to force their will upon them. By this time, moreover, the supreme commander declared that "the sweeping measures which the United States of necessity alone has taken . . . in the occupation of Japan have been largely accomplished and upon all of which action is proceeding in accordance with determined policies."[49] In other words, American occupation authorities and Japanese were fast reforming the country, and there was no need for other nations to interest themselves in the matter.

The Joint Chiefs of Staff, in the meantime, had begun a study of postwar U.S. strategy. Already in October 1945 there was the assumption, as stated by the joint intelligence staff, that "the long-term objective of Soviet foreign policy appears to be the establishment of Soviet control over the Eurasian land mass and the strategic approaches thereto."[50] In early November the service members of the joint intelligence staff quickly prepared "a list of approximately 20 of the most important targets, suitable for strategic bombing, in Russia and Russia-dominated territory."[51] From this time on, conflict with the Soviet Union became the overriding concept with the military. Even civilian officials came to accept it. As Clark Clifford, special counsel to President Truman, noted in his famous memorandum, "American Relations with the Soviet Union" (September 24, 1946), "Soviet leaders appear to be conducting their nation on a course of aggrandizement designed to lead to eventual world domination by the U.S.S.R."[52] In the following February John Hickerson, deputy director of the State Department's office of European affairs, asserted, "there must be a vigilant determination on the part of the peoples and governments of the U.S.A. and the U.K. to resist Soviet aggression, by force of arms if necessary. . . . If the lessons we learned from efforts to deal with Hitler mean anything, concessions to the Soviet Union would simply whet their appetite for more."[53] When the National Security Council was established that year to cope with urgent security problems, one of the first reports it prepared (NSC 7) was on "the position of the United States with respect to Soviet-directed world communism." The defeat of the Axis, the report pointed out, had left the world with two superpowers: "Between the United States and the USSR there are in Europe and Asia areas of great potential power which if added to the existing strength of the Soviet world would enable the latter to become so superior in manpower, resources and territory that the prospect for the survival of the United States as a free nation would be slight. In these circumstances the USSR has engaged the United States in a struggle for power, or 'cold war,' in which our national security is at stake and from which we cannot withdraw short of eventual national suicide."[54] This was the language of the Cold War which now underlay United States diplomacy in the postwar world.

The Cold War, however, primarily engaged the powers in Europe and the Middle East. The Joint Strategic Survey Committee noted in April 1947, "The area of primary strategic importance to the United States in the event of ideological [i.e., anticommunist] warfare is Western Europe, including Great Britain." Next in importance was the Middle East, then northwest Africa, Latin America, and finally the Far East.[55] The low priority assigned to the possibility of confronting Soviet aggression in the Far East was confirmed in the NSC 20-series, a set of five documents drawn up in 1948 which provided the guiding principles for America's Cold War diplomacy. According to NSC 20/4, approved by President Truman on November 24, "The will and ability of the leaders of the USSR to pursue policies which threaten the security of the United States constitute the greatest single danger to the U.S. within the foreseeable future." While the Soviet goal was world domination, the paper pointed out, the "immediate goal of top priority since the recent war has been the political conquest of western Europe." Russian armed forces were capable of "overrunning in about six months all of Continental Europe and the Near East as far as Cairo, while simultaneously occupying important continental points in the Far East." Under the circumstances, top priority should be given by the United States and the "Western democracies" to the success of the European Reconstruction Program and their increased military effectiveness.[56]

There was no such clear-cut formulation of Cold War strategy in Asia. This can best be seen in the lack of decisiveness toward the Chinese civil war which was in sharp contrast to the forcefulness exhibited in Turkey, Greece, and Western Europe. An interim report drafted by the National Security Council in March 1948 suggested that, although the long-range American objective should be "the furtherance of a stable, representative government over an independent and unified China which is friendly to the United States and capable of becoming an effective barrier to possible Soviet aggression in the Far East," in reality there was little the United States could do. It was virtually impossible to stem the tide of Communist victory in China short of massive American involvement, amounting to a virtual take-over of Chinese government and administration. Such a step would surely bring about large-scale Soviet assistance to the Chinese Communists, and in the resulting confrontation "the advantage would be with the USSR, because of its favorable geographical position and the vitality of the Chinese Communist movement." Although limited economic assistance might continue to be given to the Nationalist government, such a program "should be regarded as subordinate to the efforts to stabilize conditions in areas of more strategic importance."[57] The staff of the National Security Council reemphasized this theme when they wrote in January 1949 that the United States should regard "efforts with respect to China as of lower priority than efforts in other areas where the benefits to U.S. security are more immediately commensurate with the expenditure of U.S. resources."[58]

Unlike Europe and the Middle East, moreover, no serious thought was given to cooperating with Great Britain in devising a policy toward China or anywhere else in Asia. In the papers of the National Security Council, the State Department, and the Joint Chiefs of Staff during 1948–49, one rarely finds Britain mentioned in connection with the civil war in China. Even in considering alternative strategies for Taiwan, an island as close to the European colonial areas as to the Philippines, the United States never seriously contemplated joint action with Britain.[59] The Europecentrism of Cold War strategy made it difficult for the United States to devise a formula for cooperation with Great Britain in Asia. In 1949, as the Communist take-over of China appeared imminent, the United States government did consider "mobilization of the political and economic power of the western world to combat openly, through intimidation or direct pressure, a Chinese Communist regime." But, Secretary of State Dean Acheson pointed out, it was difficult to see "how the necessary degree of concerted action could be obtained from all western nations," in particular the United Kingdom with its large investments in and trade with China.[60]

The Cold War in the sense of American-British opposition to Soviet policy did not, in other words, quite apply to the Far East. The years 1945–49 were in fact a period of comparative retrenchment of American power from the region; as various essays in this book show, the United States did little to prevent the Chinese Communists from winning the civil war, its forces were withdrawn from Korea, it decided against making a commitment in Taiwan, and it developed no comprehensive strategy with respect to Southeast Asia. All this amounted to America's disinclination to engage the Soviet Union in a Cold War confrontation in Asia in the immediate postwar years.

This did not mean, however, that the United States had no policy at all in that region. The Cold War defined its policy in Europe and the Middle East, but in Asia the United States continued to operate within the framework established during World War II. This framework, sometimes referred to as "the Yalta system," was not as precise as the Washington Conference system of the 1920s, but it nevertheless delineated the extent of American involvement in the postwar Asia-Pacific region. According to this scheme, the United States, acting unilaterally rather than in cooperation with Great Britain, would establish control over the former Japanese islands of the Pacific, occupy Okinawa and Japan proper, agree to the retrocession of Taiwan and Manchuria to China, support eventual independence for Korea, and accept the return of Soviet power to northeast Asia. For a while after 1945, Washington saw little need to depart from such a formula. Since these outlines had been defined well before the onset of the Cold War, they should be regarded as a pre–Cold War policy.

U.S. policy in postwar Japan best exemplified this approach. Because detailed plans for the surrender, occupation, and postwar orientation of Japan had been worked out long before the end of the war, all that the United States had to do was to implement them. There were, to be sure, occasional departures from these outlines as the occupation forces under General MacArthur encountered situations that called for ad hoc responses in administering the defeated country. It is also true that Cold War perceptions began to affect American officials' view of Japan soon after the war. "Japan is the one nation," the Joint Strategic Survey Committee noted in April 1947, "which could contain large armed forces of our ideological opponents in the Far East" while the United States and its European allies were engaged in a major offensive in the West.[61] Accordingly, in 1948 the National Security Council undertook examination of policy toward Japan "in view of the serious international situation created by the Soviet Union's policy of aggressive Communist expansion."[62] By June 1949, the Joint Chiefs of Staff were anxious to make sure that the United States would be able "to derive full strategic advantage from the potentialities of Japan and to deny Japan's ultimate exploitation by the USSR."[63]

Policy toward Japan thus came to be phrased in the context of the developing Cold War. Its substance, however, did not depart drastically from wartime formulations. When George F. Kennan, head of the State Department's policy planning staff, went to Tokyo in March 1948 to confer with MacArthur, he stressed the need for "maximum *stability* of Japanese society" and an "intensive program of economic recovery" for the country. MacArthur agreed, saying that the United States had an opportunity, "through the Japanese . . . to bring to [Asians] the blessings of freedom and of a higher standard of living."[64] In Washington, the Joint Chiefs of Staff urged in June 1949 that in order to cope with "the continuing Soviet policy of aggressive communist expansion," it was essential that "Japan's democracy and western orientation . . . be established beyond all question."[65] When, toward the end of the year, the National Security Council undertook to draft a comprehensive policy paper for Asia, it summed up official views of Japan which were not so much new as reiterations of earlier themes:

A middle of the road regime in Japan retaining the spirit of the reform program . . . would in the long-run prove more reliable as an ally of the United States than would an extreme right-wing totalitarian government. Under such a regime the channels would be open for those elements in Japan that have gained most from the occupation to exercise their influence over government policy and to mold public opinion. . . . The existence of such a regime . . . will make possible the most effective exercise of United States political and economic influence in the direction of ensuring Japan's friendship, its ability to withstand external and internal Communist pressure, and its further development in a democratic direction.

The basic United States non-military objectives in Japan . . . remain the promotion of democratic forces and economic stability before and after the peace settlement.[66]

These ideas were behind the steps that led to the conclusion of the Japanese peace treaty in 1951. While the State Department and the Joint Chiefs clashed, often violently, regarding the timing for such a treaty, they both shared the conviction that America's basic objective was to ensure Japan's "Western orientation." In other words, there was little need to introduce novel concepts or strategies concerning U.S.-Japanese relations. This was in contrast to policy toward the rest of Asia. The drafting of NSC 48/2, entitled "The Position of the United States with respect to Asia,"on December 30, 1949, may be regarded as the first instance in which Washington attempted the formulation of a new Asian policy within the framework of the Cold War. In that document it was stated that the United States should support "non-Communist forces in taking the initiative in Asia," exert "an influence to advance its own interest," and initiate "action in such a manner as will appeal to the Asiatic nations as being compatible with their national interests and worthy of their support."[67] Given this assertiveness, America's decisions, in the following spring, to initiate programs of assistance to the Bao Dai regime in Vietnam and, in June 1950, to intervene militarily in the Korean peninsula, were hardly surprising. Such instances would have been unthinkable before 1949, but with the adoption of a new Asian policy they were carried out just as the United States had earlier responded to perceived Soviet threats in Persia, Turkey, or Greece. The Cold War had come to Asia. U.S. policy toward Korea, China, and Southeast Asia became comprehensible within the framework of the global bipolar confrontation.

The uniqueness of U.S.-Japanese relations consists in the fact that it did not take the coming of the Cold War in Asia before these relations were defined as part of postwar United States strategy. There was a coincidence of America's wartime and postwar approaches to Japan because they were derived from certain key assumptions: first, that the United States would continue to be the dominant outside power exercising control over Japan's destiny; and, second, that a stable, reformist, peaceful Japan would be integrated into an international order which would itself be defined in liberal terms. In this sense, there was no reversal in U.S.-Japanese relations after the onset of the Cold War. America's unilateral moves in Japan and the close, almost exclusive, relationship between the two countries were a pattern which had become discernible long before the collapse of Nationalist China or the U.S.-Soviet confrontation in Europe and the Middle East. We must, therefore, locate the origins of postwar U.S.-Japanese relations in World War II.

By the same token, Japan's emergence as America's staunch ally was not a product of the Cold War. As far as the Japanese leaders were concerned, their country's defeat demonstrated the bankruptcy of an attempt to create an anti–Anglo-American order in Asia. They would go back to the general orientation of the 1920s when cooperation with Britain and America had been the basic framework of Japanese policy and politics. Such reorientation was psychologically and intellectually easy to make because of Japanese proclivity to the idea of "cooperation." Cooperation with Germany had failed, so Japan would try it with the United States. After all, even Matsuoka Yōsuke, the architect of the Axis alliance, had written in 1940: "Even when Japan's aim is to cooperate with a certain country, Japan may fight that country on the way to the accomplishment of that end. Japan may even wage a war with that country. Such action is, however, a road to cooperation."[68] No better description, and no more prophetic statement, of the course of U.S.-Japanese relations during the 1940s could have been made.

1. The best recent study of wartime policy toward Germany is Tony Sharp, *The Wartime Alliance and the Zonal Division of Germany* (London: Oxford University Press, 1975).

2. Department of State, *Postwar Foreign Policy Preparation, 1939–1945* (Washington: 1949), pp. 67–213.

3. ST minutes, 7 May 1943, Harley Notter Papers, National Archives. (ST stands for the security technical committee of the security subcommittee.)

4. Memo of conversation with Hornbeck, by Borton, 28 October 1943, ibid.

5. ST minutes, 3 July 1943, ibid.

6. ST minutes, 26 May 1943, ibid.

7. ST minutes, 7 May 1943, ibid.

8. T 341 (Feary memo), 21 June 1943, ibid. (T stands for the territorial problem subcommittee.)

9. T 366 (Blakeslee memo), 29 September 1943, ibid.

10. T 381 (Borton memo), 6 October 1943, ibid.

11. T minutes, 17 December 1943, ibid.

12. *Foreign Relations of the United States 1944* (henceforth cited *FR*), V, 1190–94.

13. Ibid., 1202–5.

14. Ibid., 1213–14.

15. PWC 116a, and PWC 116a (Alternative), both 24 April 1944, Notter Papers. (PWC stands for the postwar programs committee.)

16. PWC 145, 26 April 1944, ibid.

17. PWC 146, 26 April 1944, ibid.

18. *FR, 1944*, V, 1257–60

19. Ibid., 1250–55.

20. *See* Walter LaFeber, "Roosevelt, Churchill, and Indochina, 1942–1945," *American Historical Review* 80, no. 5 (December 1975): 1277–95.

21. McDermott minutes, 6 October 1944, F 4501/94/23, Foreign Office Archives, Public Record Office.

22. Foulds minutes, 17 February 1944, F 931/94/23, ibid.

23. *FR, 1945*, VI, 521–29, 549–54.

24. JCS 1355, 3 May 1945, Joint Chiefs of Staff Papers, National Archives.

25. *FR, 1945*, VI, 545–47.

26. *See* Martin J. Sherwin, *A World Destroyed: The Atomic Bomb and the Grand Alliance* (New York: Knopf, 1975), ch. 8.

27. Dooman memo, 1 May 1945, SWNCC 70/1/D, SWNCC Papers, National Archives.

28. SWNCC 70/2, 23 June 1945, and SWNCC 70/3/D, 18 July 1945, ibid.

29. Department of Defense, "The Entry of the Soviet Union into the War against Japan: Military Plans, 1941–1945" (September 1955), National Archives, pp. 61–68.

30. Sargent to Churchill, 9 May 1945, F 1834/364/23, Foreign Office Archives.

31. Sansom to Foreign Office, 3 May 1945, and Sterndale Bennett minutes, 9 May 1945, F 2444/364/G 23, ibid.

32. Halifax to Foreign Office, 30 May 1945, F 3238/364/G 23, ibid.

33. Foulds minutes, 31 May 1945, F 3238/364/G 23, ibid.

34. Sansom-Foulds memo, 20 June 1945, F 3768/364/G 23, ibid.

35. Foulds to Sterndale Bennett, 27 July 1945, F 4789/364/G 23, ibid.; *FR, Conference of Berlin, 1945*, II, 1277.

36. Ibid., 1286.

37. JCS 1398/1 (SWNCC 70/3/D), 18 July 1945, JCS Papers.

38. JCS 1398/3 (SWNCC 70/5), 20 August 1945, ibid.

39. For an excellent discussion of JCS planning for the occupation of Japan, *see* Iokibe Makoto, "Beikoku ni okeru tai-Nichi senryō seisaku no keisei katei," *Kokusaihō gaikō zasshi* 74, nos. 3, 4 (October, December 1975).

40. De la Mare minutes, 3 August 1945, F 4671/584/61, Foreign Office Archives.

41. Balfour to Foreign Office, 13 August 1945, F 5110/630/G 23, ibid.

42. Foreign Office to Balfour, 12 August 1945, F 5048/630/G 23, ibid.

43. *FR, 1945*, VI, 529–35.

44. Foreign Office to Balfour, 18 August 1945, F 5403/364/G 23, Foreign Office Archives.

45. Far Eastern department memo, 11 September 1945, F 6699/364/23, ibid.

46. Foulds and Sterndale Bennett minutes, 24 September 1945, F 7331/364/23, ibid.

47. Roberts to Foreign Office, 21 October 1945, F 8717/1605/G 61, ibid; W. Averell Harriman, *Special Envoy to Churchill and Stalin* (New York: Random House, 1975), ch. 21.

48. JIC 323/1, 15 October 1945, JCS Papers.

49. MacArthur to JCS, 4 May 1946, CCS 383. 21 Japan, JCS Papers.

50. JIS 80/9, 26 October 1945, JSC Papers.

51. JIS 329, 3 November 1945, ibid.

52. Clifford memo, 24 September 1946, in Harry S. Truman Library.

53. *FR, 1947*, I, 715–16.

54. NSC 7, 30 March 1948, NSC Papers, National Archives.

55. *FR, 1947*, I, 737.

56. *See* David Rosenberg, "The U.S. Navy and the Problem of Oil in a Future War," *Naval War College Review* (Summer 1976): 53–64.

57. NSC 6, 26 March 1948, NSC Papers.

58. NSC 34/1, 11 January 1949, ibid.

59. *See* NSC 37/1, 19 January 1949, and NSC 37/3, 11 February 1949, ibid.

60. NSC 41, 28 February 1949, ibid.

61. *FR, 1947*, I, 745.

62. NSC 13/2, 7 October 1948, NSC Papers.

63. NSC 49, 15 June 1949, ibid.

64. PPS/28/2, 26 May 1948, ibid.

65. NSC 49, 15 June 1949, ibid.

66. NSC 48/1, 23 December 1949, ibid.

67. NSC 48/2, 30 December 1949, ibid.

68. Cited in R. J. C. Butow, *The John Doe Associates* (Stanford: Stanford University Press, 1974), p. 89.

The Cold War and
U.S.-Japan Economic Cooperation

Yamamoto Mitsuru

Postwar Japanese foreign policy—the way Japan responded to the international environment—will not be clear without an understanding of the important role played by economics. What, for example, did the policy-making elite consider to be the compelling tasks and objectives for the national economy? How did their perception of these tasks and objectives affect Japan's foreign policy in the context of the restraints and opportunities provided by the international environment? Probing into the interplay between foreign policy and economic considerations offers an important perspective for analysis of the last 30 years of Japanese foreign relations.

"Economic cooperation" first appeared on the agenda of U.S.-Japan relations in early 1951 when special envoy John Foster Dulles came to Japan (January 25 to February 11, 1951) to prepare for the conclusion of the San Francisco peace treaty. Here "economic cooperation" refers to the plans, expectations, speculation, illusions, slogans, or a combination of these, which proliferated at that time. The substance of "economic cooperation" with the United States remained ill defined. But in a certain sense, that very vagueness augmented the important influence exerted by the concept in the realms of government, business, and mass communication. It not only affected views of U.S.-Japan relations, but also had an impact on Japanese policy planning for economic recovery. For occupied Japan, alignment with the West was almost inevitable. That being the case, "U.S.-Japan economic cooperation" symbolized the benefits that Japan expected and hoped would accrue from that alignment. Even after the peace treaty was concluded, and on into the mid-1950s, it was a keystone of economic planning, and as far as Japan was concerned, gave powerful impetus to the Japan-American alliance.

My purpose here is to explore the background and realities of U.S.-Japan economic cooperation by identifying the roles played by the government, business, public opinion, and occupation authorities in the Japanese milieu, and portraying American responses to them. Hopefully, this will clarify how Japanese leaders perceived the international environment and the problems confronting Japan as it emerged from the protection and restrictions of the occupation. What were the fundamental assumptions and intentions behind their aspiration for U.S.-Japan economic cooperation? And, what impact did their approach have on the overall pattern of U.S.-Japan relations?

The Issue Takes Shape

After the Dulles visit, U.S.-Japan economic cooperation and the peace treaty became the urgent issues facing occupied Japan. According to Nishimura Kumao, then director of the treaty bureau of the Foreign Ministry and a key figure directly involved in the peace talks,[1] Prime Minister Yoshida Shigeru told Dulles in their first meeting that he was opposed to Japan's rearmament. Dulles was displeased. After their meeting at the Mitsui Building, they headed for SCAP headquarters to meet General Douglas MacArthur. There, Yoshida told MacArthur, "One of the questions posed by the special envoy has perplexed me. He wants to know what sort of contribution Japan, now desirous of a peace treaty guaranteeing self-reliance and independence, intends to make to the free world." MacArthur smiled at Dulles and, according to Nishimura, commented: "What the Free World desires today is that Japan not be a military power. It would not be feasible. Japan has the arms production capability. It has the labor force. Supply the materials, and make full use of that productive capacity, and thus help build the power of the Free World." MacArthur supported the prime minister and soothed Dulles's ire.

Yoshida has discussed the rearmament problem in his memoirs:[2] "After much discussion between Japan and the United States, the problem was handled in line with General MacArthur's wise and symathetic suggestions." The resulting decision was that Japan should indirectly cooperate for U.S. rearmament by utilizing its old imperial army and navy armories. A conference with the Dulles mission on the morning of February 5 was conducted at the staff level. There the Japanese presented supplementary views to what they had said previously and data to provide answers to American questions. These data also included information about residual armament production capability and the surplus productive potential of major industries.[3]

On February 16, MacArthur ordered Yoshida to look into the possibility of establishing a system of economic cooperation between Japan and the United States. On February 19, the chief of the SCAP Economic and Scientific Bureau, Maj. Gen. William F. Marquat, instructed the director-general of the Economic Stabilization Board (ESB) to adjust Japan's industrial production plans in order to accommodate America's expanding demand for armament.[4] SCAP also suggested that the ESB make a survey of unused plants and equipment in key industries and find out what their top production levels were. SCAP wanted ESB's examination of the money and materials that would be needed to put the unused facilities into operation and to expand the production capacity of these industries to necessary levels. Occupation authorities also made their own estimate of maximum productive potential. The ESB estimates were based on the following assumptions: (1) The United States would supply Japan with a portion of its defense expenditures as aid; (2) Japan would be able to obtain a level of raw materials close to what it needed; (3) Japan could expect to borrow from the United States Liberty-type ships to transport imported materials; and (4) measures would be taken for inducing foreign capital to develop electric power facilities capable of supplying adequate power.[5]

It is clear when we look at the origins of U.S.-Japan economic cooperation that the United States did not even have a blueprint and that the Japanese government projections for cooperation were based on nothing more than a number of assumptions. However, the Japanese side, particularly the business world, was immediately suffused with a sense of anticipation. As early as March 3, K. D. Morrow, special assistant to General Marquat, warned of the Japanese tendency to be impatient. He was quoted by a Japanese news report as saying, "In fact SCAP is examining various ways of placing orders to procure goods for Korea, but that does not mean we have any special plans at this time to apply the formula for U.S. National Defense orders to Japan. . . . America's aid to Japan will probably continue. However, it is too early to expect any plan for special cooperation beyond what exists at present. It should not be forgotten that there is a mountain of problems to be overcome in the Japanese economy before any such grandiose scheme can be considered."[6]

Soon thereafter an editorial appeared in one of the biggest dailies in Japan, entitled "The realities of U.S.-Japan economic cooperation." The editorial in the March 8 issue of the *Mainichi shimbun* said, "The dominant thinking in the business world is based on the optimistic assumption that the Japanese economy will undergo tremendous growth in the near future through large-volume American procurement orders and enormous capital loans, but," it warned, "such assumptions are dangerous—like counting your chickens before they hatch." The editorial suggests both a buoyant mood and strong reservations. Many other reports and similar evidence might also have squelched the optimism. In addition to the Morrow statement, Japanese correspondents stationed in the United States were relaying much more realistic views. For example, the *Asahi shimbun* of March 13, 1951, carried a report from its Washington correspondent called "U.S.-Japan economic cooperation as seen from the U.S." The article stated that there were no signs of any concrete plans taking shape. Despite such cautious statements, hopes continued to burgeon and newspapers were filled with reports on the subject. At the second meeting of the Keidanren (Federation of Economic Organizations) committee on economic cooperation with the United States, held on March 13, a draft recommendation was adopted on methods of cooperation between the Japanese and American economies. One of the statements said: "It is imperative that Japan become the factory of Asia. We believe that the concept behind the Marshall Plan can be extended to Asia to achieve that end. Japan can handle certain activities on behalf of the United States in an operation similar to what the ECA (Economic Cooperation Administration) is doing in Europe. In addition to making a contribution to democratic economic restoration and resource development in Asia, it will provide a good way for Japan to secure the raw materials it lacks."[7]

Earlier, at the end of January, eight business organizations including Keidanren, the Japan Chamber of Commerce and Industry, and Nikkeiren (Japan Federation of Employers' Associations) had compiled another opinion paper concerning the terms of the peace treaty and presented it to Dulles. One request was for the quick conclusion of a U.S.-Japan economic pact and the establishment of a U.S.-Japan economic committee. The latter would include individuals from business and finance in both countries who would represent their respective governments. The Japanese business leaders were motivated by an urgent desire for a relationship with the United States so close to be virtually an amalgamation of the two economies.

To recapitulate, Japan had no desire for rearmament. It had to devise some other ways to contribute to the cause of the Free World under the support of which Japan was to restore its sovereignty. It was a time when Japan was performing a very important function in the Korean War by fulfilling the procurement orders for American military operations. Hence, the Yoshida-Dulles conference arrived at an understanding in principle that Japan could best contribute to the Free World through economic cooperation with the United States.

Occupation authorities had also been examining the feasibility of using the Japanese productive capacity to augment military supplies in the Korean War and had carried out studies of maximum production potential in Japan. The overtures that they made to the ESB were part of that effort. The Japanese policy-makers directly linked the Yoshida-Dulles talks with the SCAP overtures to inflate their hopes for developing a self-reliant economy through U.S.-Japan economic cooperation.

Japan's Needs and Expectations

The opportunities provided by the Korean War stimulated the Japanese economy to move upward. Exports rose and diversified as the international economy shifted from a buyer's to a seller's market. Special procurement orders for military supplies for the Korean War also created new demand. Before 1950 there had been some $300 million annual deficit in current account on Japan's international balance of payments, but in that year the accounts were $40 million in the black—the first time after the end of World War II that Japan had a current account surplus. Throughout 1952 the Japanese economy benefited from the procurement orders and, although in that year there was a large trade deficit of $290 million, it was covered by military orders and UN forces' dollar spending in Japan, giving excess receipts on total current account transaction to the tune of $150 million.

Not only did the procurement orders for the Korean War help the balance of payments, they brought about increases in production and employment. During the one year and ten months following the outbreak of the war, the procurement orders gave full-time or temporary employment to 290,000 people, and created jobs for a total of 3.65 million day laborers.[8] Unlike the relief goods received through the GARIOA (Government Account for Relief in Occupied Area) and EROA (Economic Rehabilitation in Occupied Area) funds, the procurement orders had the same effects as exports creating new demand—became a built-in prop of the economy, provided employment, and raised income levels. This category of trade made up 18 percent of the total of normal exports for 1951, and 44 percent in 1952. On the one hand, Korean War procurements became a windfall for the Japanese economy, which had been in the depths of the "Dodge recession." But they also created a situation which the government's Economic White Paper for fiscal 1953 called "a distorted economy that must cling to special procurements for its survival." Without that demand, though, the relatively high prices of Japanese goods on the international market would have had to be cut, and much greater effort given to increasing exports to close the gap between imports and exports. The unexpected foreign currency revenues temporarily covered such problems.

With the peace treaty soon to be concluded, Japan was pressed with the problem of how it would be able to pay its own way. As national income levels rose and the economy expanded from the Korean War procurements, the policy-makers were confronted with many serious dilemmas in defining the optimum course toward a self-reliant economy. The council on independent economy, established in July 1950, presented a three-year economic independence plan to the government in January 1951. The plan, to be implemented beginning fiscal 1951, was based on the assumption that American aid would be extended until fiscal 1953. It projected that if a favorable balance in international payments were maintained, the living standard would be raised to 89 percent of the prewar (1934–36) level by the end of the period. In order to establish autonomy and to break away from an economy and trade structure heavily dependent on the United States, economic cooperation with the United States or something similar would be necessary. The gist of the thinking among policy planners was that without a boon like the special war procurements any plan would be infeasible.[9]

The second problem was resources. During the occupation, necessary resources and materials were supplied to Japan by the United States (i.e., SCAP), which acted as buying agent. But with the tightening of supply for some materials brought about by the worldwide armament boom, the policy planners and industry were very concerned to acquire a guaranteed flow of resources. The defense production act established in the United States in September 1950 granted the president broad powers to allocate raw materials and control prices and wages. On the international stage, in line with Western mutual defense arrangements made at the Truman-Attlee talks in December 1950, a central organization for the international raw materials conference and six commodities committees (expanded to seven in March) were set up in February 1951. These developments naturally affected Japan's import of raw materials.

The importance of resources in Japanese thinking about economic cooperation comes out in a newspaper report of the views of Komamura Sukemasa of the Gōshō Trading Company, a member of a cotton industry mission to the United States in March 1951.[10] Komamura said, "We must link the Japanese economy to American efforts toward rearmament," and that it was urgent for Japan to stop competing with the United States in buying such materials as tin and rubber. He went on to say that it was necessary to get U.S. government understanding so that imports, such as iron ore and scrap that the United States considered critical, could be obtained. Just when ideas similar to Komamura's were gaining ground in Japanese business and finance, several unavoidable occurrences not foreseen by promoters of economic cooperation with the United States dashed their optimism: first the halt on strategic goods buying by the United States (March 1951), then the slowdown on military expenditures, and a statement by Foreign Minister Jakob Malik of the Soviet Union, followed by the beginning of ceasefire talks. These developments led to a pause in stockpiling by industrial nations, and a subsequent leveling-off of international market conditions.

Finally, the third element motivating Japan toward economic cooperation with the United States was the expectation that economic ties with Southeast Asia would be reestablished by riding on U.S. aid programs. Prior to the outbreak of the Korean War, the ESB had conducted research, called the Eos project (dated June 3, 1950, and named after a Greek goddess), of conditions necessary for economic independence. "Plan A" of the project presumed that a small-scale Marshall Plan would probably be carried out in Asia. Optimistic projections and similar expectations had been occasionally expressed even before the Korean War. What prompted such thinking on the part of Japan was probably the start of American aid to Indochina and the Point Four program, included in President Truman's inaugural address of January 1949. He said, "Fourth, we must embark on a bold new program for making the benefits of our scientific advances and industrial progress available for the development and growth of underdeveloped areas."

In November 1950, Gordon Gray's report to the president was announced.[11] It drew special attention to the importance of social and economic progress in underdeveloped areas for the security and well-being of the Free World and set out a series of recommendations for encouraging aggressive development programs in Southeast Asia and elsewhere. This report became an important source of encouragement for those Japanese involved in foreign and economic policy planning to connect the Japanese role in Southeast Asia to the framework of U.S. Far Eastern policy.[12]

One thing that should be noted is the loss of trade with continental China during the Korean War. Trade with China after World War II was interrupted by the civil war and was just being restored at the time the Peking government was established in October 1949. Trade continued to expand for some time after the start of the Korean War, with Japanese exports increasing sixfold ($19,643,000) over the previous year and imports doubling to $39,531,000. Imports from China for 1950 consisted chiefly of soybeans, rice, coal, and iron ore, and the country was the fourth-ranking exporter to Japan after the United States, Australia, and Thailand.[13] With the entrance of the Chinese "volunteer army" into Korea, restrictions were placed on exports to China in December 1950, and in retaliation, China halted its exports. Because the relative proportion of exports to China out of the total was low (2.4 percent), the aggregate effect on the export trade was small, but in the import field it presented a very big problem; new suppliers had to be found for important items like coking coal, iron ore, soybeans, and manganese ore. In May 1951, the UN adopted a resolution calling for a strict embargo against China. Japan's 1951 exports to the mainland fell to one-third and imports to one-half of 1950 levels.[14] Iron ore was then obtained from the Philippines, India, Malaya, and Hong Kong, while other products were bought from the United States and Canada. Increased transportation costs meant higher prices, making Japan all the more eager to find a cheap and stable supply source of resources in Southeast Asia.

There were three factors that Japan had to consider in opening this avenue for trade: the feelings against Japan held by the people of Southeast Asia; suspicion by other nations such as Great Britain with interests in the area, toward a Japanese economic comeback; and, more than anything else, Japan's capital shortage. That is why Japan considered it mandatory to take advantage of the opportunities provided by U.S. aid programs in Southeast Asia.

Plans and Responses

SCAP headquarters and the ESB both made projections of maximum productive levels. The ESB conferred with the Finance Ministry to produce a report called "Economic policy for cooperation," and presented it to SCAP. Occupation headquarters then ordered Japan to make a plan for rapid increases in production, but there appeared no indication on the part of the U.S. government of a concrete step for placing large procurement orders.

Then, in April 1951, Marquat, as spokesman for the Japanese government, went to the United States for an on-the-spot investigation of Washington's thinking. When he returned on May 16, he made what became known as the "Marquat statement." Yoshida could not hold back his disappointment, for, as he says in his memoirs, "Major General Marquat talked much about U.S.-Japan economic cooperation, but most of it was abstract, more like a sermon."[15] There was nothing in the announcement pertaining to the special kind of program that the Japanese had hoped for so much. Marquat commented to the effect that the United States was fully aware of the advantage in Japan's taking part in the U.S. emergency procurement plan along with the European and other Western nations, based on competitive prices and quality of goods. In other words, contrary to Japanese expectations of a program in which Japan alone would receive special consideration from the United States on raw materials and financing, buying would be done on a commercial basis. It was clear that Japan had to make its own efforts in international competition, just as it would in normal export business. Marquat also stated that no overall plan existed for procurement orders over the long term, and that orders would be given by the usual methods of contract in free competition. Washington had no all-inclusive plan for Asia similar to the Marshall Plan.

Nothing indicates that Washington considered the Marquat statement very important. Rather, what they focused on is revealed by a statement made two days before; they called for a decrease in aid to Japan and announced that America would bear part of the costs for the occupation. The results obtained from Washington probably diverged sharply from what even Marquat expected. Such discrepancies in the assumptions behind policy planning show the different level of concern toward Japan held by SCAP compared with the policy-making agencies of the United States—with the possible exception of the Department of the Army, which had a direct stake in Japanese affairs.

On the other hand, it would be incorrect to assume that Washington gave no heed to the special plan desired by Japan. These questions were discussed in Washington; for example, Charles E. Wilson, director of defense mobilization, proposed to the departments of State and Defense and to the Economic Cooperation Administration (ECA) that if Japan's idle productive capacity could be combined with Southeast Asian resources, the resulting commercial and industrial structure would help lighten America's burden, contribute to the stabilization of Southeast Asia, and provide for economic integration of free nations in Asia, just as in Western Europe. In a Washington dispatch *The New York Times* reported: "What is ultimately sought by some Defense Mobilization officials is an arrangement that would move toward economic integration of free countries in the East in the same way that the Western European Governments are cooperating through the NATO and regional economic programs." It said that Wilson was believed to have proposed "exploratory talks on the question." The response from the State and Defense departments and ECA was "mixed," it added.[16]

According to the report, those favoring Japan's recovery were sympathetic to the proposal, but those who either had direct contact or knowledge of the Southeast Asian situation were skeptical. The latter group felt that even if the United States wanted to carry out such a plan there would be great obstacles. The Wilson proposal suggested that idle facilities in Japan be supplied with iron ore from the Philippines, Malaya, and India, and bauxite from Palau. Criticism of the Wilson proposal stemmed less from opposition to helping Japanese recovery by supplying resources than from the idea that those nations would probably want to develop their own industries. A chief reason that the proposal did not receive active support outside those involved in Japanese affairs was the lack of political and psychological conditions in Asia (including feelings sympathetic to a Japanese presence by the Southeast Asian nations) which would support the kind of regional integration that the Marshall Plan fostered.

Several events around the time *The New York Times* article appeared can be interpreted to mean that the United States did not consider economic cooperation with Japan as any new big plan but thought of it as a way to give Japan various opportunities under existing plans and programs. One was an announcement that a Tokyo office of ECA would be set up to purchase materials in Japan for aid to Southeast Asia. The other was the dispatch of a survey team led by Morrow from SCAP headquarters to Southeast Asia.

We can also see that there was no consensus within SCAP. Some in SCAP doubted the validity of the "top-level survey" that measured maximum productive capacity on an individual industry basis rather than measuring the relation of all industries to the aggregate. Moreover, the survey assumed that there would be a supply of raw materials, energy, and labor with no conditions on their availability, without even any concrete measures spelled out to make that assumption a reality. Officials in the industry section reportedly said that Morrow was making plans for their own sake.[17] Miyazaki Isamu, who was on ESB during the period under discussion, commented that there were two lines of thinking on this issue in SCAP: one was represented by Morrow, who felt that top priority should be given to full expansion of productive capacity in manufacturing and mining; and the other by those in the finance section, who pressed for emphasis on stability.[18]

There were differences in thinking within the Japanese government similar to those in SCAP. The ESB was more inclined to the Morrow type of approach, a method which gave precedence to industrial mobilization programs to increase material production and power supply.[19] In contrast, the process of discussion within the Finance Ministry shows that a very cautious attitude prevailed among its officials; some of them feared that although U.S.-Japan cooperation was commendable in principle, in practice it entailed the possibility that the Japanese economy would be victimized by an excess of exports over imports and, in addition, that the continuity of U.S. orders to Japan might not be guaranteed. In the initial stages of their discussions, the Finance Ministry was apprehensive about the possibility that economic cooperation would necessitate strong domestic controls over finance and raw materials.[20] They feared that "New Dealers" in SCAP, and MITI and ESB bureaucrats would inevitably push to broaden the scope of control over the economy, in steadily widening waves—an inherent characteristic of control—eventually encompassing a much broader area than originally intended. Suffice it to say for now that there was no consensus on the Japanese side; more detailed research into official documents would be required to clarify the bureaucratic politics concerning this question.

That the kind of uproar going on in Japan had no equivalent in Washington is indicated by what took place during the visit that Joseph M. Dodge made in October 1951. In his Tokyo statement he said that Japanese industrialists and others seemed to feel that the United States would provide the concrete planning for economic cooperation between the two nations, but that they were mistaken; such cooperation was something that Japan would have to conduct in order to ameliorate its balance of payments and achieve economic independence. They should consider what they themselves could do to get more orders and to increase exports.[21] Another source, a memorandum entitled "United States-Japan economic cooperation in the post-treaty era" (draft) for U.S. government internal use, which Dodge probably wrote during the period between his visit to Japan and Feburary 1952, states:

> Economic Cooperation (as a slogan) has received wide publicity in Japan but there has been little in the way of concrete or measurable results, so far. There is a tendency in Japan to look for it and focus their hopes for the future on it. However, this is manifested by little aggressive or constructive action on their part to further it. This may be partly the result of fear that they will start on a program that will not continue and will cause later and greater difficulties. Their approach to the problem is inclined to be an expectation that the United States will plan and blueprint the needs of Japan and then fit the economy of the United States into those needs— instead of the reverse. This is the inevitable result of the paternalistic care given the reconstruction of Japan in the six years of their almost complete dependence on the United States.[22]

Business conditions in Japan declined in the fall of 1951 because of several factors: a slacking off in international business which began in March, a slowdown in exports caused by Japan's relatively high prices compared to worldwide levels, and the domestic financial situation. Moreover, the convening of the peace con-

ference in San Francisco made the problems of economic independence more urgent, and financial burdens were expected to
pile up with the coming into force of the peace treaty, including
defense expenditures, repayment of GARIOA funds, payments on
prewar foreign bonds, indemnities for Allied assets and reparations
to Southeast Asian nations. This situation made people in industry
and government planners all the more eager to breathe life back
into the U.S.-Japan economic cooperation concept. These factors
and Dodge's comment that Japanese should themselves find ways
to stand on their own feet were perhaps instrumental in the formation of the liaison committee for economic cooperation by the
cabinet on November 16, 1951. The director-general of the ESB
was appointed committee chairman, and the vice-ministers and
deputies of ministries and agencies concerned served as members.
Other groups were formed as well: the supreme council for economic cooperation was launched on February 1, 1952, with the
prime minister as chairman, and economic organizations including
Keidanren jointly set up a committee to promote Japanese-
American cooperation. The report sent by Sudō Hideo, director-
general of the ESB, to Marquat, entitled "Establishment of a
viable economy and promotion of economic cooperation," represented one result of such efforts. With the end of the occupation,
however, SCAP was no longer present to promote economic cooperation, and Japan had to start taking part directly in international trade and the world economy. The first stage in U.S.-Japan
economic cooperation had come to an end.

The Japanese mission to the San Francisco conference took with
it a set of tentative projections known as "File B." Fiscal 1954 was
the general target date for these projections, but their figures had
almost no practical meaning, for they were an attempt rather to
explain the problems facing the Japanese economy than to present
any feasible basis for planning.[23] The assumption was that Japanese economic power would be raised to the maximum along lines
provided by economic cooperation with the United States. This
was the same line of thinking that had guided the calculations
for maximum production, the "top level survey" mentioned previously. At the end of the peace conference, Finance Minister
Ikeda Hayato and the governor of the Bank of Japan, Ichimada
Hisato, were scheduled to take these projections to Washington

for negotiations with the U.S. government on aid and loans. But the latter was not prepared for negotiations, and Dodge was sent to San Francisco to dissuade the two men from making their trip.

File B emphasized two points. The first was that a shortage of electric power was the bottleneck in industrial expansion and that foreign funds would be necessary to develop adequate electric power sources. The second was that Southeast Asian development would have to be encouraged.[24] When we trace the history of Japanese international affairs through the 1950s, we see that this type of thinking, which had grown with the concept of U.S.-Japan economic cooperation, was to have a long-term influence on post-peace treaty Japanese foreign policy in general, and on policy toward the United States and Southeast Asia in particular.

Conclusion

This essay is part of a larger study of the dynamic process in which the international structure of the Cold War influenced, and to some extent shaped, the pattern of Japan's foreign relations, especially as it related to domestic restraints and aspirations. As such, these conclusions can only be partial and tentative, but in this examination of the concept of U.S.-Japan economic cooperation we can make at least five general points.

(1) Asia differed from Europe because there were no existing conditions through which the United States could inspire the kind of regional unity the Marshall Plan did in Europe. Different ideas appeared at different times, but there is nothing to show that the U.S. government paid serious attention to them. There were some vague ideas or long-range visions about the alignment of the free nations of Asia with Japanese industrial power as a key element. But, on the other hand, policy-makers were confronted with the urgent, short-term task of finding effective ways to fulfill pressing U.S. procurement needs. Perhaps these two factors combined to arouse the Japanese expectation of a cooperative scheme among Japan, the United States, and Southeast Asia, which, however, never came to pass. Japanese leaders entertained such a plan probably because they mistook what was actually either a long-range

vision or short-term measures on the part of the United States for a workable, ongoing plan.

(2) At the time Japan set out on the road to independence it was virtually isolated in the international environment. Cut off from the continent and deprived of a political and psychological base in Southeast Asia, Japan became a member of the Free World, but its relations were in actuality restricted to the United States. Moreover, the connections formed were ones in which Japan's primary value was considered to be its availability for military purposes. Although the Japanese and West German situations were the same in the sense that both were defeated nations in World War II and U.S. allies during the Cold War, they were actually quite different. West Germany received support through the development of regional linkages such as the Marshall Plan, OEEC, ECSC, and eventually the European economic market. That is probably one reason why Japan, a nation which sought independence, at the same time desired continued U.S. patronage through a formula like U.S.-Japan economic cooperation.

In this connection, it should be noted here that Japan's aspiration to economic penetration, under U.S. protection, of Southeast Asian countries apparently constituted one of the principal justifications for the Domino theory in Washington's Asia policy. The following passage in Secretary of State Dulles's address, delivered over radio and television networks midway in the Geneva conference of 1954, serves as an example: "Let me turn to the problem of Southeast Asia. . . . Communist conquest of this area would seriously imperil the free world position in the Western Pacific. It would, among other things, endanger the Philippines, Australia, and New Zealand, with all of which the United States has mutual-security treaties. It would deprive Japan of important foreign markets and sources of food and raw materials."[25]

(3) There is a high degree of self-centeredness in Japan's attitude toward the outside world. Dodge aptly observed that the Japanese were inclined to expect the United States to both draw plans to fit the needs of Japan and make adjustments in the American economy accordingly. The same is true of resource development in Southeast Asia. There, too, any consideration, observa-

tion, or analysis of how people in that area might react to a Japanese comeback was overshadowed by concern for Japan's own needs. There was an almost total lack of awareness of the complex problems which would inevitably arise if and when the United States carried out a plan in Southeast Asia in which Japan was given a privileged role.

(4) The plans made for a self-reliant economy were developed out of thinking and methods that focused on material mobilization with which the government bureaucracy had become familiar under wartime economic control. A complete statement cannot be made without further study of how the ministries and agencies formulated their policies, but it is perhaps safe to conjecture that little, if any, consideration of the overall domestic economic policy and long-range post-independence foreign policy went into the process of such deliberations. The policy-makers were more preoccupied with their own figures and statistics.

(5) Words, or, better, slogans, rather than any real substance, were what impressed the promoters of the cooperation idea, both in government and business. Policy was, at the same time, pulled along by optimistic forecasts and expectations that fit with Japan's needs rather than being based on an awareness of reality. Once things started, officials fell in with a follow-the-leader mentality, as is clearly shown throughout the drama of U.S.-Japan economic cooperation. The bureaucratic apparatus has a built-in method of making "alibis" for whatever is the outcome of a policy decision. Thus, officials can criticize others in case of failure, while they can also avoid charges of obstruction in case of success. Such a defense mechanism only serves to increase the level of illusion in the policy-making process.

1. Nishimura Kumao, *San Furanshisuko tai-Nichi kōwa jōyaku* (Tokyo: Kajima ken-kyūjo shuppankai, 1970), pp. 88–89.

2. Yoshida Shigeru, *Kaisō jūnen*, vol. 2 (Tokyo: Shinchōsha, 1957), p. 162.

3. Nishimura, *San Furanshisuko*, p. 92.

4. Economic Planning Agency, ed., *Sengo keizaishi—Sōkan hen* (Tokyo: Keizai kikakuchō, 1957), pp. 362–65.

5. Ibid.

6. *Asahi shimbun*, 4 March 1951, accredited to Kyōdō News Service.

7. *Nihon keizai shimbun*, 14 March 1951.

8. Economic Stabilization Board, *Tokuju hakusho* (21 July 1952).

9. Economic Planning Agency, ed., *Sengo keizaishi—Keizai seisaku hen* (Tokyo: Keizai kikakuchō, 1960), pp. 321–22; *Sengo keizaishi—keizai antei hombushi* (Tokyo: Keizai kikakuchō, 1964), pp. 241–43. *See also* Miyazaki Isamu, "Sengo keizai keikaku no keifu to sono haikei (II)" in *Nihon no keizai keikaku—Sengo no rekishi to mondai*, ed. Hayashi Yūjirō (Tokyo: Tokyo keizai shimpōsha, 1957), pp. 134–36.

10. *Asahi shimbun*, 4 March 1951, report from the Washington correspondent.

11. "Report to the President on Foreign Economic Policies" (10 November 1950).

12. Hagiwara Tōru, ed. *Kōwago no gaikō (II)—Keizai*, vol. 1 (Tokyo: Kajima kenkyūjo shuppankai, 1972), pp. 100–102.

13. Ministry of International Trade and Industry, *Tsūshō hakusho—Shōwa 26 nendo* (1951), pp. 91–92.

14. Ibid., 31–32, 91–92.

15. Yoshida, *Kaisō jūnen*, vol. 3, p. 244.

16 *The New York Times*, 22 July 1951. Reports to the same effect appeared through AP and AFP wire services in *Sankei shimbun*, 24 July, and *Asahi shimbun*, 25 July.

17. *Sengo keizaishi—Keizai seisaku hen*, p. 258.

18. Miyazaki, "Sengo keizai keikaku," p. 137.

19. Ibid., p. 138.

20. Ministry of Finance, "Keizai kyōryoku ni tsuiteno mondaiten," mimeographed (Morinaga papers, Finance Minstry, 25 May 1951).

21. *Sengo keizaishi—Keizai antei hombushi*, pp. 265–66.

22. Joseph M. Dodge, "United States-Japan Economic Cooperation in the Post-Treaty Era," draft (Joseph M. Dodge papers, Burton Historical Collections, Detroit Public Library).

23. *Sengo keizaishi—Keizai seisaku hen*, pp. 298–99.

24. Ibid., p. 299.

25. *Department of State Bulletin* (17 May 1954), 740.

Appendix
Summary of the Proceedings of the International Symposium (1975)

Editors' note: This summary is drawn from the "Proceedings of the International Symposium" of a conference held in Kyoto in November 1975, where most of the papers in this volume were first presented. The Proceedings, published in Japanese in one volume, was based on the massive "Stenographic Record of the International Symposium," which was completed with the cooperation of a pool of student stenographers from Kyoto and Doshisha universities under the supervision of Asada Sadao. This summary focuses on four main themes of discussion at the conference. Unfortunately, many important issues and statements by participants could not be included in this summary.

The Significance of Research on the Cold War in Asia

Could Japanese scholars make significant contributions in a field where Western scholars had already done so much more? This was a question that had been posed long before the symposium by Ichimura Shin'ichi (Kyoto University). Hayashi Kentarō (University of Tokyo), Nagai Yōnosuke (Tokyo Institute of Technology), and others suggested that Japanese scholars should be able to examine the debate between orthodox and revisionist Western scholars in terms of the sociology of knowledge in order to point up peculiarities of this debate. Furthermore, they should be able to analyze the structure of the international environment in postwar Asia from a Japanese perspective.

This subject was raised again at the Kyoto symposium by D. C. Watt (London School of Economics and Political Science), who, as a British scholar, represented a European viewpoint at the conference. Watt stated that the debate on the Cold War in the United States had a peculiarly American character. As a member of a pluralistic society composed of many ethnic groups, the American scholar performed an especially important function in the process of the formation of a national self-consciousness. Scholars served as links in America's long process of groping for a national identity. According to Watt, most of the revisionist scholars in the United States felt that American society had betrayed its earliest ideals and become contaminated and decadent. This atavistic reaction to the disasters which had overtaken America's policy in Southeast Asia was of obvious interest historically, that is, to historians of America. It had nothing, strictly speaking, to do with the historical elucidation of American foreign policy as such. As a British scholar able to view this situation objectively, Watt pinpointed this tendency to debate American policy in pseudo-theological, para-ethical terms as a special characteristic of American study of the Cold War.

At the end of the summing-up session, Watt stated that his visit to Japan had confirmed for him the fact that the attitudes of Europe and Japan toward the superpowers had much in common. One of the most important results of this international conference was the confirmation of the uniqueness of Japanese studies of the Cold War—studies that differed from those of American scholars. At a panel discussion sponsored by the publishers of the influential *Chūō kōron* magazine, Walter LaFeber (Cornell University) expressed the opinion that the conference had revealed more blind spots in research in the United States than he had imagined.

Most of the foreign participants, including John Gaddis (Ohio University) and George Kahin (Cornell University), agreed that the conference represented a type of international scholarly gathering which was rarely seen, one at which Japanese social scientists and Western scholars, using identical primary sources, were able to exchange frank views on areas other than Japan. As opposed to the foreign participants, who were mostly historians, the Japanese participants included political scientists, sociologists, cultural anthropologists, and area specialists. The many bold views and new hypotheses produced by this interdisciplinary approach of the Japanese at the conference made it an epoch-making event.

The Expansion of the Cold War into Asia

Special note should be made of the fact that the conference participants were almost in complete agreement on the important problems of how, why, and when the Cold War spread from Europe to Asia and escalated to the "hot wars" of Korea and Vietnam. These problems could be divided into two parts.

First, there was the question of the differences between the structure of the Cold War in Europe and that in Asia. In Europe, the United States and the Soviet Union came to realize the impossibility both of war and of compromise through diplomatic negotiation. As a result, the two nations acted unilaterally on such issues as Eastern Europe, Germany, and the Middle East. The Cold War in Europe, however, differed from that in Asia in that it never reached the level of a "hot war." Why? Nagai suggested that the responses of the superpowers to each other in the form of unilateral actions meant a warlike intent was kept under control at nonmilitary levels—ideological, political, economic, and cultural—because of the tremendous destructive nature of a nuclear war. Moreover, in terms of the "containment line," in Asia there were larger gaps between the boundaries of the interstate system and of ideology than in Europe (e.g. the differences between ANZUS and SEATO in Asia and NATO in Europe). Both Akira Iriye (University of Chicago) and Gaddis suggested that nuclear weapons perhaps prevented the U.S.-Soviet confrontation from developing into a hot war. The "weapons of ultimate violence," in Gaddis's words, may have been responsible for the "ultimate peace."

Watt emphasized that a "norm of behavior" for the interstate system had developed over a long period of time in Europe, promoting a degree of self-restraint on the part of the powers since the behavior of other nations could be predicted with some accuracy. However, he added, neither the Soviet Union nor the United

States recognized the other as part of the same system. Rōyama Michio (Sophia University) stated that most of Asia, except for Japan and Thailand, had been colonial or semi-colonial and therefore that the process of modern nation-building had been incomplete.

Iriye and Nakajima Mineo (Tokyo University of Foreign Studies) called attention to the structural differences in the postwar Yalta system with regard to Asia and Europe. According to Iriye, the Yalta framework for dividing the postwar world into spheres of influence was much more explicit in Europe than in Asia. In such a perspective, it was not surprising that the United States should ultimately act unilaterally in Korea or Indochina. Viewed on a global level, Nakajima said, the reasons for the escalation of the Cold War into a hot war in Asia could perhaps be traced to the treatment of Asia as a region peripheral to the center of civilization, Europe.

This point may be related to the idea put forth by Kahin concerning the differences between Europe and Asia in terms of the "stakes" and "risks" involved. In this sense, there were more opportunities for the United States and the Soviet Union to take "risk-free" unilateral actions in Asia than in Europe. That this held true for the Soviet Union as well as the United States was brought out by Watt in his comparison of Austria in 1947–48 and Korea in 1950. Although the situation in these two countries was similar, the Soviet Union stopped the Austrian Communist paramilitary guards from marching on Vienna, while it did not stop the North Koreans from crossing the 38th parallel. Kamiya stated that hot wars caused by major or limited military exercises had their origin in an ignorance of Asia, as witnessed in the case of General Hodge in South Korea.

The second part of this larger issue—the question of why and when the European Cold War expanded into Asia—caused a very lively discussion and debate among the conference participants. Watt urged them to consider separately the two stages of the origin of the Cold War and its subsequent escalation. Although the European Cold War began in the late fall of 1947, one would have to say that the Asian Cold War did not begin until the second half of 1949 in order to be able to differentiate between the stages of origin and escalation. (Moreover, for Britain it began not in

China but in Malaya.) Iriye stated that, until 1949, American involvement in Asia had declined, with the Truman administration giving precedence to Europe in its foreign policy. Thus, it could be said that the Cold War did not operate as a well-defined strategic concept for the United States in Asia at the very time that the European Cold War was intensifying. Nagai started an energetic debate on this subject. He argued that the expansion and application of the Truman administration's European-oriented Cold War doctrine in Asia was not due to the outbreak of the Korean War. Rather, this shift was prompted by the sudden change in American public opinion caused by two strong shocks in the summer of 1949—the "loss of China" and the "loss of atomic monopoly." (On a deeper level of analysis, however, this change was due to the historical conflict between two national identities—that of America as a "continental empire" and America as a "sea power.") The change in public opinion in 1949 was clearly reflected in the two presidential recommendations NSC 48/1 and NSC 48/2. The NSC 68 document also showed that the momentum toward a zero-sum game of the "globalization of containment" had by then become thoroughly internalized within American public opinion, the Congress, and the administration before the Korean War.

Kahin noted that the function of American public opinion in decision making changed after the spring of 1949. Though LaFeber's argument that the Truman administration skillfully manipulated public opinion and Congress might be generally correct, nevertheless, Kahin would argue that from the spring of 1949 at least, American policy was carried out on the basis of public opinion. There was discussion of the theory of "public opinion as rear guard," introduced by Tsujimura Akira (Univerity of Tokyo), a sociopsychologist specializing in public opinion research.

Hata Ikuhito (Ministry of Finance) noted that Asia became a Cold War crisis spot in global terms between the spring of 1949 and 1950. Starting with the crossing of the 38th parallel in Korea, and then with the problems in the strait of Taiwan and Vietnam, a crisis situation quickly developed in Asia. But the postwar environment of Asia had been determined before the Korean War. LaFeber also thought that one could see, in the totality of American policy in 1949, a process of convergence and merger of the "esoteric" and "exoteric" elements in official rhetoric.

American-Chinese-Soviet Relations at the Time of the Korean War

The conference devoted some sessions to the discussion of the relations between the United States, China, and the Soviet Union at the time of the Korean War. Gaddis and Fukuda Shigeo (Nagoya University) emphasized the importance of viewing the Korean War as a problem involving "internal struggles" in each of the countries. It is probable that the "internal struggle" aspect of the Korean War—for long seen as an "international civil war"—will gradually become more important. For this reason, the work of Okonogi Masao (Keiō University), who analyzed the nature of the domestic political confrontation on the Korean peninsula based on a detailed study of primary Korean sources, received high praise from Gaddis and many other participants.

The Korean War, however, had a stronger international aspect than the Vietnam War. In dealing with this issue, the conference focused on the problem of the connection between the complicated internal politics of the Korean peninsula and the foreign policies of the United States, China, and the Soviet Union. In this connection, Robert M. Slusser's (Michigan State University) paper on the Korean policy of Stalin stimulated a lively debate, especially regarding his bold hypothesis that Stalin's wartime policy had aimed at attaining a warm-water port in northeast Asia. According to Kimura Hiroshi (Hokkaidō University), this was a "brilliant hypothesis," but one which was based on negative evidence, what Slusser called Stalin's "strategic silence" during the war. Kimura stated that there was still need for a complete investigation of the sources in order to determine whether Stalin's silence was "meaningful" or not. From the viewpoint of the recently developed "bureaucratic politics" model, Gaddis stressed that one could not judge on the basis of results alone whether Stalin's silence was the "strategic rationality" of an "actor," an accident or mistake, or the product of divisions within the bureaucratic structure. Gaddis also emphasized in his own paper the large gaps between "result" and "intention" in history, and pointed out the role of accidents or mistakes in American policy toward Korea from 1945 to 1950. In response, Slusser argued that his theory concerning Stalin's diplomacy was based on more than mere negative evidence and cited some evidence from official Soviet documents, one of which was the State Defense Committee's order of July 1945, the "Order Relating to the Development of Harbor Facilities in the Far East."

In connection with the problem of Sino-Soviet relations over the Korean War, Nakajima Mineo stated that Stalin's designs on Manchuria and Outer Mongolia were one of the basic causes of the Sino-Soviet split. He criticized Slusser for not clearly differentiating between the position of Outer Mongolia, Manchuria, Korea, and "other parts of China." Stalin's intent, as revealed in the Kao Kang incident, was to weaken a united China under Mao Tse-tung by turning the northeast into an independent region. Therefore, Nakajima argued, it was inappropriate to deal with the ports of Vladivostok, Port Arthur, Dairen, and Inchong as one unit. Slusser in turn replied that he found it difficult to accept Nakajima's opinion that Stalin considered the Korean peninsula a buffer zone. On the contrary, according to Slusser, Stalin saw Korea more as a great power vacuum than as a buffer zone. For Stalin, Korea was an integral part of the "Soviet occupation zone" over which the right of control could not be relinquished to the United States, China, or Japan.

At a session on "The Cold War and China," the conference took up the question whether or not it would have been possible for American policy to have divided China and the Soviet Union. There was also heated debate over the nature of the policy of "leaning to one side" of the Mao regime in China. Okabe Tatsumi (Tokyo Metropolitan University) skillfully pointed out the fallacy of interpreting U.S.-Soviet-Chinese relations in 1949 by using a kind of "billiard ball" or "power politics" approach which relies on hindsight derived from the present Sino-Soviet split. Criticizing the views of Nakajima and others quoted in Allen Whiting's (University of Michigan) paper, Okabe argued that the Soviet Union had a status in the eyes of China "different in nature" from that of other countries. Russia, to the Chinese, was a friendly nation which served primarily as a model for the

Chinese domestic social system. The policy of "leaning to one side," therefore, was definitely not just a diplomatic policy or strategy.

In reference to America's failure to take advantage of the Sino-Soviet rift, Iriye stated that the opinions of the chief of staff concerning recognition of the new People's Republic of China at the end of 1949 were concluded much more in the framework of the U.S.-Soviet global confrontation than that of the State Department. Therefore, he argued, one of the reasons the American government did not take advantage of the Sino-Soviet split was that the pressure for a tougher policy toward China from the military had grown stronger toward the end of 1949. LaFeber countered with the observation that bureaucratic politics was not so crucial at that juncture because Truman and Acheson never seriously considered recognizing the Communist Chinese regime anyway.

LaFeber raised an important question concerning American policy toward Korea: why, when American policy toward Japan in 1947–48 was moving toward using the country as a base in its Cold War strategy and reviving its industry, did not the United States take over Korea in connection with this new Japanese policy? Gaddis answered that Korean policy was a "blind spot" in American government policy making at the time. The United States lacked a strategic view which considered Japan and Korea together as a set. LaFeber also brought up the fact that, in the same way, the American government did not really consider the importance of the impact on Stalin of its independent peace making with Japan.

Continuities and Discontinuities in U.S. Policy toward Japan

Iriye told the conference in his paper that American postwar policy toward Japan developed from earlier wartime planning and was from there on consistent and basically unchanging. The main themes of American policy, according to Iriye, were to have the United States play the most important role in postwar Japan and to pursue a liberal policy based on capitalistic internationalism. American policy toward Japan was much more consistent than its policy toward Southeast Asia, the Korean peninsula, or China. It was even more consistent than American policy in Europe toward Germany, Italy, and France. Hosoya Chihiro (Hitotsubashi University) responded to Iriye's presentation with an objection to evaluating the consistency of American policy toward Japan on the basis of bureaucratic politics. This response triggered a very minute discussion on the decision-making process involved in American occupation policy in Japan. This discussion was based on American and British documents, the works of Hugh Borton and other Western scholars, and the recent studies of Hata, Iokibe Makoto (Hiroshima University), and other Japanese scholars. Hosoya objected to the fact that Iriye's paper focused on the Japan specialists in the State Department. He argued that it was necessary to pay more attention to the problem of coordination and interaction between the State Department and the military. Continuing along this line of discussion, Nagai wanted to know whether there was not a structural difference between the Roosevelt and Truman administrations in the interaction of the top political level and the middle professional level in the decision-making process. Was not the middle professional level ignored during FDR's administration, or, to exaggerate slightly, was not the State Department merely shuffling papers in this period?

Rather than deal only with the one-way intentions of the United States where policy was decided, Hata, Rōyama, and Yamamoto Mitsuru (Hōsei University) raised questions concerning economics, politics, and security from the standpoint of the Japanese domestic political situation. For example, they discussed the bargaining on the emperor system and the behind-the-scene maneuvers between George Kennan and Douglas MacArthur over NSC 13/3, which dealt with Article IX of the Japanese constitution.

The conference agreed that the successful realization of America's preliminary plans for Japan was due, more than anything else, to the fact that, in the Far East, the United States held the dominant power of control over Japan. At the same time, as Watt, Hosoya, and Bamba Shin'ya (Tsuda College) pointed out, the activities of Australia, Canada, and New Zealand—the former British colonies—must not be overlooked. Moreover, it was important, as Kōsaka Masataka (Kyoto University) noted, that Japan had a peculiar geopolitical situation as an island nation.

To sum up some of the conclusions of the conference: in the context of U.S.-Soviet relations between 1947 and 1949, there was no Cold War strategy based on a coherent strategic doctrine in Asia as there was in Europe. In that sense, the Cold War in Asia could be said to have begun in earnest in the year 1949.

Contributors' Biographies

ARUGA TADASHI is a graduate of the University of Tokyo (B.A. 1953, M.A. 1955). He has also studied at Princeton University and the University of Wisconsin. He has taught at International Christian University and is now professor of diplomatic history at Seikei University in Tokyo. He is the author of *Amerika seijishi* [The Political History of the United States] (rev. ed. 1972) and *Gendai Amerika ron* [The United States Today] (1971).

JOHN LEWIS GADDIS is professor of history at Ohio University. He has also taught at Indiana University Southeast and most recently has been Visiting Professor of Strategy at the U.S. Naval College. He has written a great deal on the Cold War, his major publication being *The United States and the Orgins of the Cold War, 1941–1947* (1972). *Russia, the Soviet Union, and the United States: An Interpretive History* will appear in 1977.

AKIRA IRIYE is a graduate of Haverford College (B.A. 1957) and Harvard University (Ph.D. 1961) and is presently professor of history at the University of Chicago. He is the author of *After Imperialism: The Search for a New Order in the Far East* (1965), *Across the Pacific: An Inner History of American–East Asian Relations* (1967), *Pacific Estrangement: Japanese and American Expansion* (1972), and *The Cold War in Asia* (1974), and editor of *U.S. Policy in China* (1968) and *Mutual Images: Essays in American-Japanese Relations* (1975).

ITŌ TAKAYUKI graduated from the University of Tokyo (B.A. 1965, M.A. 1967) and is now associate professor of international relations at the Slavic Institue, Hokkaidō University. He has also studied at the Free University of Berlin (1968–72) and the University of Warsaw (1971). He has contributed several articles on Eastern Europe to *Surabu kenkyū* [Slavic Studies], among them "Tōō ni kansuru rengōkōku no sensō mokuteki 1941–1945" [Eastern

Europe in the Allied War Aims 1941–1945] (1976), and "Dainiji taisen go no Tōō" [Eastern Europe after World War II] in *Tōōshi* [East European History], ed. Yada Toshitaka (1976).

GEORGE McT. KAHIN is A. L. Binenkorb Professor of Government and International Relations at Cornell University. He received his B.A. degree from Harvard University, his M.A. from Stanford University, and his Ph.D. from Johns Hopkins University. He is the author of *Nationalism and Revolution in Indonesia* (1952), co-author of *The United States in Vietnam* (1967), and editor of *Major Governments of Asia* (1963) and *Government and Politics of Southeast Asia* (1964).

WALTER LAFEBER, presently professor of history at Cornell University, received his B.A. degree from Hanover College, his M.A. from Stanford University, and his Ph.D. from the University of Wisconsin. He has also been Commonwealth Lecturer at the University of London. He is the author of *New Empire: An Interpretation of American Expansion, 1860–1868* (1963) and *America, Russia, and the Cold War, 1945–1971* (3rd ed. 1975) and co-author of *John Quincy Adams and American Continental Empire* (1965) and *The American Century: A History of the United States since the 1890's* (1975).

NAGAI YŌNOSUKE, a graduate of the University of Tokyo (B.A. 1950) and Hokkaidō University (S.J.D. 1960), is now professor of political science at the Tokyo Institute of Technology. Between 1962 and 1964 he was a visiting scholar at the Yenching Institute, Harvard University. He is the author of *Heiwa no daishō* [The Price of Peace] (1967), *Jūkōzō shakai to bōryoku* [Violence in a Society with a Flexible Frame] (1971), *Seiji ishiki no kenkyū* [Studies on Political Consciousness] (1971), and *Takyoku sekai no kōzō* [The Structure of the Multipolar World] (1971).

NAKAJIMA MINEO is a graduate of the Tokyo University of Foreign Studies (B.A. 1960) and the University of Tokyo (M.A. 1965). He has been special assistant to the Japanese consulate general in Hong Kong (1968), and is presently associate professor of international relations and contemporary Chinese studies at the

Tokyo University of Foreign Studies. Among his publications are *Gendai Chūgoku ron—Ideorogī to seiji no naiteki kōsatsu* [On Contemporary China—Political and Ideological Considerations] (rev. ed. 1971), *Chūgoku-zō no kenshō* [Verification of China's Images] (1972), and *Gendai Chūgoku to kokusai kankei* [Contemporary China and Its International Relations] (1974).

OKABE TATSUMI, a graduate of the University of Tokyo (B.A. 1955, M.A. 1957, Ph.D. 1973), is presently professor of international relations at the Tokyo Metropolitan University. He has been a Fulbright Scholar at the University of Washington (1960–61), a researcher at the Japanese embassy in Singapore (1966–67), and a visiting professor at Nanyang University, Singapore (1973–74). His publications include *Gendai Chūgoku no taigai seisaku* [Contemporary China's Foreign Policy] (1971), *Tōnan Ajia to Nippon no shinro* [Southeast Asia and Japan's Future Policy] (1976), and *Chūgoku no tainichi seisaku* [China's Japan Policy] (1976).

OKONOGI MASAO received his B.A. and M.A. degrees from Keiō University in Tokyo (1969, 1971) and has completed the doctoral course at the same university. He has also studied at Yonsei University in Seoul (1972–74). He is presently lecturer on Korean studies at Keiō. He is co-editor of *Chōsen mondai sengo shiryō* [Materials on Postwar Korean Problems] (1976),

ROBERT M. SLUSSER is professor in the department of history, Michigan State University. He is the author of *The Berlin Crisis of 1961* (1973), and co-author of *Calendar of Soviet Treaties, 1917–1957* (1959), *The Theory, Law, and Policy of Soviet Treaties* (1962), and *Soviet Foreign Policy, 1928–1934: Documents and Materials* (1967).

TANIGAWA YOSHIHIKO, a graduate of Kyushu University (B.A. 1951, Ph.D. 1969), is professor of international relations at the same university. He has also been a visiting scholar at the Yenching Institute, Harvard University (1958–60). Among his publications are *Tōnan Ajia minzoku kaihō undō shi* [History of National Liberation Movements in Southeast Asia] (1969) and *Tōnan Ajia no minzoku kakumei* [National Revolutions in Southeast Asia] (1971).

D. C. WATT, professor of international history, London School of Economics and Political Science, University of London, is a graduate of Oxford University (B.A. 1951, M.A. 1954). Among his numerous publications are *Britain Looks to Germany* (1965), *Personalities and Policies* (1965), and *Too Serious a Business* (1975), and he is co-author of *Survey of International Affairs* (1966, 1970).

ALLEN S. WHITING received his A.B. degree from Cornell University (1948) and his M.A. and Ph.D. degrees from Columbia University (1952, 1954). His research has taken him to Taiwan, Hong Kong, and Japan, and his teaching experience to a number of universities, among them Northwestern, Michigan State, and the University of Michigan, where he is now professor of political science and associate of the Center for Chinese Studies. He is the author of *Soviet Policies in China 1917–1924*, (1954), *China Crosses the Yalu: The Decision to Enter the Korean War* (1960), and *The Chinese Calculus of Deterrence: India and Indochina* (1975).

YAMAMOTO MITSURU, a graduate of the University of To-kyo (B.A. 1950), is now professor of international relations at Hōsei University in Tokyo. He is the author of *Gendai no keizai gaikō* [Economic Diplomacy Today] (1972), and *Jishu gaikō no gensō* [The Illusion of the Diplomacy of Independence] (1973), and co-author of *Gendai Nihon keizai* [Contemporary Japanese Economy] (1976).

YANO TŌRU, a graduate of Kyoto University (B.A. 1959, S.J.D. 1968), is associate professor at the Center for Southeast Asian Studies, Kyoto University. From 1968 to 1969 he was associate professor of international relations at George Washington University. He has written *Tai Biruma gendai seijishi kenkyū* [Studies in Contemporary Thai and Burmese Political History] (1968), *Nihon no nanshin to Tōnan Ajia* [Southeast Asia and Japan's Southward Expansion] (1975), and *Nanshin no keifu* [Genealogy of Japan's Southward Expansion] (1975).

Index

441